THE RENEWAL OF ISLAM

FITZROY MORRISSEY is a Fellow of Pembroke College, Oxford, and Associate Professor of Islamic Studies and Law at the Faculty of Asian and Middle Eastern Studies, University of Oxford. A historian of Islam with a particular interest in Sufism, Islamic law and comparative religion, he is the author of *A Short History of Islamic Thought* (Head of Zeus 2021).

Also by Fitzroy Morrissey

A Short History of Islamic Thought
Sufism and the Scriptures: Metaphysics and Sacred History in the Thought of ʿAbd al-Karīm al-Jīlī
Sufism and the Perfect Human: From Ibn ʿArabī to al-Jīlī

Fitzroy
Morrissey

THE
RENEWAL
OF
ISLAM

Thinkers and Believers
of the Modern Era

An Apollo Book

First published in the UK in 2026 by Head of Zeus,
part of Bloomsbury Publishing Plc

Copyright © Fitzroy Morrissey, 2026

The moral right of Fitzroy Morrissey to be identified as the author of this work has been asserted in accordance with the Copyright, Designs and Patents Act of 1988.

All rights reserved. No part of this publication may be: i) reproduced or transmitted in any form, electronic or mechanical, including photocopying, recording or by means of any information storage or retrieval system without prior permission in writing from the publishers; or ii) used or reproduced in any way for the training, development or operation of artificial intelligence (AI) technologies, including generative AI technologies. The rights holders expressly reserve this publication from the text and data mining exception as per Article 4(3) of the Digital Single Market Directive (EU) 2019/790.

Scripture quotations taken from The Holy Bible, New International Version®, NIV®. Copyright © 1973, 1978, 1984, 2011 by Biblica, Inc. Used with permission of Zondervan. All rights reserved worldwide.

9 7 5 3 1 2 4 6 8

A catalogue record for this book is available from the British Library.

ISBN (HB): 9781804542170
ISBN (EPUB): 9781804542156

Cover design: Gemma Gorton
Typeset by Six Red Marbles India

Printed and bound in Great Britain by Clays Ltd, Elcograf S.p.A.

Bloomsbury Publishing Plc
50 Bedford Square, London, WC1B 3DP, UK
Bloomsbury Publishing Ireland Limited,
29 Earlsfort Terrace, Dublin 2, D02 AY28, Ireland

HEAD OF ZEUS LTD
5–8 Hardwick Street
London, EC1R 4RG

To find out more about our authors and books
visit www.headofzeus.com
For product safety related questions contact productsafety@bloomsbury.com

'This is what the Lord says:
"Stand at the crossroads and look;
ask for the ancient paths,
ask where the good way is, and walk in it,
and you will find rest for your souls."
But you said, "We will not walk in it."'

(Jeremiah 6:16, NIV)

Contents

Preface: Reform, Resistance and Renewal ix

1. Dreaming of Renewal 1
2. Harmonizing the Tradition: Shah Wali Allah 15
3. Returning to Fundamentals: Zaydi Traditionalism and Wahhabism 34
4. Following the Prophet: The Muhammadan Path 63
5. Following the Imams: Shi'ism in the Eighteenth and Nineteenth Centuries 101
6. Engaging with Modernity I: Islamic Renewal in Colonial India 140
7. Engaging with Modernity II: Islamic Renewal in the Modern Middle East 187
8. Defending God's Sovereignty 237

Acknowledgements 282
Notes 284
Index 341

Preface

Reform, Resistance and Renewal

In July 1907, Ignaz Goldziher, a Hungarian Jewish scholar widely regarded as the father of the modern academic study of Islam, received a letter from Duncan Black Macdonald, a Scottish-born orientalist and Christian missionary based at the Hartford Theological Seminary in Connecticut. Macdonald wrote of how much he looked forward to the completion of Goldziher's *Lectures on Islam*, a series of six lectures originally intended to be delivered in the United States but only published in book form in 1910, in which Goldziher claimed to have 'dealt exhaustively with the history of the development of Islam'.[1] Macdonald told his colleague how he was particularly looking forward to reading the last lecture on 'Modern Movements' in Islam, for, he wrote, 'Islam really is moving'.[2]

Goldziher had first-hand knowledge of modern developments in Islam. In 1873, while still in his early twenties, he had gone to the Middle East for a year, spending time in Damascus, Cairo and Constantinople. In Cairo he studied at al-Azhar, the chief centre of learning in Sunni Islam, and met Jamal al-Din al-Afghani (d. 1897), an anti-imperialist activist, teacher of Islamic philosophy and pioneer of Muslim modernism, whose leading student, the Egyptian religious scholar Muhammad 'Abduh (d. 1905), would become the most important representative of Islamic reform in the late nineteenth century. In Damascus he befriended Tahir al-Jaza'iri (d. 1920), 'the Muhammad 'Abduh of Syria', a collector of Arabic manuscripts, educationalist and religious reformer who encouraged a return to the scriptural sources of Islam and was unapologetic about taking what was good and true from Shi'ism, the rationalist Mu'tazili school of Islamic theology and the Aristotelian tradition of Islamic philosophy.[3] 'I hope that you still remember your Hungarian friend, who sought your hospitality in Syria in 1290 [of the Islamic calendar; 1873 AD], gaining enlightenment from its scholars, frequenting its learned men and litterateurs,' Goldziher wrote to al-Jaza'iri several decades later. 'By God almighty, your memory has not faded from my soul or my mind, nor has the memory of the enlightened friends.'[4] In his personal diary, Goldziher remembered his time in Damascus as 'the most beautiful' period of his life. 'I truly entered in those weeks into the spirit of Islam to such an extent,' he wrote, 'that ultimately I became inwardly convinced that I myself was a Muslim and judiciously discovered that this was the only religion which, even in its doctrinal and official formulation, can satisfy philosophical minds.' His aim, he added, was to 'elevate' his own Jewish religion to 'a similar rational level'.[5]

In his *Lectures on Islam*, Goldziher outlined a framework for thinking about the reformist tendencies he had encountered during his 'Muhammadan year'. Key to this framework are the concepts of *sunnah*, the authoritative custom or practice of the Prophet Muhammad, and *bid'ah* (pl. *bida'*), deviation or 'innovation' from prophetic practice. While pious and faithful Muslims, he notes, have always sought to conform to the Sunnah of the Prophet and to avoid innovations, the notion of what constitutes *sunnah* has also constantly been adapted to accommodate new ideas, practices and institutions in the name of the consensus and common interest of the Muslim community. In the modern period, he observes, this freedom to adapt to new circumstances has enabled Muslim countries to borrow from the West practices and institutions such as printing, insurance, savings banks and constitutional government. Yet, Goldziher continues, though this tendency also existed in premodern Islam, there has always been a minority of Muslims who were opposed to such a flexible and adaptive approach and sought to narrow the scope of 'good' or acceptable innovations as far as possible. 'In the internal history of Islamic movements,' he writes, 'we witness a continual struggle of *sunnah* against *bid'ah*'. As an example, he cites the long battle waged by 'rigorists' such as the fourteenth-century Damascene scholar Ibn Taymiyyah (d. 1328) – and his modern heirs the Wahhabis of central Arabia – to purify Muslims' ritual practice of all traces of polytheism.[6]

Both the struggle to combat innovations in the name of the Sunnah *and* the effort to adapt Islam to changing circumstances are best understood as examples of *tajdid* – that is, as attempts to 'renew' Islam. This was a concept that Goldziher treated elsewhere in his work. In 1871 – two years before his travels in the Middle East – Goldziher published an article on Jalal al-Din al-Suyuti (d. 1505), a prolific and influential religious scholar of fifteenth-century Egypt known for his mastery of all the major disciplines of Islamic learning. Goldziher's article focuses on a treatise written by al-Suyuti at the very end of the ninth Islamic century (the fifteenth century of the Christian calendar). The treatise is devoted to a Hadith, or saying of Muhammad, in which the Prophet announces that, at the beginning of every century, God will send someone to 'renew' the religion. Al-Suyuti's purpose in writing it was to claim for himself the title of *mujaddid*, the 'renewer' of Islam for his century.[7]

While the idea of *tajdid* had been around since at least the eleventh century AD, before al-Suyuti it was rarely employed as a mechanism for the development of Islamic thought.[8] As the scholar of Islam Ella Landau-Tasseron has found, in the medieval period the term *mujaddid* was mainly an honorific title applied within the Shafi'i school of Islamic law (which, along with the Hanafi, Maliki and Hanbali schools, is one of four *madhhabs* or schools of law recognized in Sunni Islam).[9] Al-Suyuti, however, seems to have meant something more concrete by the term. He believed that, thanks to the negligence of his fellow Muslims, the Islamic cultural heritage was in danger of being lost, and that it was his 'mission' to preserve it.[10] He also claimed to be a *mujtahid* – that is, a scholar capable of working out the divine law directly from the scriptural sources using his or her *ijtihad* or independent reasoning – and made this ability central to his claim to be the *mujaddid*.[11]

As a commentator on the Qur'an, a scholar of Hadith, a Shafi'i legal theorist, a Sufi mystic and an Ash'ari theologian (the Ash'aris being, alongside the Maturidis, one of the two orthodox schools of Sunni theology), al-Suyuti was an embodiment of the Islamic intellectual tradition in its post-classical period (which dates from roughly the twelfth century AD onwards). At the same time, in claiming to be a renewer and a *mujtahid*, he prepared the way for modern Islam. From his time onwards, the notion of *tajdid* became a mechanism from within the Islamic tradition for renewing that same tradition. The Muslim thinkers and believers who sought to lead that renewal would claim, like Duncan Black Macdonald, that Islam was 'moving'. They aimed, however, not to bring Muslims to a place that was entirely new, but rather to lead them back to what they saw as true Islam. 'Their aim and vocation,' wrote Goldziher of the Wahhabis, 'is the restoration of early Islam.'[12] Yet the Wahhabi vision of original Islam was by no means the only one. Others sought to recover the religion that, in Goldziher's words, 'could satisfy philosophical minds', while still others took inspiration from the mystical tradition of Sufism. What they shared was a sense that Islam as it was being lived by Muslims was not the religion that had been taught by the Prophet—that their fellow believers, as God had said of the Children of Israel in the Biblical book of Jeremiah, were refusing to walk in the 'good way' that was 'the ancient paths'. What they wanted was to make Islam as it actually was conform to Islam as it ought to be.

1

Dreaming of Renewal

In October 1728, 'Abd al-Ghani al-Nabulusi (d. 1731) had a momentous vision. Al-Nabulusi, a Sufi and religious scholar from Ottoman Damascus, had seen the Ka'bah, the cubic building in Mecca to which Muslims direct their prayers and go on pilgrimage, in a state of ruin. 'I saw a vision that the four corners of the Ka'bah had collapsed to the ground,' he related to one of his disciples. 'I rebuilt them all as I was standing there, without touching them with my hands.'[1]

A prolific author, like al-Suyuti, of works on a wide variety of subjects, al-Nabulusi was no stranger to dreams and visions. His most widely read book is a manual of dream interpretation, *The Perfuming of Mankind in the Interpretation of Dreams*, which he completed in 1685.[2] Arranged alphabetically for ease of use, under the Arabic letter *kaf* the manual contains an entry on the symbolism of the Ka'bah. In a dream, al-Nabulusi explains, the Ka'bah symbolizes a caliph (the successor of the Prophet Muhammad as head of the Muslim community), a vizier or a leader, and to see it in a dream is a harbinger of good things.[3] In the interpretation of al-Baytamani (d. 1761), the disciple to whom al-Nabulusi related his dream of 1728, the ruined Ka'bah stood not just for the caliph, but for the Muslim community or *ummah* as a whole. Al-Nabulusi's rebuilding of the House of God symbolized his status as a renewer of the faith. 'Surely,' al-Baytamani writes in his biography of his teacher, 'this is a sign of his renewal of Islam.'[4] Al-Nabulusi, in other words, was the *mujaddid*, the 'renewer' of Islam whom the Prophet had predicted would appear at the beginning of every century.

The vocation of the *mujaddid* is to restore the true faith in periods of moral and doctrinal decay, and al-Nabulusi certainly had a low opinion of the spiritual condition of his time. Evoking the age-old motif of *fasad al-zaman*, 'the corruption of the time', he wrote, 'Know that the time has become greatly corrupt, and people have become very harmful, for they distract you from worshipping God, so that you barely derive anything from [divine worship], then they corrupt what you have managed to derive, so that barely anything of it remains secure for you.'[5] These lines appear in a short treatise on withdrawing from society in times of corruption, *The Perfecting of the Attributes in Staying at Home*, which al-Nabulusi wrote in 1685, six years into a seven-year retreat during which he is said – probably with some exaggeration – to have barely left his house.[6]

Al-Nabulusi's withdrawal from society reflected his sense of despair at the direction in which his native Damascus was heading. His works from around this time abound in condemnations of the *jahl* and *ta'assub* – that is, the 'ignorance' and 'fanaticism' – of those he called 'pseudo-jurists' or 'the jurists of the masses', who wrongfully attacked Sufis like himself and the followers of other schools of law, provoking *fitnah*, a term signifying both civil strife and moral degeneration, within the Muslim community.[7] For instance, in a 1677 treatise on the permissibility of listening to musical instruments, al-Nabulusi laments that discord between Muslims has been stirred up by legal opinions issued by 'ignorant jurists, most of whom are villagers and tradesmen, who have memorised a few legal issues and so think they are perfect', and whose competence in legal matters the masses are not qualified to judge.[8] These pseudo-jurists' hearts, al-Nabulusi explains, are filled with pride and love of this world, and their fatwas are based not on a proper examination of the sources of God's law or sound knowledge of the books of the legal schools, but on their emulation of earlier scholars' opinions without reference to the relevant scriptural evidence – an activity known as *taqlid* – as well as on rational syllogisms and the 'delusions of their souls'.[9]

These criticisms were directed against Turkish scholars who had settled in Damascus and who were followers of the Qadizadeli movement. Named after Qadizadeh Mehmed (d. 1635), a preacher at several of the imperial mosques of Istanbul – including, from 1631, the famous Hagia Sophia – the Qadizadeli movement was mainly made up of middle-ranking religious scholars preaching in and around the mosques of Istanbul and other Ottoman cities in the decades between 1620 and 1680. The Qadizadelis were puritans whose vision of Islamic renewal was based on stripping away 'innovations' – *bidaʿ* – in social and religious practice, particularly those associated with the popular Sufi orders.[10] Yet though they are often portrayed as anti-Sufi fundamentalists, the Qadizadelis in fact drew on a sober, Shariʿah-minded Sufism, particularly of the kind associated with the resolutely Sunni Naqshbandi Sufi order.[11] Moreover, far from being fundamentalists – in the sense of seeking to bypass the classical tradition in order to get back to the fundamental sources – the leaders of the movement were firmly rooted in the Maturidi school of Islamic rationalist theology (the other school of theology, besides the Ashʿari school, in Sunni Islam) and the Hanafi school of Islamic law (one of the four Sunni *madhhabs* or schools of jurisprudence).[12] Reflecting this grounding in the Islamic intellectual tradition, the Qadizadeli scholar Ahmad al-Rumi al-Aqhisari (d. 1632) writes in *The Councils of the Pious*, an influential 'manifesto for reform' produced in the early seventeenth century,[13] that 'the renewer of religion' – that is, the *mujaddid* – 'must be one who knows both the outward and inward religious sciences', meaning the 'outward' sciences of theology and law, and the 'inward' science of Sufism.[14]

In this and other respects the Qadizadelis were following Mehmed Birgivi (d. 1573), a sixteenth-century Anatolian religious scholar who had similarly struggled for the moral reform of Ottoman society. Writing within the context of a broader Ottoman movement to define and impose Sunni Islam in the wake of the Ottoman Empire's wars against the Shi'i Safavids and the Christian Habsburgs, Birgivi aimed at the 'purification' of the hearts of Muslim believers and the 'correction' of their doctrine.[15] Like al-Nabulusi, his starting point was the religious and moral decline of the Muslim community. 'Ignorance (*jahl*) rules supreme amongst merchants, craftsmen, day labourers and associates in commercial partnerships,' he writes in *The Muhammadan Path*, his major work on moral reform. 'They do not respect the [religious] law and its conditions in their worldly transactions; their transactions become invalid, corrupted and reprehensible. What they gain or acquire is unlawful or repulsive.'[16] In this deplorable situation, Muslims needed to cling to the Qur'an and the Sunnah of the Prophet, avoid unwarranted innovations in faith and practice, and practice 'moderation' in their behaviour.[17] The basis of correct piety, in Birgivi's view, is right intention, *niyyah salihah*, and one of the greatest evils is sanctimonious hypocrisy, or *riya'*.[18] By reforming the inner dispositions of individual believers, he thought, society itself could be reformed. This was a vision of renewal inspired by the sober, ethically minded Sufism of the great al-Ghazali

(d. 1111), whose *Revival of the Religious Sciences* Birgivi quoted often, and who, four centuries before al-Suyuti, had claimed to have been selected by God to revive Islam.[19] It also drew from an Islamic ethical tradition that was ultimately rooted in Aristotle.[20]

As Birgivi's references to 'commercial partnerships' and 'worldly transactions' indicate, among his major concerns were ethical abuses related to money. One of the principal targets of his ire was the so-called 'cash endowment'. As defined by the Ottoman historian Jon E. Mandaville, this practice, which emerged in the Ottoman Empire in the early fifteenth century, involved 'the establishment of a trust with money the interest from which might pay the salary of a teacher, or preacher, or even unashamedly pass into the pocket of the founder of the trust'.[21] Since paying or receiving interest – called *riba* – is forbidden in Islamic law, to Birgivi, this practice was a clear example of the moral and religious decay of Ottoman society. Refuting the arguments of Ebu-s-Su'ud (d. 1574), the chief mufti of the empire and a defender of the cash endowment, Birgivi identified it as one of the 'great evils' of his time.[22] In *The Muhammadan Path*, he listed taking interest as one of the 'seven great offenses' alongside polytheism, magic, murder, the appropriation of an orphan's possessions, desertion from the army on the day of battle and the slander of innocent believing women.[23]

Qadizadeh Mehmed, the preacher from whom the Qadizadelis took their name, had studied with the disciples of Birgivi in his hometown of Balıkesir, in western Anatolia, and, like Birgivi, the Qadizadelis taught that social reform began with the purification of the individual believer's inner self.[24] In their drive for individual and societal purification, they carried forward Birgivi's concern for financial abuses. Among the hundred topics treated in the Qadizadeli treatise *The Councils of the Pious* are 'lawful earnings', 'the prohibition of monopolies', 'the fates of traders in the hereafter', 'trading, truthfulness, and trustfulness', 'the true nature of usury' and 'forward buying and other contracts'.[25] Yet their main concern was with the eradication of illicit innovations associated with the Sufi orders. Some of the activities that they targeted were age-old Sufi rituals, such as the vocal *dhikr* or recital of the name of God, the Sufi mystical concert known as *sama'* (literally meaning 'hearing') and the visitation of shrines, or *ziyarah*, to seek a saint's intercession with God. But they also took aim at new social practices such as the drinking of coffee and smoking of tobacco, both of which had become wildly popular in the decades preceding the rise of the Qadizadeli movement.

According to the Ottoman historian Ibrahim Peçevi (d. 1650), coffee, which had first been cultivated in Yemen and Ethiopia, was introduced to Istanbul in the year 1555, when two Syrian merchants, one from Aleppo and the other from Damascus, opened coffeehouses in the Ottoman capital. These coffeehouses, in the words of Peçevi, quickly 'became meeting-places of a circle of pleasure-seekers and idlers', with the result that the religious scholars declared that it was better to visit a tavern than a coffeehouse, and the preachers in the mosques 'made great efforts to forbid it'.[26] Tobacco reached Istanbul around half a century later. Peçevi relates that 'English infidels' brought it to the Ottoman lands in 1600 or 1601, and soon not only 'pleasure-seekers and sensualists', but even many great religious scholars had become addicted to it.[27] Coffee, in particular, was associated with the Sufi orders, since the Sufis were said to drink it to help them stay awake for their night-time devotions. In 1633, apparently under the influence of Qadizadeh Mehmed's preaching, the Ottoman sultan Murad IV (r. 1623–40) banned both coffee and tobacco, closed the coffeehouses and reportedly executed thousands of smokers for refusing to give up the habit.[28] These stringent provisions were justified through the new legal principle of *taqyid al-mubah*, the ruler's right to 'restrict what is legally permissible' in the interest of the common good.[29]

Murad IV's prohibitions were not to last, however. After the sultan's death in 1640, the Ottoman chief mufti issued a fatwa declaring that tobacco was permitted. Writing in 1656, the Ottoman 'gentleman scholar' Katib Çelebi (d. 1657) observed, 'Occasional reprimands from the [Ottoman] Throne to smokers have generally been disregarded, and smoking is at present practised all over the habitable globe.'[30] As for the coffeehouses, Katib Çelebi relates that, though they had yet to recover in the imperial capital, nevertheless 'in cities and towns outside Istanbul, they are opened just as before', for 'such things do not admit of a perpetual ban'.[31]

That said, when 'Abd al-Ghani al-Nabulusi was writing in the 1670s and 1680s, Qadizadeli puritanism remained influential, especially in the Arab provinces of the Ottoman Empire. In Cairo and al-Nabulusi's native Damascus, Qadizadeli preachers used *The Muhammadan Path* of Birgivi to rail against Sufi music, the cult of tombs, and smoking.[32] Al-Nabulusi met the Qadizadeli challenge head on, authoring a commentary on *The Muhammadan Path* in which he sought to reappropriate Birgivi's legacy from those he called *ahl al-ta'assub* – 'the people of fanaticism'.[33] He also wrote books arguing for the permissibility of the visitation of tombs, listening to music and smoking.

These works give a clear insight into al-Nabulusi's vision of a renewed Islam. Like Birgivi, he emphasizes that actions ought to be judged according to the intention or *niyyah* of the person doing them.[34] This principle is rooted in a famous Hadith – 'Actions are according to intentions' – which is the first prophetic report recorded in the canonical collection of al-Bukhari, the most important book, for Sunni Muslims, after the Qur'an.[35] Yet whereas the Qadizadelis took the Prophet's stress on intention as the basis for a critique of the morals of other Muslims, al-Nabulusi emphasized the importance of being charitable towards one's fellow believers. A person's intention, he observes, is a matter of the heart, which only God can know.[36] Given this, Muslims are obliged to follow the Prophet's injunction to 'think well' of one another – a principle, well anchored in the classical Islamic tradition, known as *tahsin al-zann*.[37] And rather than erring on the side of prohibiting activities of uncertain legal status, scholars should apply the juristic norm that things are allowed in principle, unless there is an explicit Qur'anic verse or Hadith report indicating that they are forbidden – a norm termed *al-ibahah al-asliyyah*, or the 'original permissibility' of things.[38]

This attitude of tolerance is to be extended, in al-Nabulusi's view, to all Muslims, that is, to ordinary believers as much as to learned scholars. Insisting that the divine law applies equally to all, al-Nabulusi argues that listening to music is allowed for all believers, whether they are from 'the common people of limited understanding' or 'the perfect elite' – a position that diverges from earlier Sufi texts, which tend to restrict listening to Sufi music to the initiated.[39] He likewise condemns those who conceal God's commandments from the masses on the basis of the esoteric principle that the divine law contains 'hidden knowledge'.[40] Similarly, the four travelogues that al-Nabulusi wrote to document the journeys that he undertook through Syria, the Holy Land, Egypt, and the Hijaz between 1689 and 1700 display, in the words of the historian Steve Tamari, his delight at 'encounters with peasants and the general public' and his 'profound respect for the insights and knowledge of (even illiterate) villagers'.[41] He even taught *The Ringstones of Wisdom*, the most important book on Sufi metaphysics by his intellectual hero Ibn 'Arabi (d. 1240), in open lectures at the Umayyad Mosque of Damascus;[42] indeed, al-Nabulusi wrote a commentary on that extremely difficult and obscure text with the explicit intention of making it accessible to the ordinary believer – in a striking departure from the practice of previous commentators to explain Ibn 'Arabi's text in highly technical philosophical language.[43]

Al-Nabulusi's egalitarianism is not totally unqualified, however. He holds that there are three levels of belief that are of increasing merit: belief based on blind emulation – *taqlid* – and submission to authority, belief based on rational demonstration, and, finally, belief based on mystical 'witnessing'.[44] He also divides Muslim believers into three categories that correspond to these levels of belief: the masses, who utter theological doctrines with their tongues and believe them in their hearts; the elite, who establish rational proofs for their belief; and the elite of the elite, whose belief is mystically drawn from the light of God.[45]

Al-Nabulusi relates his threefold hierarchy of belief in a commentary that he wrote on *The Mother of Proofs*, a summary of the Islamic creed by the fifteenth-century North African scholar Muhammad ibn Yusuf al-Sanusi (d. 1490). A native of Tlemcen in today's northwestern Algeria, al-Sanusi was a theologian of the Ash'ari school who argued that all Muslims, even ordinary believers, should understand the rudiments of *kalam* – that is, rational theology. Those who were unable to give a rational explanation of their belief, but relied instead on blind emulation or *taqlid*, he held, were either sinners or unbelievers. He wrote *The Mother of Proofs*, along with several other creedal works, to help spread theological knowledge within the Muslim community, and over the course of the seventeenth century and afterwards, his works became very popular in the central Islamic lands, including in Cairo, Damascus and the Hijaz.[46] His influence was also felt among the Qadizadelis, who, as we have seen, were not averse to rational theology. The Qadizadeli scholar Ahmad al-Rumi al-Aqhisari, for instance, wrote a treatise on the insufficiency of *taqlid* that consisted of a series of extracts from al-Sanusi's works.[47]

Like his commentary on Birgivi's *Muhammadan Path*, al-Nabulusi's commentary on al-Sanusi's creed can partly be seen as an attempt to reclaim the legacy of a prominent earlier thinker from the Qadizadelis. Both his perspective and that of al-Sanusi and the Qadizadelis express a kind of egalitarianism – al-Nabulusi's insofar as he affirms that the ordinary believer's faith is true, even when it is based on imitation, and al-Sanusi's insofar as he credits the average Muslim with the ability to handle rational arguments for Islamic belief. Furthermore, although al-Nabulusi privileges mystical knowledge, he does not limit that knowledge to a special class of believers, as earlier Sufis had done. As we have seen, he taught the mystical works of Ibn 'Arabi to anyone and everyone, suggesting that, in his view, mystical 'witnessing' is accessible to all.

Al-Nabulusi's charitable attitude towards his contemporaries extended not only to ordinary Muslims but also to followers of other faiths; indeed, he has been celebrated by modern scholars for his 'religious pluralism', 'Abrahamic' perspective and 'religious tolerance'.[48] A good example of his open-mindedness towards other religions is to be found in a polemical treatise written in response to criticisms made against him by a certain Turkish scholar, presumably a Qadizadeli. Al-Nabulusi insists in this treatise that Jews and Christians living under Muslim rule who pay the *jizyah* – the poll tax required of protected minorities, or *dhimmis*, in Islamic law – 'have the same rights and duties as the Muslims'.[49] Indeed, he indicates that *dhimmis* can be 'led by God to inner faith' – belief, like intention, being a matter of the heart which only God can know – in which case they will 'enter paradise along with the Muslims'.[50] This tolerant attitude manifested itself in al-Nabulusi's personal dealings with non-Muslims, especially Christians. His travel writings record his visits to Christian holy sites such as the Church of the Nativity in Bethlehem, where he sought 'a blessing by means of the relics of the infallible prophet' – meaning Jesus – and got on splendidly with the resident monks, whose melodies he particularly enjoyed. In the Armenian monastery in Jaffa, similarly, he wrote of his attainment of 'perfect happiness, and the most complete purity and joy'.[51] In 1712, al-Nabulusi wrote a response to three questions on the nature of God posed by the Greek Orthodox Patriarch of Antioch Athanasius Dabbas (d. 1724), whom he addressed as 'one of our brothers in spiritual practice, whose noble souls and subtle essences have become moons in the heavens of monotheism'.[52]

Al-Nabulusi's vision of a renewed Islam cannot be understood without an appreciation of his debt to Ibn 'Arabi, the Sufi thinker known to his followers as *al-shaykh al-akbar* – 'the Greatest Master'. Al-Nabulusi's devotion to this thirteenth-century mystical theorist, who was born in al-Andalus but eventually settled in Damascus, was intense. In 1707 al-Nabulusi moved to the Salihiyyah district on the outskirts of Damascus out of a desire to be near to the mausoleum of Ibn 'Arabi, which the Ottomans had renovated after they conquered the city in 1516. He dreamt often of Ibn 'Arabi, whom he saw as a father figure. 'It is well-known that I draw upon the Shaykh's words in all my states,' he wrote, 'and that his books, in accord with the Qur'an, the Sunnah, and the consensus of the pious forefathers, are the pillar of my belief.'[53]

Ibn 'Arabi's Sufi metaphysics centres on the idea that there is only one existence, the existence of God, which reveals itself in limited forms within the created realm. Al-Nabulusi was a passionate defender of the doctrine of *wahdat al-wujud* – 'the unity of existence' – as this controversial idea came to be known among Ibn 'Arabi's later interpreters.[54] One of the potential implications of this doctrine is a kind of religious pluralism: if everything is a manifestation of God's existence, then everything that is venerated – whether a Christian cross, the stars or an idol – is in some sense divine.[55] In this sense, for Ibn ʿArabi, anyone who worships anything is a monotheist, a view that anticipates the twentieth-century philosopher Eric Voegelin's insight that 'in all polytheism is latent a monotheism which can be activated at any time'.[56] Al-Nabulusi's charitable attitude towards non-Muslims is probably best understood in this context; hence, in a commentary on a text by ʿAbd al-Karim al-Jili (d. 1408), another prominent follower of Ibn ʿArabi, he explains that, from the perspective of the mystical 'reality' termed *al-haqiqah* – albeit not from the perspective of the divine law – all religions are true.[57] Another relevant feature of Ibn ʿArabi's thought is his emphasis on the flexibility and ease of the Shariʿah. Again, fidelity to what has been called Ibn ʿArabi's 'school of mercy' helps explain al-Nabulusi's emphasis on thinking well of other Muslims.[58]

Al-Nabulusi's adherence to Ibn ʿArabi's mystical perspective also led him to take an ambivalent view on the rational sciences. As we have seen, al-Nabulusi regarded rational ways of knowing as inferior to mystical ones, and though he was not opposed to rational theology *per se*,[59] he did adopt a hostile stance towards Aristotelian logic, which he condemns in his commentary on Birgivi's *Muhammadan Path* as 'pure harm for Muslims'.[60] In this regard at least, al-Nabulusi's Ibn ʿArabi-inspired vision ironically comes close to the scripturalist vision of reform inspired by Ibn ʿArabi's great critic, the fourteenth-century Hanbali scholar Ibn Taymiyyah, a campaigner for a purified Sunnah whose reputation was being rehabilitated in this period, and who like Ibn ʿArabi was opposed to rational theology and Aristotelian logic.[61] Indeed, one of those who led the recovery of Ibn Taymiyyah's perspective, the Medina-based Sufi Ibrahim al-Kurani (d. 1690), was also a zealous defender of Ibn ʿArabi's doctrine of the unity of existence.[62] Al-Nabulusi met al-Kurani's sons and students during his travels in the Hijaz, and read and debated al-Kurani's writings on Sufism and theology, authoring a critical commentary on his views on divine causality and human agency.⁶³

Finally, al-Nabulusi drew on Ibn 'Arabi's theory of sainthood, or *walayah*. According to Ibn 'Arabi, the saints walk in the footsteps of the prophets. Just as there is a 'Seal of Prophets' – the title applied to Muhammad in Qur'an 33:40 – so too is there a 'Seal of Muhammadan Sainthood'. This special individual brings sainthood to perfection just as Muhammad had perfected prophethood, and knows things that only he and Muhammad are allowed to know.⁶⁴ Ibn 'Arabi saw himself as the Seal of Muhammadan Saints, and al-Nabulusi likewise appears to have claimed the title for himself; at least, his disciples saw him as the Seal.⁶⁵ This idea, and what it implies about his special connection with the Prophet, must have shaped his self-perception as the renewer of the age.

Al-Nabulusi's vision of renewal, along with the vision of his Qadizadeli opponents and their forbear Birgivi, typify many characteristics of Islamic thought in the early modern period. These include the assumption of the mantle of *tajdid* as a response to the supposedly decrepit state of Islam and the Muslim community in their time; an extensive, but not uncritical, engagement with the post-classical intellectual tradition, including the mainstream Sunni disciplines of jurisprudence, rational theology and Sufism, and reliance on the thought both of Ibn 'Arabi and his opponent Ibn Taymiyyah; an eagerness to respond to novel practices and ideas, either by denouncing them as innovation or by integrating them into an acceptably Islamic way of life; a critical attitude towards *taqlid* – the blind emulation of authority – and *ta'assub*, or fanaticism for one's school of law; serious and often sympathetic reflection on non-Muslim ways of life and thinking; and a move towards egalitarianism. Those last two features, in particular, feel strikingly modern, especially in light of the Islamic tradition's emphasis on hierarchy, both within the

Islamic community itself and between Islam and other religions.[66] Al-Nabulusi has in fact been identified by several modern scholars as the herald of an Islamic enlightenment or Arab renaissance.[67] While this assessment should be qualified by a recognition of the deep roots of al-Nabulusi's thought in the medieval Islamic tradition – particularly the metaphysical Sufism of Ibn ʿArabi – he is undoubtedly an important early contributor to the making of modern Islam.

2

Harmonizing the Tradition: Shah Wali Allah

Al-Nabulusi was by no means the only early modern Muslim scholar to envision himself – quite literally – as a renewer of the faith. In 1731, the Indian Sufi and religious scholar Shah Wali Allah of Delhi (d. 1762) was in the holy city of Mecca. One day, after he had performed the afternoon prayer, the spirit of the Prophet Muhammad appeared to him, covered him in a garment and breathed into his heart, in an act that Shah Wali Allah took to be an 'explanation of religion'.[1] Later – Shah Wali Allah specifies that it was the night of 14 August 1731 – he had another vision in Mecca, in which the Prophet's grandsons, Hasan and Husayn, came to his house and handed him Muhammad's pen and cloak – symbols, respectively, of the Prophet's knowledge and inheritance.[2] These were just two of many dreams and visions with which Shah Wali Allah was blessed in the fourteen months he spent in Mecca and Medina between 1731 and 1732. In *The Effusions of the Two Sanctuaries*, he records forty-seven in all, which he understood to be indications of his election as the *mujaddid*. 'The greatest divine blessing that was bestowed on me,' he writes in his autobiography, 'is that

I was vested with the robe of opening a new age (*khil'at-i fatihiyyat*) and the success of subsequent ages was placed in my hands.'[3]

Shah Wali Allah was born near Delhi in 1703, in the final years of the reign of 'Alamgir, the last of the great Mughal emperors. His father and first teacher, Shah 'Abd al-Rahim (d. 1726), was a scholar of the Hanafi school of law, who had contributed to the compilation of *The Fatwas of 'Alamgir*, a major compendium of Hanafi law written at the instigation of the Mughal emperor. Shah 'Abd al-Rahim was also a Sufi of the Naqshbandi order and the founder of the Rahimiyyah madrasah in Delhi, a seminary whose curriculum emphasized study of the Qur'an and Hadith over and above the rational sciences of theology and logic – though not to the total exclusion of the latter. This focus on the scriptural sources, which would become a marked feature of Shah Wali Allah's own thought as well as the thought of those inspired by him, distinguished the Rahimiyyah madrasah from the Farangi Mahall tradition in Lucknow, whose curriculum, the *dars-i nizami*, emphasized the rational sciences and was, in the words of the historian Francis Robinson, 'the dominant system of Indian Islamic education' from the eighteenth to the twentieth century.[4]

Shah Wali Allah received his early education at home. A precocious child, in his autobiography he recalls having memorized the Qur'an at the age of seven before moving on to the study of 'Persian books and treatises'. He was married at fourteen, and the following year was initiated by his father into the Naqshbandiyyah. 'I became a disciple of my father,' he writes, 'and devoted myself to the occupations of the Sufi, especially those of the Naqshbandi shaykhs.'[5] More specifically, Wali Allah's Naqshbandi affiliation was to the Mujaddidi branch of that Sufi order. As its name suggests, the notion of renewal was central to the Mujaddidi tradition. Its founder, the early modern Indian scholar Ahmad Sirhindi (d. 1624), was regarded by his followers as nothing less than *mujaddid-i alf-i thani* – 'the renewer of the second Islamic millennium'. Writing against the backdrop of the Mughal Emperor Akbar's attempt to establish a universalist religion of 'Total Peace', which the *mujaddid* saw as an attempt to 'obliterate' Islam, Sirhindi described himself as living in a time 'full of darkness'. He explained this situation by way of a novel theory that, in the thousand years since his death, the Prophet Muhammad had gradually turned his attention away from his community and become a pure spirit, completely absorbed in God. This situation, Sirhindi asserts, has led God to send a 'man of perfect knowledge' – the *mujaddid* – who takes on the 'perfections' of the prophets of the pre-Islamic period and, like the Qur'anic Jesus, is supported by the Holy Spirit.[6] This potently millenarian understanding of renewal is combined in Sirhindi's thought with a 'juristic' form of Sufism that emphasizes the harmony of ecstatic mysticism and the Shari'ah, along with a systematic articulation of the Sufi path.[7] These three features of his thought formed the basis of the Mujaddidi path, which, from its centre at Sirhind in northern India, spread rapidly across Central Asia and into the Ottoman Empire over the course of the seventeenth and eighteenth centuries, becoming one of the major Sufi orders of the early modern Islamic world.

At the same time as Wali Allah joined the Mujaddidi order, he was enrolled at his father's Rahimiyyah madrasah, and studied the major books of Hadith, Hanafi law and practical and theoretical Sufism, as well as philosophical theology and other rational sciences such as astrology and medicine.[8] When he was sixteen his father died: on his deathbed, Shah 'Abd al-Rahim permitted his son to initiate others into Sufism and to guide their spiritual development. Alongside this role as Sufi guide, Shah Wali Allah also inherited his father's position as professor at the Rahimiyyah, and he spent the next twelve years teaching books on the religious and rational sciences and studying the law books of the four Sunni legal schools, with a particular focus on their use of Hadith.

In late 1731 Shah Wali Allah went on pilgrimage to Mecca. He remained in the Hijaz until the end of the following year, taking the opportunity afforded by residence in Medina, the city of the Prophet and a major centre of Hadith studies in this period, to continue his study of Hadith. He immersed himself in the six collections of Hadith recognized as canonical in Sunni Islam, as well as the *Well-Trodden Path* of Malik (d. 795), a law book-cum-Hadith collection, compiled by the founding father of the Maliki school of law, which contains sayings of Muhammad's Companions as well as of the Prophet himself. Among his teachers was Abu Tahir Muhammad al-Kurdi (d. 1733), the son of Ibrahim al-Kurani, whom we have met as correspondent of al-Nabulusi and a key figure in the revival of Ibn Taymiyyah. Like his father, al-Kurdi was both a Hadith scholar and a Sufi, whose 'all-encompassing frock', in Shah Wali Allah's words, 'comprehend[ed] all the garments of the Sufis'.[9] (The Sufi frock, or *khirqah*, is a symbol of initiation, similar to the Prophet's cloak mentioned earlier.) This marriage of Hadith scholarship and Sufism was to characterize Shah Wali Allah's perspective too.

Besides his Hadith studies, Shah Wali Allah spent much of his time in Medina praying at the Prophet's tomb. It was in the course of these devotions that he experienced several of the visions in which, so he believed, he was instructed to undertake the renewal of the faith. Shah Wali Allah sets out his understanding of the role and qualities of the *mujaddid* in *The Divine Elucidations*, a work mainly devoted to Sufi metaphysics, and which reveals the influence on his thought of Ibn 'Arabi. Shah Wali Allah identifies the renewer as 'the perfect one' – *al-kamil* – a title that evokes Ibn 'Arabi's notion of 'the perfect human', the human being who is the most perfect and complete reflection of God's names and attributes. According to Shah Wali Allah, the perfect one possesses a comprehensive, divinely inspired knowledge, which enables him to understand all that the Prophet taught and to discern the hidden meanings – the *asrar* – of the divine commandments. He – and Shah Wali Allah assumed the renewer to be male – is a master of the Islamic intellectual disciplines of Hadith, jurisprudence and theology, and is on a mystical path that encompasses all the Sufi orders in existence today. Because of this, he is able to correct the three principal errors into which contemporary Muslims have fallen, namely, an obsession with the logical reasoning of the philosophers, 'to the point,' Shah Wali Allah writes, 'that religious doctrines can scarcely be discussed without being mixed up with logical debates'; an overzealous attachment to Sufi shaykhs, at the expense of focusing on the Qur'an and Hadith; and a fanatical belief in the superiority of their own *madhhab* or school of law. Adopting the mantle of the renewer, the perfect one will 'abrogate' all the Sufi orders and all the schools of law – just as the Qur'an, according to Islamic doctrine, has abrogated all the earlier scriptures – and will lead his fellow believers back to a proper understanding of scripture.[10]

These, in brief, are Shah Wali Allah's leading ideas. They are elaborated in greater detail in *God's Conclusive Proof*, widely regarded as Shah Wali Allah's most important work. Like other proponents of renewal, Wali Allah's starting point is the sorry state of Islam in his time. 'I am in an era of ignorance (*jahl*), tribalism ('*asabiyyah*), and following the passions,' he laments at the beginning of the book, 'in which every person admires his own ruinous opinions and being the contemporary of someone is the basis of disagreement.'[11] These accusations recall al-Nabulusi's denunciation of the ignorance and fanaticism of the 'pseudo-jurists' of his own time. Even more than al-Nabulusi, Shah Wali Allah, who was educated in the Hanafi school, but often preferred the position of the Shafi'i *madhhab* on a given issue and was a devoted reader of one of the foundational texts of the Maliki school, was passionately opposed to zealous attachment to one's school of law. He regarded *madhhab*-fanaticism as one of the major symptoms of Islamic decline, and wrote a book, *A Fair Explanation of the Cause of Difference*, in which he accounts for the historical divergence between the four Sunni schools of law and criticizes those scholars who practise *taqlid*, the blind emulation of their school's position. In another work, *The Necklace on the Rules of Ijtihad and Taqlid*, he asserts that *ijtihad* – the exertion of mental effort to independently derive God's law from the scriptural sources – will remain a duty that must be undertaken by at least some members of the Muslim community until the end of time – in keeping with the view of al-Suyuti, but in contradiction of the view held by many scholars that the 'gate of *ijtihad*' had closed at some point in the medieval period.[12]

Shah Wali Allah's advocacy of *ijtihad* was not totally unqualified. Drawing on classifications outlined by medieval Sunni scholars, he holds that there are different degrees of *ijtihad*, with 'unrestricted *ijtihad*' – a form of interpretation that does not take account of the established doctrine of the schools – limited to the founders of the four schools of law. While advocating an eclectic approach to legal doctrine and tolerance of diversity between the schools, Wali Allah asserts that it would be wrong for scholars to abandon their school entirely – he describes himself as a *mujtahid* within the bounds of the *madhhab* – and insists that ordinary believers who are not experts in the Qur'an and Sunna ought to practise *taqlid*. That said, these ideas were evidently outlined in the hope of bringing about a reconciliation – what he termed *tatbiq* – between the schools of law, and particularly between the Hanafi and Shafi'i *madhhabs*, the dominant schools of law in India, neither of which, he thinks, has a monopoly on the correct interpretation of the law. In seeking to reconcile the schools of law in this way, Shah Wali Allah was following in the footsteps of the fourteenth-century Hanbali scholar Ibn Taymiyyah, whose thought, as already noted, was experiencing a revival in the circles of Hadith scholarship that Wali Allah had frequented in Medina, and who had likewise attempted to bring together what was best from each of the schools of law.[13] In condemning *taqlid* of the schools and calling for *ijtihad*, Shah Wali Allah helped pave the way for a more radical rejection of the authority of the schools in the nineteenth and twentieth centuries – a theme that we shall encounter in later chapters of this book.[14]

Ijtihad involves going back to the fundamental sources, and Shah Wali Allah's solution to the tribalism and ignorance that he saw all around him was to redirect his coreligionists' attention to the Qur'an and Hadith. One aspect of this return to the sources involved removing the layers of interpretation that had covered over the original meaning of the Qur'an. Shah Wali Allah wrote a book, *The Great Victory on the Principles of Exegesis*, in which he outlines a method for reading the Qur'an on its own terms. Instead of focusing on the historical contexts in which the verses of the Qur'an had supposedly been revealed, as the Qur'an commentators usually did, readers should consider God's purposes in revealing those verses. Those purposes, which would remain eternally valid, are 'the purification of the hearts of the people, repudiation of their corrupt beliefs and eradication of their evil actions'.[15] Commentators should 'let the Qur'anic narratives speak for themselves', taking the Qur'an as the basis for their belief rather than reading their pre-existing beliefs into God's word.[16] And students should first study the Qur'an without the aid of a commentary, in order to avoid having their understanding of the text shaped by the commentary literature – a method of teaching the Qur'an that Shah Wali Allah inherited from his father.[17] In this way, Wali Allah, who like al-Nabulusi before him, was disparaging about Aristotelian logic and philosophy more generally, sought to chart a path away from 'the method of the logicians', whose rational demonstrations, he thought, had obscured the true meaning of the sacred text, which ought to be read on its own terms.[18]

Another important component of Shah Wali Allah's renewed focus on scripture was Qur'an translation. In 1738, six years after his return to Delhi from the Hijaz, he produced a complete translation of the Qur'an into Persian, the major language of Islamic literary culture in South Asia, inserting the Persian translation in the lines between the original Arabic text.[19] Contrary to widespread assumptions that the Qur'an cannot be translated – or at least that it was not translated before the modern period – Shah Wali Allah's translation was by no means the first rendering of the Qur'an into Persian. Written Persian translations of the Islamic scripture go back to the tenth century AD, that is, to the very period when spoken Persian was formalized into a written language.[20] Even before that, in the eighth century, the founding fathers of the Hanafi legal school to which Shah Wali Allah belonged allowed Persian-speaking Muslims to use translations of Qur'anic verses during their ritual prayers.[21] In the medieval Maghreb, similarly, some jurists allowed Berbers who did not know Arabic to pray in their own language.[22] In Wali Allah's native India, the translation of the Qur'an into Persian had been going on since the turn of the thirteenth/fourteenth century.[23] Often these translations were intended to be used as teaching aids in the madrasah, as Shah Wali Allah's also was.[24]

What set Shah Wali Allah's translation apart was its explicitly democratizing orientation.[25] In the introduction to the work, he explains that his goal in producing a translation is to make the Qur'an accessible to 'the sons of soldiers and craftsmen' and those without the time or ability to pursue a scholarly education – language reminiscent of the justifications for the vernacular translation of the Bible provided by Protestant Reformers such as William Tyndale and John Calvin.[26] Like the Protestant Reformers, by giving ordinary believers direct access to scripture, Shah Wali Allah sought to undermine the authority of intermediaries standing between the believer and God. In his case, this meant the religious scholars and Sufi shaykhs whose ignorance and tribalism he blamed for the sorry condition of contemporary Islam.[27]

This concern for making the Qur'an intelligible to ordinary believers recalls the egalitarian tendency that we saw in the thought of Shah Wali Allah's fellow 'renewer' al-Nabulusi. It was a concern that was carried forward by Shah Wali Allah's sons. At his father's request, in the mid-eighteenth century Wali Allah's son Shah Rafi' al-Din (d. 1818) produced a literal translation of the Qur'an into Urdu, which was then emerging as a major Islamic language of northern India. In 1790, another of Wali Allah's sons, Shah 'Abd al-Qadir (d. 1815), made a more readable translation – pointedly titled *The Clarifier of the Qur'an* – into what he called 'commonly used Hindi [that is, Urdu]', avoiding Persian and Arabic loanwords to make the meaning of the sacred text clear to those Muslims who had not been educated in those languages of Islamic high culture. A third son, Shah 'Abd al-'Aziz (d. 1824), wrote a Qur'an commentary in simple Persian, and would give public lectures on the Qur'an on Tuesdays and Fridays, which thousands of people are said to have attended – again recalling al-Nabulusi's public lectures on Ibn 'Arabi.[28]

As much as the project of making the Qur'an accessible was central to Shah Wali Allah's vision of renewal, his major focus was Hadith. 'The main focus and summit of the sciences that give certain knowledge, and the foundation and basis of the religious disciplines,' he writes in the introduction to *God's Conclusive Proof*, 'is the science of Hadith.'[29] Indeed, later in the book, in a chapter on how to rank books of Hadith, he puts the point even more strongly, arguing that 'the only way to knowledge of the divine laws and commandments is through the reports (*khabar*) of the Prophet'.[30] In that same chapter, Wali Allah explains that Hadith books are ranked according to two criteria: first, the extent to which the prophetic reports collated within them are widely circulated among Hadith scholars, and second, the extent to which leading jurists have been able to derive laws from those reports and base their legal doctrine on them. According to these criteria, three collections of Hadith fall into the first rank: the *Authentic Collections* of al-Bukhari and Muslim – the two most authoritative Hadith books in Sunni Islam – and Malik's *Well-Trodden Path*.[31]

As already noted, Shah Wali Allah revered the *Well-Trodden Path* of Malik.[32] He wrote two commentaries on the text, one in Arabic and the other in Persian, and cited with approval the statement of al-Shafi'i (d. 820), the founding father of one of the other schools of law and the jurist responsible for making prophetic Hadith the basis of Islamic law, that the *Well-Trodden Path* was 'the soundest book after the Book of God' – that is, the Qur'an.[33] Wali Allah's appreciation for Malik's work reflects his lack of partisanship for his own Hanafi school of law. Indeed, he compares the *Well-Trodden Path* favourably to the work of the late eighth-century jurists Abu Yusuf (d. 798) and Muhammad al-Shaybani (d. 805), who along with Abu Hanifah (d. 767) are recognized as the founders of the Hanafi school.[34] Malik's Hadith, so the argument goes, are the most reliable, and fidelity to Hadith trumps fidelity to one's school of law.

In the preface to *God's Conclusive Proof*, Shah Wali Allah explains that the science of Hadith has four levels. These are, first, the art of discerning whether a Hadith is an authentic statement of the Prophet; second, the art of working out the meaning of strange or difficult Arabic terms found in the reports; third, the art of deriving substantive laws from the Hadith reports and drawing analogies on the basis of those laws; and fourth, 'the science of the mysteries of religion, which seeks the inner wisdom and rationales behind the commandments'. Of these levels, he says, the fourth is the most profound, for it gives the scholar clear and certain insight into the meaning of the law. It is accessible only to those who have combined mastery of the outward sciences of the law and Hadith with 'divinely inspired knowledge', that is, mystical illumination of the kind that Shah Wali Allah had himself received while in the Hijaz.[35] Indeed, as we have seen, he associates knowledge of the hidden meanings of the law with the renewer of the faith.

Shah Wali Allah gives, as examples of the 'inner wisdom' – or *hikam* – of the law, the pillars of Islam and other foundational divine commandments. The reason for the ritual prayer is to encourage Muslims to 'remember God and converse with Him'; the rationale for almsgiving is 'to ward off the sin of stinginess and to meet the needs of the poor'; the purpose of fasting is 'to subjugate the lower self'; and the aim of the Hajj pilgrimage is 'to magnify the emblems of God' in Mecca. Turning to criminal law, Shah Wali Allah asserts that the purpose of the law of retaliation is to prevent murder, just as the purpose of the *hudud* – the fixed penalties laid down by God for certain offences, such as cutting off the thief's hand – is to prevent sins. Jihad was likewise instituted 'to elevate God's word and to put an end to discord', while the laws concerning social transactions – what are called the *muʻamalat* – and disputes had been laid down to establish justice within society.[36]

These examples point towards an idea that is central in Shah

Wali Allah's thinking, namely that the Shari'ah works towards the benefit of all, that is, according to what he calls *al-masalih al-kulliyyah*, 'the universal benefits' of the law. The idea that the divine law was established for the benefit of mankind was not a new one in Islamic legal thinking. As the scholar of Islamic legal theory Robert Gleave has written, 'Most Sunni legal theorists subscribe to the view that the *Shari'a* has aims, and principal amongst these is the promotion of the "benefits for the believers" (*maṣāliḥ al-'ibād*).'[37] Indeed, the key juristic method of analogy, or *qiyas*, depended on this view, for analogy worked by taking the reason or aim underlying a law found in the scriptural texts (for instance, the Qur'an's prohibition of wine aims at preventing intoxication and the resultant neglect of prayer) as the source for a new rule (such as the prohibition of other kinds of alcohol).[38] On this basis a theory was developed that the law has five essential aims or *maqasid*, namely, the protection of religion, life, progeny, property and reason, with the 'ultimate goal' of protecting the public benefit (*maslahah*, the singular form of *masalih*).[39] This resulted in rational justifications of the law that sound similar to Shah Wali Allah's. For instance, the eleventh-century political theorist and Shafi'i jurist al-Mawardi (d. 1058), who observes that God laid down laws as a way to establish 'benefits for creation' (*masalih al-khalq*),[40] suggests that the reason for the Ramadan fast is to create sympathy for the condition of the poor.[41] While the idea that the law has aims cut across the schools of law – one of its major theorists was al-Ghazali, who was also a Shafi'i – the notion that the law could be worked out based on what was conducive to the public benefit was particularly associated with Malik and his school.[42] Given that Wali Allah's own Hanafi school tended not to make use of the concept, his emphasis on public benefit is another sign of his willingness to go beyond the bounds of his school.

Where Shah Wali Allah diverges from earlier Sunni jurisprudence is in connecting the identification of the purposes of the law to his own mystical experience. Yet here too there was a precedent in the medieval tradition. Sufis such as Ibn 'Arabi and, in his mystical writings, al-Ghazali, had outlined the inner 'mysteries' and 'wisdom' – the same terms used by Shah Wali Allah – of the pillars of Islam. For example, in the book on the mysteries of fasting in *The Revival of the Religious Sciences*, an influential work in which he attempted to infuse jurisprudence with Sufi spirituality, al-Ghazali explains that fasting is a means of vanquishing Satan, the enemy of God, for Satan works through man's appetites, which are strengthened by eating and drinking.[43] For Ibn 'Arabi, similarly, fasting 'shackles' the devils and enables the one fasting to draw near to God by taking on the divine attribute of 'everlastingness'.[44]

While not unprecedented, however, Shah Wali Allah's thinking about the aims and benefits of the law is remarkable insofar as he takes those aims and purposes as the starting point for a comprehensive vision of ethico-religious and socio-political renewal. Shah Wali Allah's ethics are rooted in a distinction he makes between the two aspects of human nature, which he calls the 'angelic' and 'animalistic' faculties in man. These terms, which are rooted in ancient Greek ethical theory and mediated through the classical Islamic tradition of philosophical ethics, respectively denote man's rational soul, which is directed towards heavenly things, and his passions or desires, which are turned towards earthly affairs.[45] According to Shah Wali Allah, 'true happiness' consists in the submission of one's animalistic nature to one's rational or angelic soul.[46] This can be achieved through fulfilling the acts of worship prescribed by the divine law and by the practice of four cardinal virtues: purity, humility before God, magnanimity and justice.[47]

While he promotes the cultivation of reason over the

indulgence of the passions, Shah Wali Allah's ethical vision is not one of philosophical escapism. Condemning both the extreme asceticism of renunciant Sufis and the extreme rationalism of the philosophers, he asserts that the best of the 'perfect humans' are those in whom there is a harmony or balance between the angelic and animalistic faculties, for 'the best things are the moderate ones'.[48] This moderation, which is rooted both in Aristotle's theory of the golden mean and in the Qur'an's description of Muslims as *ummat al-wasat* – 'the middle community' (Q. 3:110) – reflects the profoundly social orientation of Shah Wali Allah's ethics and his wider vision of renewal.

That vision, it should be remembered, was a response to what he saw as the deep moral and political decay of the Mughal society in which he lived. In *The Divine Elucidations*, Wali Allah laments the fact that Mughal officials drink wine in public and tolerate the existence of brothels, taverns and gambling dens, and that 'in this Empire' the *hudud* penalties 'have not been enforced for six or seven centuries'.[49] Just as serious was the corruption of the Mughal system of taxation and public spending. There are, he explains in *God's Conclusive Proof*, two 'predominant reasons' for 'the ruin of countries in this time': first, the depletion of the treasury, because people have taken from it 'without undertaking anything for the public benefit' – again, he uses the term *maslahah* – and second, 'the imposition of heavy taxes on farmers, merchants and craftsmen' to the point that they are ruined and the strong among them rise up in rebellion. 'The city will only flourish,' he writes, 'if taxes are light and protections are set up to the necessary extent.'[50] Shah Wali Allah here echoes the theory of taxation of the famous North African philosopher of history Ibn Khaldun (d. 1406), who would be cited by Ronald Reagan as a pioneer of supply-side economics.[51]

In response to the decay of Mughal society, Shah Wali Allah

developed his theory of what made for a morally and materially prosperous society. Key to this theory is the concept of the *irtifaqat*, a term that Wali Allah appears to have coined himself, and which denotes those things that support civilization. The ability to work out these civilizational supports through the use of reason, Wali Allah observes, is one of three things that distinguish man from other animals, along with a 'universal outlook' – meaning that humans do things not simply to satisfy their bodily needs, but with some larger, rationally derived benefit in mind – and a concern for elegance and beauty.[52]

Wali Allah arranges the things that support civilization into four levels that correspond with different levels of civilizational progress. The first level consists of those things that are shared by all human societies, both rural and urban, such as language, agriculture, the cooking of food, homes to shelter people from the heat and cold, clothing, mating and customs for resolving conflicts. The second level, by contrast, is reached only by those whom Shah Wali Allah calls 'the inhabitants of civilized areas and settled villages within the righteous regions'. At this level, people attain 'the art of the proper means of living'. This means that, when considering the things found at the first level of civilizational progress, they are able to choose those things that are most beneficial and least harmful. They do so through the application of 'correct experience', through the judgement of those among them who by their nature possess 'perfect temperaments', and in the interest of promoting good relations and cooperation between people and other higher aims of the divine law.[53] In practical terms, this means that, at this second level of civilizational development, people develop economics, mastering the arts of household management and economic transactions.[54]

However, says Shah Wali Allah, when this second level has been perfected, economic exchange leads to greed, envy and discord, and people dominated by base desires come to the fore, with the result that it becomes impossible to put the civilizational supports into practice. People are therefore forced, he writes, 'to establish a king to judge with justice between them, to restrain the disobedient among them and to collect and spend taxes'.[55] This entails the emergence of politics, which, as Shah Wali Allah defines it, is the wisdom of maintaining good relations between the inhabitants of a city. Wali Allah's political ideas are rooted in the Platonic political philosophy of the medieval Islamic philosophical tradition, particularly as expressed by al-Farabi (d. 950/1), who famously articulated a vision of a perfect city governed by a philosopher-prophet.[56] Since a city is made up of many people, Wali Allah observes, it is not possible that they will all agree to the city's customary way of doing things, nor that one person will be able to reproach another for deviating from that customary practice unless he or she possesses a special rank. A city's affairs will therefore only be properly organized, Wali Allah concludes, if there is a single individual whom the religious and political elite agree to obey.[57] This individual, whom Shah Wali Allah calls a king, must be brave, temperate and wise, and should be guided in his decisions by the *maslahah* or public benefit, which as we have seen is a concept that is central to Wali Allah's understanding of Islam.[58]

In Shah Wali Allah's theory, the emergence of a king in each city leads to the fourth and final stage of civilizational development, which is initiated when these kings abandon 'rightly guided custom' and struggle among themselves for power, exchanging the 'universal outlook' that is proper to mankind for 'partial outlooks'. This compels people to set up a higher authority, called a caliph, to restrain the tyrannical kings and combat, with force, 'savage souls' and 'people spreading corruption on earth'.[59] Since the caliph is tasked with maintaining concord within the city, which is a 'mixture' of very heterogenous elements, he must be among those whom Shah Wali Allah calls 'the people of harmony', whose angelic and animalistic faculties are in a state of balance.[60] He should have eyes in every quarter and must possess a 'penetrating insight' into human nature.

This insight, Shah Wali Allah indicates, is divinely inspired. Wali Allah includes the caliph among the *mufahhamin*, those people who have been enabled by God to understand the true nature of things, a category that also includes the prophets and renewers of the faith.[61] This view of the caliph as the divinely guided leader of the community, in both its religious and political affairs, seems in fact to have been the original meaning of the caliphate in the first centuries of Islam.[62] Drawing on earlier Sufi ideas, particularly from the philosophical Sufi tradition of Ibn 'Arabi, in *The Divine Elucidations* Shah Wali Allah distinguishes between two dimensions of the caliphate, the 'manifest' and the 'hidden', where the manifest caliphate denotes the caliph's responsibility for establishing justice and imposing God's law, and the hidden caliphate signifies his duties as a teacher of scripture and divine wisdom and a guide in spiritual purification.[63] The union of these two dimensions of the caliphate – the political and the mystical – is the basis of the ideal state.

One of the noteworthy features of Shah Wali Allah's political philosophy is its universality. There is nothing specifically Islamic about the 'supports of civilization' or the forms of government proper to each stage of civilizational development. As an example of the appointment of a caliph, Wali Allah cites not the 'rightly guided' caliphs of early Islamic history, but the story of the Biblical prophet Samuel, who, according to the usual interpretation of Qur'an 2:246, was asked by the Children of Israel to appoint a king over them (the Biblical Saul) so that they could fight in the way of God.[64]

This openness to the history and experience of non-Islamic

societies reflects Wali Allah's interest in identifying points of unity underlying the apparent diversity of creation. 'There is no multiplicity that does not begin with unity,' he writes, in a statement that evokes the Ibn 'Arabi tradition's belief in *wahdat al-wujud*, 'the unity of existence'.[65] This principle is the philosophical foundation of Shah Wali Allah's concern for reconciling the different schools of Islamic law and the various Sufi orders. It also leads him to take, like al-Nabulusi, an open-minded view of religious diversity. Drawing on the Qur'an's identification of Muhammad's message with that of the earlier prophets, Wali Allah asserts that the 'root' of religion is one, even if the paths and methods are many. This common root consists of the things that all the prophets agreed on, including the unity and transcendence of God, the need to submit to Him and obey Him, God's determination of all things, the final judgement and resurrection of man, pious acts such as pilgrimage, fasting and prayer, and customs such as marriage, establishing justice and spreading God's word.[66]

These features are shared by what Shah Wali Allah calls the 'heavenly religions', meaning Judaism, Christianity and Islam;[67] indeed, inspired by the Qur'an's frequent references to 'the religion of Abraham', he seems to anticipate the twentieth-century idea of the 'Abrahamic' religions.[68] But, reflecting his South Asian environment, Wali Allah also looks beyond the three Abrahamic faiths, and again finds a basis for agreement. All religions on earth, he asserts, teach belief in and reverence for their founder and have an idea of normative custom and divine law – that is, *sunnah* and *shari'ah*.[69] All religions likewise agree that there are certain times of day – namely, just before dawn, just after midday, after dusk and from midnight to just before daybreak – that are best suited to performing acts of worship,[70] while 'the principle of pilgrimage is found in every religious community'.[71] Even the pre-Islamic Arabs – the people of what the Islamic tradition calls *jahiliyyah* or the time of ignorance – believed in God's creation and management of the world, His transcendence and determination of events, His requital of good and evil, and in the existence of angels and prophets.[72] These commonalities are rooted in the fact that, according to Islamic theology, humans share a *fitrah*, or primordial disposition, which naturally inclines them to worship the one true God.[73]

Nevertheless, as Wali Allah sees it, humans' primordial dispositions can be corrupted by their physical nature or lower selves, man-made conventions and misunderstanding. These forms of corruption, when present on a societal scale, lead to the spiritual decline that necessitates religious renewal, just as it was the introduction of corrupt practices and beliefs, among both the pre-Islamic Arabs and the Jews and Christians, that induced God to deliver the Qur'an to Muhammad.[74] Shah Wali Allah's open-mindedness towards other religions, and towards other Islamic denominations, should not be mistaken, therefore, for indifference. Islam, he insists, is the 'natural religion', and has abrogated the religions that came before it.[75] This is why the corruption of Islam in his own time is so deplorable, and renewal so pressing.

Shah Wali Allah was a great harmonizer, seeking and finding unity between scripturalism and mysticism, spirituality and this-worldliness, the schools of law and the Sufi orders, and Islam and other religions. This ability to harmonize the tradition made him extremely influential. As we shall see, in the centuries after his death in 1762, numerous Islamic movements would emerge, primarily, but not only, in South Asia, which were inspired by one element or another of his vision of renewal. Nevertheless, there were also other forces of renewal emerging around this time, some of which did not share his tolerance of spirit.

3

Returning to Fundamentals: Zaydi Traditionalism and Wahhabism

It was not only Sufis who had visions. Around 1792, three years before becoming chief judge of the Qasimi Imamate of Yemen, Muhammad al-Shawkani (d. 1834) had a dream in which he saw himself in conversation with Ibn al-Amir al-San'ani (d. 1769), another Yemeni scholar who had been preacher at the Great Mosque of Sanaa and had died over two decades previously. Ibn al-Amir was walking on foot, while al-Shawkani was riding in a group. When he saw Ibn al-Amir, al-Shawkani got down and greeted him, and a discussion between them ensued. Ibn al-Amir said to al-Shawkani, 'Be precise about the chain of transmission [of Hadith reports] and apply yourself eagerly and meticulously to the interpretation of the speech of the Messenger of God.' It occurred to al-Shawkani that Ibn al-Amir was referring to the fact that he was teaching the Hadith collection of al-Bukhari at the Great Mosque of Sanaa, to a group which included scholars and common people, and would explain the words of the Hadith reports in terms that the commoners could understand. Just as he was about to mention this, Ibn al-Amir said to him, 'I know that you are teaching a group that includes common people, but be precise about the chains of transmission, and apply yourself eagerly and meticulously to the interpretation of the speech of the Messenger of God.' Then al-Shawkani asked him about the state of the scholars of Hadith in the afterlife, and Ibn al-Amir said that on account of their Hadith scholarship they were in paradise, or between the hands of God, the All-Merciful. Then he cried out with a loud cry, embraced al-Shawkani and left.[1]

When al-Shawkani asked an expert in dream interpretation what Ibn al-Amir's actions symbolized, he was told that he would experience similar trials to the older scholar. Such was the destiny of anyone who sought to combat what they regarded as the decline of Islam, for, like the Qadizadelis, al-Nabulusi and Shah Wali Allah, both scholars strove for the renewal of the faith. In the biographical dictionary that he compiled devoted to religious scholars who lived after the seventh Islamic century, al-Shawkani describes his predecessor as 'one of the leaders who renewed (*mujaddidun*) the milestones of the religion'.[2] And while al-Shawkani never claimed to be the *mujaddid* himself, he does refer to the *mujaddid* tradition when lamenting the decline of Islam, and his disciples explicitly identified him as the renewer of his age.[3]

Al-Shawkani, Ibn al-Amir and the Qasimi dynasty which they served were Zaydis, a branch of Shi'i Islam named after Zayd b. 'Ali, a descendant of the Prophet who had led a failed revolt against the Umayyad caliphate in the Iraqi town of Kufa in 740. Shi'ism is distinguished from the majority Sunni form of Islam by its attitude to religious authority. The Sunnis delegate authority in religious matters to the ulema, the scholars qualified to interpret the Qur'an and Sunnah of the Prophet. The Shi'ah, by contrast, believe in the religious authority of their Imams, who must be members of *ahl al-bayt*, that is, the family of the Prophet. Most Shi'ah believe that this knowledge is divinely inspired, comprehensive and infallible. The Imams, according to a tradition recorded in the books of the Twelver Shi'ah, the majority form of Shi'ism, are *muhaddathun*, 'spoken to' by the angels. The Twelvers, as well as the Isma'ilis, a smaller branch of Shi'ism, also restrict the Imamate to the descendants of the Prophet through his daughter Fatimah and her husband 'Ali ibn Abi Talib, and hold that an Imam is chosen through the explicit designation, or *nass*, of his immediate predecessor.[4] In the view of the Zaydis, by contrast, any *sayyid*, or descendant of the Prophet, can theoretically become the Imam. For them, the Imam's religious knowledge is not divinely inspired but acquired through study. The Imam must accordingly be a *mujtahid*, a scholar able to derive the law independently from the scriptural sources through *ijtihad*. He must also be a military leader. Inspired by the Imam after whom they were named, the Zaydis insist that only those descendants of the Prophet who engage in *da'wah* – calling people to the true Imamate – and lead an armed uprising against unjust rule are qualified to be the Imam.[5]

The historic heartlands of Zaydism are in northern Yemen, where Zaydi Imams ruled from the time of Imam al-Hadi (d. 911), the archetypal Zaydi Imam and most important point of reference for the Zaydi school of law (known, after him, as the Hadawi *madhhab*), until the republican revolution of 1962.[6] At the end of the sixteenth century, the Imamate was acquired by the Qasimi dynasty, descendants of al-Hadi who, in the following century, expelled the Ottomans, expanded Zaydi control over the rest of the country, including the traditionally Shafi'i southern lowlands, and supervised a flourishing economy that depended on the export of coffee.[7] Yet, by the early eighteenth century, this rosy picture of Zaydi rule was discoloured by three processes. First, the loss of the important port town of al-Shihr, in the Hadramawt region of eastern

Yemen, along with the decline in global coffee prices, seriously weakened the economy of the Imamate. Second, whereas the early Qasimis had been, in accordance with the Zaydi theory, 'men of the pen and the sword', the later Imams ceased to live up to this ideal, nor indeed did they claim to do so. Third, the enlargement of the Qasimi state in the seventeenth century led to Zaydi religious scholars coming into much closer contact with the Shafi'i scholars of southern Yemen, accelerating a process that had begun with the Zaydi scholar Muhammad ibn Ibrahim al-Wazir (d. 1436) in the fifteenth century, whereby Zaydi scholars turned increasingly to the study of Sunni religious texts, particularly their canonical collections of Hadith.[8]

The result of this last process was the emergence of Zaydi traditionalism, a movement in which Ibn al-Amir and Muhammad al-Shawkani, the scholars whom we met at the beginning of this chapter, played a major role. 'Traditionalism' is a term used in the study of Islam to denote the method of *ahl al-hadith*, 'the partisans of Hadith', those religious scholars who seek to base theology, and especially the law, on the Qur'an and Hadith, to the exclusion of rational procedures and the inherited traditions of the legal schools. Traditionalists, in other words, go back to the fundamentals. In the case of Zaydi traditionalists like Ibn al-Amir and al-Shawkani, this meant bypassing the legal manuals of the Hadawi school of law and deriving the law directly from the words of the Prophet, as recorded in the Sunni books of Hadith. As al-Shawkani heard his traditionalist predecessor say to him in his dream, it meant applying oneself 'eagerly and meticulously to the interpretation of the speech of the Messenger of God' as it had been set down in books like the celebrated *Authentic Collection* of al-Bukhari that he taught in the Great Mosque of Sanaa.

Working out the law directly from the scriptural sources

is the definition of *ijtihad*, and it was *ijtihad* that the Zaydi traditionalists applied as the 'cure' for the 'illnesses' that had infected the Zaydis of Yemen and explained the decline of the Qasimi state. As with other eighteenth-century renewers, those illnesses consisted, as they saw it, in *madhhabiyyah*, 'madhhabism', or fanatical devotion to one's school of law, and especially in *taqlid*, which al-Shawkani defines as seeking an answer to a question of law not from the Book of God or the Sunnah of the Prophet but from the *madhhab* that one follows.[9] The merit of the traditionalists, al-Shawkani writes in his biographical entry for Ibn al-Wazir, the founding father of Zaydi traditionalism, is that 'they limit themselves to the texts of the Book and the Sunnah and cast off *taqlid*'. He thinks this is meritorious, because, while the scriptural texts provide certain knowledge of God's law, the legal manuals of the Zaydi-Hadawi *madhhab*, which provide the basic material for *taqlid*, are based on fallible human *ra'y* or 'opinion'.[10]

The depiction of post-classical Islamic jurisprudence as being locked in a rigid mindset of *taqlid*, in contrast to the creative *ijtihad* of the formative period, is something of a caricature of the late-medieval Islamic legal tradition. In fact, as the historian of Islamic law Wael Hallaq has shown, the so-called 'gate of *ijtihad*' was never definitively 'closed', and post-classical jurists continuously sought to adapt legal rules to changing social circumstances by sifting, selecting and updating norms found in earlier authoritative texts within their schools – activities referred to by the terms *tarjih* and *tashih*, which denote 'rule-formulation' and 'rule-review' in this context.[11] Furthermore, *taqlid* can perhaps best be seen as a form of what Sherman Jackson, another scholar of Islamic legal history, has termed 'legal scaffolding', that is, as an attempt to show that one's legal interpretations are built on the teachings of earlier authority figures.[12] Nevertheless, it is true that, from around the thirteenth century onwards, Muslim jurists tended not to think the law anew through a fresh interpretation of the scriptural sources. Instead, they undertook a kind of codification of the rules of their respective schools – exemplified in the growth of the legal genre of the *mukhtasar* or 'summary' of the law – as a way of achieving greater consistency, uniformity and predictability in the law.[13]

The Zaydi traditionalists' condemnation of the unthinking emulation of one's school of law was harsh and unmitigated. Lamenting the fact that the 'innovation of madhhabism' had led Muslims to prefer the opinions of later scholars to the explicit declarations of the Prophet Muhammad, Ibn al-Amir writes of the need for people to 'wash their minds of the filth of fanaticism and cut through the substance of madhhabism's devilish insinuations'.[14] Al-Shawkani likewise warns that *madhhab*-fanaticism invariably leads to bloodshed and the violation of the divine law, and condemns *taqlid* as a reprehensible innovation from the Sunnah of the Prophet.[15] Muftis and judges who practise *taqlid*, he complains, 'turn their ignorance into law',[16] and to claim that the gate of *ijtihad* has been closed amounts to 'abrogating the Shari'ah'.[17]

Those who are qualified to derive the law from the scriptural sources, al-Shawkani argues, are forbidden from relying on *taqlid*. Contrary to those Zaydis who advocated reliance on the legal manuals of the Hadawi school, al-Shawkani asserts that this prohibition of *taqlid* is the opinion of the Zaydi Imams themselves.[18] Indeed, he says, the Zaydi tradition in which he had been raised was particularly given to *ijtihad*. 'Adherence to the texts of the Book and the Sunna', he writes, is a 'special characteristic' of the Yemeni Zaydis, who 'do not rely on emulation in any way or form',[19] and the Imams had always studied the Sunni collections of Hadith.[20] That said, neither al-Shawkani nor Ibn al-Amir confined himself to the Zaydi-Hadawi school. Ibn al-Amir's major work was a commentary on a collection of Hadith pertaining to legal topics compiled by the fifteenth-century Shafi'i scholar Ibn Hajar al-'Asqalani (d. 1449), while al-Shawkani wrote a similar commentary on a collection of legal Hadith made by the grandfather of Ibn Taymiyyah, who like his famous grandson was an adherent of the Hanbali school. In fact, along with the Andalusian scholar Ibn Hazm (d. 1064), an independent-minded jurist of the literalist Zahiri school, and earlier Zaydi traditionalists like Ibn al-Wazir, Ibn Taymiyyah was al-Shawkani's intellectual hero, just as he was for many other reformers of this and later periods.[21]

There was a theoretical basis to this engagement with non-Zaydi sources. Whereas Shah Wali Allah had presented himself as a *mujtahid* within the bounds of his Hanafi *madhhab*, al-Shawkani rejected this restricted type of *ijtihad* as a contradiction in terms.[22] Both he and Ibn al-Amir argued instead for the continued existence of 'unrestricted *ijtihad*', the free and independent legal reasoning that Wali Allah had ascribed to the founders of the schools of law, and which al-Shawkani discerned in the writings of iconoclastic intellectuals like his heroes Ibn Hazm and Ibn Taymiyyah. To assert that this kind of *ijtihad* had died out with the founders of the *madhhabs*, the Zaydi traditionalists contended, was to suggest that God's grace was limited to people who lived in certain eras.[23] Indeed, they argued, it was in many ways *easier* to undertake *ijtihad* now than it had been in earlier times, for contemporary scholars were more knowledgeable than their predecessors thanks to the greater availability of books on Hadith and the Arabic language.[24] Al-Shawkani's biographical dictionary of religious scholars who had lived since the seventh Islamic century – the thirteenth century AD – aimed to prove the point that jurists had continued to exercise *ijtihad* throughout the post-classical period and into the very recent past.[25] Ibn al-Amir is accordingly described in that work not only as the renewer of his time but also as 'the unrestricted *mujtahid*', a rank that al-Shawkani claimed to have reached himself before the age of thirty.[26]

This unrestrained exercise of legal reasoning had practical consequences, and often got the Zaydi traditionalists into trouble with their more conservative contemporaries. As we have seen, al-Shawkani was very conscious of the difficulties that his predecessor Ibn al-Amir had had to endure as a result of his traditionalist views. Ibn al-Amir underwent many trials at the hands of his contemporaries, al-Shawkani writes in his biographical dictionary, and the common people planned to kill him on one occasion after another, 'but God protected him from their treachery and deceit and preserved him from their evil'.[27] Indeed, Ibn al-Amir was made preacher at the Great Mosque of Sanaa in 1738 or 1739. Yet more trouble was soon to follow. First there was the controversy that ensued when Ibn al-Amir neglected to mention the name of the Imam in the Friday sermon, this being one of the formal means by which the legitimacy of the Imam was acknowledged, following which Ibn al-Amir was briefly imprisoned. Then came the uprising of the tribes of the notoriously lawless Jabal Barat region, who, urged on by Zaydi scholars whom al-Shawkani calls 'the devils among the jurists', accused Ibn al-Amir of having almost obliterated the Hadawi *madhhab* on account of his use of Sunni books and his adoption of legal positions that were characteristic of the Sunni schools of law.[28]

The issue that caused the most friction concerned Ibn al-Amir's views on how to perform the ritual prayer, particularly the issue of *raf' al-yadayn*, 'the raising of the hands' during prayer. The question of whether, and if so when, worshippers should raise their hands when performing the five daily prayers was one on which there was *khilaf* – disagreement between the schools of law. This apparently arcane issue, which has been described as 'one of the most controversial questions of Muslim ritual', had been vigorously debated since at least the ninth century AD. It is significant not only because how a person prays is a visible indicator of which legal school he or she belongs to, but more fundamentally because it concerns how to worship God correctly.[29] Among the Sunnis, the Hanafi and Maliki schools hold that the hands should be raised only when saying *Allahu akbar* – 'God is most great' – at the beginning of the prayer, while the Shafi'is and Hanbalis repeatedly raise their hands when bowing and rising during the prayer. The reason for this disagreement, as with most forms of *khilaf*, is that there are conflicting Hadith reports on the issue, as well as a conflict between the Hadith and the customary practice – or *'amal* – of Medina, which Malik and his school hold to be authoritative.[30] There is also an interreligious dimension to the debate: raising the hands during prayer was associated with Jewish practice, on the basis of a Hadith in which Jabir ibn 'Abd Allah, a Companion of the Prophet who had been on the pilgrimage to Mecca with Muhammad, related that only the Jews raised their hands when they saw the House of God.[31] Those who sought to limit the practice sometimes did so on the basis of another Hadith, in which the Prophet warned, 'Whoever imitates a people becomes one of them.'[32]

The Zaydis did not raise their hands when performing the ritual prayer. Yet, based on their study of the Sunni Hadith collections and the major texts of Shafi'i law, the Zaydi traditionalists regarded raising the hands repeatedly during the prayer as a *sunnah*, or normative custom. 'Whoever says that this [that is, raising the hands] is an innovation,' Ibn al-Amir quotes the Hadith collector al-Bukhari saying, 'defames the Companions.'[33] Citing the Hadith report, 'When he [that is, the Prophet] got up to pray he raised up his hands', as well as the opinions of Shafi'i scholars and the Zahiri Ibn Hazm, al-Shawkani likewise argues that there is a consensus within the Islamic community on the necessity of lifting the hands at the beginning of the prayer. In response to those Zaydis who reject this practice, he further notes that the Hadith about the Prophet raising his hands when he rose to pray is cited by Zayd ibn 'Ali, from whom Zaydism got its name, in the legal text attributed to him, and that the majority of Zaydi Imams recommended it.[34] As with his claim that *ijtihad* had been commanded by the Imams, in making this point Shawkani was seeking to present his traditionalism as an authentic expression of the Zaydi tradition, even while he was reforming that tradition in an unmistakably Sunni direction.

In keeping with his views on the ongoing necessity of *ijtihad*, besides undertaking independent reasoning himself, al-Shawkani also sought to perpetuate *ijtihad* through education. In *The Etiquette of Seeking Knowledge*, al-Shawkani outlines a programme of study for those aiming to become a *marja'* – or reference point on the content of the divine law – through their teaching and their writing of books and fatwas. An aspiring scholar of this rank, he explains, must pursue a curriculum consisting of sixteen scholarly disciplines, from grammar and logic, through legal theory, the interpretation of the Qur'an and the sciences connected to the study of Hadith, to history, poetry and the natural sciences. Of these subjects, al-Shawkani considered the study of the prophetic Sunnah to be the most important, describing it as 'a lantern to all other sciences'.[35] Like Shah Wali Allah and other reformers of the period, the Zaydi traditionalists' programme of renewal was centred on a recovery of the practice and piety of the Prophet, hence this emphasis on the study of Hadith. In fact, al-Shawkani encouraged those who wished to practise *ijtihad* to bypass, in their minds, the centuries intervening between themselves and Muhammad and envision themselves as Companions of the Prophet: the *mujtahid*, he writes in his treatise on education, 'imagines himself present at the time of prophecy and the coming of revelation', and should pretend that no *mujtahid* has preceded him, for 'the legal provisions relate to him as they did to the Companions, without any difference'.[36]

While his sixteen-part curriculum was for those who aimed to become 'unrestricted' *mujtahids* like himself, al-Shawkani also opened the door to ordinary Muslims who had not received so extensive an education to undertake *ijtihad*. In his view, anyone who knew enough Arabic to understand the Qur'an and Sunnah, along with the essentials of legal theory, was a *mujtahid* of a sort. Ordinary Muslims who did not have direct knowledge of scripture should ask a qualified scholar to provide them with the proof texts for the different views on a legal question, and should then make up their own minds on the basis of their common sense, a process that constituted 'following' – in Arabic, *ittibaʿ* – rather than *taqlid* or blind emulation.[37] In *The Etiquette of Learning*, al-Shawkani accordingly sets out study courses for lower categories of religious scholar alongside the curriculum suitable for the advanced *mujtahid*.[38] As we saw at the beginning of this chapter, he also practised what he preached, teaching the Hadith collection of al-Bukhari to ordinary Muslims at the Great Mosque of Sanaa, much as al-Nabulusi had taught Ibn ʿArabi to all comers at the Umayyad Mosque in Damascus. As the historian of early modern Islam Ahmed Dallal has written, this effort to widen participation in legal reasoning contributed to a kind of 'democratization of knowledge' in modern Islam, reinforcing the popularizing tendency initiated by Shah Wali Allah and his sons.[39]

That said, like al-Nabulusi, al-Shawkani, who himself came from an aristocratic Zaydi family, was by no means an unqualified egalitarian. 'Nobility of descent', he explained, was the most important factor in predisposing a person to acquire knowledge. Members of 'lowly' professions such as tailors, weavers and butchers had an inherently 'base disposition', which meant that people of those backgrounds who acquired a measure of scholarly knowledge often became conceited, with the result that religious scholars got a bad name – language reminiscent of al-Nabulusi's dismissal of the so-called 'jurists of the masses'.[40]

When it came to the treatment of non-Muslims, too, the Zaydi traditionalists took a harsh view. According to a Hadith report recorded in the canonical Sunni collection of al-Bukhari, on his deathbed the Prophet had ordered that the *mushrikun* – the Qur'anic term for those who associate others with God – be driven out of the Arabian Peninsula. In the view of the Zaydi Hadawi school, this command was qualified by another report, in which the Prophet ordered that 'the Jews of the people of Hijaz' be expelled from Arabia. The Zaydis interpreted this Hadith to mean that the Jews were only barred from the Hijaz, the region of western Arabia in which the sacred cities of Mecca and Medina were located, but not from Yemen or other parts of the peninsula.[41] The Zaydi Imams had accordingly allowed Jews to live in Yemen as *dhimmis*, protected yet second-class members of society, who were subject, at least in theory, to the conditions set out in the so-called 'Pact of 'Umar', the historic treaty which defined the legal status of the non-Muslim subjects of an Islamic polity. These conditions included prohibitions on building new churches or synagogues or repairing old ones, on conducting religious ceremonies in public spaces and on proselytizing members of other religions, while the dhimmis also promised, among other things, not to wear Muslim dress, adopt Muslim names, sell alcohol to Muslims or prevent their co-religionists from embracing Islam. Protected non-Muslims also paid the *jizyah* poll tax, which was an important source of revenue for the public treasury.[42]

In the 1660s, however, this state of affairs was disrupted in the wake of a wave of messianic activity that followed the appearance in the Ottoman Empire of the self-declared

Jewish messiah – and later convert to Islam – Sabbatai Zevi (d. 1676). In reaction to this Jewish messianism, which many Muslims feared could form the basis for political revolution, the Zaydi Imam al-Mutawakkil Isma'il (r. 1640–76) undertook several repressive measures against his Jewish subjects, culminating in the order, from his own deathbed in 1676, that the Jews be expelled from Yemen – 'an occurrence', as the historian of Jewish life in the Islamic world S. D. Goitein wrote, 'very common in Christian Europe but absolutely unheard of in Arab Islam'.[43] In 1679, the order was carried out: the synagogue in Sanaa was destroyed and a mosque – called the Mosque of the Expulsion – built in its place. The Jews of the capital were driven to the Mawza' region, near the port of Mocha, with the aim of deporting them to India. Many died during the hard journey, though the survivors were soon allowed to return.[44]

These events reopened the question among Zaydi scholars of whether the existence of a Jewish community in Yemen violated the Prophet's dying wish. In 1725, responding to a claim by the chief rabbi of the Yemeni Jewish community that he had issued a fatwa permitting *dhimmis* to sell alcohol to Muslims (in violation of the Pact of 'Umar), Ibn al-Amir wrote a short treatise in which he urged the Imam to expel the Jews once and for all. The Prophet's deathbed command demanded it, he explained, and this was only confirmed, not qualified, by the Hadith about the Jews of the Hijaz. Nor was there any *maslahah*, or public benefit, in allowing the Jews to remain, as some contended, and it was likewise wrong to assume, as a statement attributed to Imam 'Ali indicated, that a mistaken pardon is better than a mistaken punishment. When the fundamental texts were clear, they had to be implemented.[45]

In maintaining this strict view, Ibn al-Amir was following the opinion of another Zaydi traditionalist, Salih al-Maqbali (d. 1696), who had played a key role in the events of 1679.

Al-Shawkani, likewise, was an advocate of expulsion. Yet the traditionalists were opposed by other prominent scholars, including two of Ibn al-Amir's teachers, who upheld the long-standing Zaydi view that the Prophet's command to expel the polytheists from the Arabian Peninsula did not apply to the Jews of Yemen. After the temporary banishment of 1679, no further expulsions were implemented by the Qasimi Imams, though the Jews of Yemen were subjected to other forms of persecution, such as occurred in 1761, when, on the advice of Ibn al-Amir and other traditionalist scholars, the Imam al-Mahdi (r. 1748–85) ordered the destruction of fourteen synagogues along with several Jewish houses in Sanaa.[46] The persecution intensified after al-Shawkani became chief judge in 1795. He wrote no fewer than three treatises arguing for the implementation of the so-called 'latrines' edict', which obliged Jews to collect faeces and other rubbish from the houses and public places of Sanaa, on the grounds that this humiliating practice was in keeping with the legal prescription that the *dhimmis* be 'abased'. He likewise wrote two treatises justifying a decree of uncertain provenance – which was in fact a breach of Islamic law – that Jewish orphans should be converted by force to Islam.[47] That said, al-Shawkani's commitment to sticking close to the revealed texts sometimes led him in a more tolerant direction. For instance, he argued against the imposition of extra taxes on the *dhimmis*, on the grounds that only the *jizyah*, or poll tax, was mentioned in the Qur'an.[48] He also displayed an uncommon interest in Jewish and Christian beliefs and scriptures and stressed those elements that were shared by the three Abrahamic monotheism, writing a treatise on *The Agreement of Religions on the Oneness of God, the Hereafter, and Prophethood* and another on the legitimacy of citing the Bible.[49]

As repugnant as their intolerant attitude towards the Jews of Yemen is to a modern reader, what is most striking about the views of the Zaydi traditionalists – from their insistence on the continued existence of *ijtihad* to their efforts at widening access to the tools required to undertake it – is the note of optimism that resounds through their programme of renewal. Talk of renewal is often associated with pessimism about the state of the Muslim community, where renewal is a response to a decline that is seen in many ways as inevitable. Ibn al-Amir and al-Shawkani do speak of decline and are undeniably proud of their status as dissident intellectuals in a time of moral and intellectual corruption. Yet true renewal, for them, is possible, because there will always be unrestricted interpreters of the law, who are able to draw out from the scriptural sources legal rulings that are relevant for contemporary problems. Indeed, because the leading scholars of the present age are in many respects better placed to interpret the law than their predecessors, not just the renewal of Islam but actual *progress* in our understanding of the faith can be attained.

The perennial barrier to the realization of true Islam, of course, was *taqlid*. Its corrosive effects were especially visible in those religious practices which, as the Yemeni reformers saw it, undermined the principle of monotheism. Of particular concern to the Zaydi traditionalists was the cult of saints, which the scholar of Sufism Alexander Knysh has described as 'a salient feature of Yemeni Sufism'.[50] At the beginning of the nineteenth century, al-Shawkani wrote a book titled *The Well-Strung Pearl on the Sincere Expression of Monotheism*, in which he took aim at those he called *quburiyyin* – 'people who frequent graves' – who seek the intercession of dead saints by visiting their tombs. In this text, which would become an important source for twentieth-century Salafi reformers, al-Shawkani argues that, while it is permitted to seek the aid and assistance of the living in those matters over which human beings have control, it is pure *shirk* ('associating' others with God, or polytheism) and *kufr* (unbelief) to ask the dead to help accomplish things that are under the sovereignty of God alone, such as the salvation of their souls. Although there is nothing wrong with visiting the graves of prophets, Imams and Sufi saints *per se*, those who speak to the dead in terms fitting only for God – like the group from northern Yemen who, visiting the tomb of the Zaydi Imam al-Mahdi Ahmad ibn al-Husayn (d. 1258), addressed him as *arham al-rahimin*, 'the most merciful of the merciful' – are no better than polytheists.[51]

These condemnations were rooted in an understanding of *tawhid*, the fundamental Islamic doctrine of monotheism, which al-Shawkani and the Zaydi traditionalists had inherited from the medieval reformer Ibn Taymiyyah, who stressed the importance not just of *believing* that there is only one God, but also of *worshipping* this one God to the exclusion of all others.[52] This idea is articulated in systematic form in Ibn al-Amir's treatise *Purifying Doctrine from the Filth of Heresy*, another source of inspiration for Salafi reformers in the twentieth century. Noting that he felt obliged to write the treatise 'because I saw and realised that the common people were taking God's servants as His equals, in towns and villages and in all the lands – in Yemen, Syria, Najd, Tihamah, and all the Islamic regions', Ibn al-Amir explains that there are two kinds of *tawhid*. First, there is the monotheism which recognises God as the Lord and Creator of all, a kind of monotheism that even the *mushrikun* – the polytheists who associate others with God – acknowledge. But there is also a second kind of monotheism, which singles out God alone for *'ibadah* or worship. The prophets, he continues, had been sent to confirm the first kind of monotheism, and to lead the polytheists away from *shirk al-'ibadah*, 'polytheism in worship', which includes invoking, taking refuge in or seeking the intercession of others besides God, and towards the monotheism of the second kind. Most importantly, God does not accept the first kind of monotheism unless it is accompanied by the exclusive worship of Him. Acknowledging God as Lord and Creator, in other words, is not enough to be saved; a believer also needs to put this belief into practice.⁵³

The distinction between these two kinds of monotheism – what is called *tawhid al-rububiyyah*, the monotheism of God's lordship, on the one hand, and *tawhid al-'ibadah*, the monotheism of worship, or *tawhid al-uluhiyyah*, the monotheism of God's divinity, on the other – and the assertion that true monotheism entails the exclusive worship of God as well as the recognition that God is one, was the guiding principle of another movement of renewal that emerged in the eighteenth century. Described by Ignaz Goldziher as 'one of the most remarkable theological and military movements in the history of the Arab people', it would go on to leave a major imprint on modern Islam.⁵⁴ Those who adhered to this movement referred to themselves as *al-muwahhidun*, 'the true monotheists', as a way of claiming that they alone were properly practising *tawhid*. Their opponents called them *al-wahhabiyyun*, the Wahhabis, after their founder, Muhammad ibn 'Abd al-Wahhab (d. 1792).

A native of 'Uyaynah, the largest town in the central Arabian region of Najd, Muhammad ibn 'Abd al-Wahhab received his early education from his father, a Hanbali scholar and judge, before embarking on a series of travels which took him to the Hijaz, the Iraqi town of Basra and the oasis of al-Ahsa in eastern Arabia.⁵⁵ In Medina he attended the same Hadith study circles that had been frequented by Shah Wali Allah. Among his teachers was an Indian scholar of the Naqshbandi Sufi order and Hanafi school of law, Muhammad Hayat al-Sindi (d. 1750), who had taught Abu Tahir al-Kurdi, one of Wali Allah's teachers, and the son of al-Nabulusi's correspondent Ibrahim al-Kurani. According to Wahhabi sources, on being asked by Ibn 'Abd al-Wahhab his opinion of those who sought intercession at the tomb of the Prophet, al-Sindi anticipated his student's later opposition to the cult of holy men by quoting Moses' rebuke of an idol-worshipping people whom the Children of Israel wished to imitate: 'Surely this they are engaged upon shall be shattered, and void is what they have been doing' (Q. 7:139).[56] Al-Sindi, and Ibn 'Abd Wahhab's other principal teacher in the holy cities, 'Abd Allah ibn al-Sayf, another native of Najd, may have also passed on to him an admiration for the writings of Ibn Taymiyyah, the most cited scholarly authority in Ibn 'Abd Wahhab's own works, as well as the characteristic feature of eighteenth-century reform: the traditionalist insistence on deriving doctrine directly from the Hadith instead of *taqlid*.[57]

Returning to Najd in the 1730s, and by now apparently convinced that the Islam of his time had been corrupted by practices that amounted to polytheism, Ibn 'Abd Wahhab settled in the town of Huraymila, where his father was the judge.[58] In Huraymila he compiled his most-studied work, *The Book of Monotheism*, a collection of Qur'anic verses and prophetic Hadith with brief commentary, arranged into sixty-six chapters, the titles of which indicate how many of the practices prevalent in Najd and the wider region amounted to *shirk*, that is, to a violation of 'the monotheism of divinity', the worship of God to the exclusion of all else. These included seeking *barakah*, or blessing, in trees and stones, seeking protection or help from other than God, and adorning, visiting or praying at the graves of the righteous.[59] This text was widely copied throughout Najd and seems to have been used as a kind of textbook for inculcating into students Ibn 'Abd Wahhab's strict notion of monotheism.[60]

Ibn 'Abd Wahhab's denunciation of popular religious practices, as well as what he regarded as the 'deviant' sexual activity of the town's inhabitants, made him many enemies in Huraymila. With his life apparently threatened, and his father, who disapproved of his son's zealotry, having died in 1741, he returned to his hometown of 'Uyaynah. There he made an alliance with the ruler of the town, 'Uthman ibn Mu'ammar, whose expansionist policies he promised to support in exchange for the ruler's propagation of the true doctrine of *tawhid* – a foretaste of the similar pact he would strike with Muhammad ibn Sa'ud a few years later.[61] In 1742, he wrote a letter to the inhabitants of Basra on the meaning of the first half of the Islamic declaration of faith – 'There is no god but God' – in which he set out his core ideas. *Shirk*, the association of others with God, he laments, has spread throughout the Islamic world, particularly in the form of the supplicatory prayers that people offer at the tombs of prophets and saints. True monotheism means worshipping God alone, and 'worship' involves seeking aid and assistance as well as veneration and prayer.[62] Up to this point, Ibn 'Abd al-Wahhab's position, which was evidently rooted in Ibn Taymiyyah's distinction between the two types of *tawhid*, was very close to that of the Zaydi traditionalists and their strictures against the *quburiyyin*. Indeed, Ibn al-Amir was initially sympathetic to the Najdi reformer, writing a poem in which he identified his own views on the idolatrous nature of many aspects of shrine religion with those of Ibn 'Abd al-Wahhab and advised the latter to persevere in the face of the misunderstanding and hostility of his contemporaries.[63]

Yet Ibn 'Abd al-Wahhab then went further than the Zaydi traditionalists. Besides directing all worship to God, true monotheists must directly challenge those who engage in *shirk*. 'Do not think,' he writes, 'if you say, "This is the truth. I follow it and I abjure all that is against it, but I will not confront them and I will say nothing concerning them," do not think that that will profit you. Rather, it is necessary to hate them, to hate those who love them, to revile them, and to show them enmity.'[64] For Ibn 'Abd al-Wahhab, 'the true test of faith', as the historian of Wahhabism Cole Bunzel has put it, is the duty of *bughd wa-'adawah*, showing 'hatred and enmity' to those guilty of associating others with God.⁶⁵ This is a Qur'anic phrase, used in scripture in both a negative context (the hatred and enmity that Satan desires to instil in those who drink wine and gamble [Q. 5:91]) and in a positive sense (the hatred and enmity shown by Abraham and his followers to the polytheists of their time [Q. 60:4]). It was in this latter sense that Ibn 'Abd al-Wahhab used the term. In his view, worshipping God alone, and confronting those who violated monotheistic worship, was the true Abrahamic monotheism.

In practical terms, showing hatred and enmity meant practising *bara'ah*, another term used by the Qur'an in relation to Abraham, which denotes 'disassociating' oneself from the polytheists (Q. 43:26, 60:4), and *takfir*, the declaration that those who engaged in what Ibn 'Abd al-Wahhab regarded as polytheism were outside the fold of Islam.⁶⁶ Indeed, drawing on Ibn Taymiyyah, Ibn 'Abd al-Wahhab went further by advocating what his biographer Michael Crawford has called 'secondary *takfir*', the view that anyone who did not condemn those engaged in polytheistic practices as unbelievers was himself an unbeliever.⁶⁷ And the consequence of declaring people unbelievers was that, once the *da'wah* or 'summons' to true monotheism had been rejected, jihad, which in this context unequivocally meant armed struggle, ought to be waged against them. For Ibn 'Abd al-Wahhab, jihad is 'the first of the works of Islam', and those who waver in performing this 'absolute duty' are guilty of 'preferring the ephemeral to the eternal, and selling pearls for dung and goodness for evil'.⁶⁸

This was not simply a theoretical position. In 1744 or 1745, Ibn 'Abd al-Wahhab was ordered to leave 'Uyaynah following an incident in which he ordered that a woman who confessed to adultery be stoned.⁶⁹ He moved to Dir'iyyah, the second largest town in Najd, which was ruled by Muhammad ibn Saʿud. Soon after his arrival, Ibn ʿAbd al-Wahhab and Ibn Saʿud are said to have made a pact similar to the agreement that Ibn ʿAbd al-Wahhab had made with Ibn Muʿammar in ʿUyaynah. 'The *shaykh*,' writes the nineteenth-century Wahhabi chronicler Ibn Bishr (d. 1873), referring to Ibn ʿAbd al-Wahhab, 'promised the ruler earthly success provided he abandoned non-Islamic taxes and committed himself to *tawhid*. He told him that whoever adhered to *tawhid*, acted on it, and supported it would master both country and people.'[70] In return, Ibn Saʿud pledged to stamp out polytheism in Najd, if necessary by force. 'From then on,' explains the scholar of Islam Henri Laoust, 'it was impossible to separate the destiny of the shaykh from that of the Saʿuds.'[71] The three Saudi states that controlled Najd and various other parts of Arabia in the years 1744 to 1818, 1824 to 1891 and 1902 to 1932, as well as, most significantly, the Kingdom of Saudi Arabia that was founded in 1932, would all propagate the Wahhabi interpretation of Islam.

As the accounts of his pact with Ibn Saʿud indicate, the main target of Ibn ʿAbd al-Wahhab's reforming zeal was his native region of Najd, where, Ibn Bishr relates, 'polytheism had spread at that time ... and the belief in trees, stones and graves had multiplied'.[72] In the first instance, this meant reforming the only loosely Islamized Bedouin of the Arabian Desert. Though Wahhabism is sometimes mistakenly characterized as the product of a desert mentality, in fact Ibn ʿAbd al-Wahhab reserved some of his sharpest criticism for the Bedouin, condemning their customary tribal law as *hukm al-taghut*, 'idol's rule', and attacking, among other things, their principle of retaliation and their violation of the Islamic legal injunctions which gave women the right to inherit.[73] The unbelief of the Bedouin, he writes in one epistle, is many times worse than that of the Jews.[74]

Nor did the townspeople of Najd escape Ibn ʿAbd

al-Wahhab's campaign to purify the practice of monotheism. When the Bedouin came down to the settled areas at the time of the harvest, Ibn Bishr relates, they brought with them healers who indulged in all sorts of polytheistic rites, such as animal sacrifices to deities other than God, which they propagated among the gullible town dwellers.[75] One of the first acts that Ibn 'Abd al-Wahhab carried out after concluding his pact with Ibn Mu'ammar, the ruler of 'Uyaynah, was to send a group of followers to cut down a group of sacred trees from which the people of 'Uyaynah would seek blessings. Ibn 'Abd al-Wahhab is reported to have cut down the most revered tree himself.[76]

Yet though his focus was on Najd, Ibn 'Abd al-Wahhab was also concerned with how Islam was being practised beyond his immediate vicinity. Two groups were especially touched by his polemics, namely, the Sufis and the Shi'ah. Ibn 'Abd al-Wahhab's relationship with Sufism is more complicated than the stereotypical image of bitter conflict between Wahhabis and Sufis would suggest. Sufis were few and far between in Najd and appear only rarely in Ibn 'Abd al-Wahhab's writings.[77] Ibn 'Abd al-Wahhab's followers maintained that they were not opposed to a 'purified' or reformed version of Sufism, their founder having been conscious of the importance of inner piety.[78] Indeed, his grandson Sulayman ibn 'Abd Allah Al al-Shaykh (d. 1818), an important Wahhabi scholar during the first Saudi state, in a book explaining the meaning of *tawhid*, stresses that love of the divine – a characteristic feature of mystical piety – is an essential component of undivided worship of the one God. 'The word *'ibadah* [that is, worship],' he writes, 'entails the perfecting of humility through the perfecting of love, so the worshipper must love the worshipped deity perfectly.'[79] In so doing, he was drawing on the mystical dimension of the piety of Ibn Taymiyyah, who, as the leading scholar of his thought Jon Hoover has written, 'often uses love as a synonym for worship'.[80] Sulayman also uses Sufi terminology in describing *'ubudiyyah*, the condition of being a servant or worshipper of God, as the noblest of the *maqamat* or 'stations' reached by Muhammad, the 'stations of the path' being a key concept in Sufism.[81]

That said, certain kinds of Sufism were irreconcilable with Wahhabi doctrine. The metaphysical monism of Ibn 'Arabi and the passionate mystical love poetry of the revered Egyptian poet Ibn al-Farid (d. 1235) were especially detested by Ibn 'Abd al-Wahhab, who described their teaching (like the beliefs of the Bedouin) as 'worse unbelief than that of the Jews and Christians' and declared that anyone who followed it – a group that would include al-Nabulusi as well as Shah Wali Allah – was an unbeliever.[82] The philosophical Sufi tradition of Ibn 'Arabi had elevated the Prophet Muhammad into 'the perfect human', asserting that the world had been created out of Muhammad's primordial light. One of the aspects of Sufi-influenced Islam that Ibn 'Abd al-Wahhab particularly loathed was the excessive veneration of the Prophet. He is accordingly accused of having burned *The Proofs of Good Deeds*, a widely used collection of prayers for the Prophet written by the fifteenth-century Moroccan Sufi al-Jazuli (d. 1465), in which 201 names of honour are ascribed to Muhammad and the believer prays for the intercession of the Prophet and a vision of him in this life.[83] Copies of al-Jazuli's prayer book were among the books destroyed by the Wahhabis during their rule over the Hijaz between 1805 and 1812.[84] Similar was Ibn 'Abd al-Wahhab's attitude to *The Mantle Ode* of the thirteenth-century Egyptian poet al-Busiri, another much-loved work of Prophet-centred mystical piety, described by the nineteenth-century explorer Richard Burton 'as universally read by the world of Islam'.[85] In Ibn 'Abd al-Wahhab's view, the verses, 'O most noble of creation, none have I to seek refuge in / but you ...', which al-Busiri addressed to the Prophet, were nothing short of *shirk akbar*, 'greater polytheism', that is, the kind of polytheism that makes a person an unbeliever.[86]

The Wahhabis regarded Muhammad as a prophet worthy of emulation rather than a mediator with God or a semi-divine being with whom a believer should seek mystical union. The Anglo-Irish peer George Annesley, Viscount Valentia, who travelled through Yemen at the beginning of the nineteenth century, relates from a 'good friend' of his who was 'avowedly a Wahabee' that Ibn 'Abd al-Wahhab's followers held that Muslims need not pray for God's blessing on the Prophet more than once in their lives and should not invoke the Prophet to intercede with God on their behalf, 'for his intercession will be of no avail'.[87] The Swiss traveller Johann Ludwig Burckhardt, who was in the Hijaz in 1814–15, likewise notes that 'the Wahaby forbids the pilgrimage to Mohammed's tomb at Medinah', for he 'regards Mohammed as a prophet, but merely as a mortal to whom his disciples pay too much veneration'.[88]

This hostility to the idea of human mediation with God also determined the Wahhabi attitude to the cult of saints. While the veneration of holy men was not unique to the Sufi orders, being a characteristic feature of popular religion in the premodern Islamic world, it was often associated with Sufism, and Ibn 'Abd al-Wahhab regarded this kind of mystical religion as polytheism and unbelief. 'Believing in the pious,' he wrote, '... is polytheism and whoever engages in this is an unbeliever.'[89] Particularly egregious were those practices linked to *ziyarah*, or the visitation of saints' tombs, such as those of the revered Sufis Ahmad al-Badawi (d. 1276) at Tanta in Upper Egypt or 'Abd al-Qadir al-Jilani (d. 1166) in Baghdad.[90] 'Touching the graves or visiting them with the intention of invoking [the dead],' Ibn 'Abd al-Wahhab affirms, 'do not belong to the religion of the Muslims.'[91] Here he was again following Ibn Taymiyyah, who, in Jon

Hoover's words, had undertaken a 'jihad against error in grave visitation'.[92]

Yet though Ibn Taymiyyah had criticized the practice of visitation, he had never actually taken it upon himself to destroy the tombs of the righteous. In this respect the Wahhabis went much further. 'Wherever the Wahabys carried their arms,' writes Burckhardt, 'they destroyed all the domes and ornamented tombs.'[93] When Saʿud ibn ʿAbd al-ʿAziz (r. 1803–14), the ruler of the first Saudi state, conquered Mecca in 1803, he wrote to the Ottoman sultan Selim III, announcing proudly, 'I destroyed all the tombs which they idolatrously worshipped'.[94] The domes over the houses in which the Prophet, his first wife Khadijah, his son-in-law ʿAli and the first caliph Abu Bakr were said to have been born were razed to the ground, while both the Maʿlah cemetery near Mecca, which was believed to contain the tomb of Khadijah, and the Baqiʿ cemetery in Medina, where many notable Companions and descendants of the Prophet were buried, were also vandalized, as proof of the Wahhabis' commitment to Ibn Taymiyyah's principle that no place is inherently sacred.[95]

Even more so than in Sufism, the idea of human mediation with God, and the accompanying practice of visitation, are essential features of Shiʿi Islam. The Imams, according to a tenth-century Twelver Shiʿi creed, are the 'gates of God and the road to Him'; like Noah's ark, those who board the Imam's ship will obtain salvation, while those who do not will perish.[96] Pilgrimage to the shrines of the Imams at Najaf, Karbala, Kadhimiya and Samarra in Iraq and Mashhad in Iran is an important feature of Twelver piety, one of its principal purposes being to seek the Imams' intercession with God.[97] For the early Wahhabis, Michael Crawford observes, the Shiʿah were therefore the 'archetypal associationists', that is, practitioners of *shirk*.[98] Writing to a prominent Shiʿi scholar in Najaf in the late eighteenth century, the Saudi leader ʿAbd al-ʿAziz (d. 1803), the son of Muhammad ibn Saʿud and father of Saʿud ibn ʿAbd al-ʿAziz, declared that the Shiʿi practice of visiting the tombs of their Imams was equivalent to polytheism, to which the Shiʿi scholar responded that seeking the Imams' intercession with God was in fact an affirmation of God's unity and omnipotence.[99]

When the Saudi-Wahhabi forces took the Iraqi city of Karbala in 1801, they desecrated the tomb of Husayn, the Prophet's grandson and the third Imam, whose martyrdom at the hands of the Umayyads at Karbala in 680 is a trauma of cosmic significance in Shiʿism, commemorated annually on ʿAshuraʾ, a day of deep mourning and lamentation for Shiʿi Muslims.[100] 'The Muslims,' writes the Wahhabi chronicler Ibn Bishr, by which he means the true Wahhabi monotheists, '... destroyed the tomb erected above the grave of al-Husayn (as claimed by those who believe in it); they took what was inside and around the shrine; and they took the monument that was placed above the grave and studded with emeralds, rubies, and jewels.'[101] Whereas Ibn Taymiyyah had refused to declare 'moderate' Shiʿah unbelievers,[102] Ibn ʿAbd al-Wahhab called all Shiʿi Muslims *Rafidah*, 'Rejecters', a term of abuse denoting their rejection of the caliphs Abu Bakr and ʿUmar, and deemed them, like the pagan Bedouin and the followers of Ibn ʿArabi, worse in their polytheism than the Christians and Jews.[103]

Ibn ʿAbd al-Wahhab's crusade against intercession, the visitation of tombs and other characteristic features of the Islam of his time, Sunni as well as Shiʿi, earned him numerous enemies. Beginning in the 1740s, and continuing throughout the eighteenth and nineteenth centuries, countless treatises were written condemning Ibn ʿAbd al-Wahhab and his followers as extremists who misunderstood Islam and threatened the harmony of the Islamic community with their sectarian violence. The opposition began close to home. Ibn ʿAbd al-Wahhab's father took a dim view of his son's enthusiasm for religious reform, and his brother Sulayman, who succeeded their father as *qadi* (Islamic judge) of Huraymila, was likewise hostile to the Wahhabi message, criticizing his brother for misreading Ibn Taymiyyah and for treating regions outside of Saudi-Wahhabi control as 'the abode of war', that is, lands of unbelief which needed to be subdued for true Islam.[104] Like other critics of Wahhabism, Sulayman likened the Wahhabis to the Kharijites, the archetypal violent extremists of early Islamic history who had rebelled against, and then killed, the fourth caliph 'Ali and declared any Muslim who committed a major sin to be an apostate who deserved death.[105] The Wahhabis' opponents also compared them to the Qaramitah, an Isma'ili Shi'i movement which in 930 had massacred the pilgrims in Mecca and stolen the black stone from the Ka'bah.[106] Ibn 'Abd al-Wahhab was himself said to be a new Musaylimah, a contemporary of Muhammad who is regarded in the Islamic tradition as the paradigmatic false prophet.[107]

What was most repulsive, in the view of the Wahhabis' critics, was their all too free and easy use of *takfir*, that is, their calling other Muslims unbelievers. It was this that turned Ibn al-Amir, who as we have seen was initially sympathetic to Ibn 'Abd al-Wahhab, against the Wahhabi reformer. Withdrawing the poem that he had written in support of Ibn 'Abd al-Wahhab, the Zaydi traditionalist wrote a second poem in which he condemned the violence that he had wreaked upon the Muslim world as a result of his broad definition of unbelief:

> Explain to me, explain to me, why did you shed their blood,
> Why did you plunder their wealth deliberately, with full intention,
> When both have been made inviolable by their profession that

There is no God but the glorious all-powerful God?[108]

For many anti-Wahhabi polemicists, Ibn 'Abd al-Wahhab's misuse of *takfir* showed that it was he who was the real unbeliever. 'If he is of sound mind,' wrote one Hanafi contemporary, 'then he is an unbelieving heretic whose killing is a duty for all who are capable of getting hold of him.'[109]

As Ahmed Dallal has argued, Ibn 'Abd al-Wahhab's predilection for *takfir* makes him an outlier among eighteenth-century Islamic reformers.[110] Nevertheless, certain key features of Wahhabi teaching are representative of a broader trend in Islamic renewal before the era of European colonialism. The Wahhabi hostility to the idea of mediation between man and God reflects a tendency towards egalitarianism that can also be found in the thought of al-Nabulusi, Shah Wali Allah and the Zaydi traditionalists. As we have seen, in Ibn 'Abd al-Wahhab's doctrine, salvation is obtained through *tawhid*, meaning both the belief in and exclusive worship of the one God who created the heavens and the earth. The meaning of *tawhid* is clearly set out, as he understands it, in the Qur'an and Hadith, and it is the duty of all Muslims, 'male and female and learned and unlearned alike', to study these texts and put their teachings into practice.[111] It is as easy, therefore, for a humble believer to be saved as for a learned jurist or saintly mystic, and that humble believer does not have to rely on the jurist or saint for his or her salvation. 'Everyone,' as Michael Crawford aptly puts it, 'was equidistant from God.'[112]

Wahhabism is sometimes compared in this regard to Protestant Christianity. 'The religion of the Wahabys,' Johan Ludwig Burckhardt writes, 'may be called the Protestantism or even Puritanism of the Mohammedans.'[113] Besides their emphasis on scripture and opposition to the idea of saintly mediators, the Wahhabis' attacks on supposedly frivolous activities such as music, smoking and coffee-drinking are also reminiscent of the campaigns of Christian Puritans, as well as the earlier struggles of the Qadizadelis.[114] Yet the key teaching of the Protestant Reformers was that salvation is attained through faith alone. For the Wahhabis, by contrast, faith in the one God needs to be accompanied by the exclusive worship of that God and adherence to His law, meaning that salvation is attained through a combination of faith and works.

In the view of the Wahhabis themselves, Ibn ʿAbd al-Wahhab was above all a *mujaddid*. Ibn Bishr opens his history of the Wahhabi mission with the observation that God periodically 'sends to this community someone to renew its religion and revive the customs of its Prophet', the implication being that Ibn ʿAbd al-Wahhab is such a renewer. The task of the *mujaddid*, Ibn Bishr explains, is twofold. Negatively, the renewer is tasked with removing from God's religion any form of polytheism along with the innovations which lead people astray. Positively, he must establish true monotheism, ensuring the spread of the declaration that there is no god but God.[115] Such, in a nutshell, is the Wahhabi message.

Ibn ʿAbd al-Wahhab, who seems to have conceived of himself as a *mujaddid*, claimed that understanding the true meaning of the Islamic declaration of faith was a blessing that had been given to him directly by God.[116] The Wahhabi chroniclers similarly write of how God had 'opened the breast' of the Najdi renewer, an expression that is used about the Prophet in the Hadith corpus.[117] In asserting that his programme of renewal was divinely inspired, Ibn ʿAbd al-Wahhab was echoing the claims made by al-Nabulusi and Shah Wali Allah. Yet his programme of renewal had a much harder edge than theirs. The Qurʾanic verses 'kill the polytheists' (Q. 9:5) and 'strive [that is, practise *jihad*] in the cause of God' (Q. 22:78), Ibn Bishr explains, speak directly to the mission of the *mujaddid*.[118] For the Wahhabis, the renewal of Islam would have to be brought about by force.

4

Following the Prophet: The Muhammadan Path

Describing the process of *ijtihad*, al-Shawkani encouraged the scholar to envision himself as a Companion of the Prophet. For the Zaydi traditionalist, this was an exercise of the imagination. For many Sufis of the eighteenth and nineteenth centuries, by contrast, it was actually possible to *become* a Companion of the Prophet through mystical visions of Muhammad. Such visions were thought to be the result of repeatedly praying for the Prophet. They could take place when the mystic was awake or asleep, and are sometimes described in terms of union with the Prophet or 'annihilation' – *fana'* – in him, a concept that went back to Ibn 'Arabi.[1] They enabled the mystic to take his or her understanding of Islam directly from the Prophet himself and in this way to bypass and transcend both the schools of law and the existing Sufi orders. Those orders, or *tariqahs* (literally, 'paths'), these mystics believed, culminated in a new path that was in fact the original and most comprehensive mystical way. This was *al-tariqah al-muhammadiyyah*, the Muhammadan Path.[2]

The term *al-tariqah al-muhammadiyyah* had been used by the sixteenth-century Ottoman scholar Mehmed Birgivi as the title of his book on ethical reform. Birgivi, however, used the term to denote the importance of studying Hadith and emulating the moral virtues of the Prophet.[3] The mystical use of the term may owe something to 'Abd al-Ghani al-Nabulusi, who, as we have seen, was a commentator on both Birgivi and Ibn 'Arabi. The concept of the mystical Muhammadan Path, however, emerges in several parts of the early modern Muslim world almost simultaneously in the generation after al-Nabulusi.

One route came from India, and the work of the Persian poet Khwaja Mir Dard (d. 1785) and his father Nasir Muhammad 'Andalib (d. 1759). A Sufi of the Mujaddidi branch of the Naqshbandi order, Nasir Muhammad was born in Delhi in 1693/4, into a family of *sayyids* – descendants of the Prophet – who were close to the Mughal emperors. One of his teachers in Sufism was a grandson and successor of Ahmad Sirhindi, the renewer of the second Islamic millennium, after whom the Mujaddidi order was named. This grandson of Sirhindi's, Pir Muhammad Zubayr (d. 1740), was the fourth and final Mujaddidi *qayyum-i zaman*, 'the everlasting of the age', a title invented by Sirhindi to denote the perfect mystic of the time, 'the vicar of God on earth', who acts as a mediator between God and creation. 'Like a minister to a king,' writes Sirhindi, '... the business of created beings is conducted through him'.[4] Another of Nasir Muhammad's Mujaddidi masters, the ecstatic Sufi poet and musician Shah Sa'd Allah Gulshan (d. 1728), who played an important role in the development of poetry in Urdu, introduced him to the writings of Ibn 'Arabi and the verses of his teacher, the great sixteenth-century Indo-Persian poet Bidel (d. 1721). Gulshan also gave Nasir Muhammad the pen name 'Andalib, 'the Nightingale', by which he became known.[5]

Around 1734, during a week-long spiritual retreat, 'Andalib had a vision of Hasan, the grandson of the Prophet, just as

Shah Wali Allah had seen Hasan and his brother Husayn only a few years previously in Mecca. According to the narrative related by his son, Mir Dard, 'Andalib told him that the holy spirit of Hasan had appeared to him and placed 'inspirations' into his heart, telling him to pass these on to others. When 'Andalib asked Hasan whether he should call this teaching the 'Hasani' path, the Prophet's grandson replied that the path was not his, but Muhammad's: 'Our name stems from the name of Muhammad, our mark is the mark of Muhammad, our love is the love of Muhammad, and our invitation is the invitation of Muhammad,' he said, '... My way is the way of the Prophet, and my path the Muhammadan path (*tariqa-yi Muhammadiyya*). I only finish what has already been revealed.'[6]

'Andalib accordingly named his way *tariqah-yi khalis-i muhammadiyyah*, 'The Pure Muhammadan Path', a name that implied that he was filtering out the 'impurities' of the existing spiritual paths through a renewal of the 'pure' religion of the Prophet.[7] The teachings of that pure religion were elaborated in *The Nightingale's Lament*, a massive work in prose and poetry that 'Andalib first composed orally over the course of three days in Urdu on hearing of the death of his beloved teacher Pir Muhammad Zubayr in 1740, shortly after the ruler of Iran Nader Shah's devastating conquest of Delhi. The expanded written text, which 'Andalib dictated to Mir Dard in Persian, was composed, he states, 'for every man and woman', 'from king to pauper, from elite to commoner', another indication of the democratizing tendency in eighteenth-century Islamic thought.[8] The book revolves around an allegorical tale of two lovers, Prince Mihr Jahangir and an ascetic's daughter, who are transformed by the ascetic's curse into a nightingale and a rose, leading to a quest to find a special jewel that would break the curse.[9] Within this frame story, however, are interspersed long reflections on Islamic mysticism, theology, philosophy and law, retellings of traditional Indian tales, and discussions of Hindu philosophy and yoga, through which the reader is instructed in the Pure Muhammadan Path.[10]

That path, 'Andalib indicates, consists in the emulation of Muhammad's character, customs and teachings, as they are recorded in the Hadith. Like Shah Wali Allah, 'Andalib stresses that Hadith are the criterion for assessing all ideas and actions.[11] By following the Hadith, the 'Pure Muhammadans' are able to unite the Shari'ah and the *tariqah* – the divine law and the spiritual path – observing the Prophet's legal prescriptions with precision while also purifying their souls.[12] Since the Hadith are 'the comprehensive texts', giving guidance on all issues,[13] the Pure Muhammadan Path is a comprehensive path, meaning that those who follow it are able to overcome the sectarian divisions – between Sunnis and Shi'ah, the schools of law and the Sufi orders – that have blighted the Islamic community. 'My way and approach is assimilation,' writes 'Andalib, using language that again closely echoes that of his compatriot and contemporary Shah Wali Allah. 'My path is all-encompassing of the status and states of the different ways and approaches.'[14]

Of particular concern to 'Andalib was the reconciliation of the conflict between Sufis of the so-called *wujudi* and *shuhudi* perspectives, that is, between those who professed *wahdat al-wujud*, 'the oneness of being', the doctrine associated with Ibn 'Arabi and his followers, and those who upheld *wahdat al-shuhud*, 'the oneness of witnessing', the idea, associated with Sirhindi, that the unity between God and creation witnessed by the mystic is merely a subjective experience, not an objective metaphysical reality. Where Shah Wali Allah sought to harmonize *wahdat al-shuhud* and *wahdat al-wujud* as two stations along the same mystical path,[15] 'Andalib was far more sympathetic to the *shuhudi* perspective, criticizing the *wujudis* in harsh terms for having misinterpreted Ibn 'Arabi and accusing them of only pretending to be Sufis.¹⁶ He also criticized radical asceticism, preferring the worldly approach that was characteristic of the Naqshbandi Sufi tradition, which preached *khalvat dar anjuman* or being alone with God *within* society.¹⁷ This, 'Andalib explains, was the practice of the 'rightly guided' caliphs; it means, among other things, choosing marriage over celibacy – 'a married dervish,' he writes, 'will be a hundred times superior to a single dervish' – and looking after one's body, which is one of the benefits of yoga, in which 'Andalib displays a remarkable interest for a Muslim writer.¹⁸

'Andalib calls the restorer of pure Islam not the *mujaddid* but the *nasir*, or 'helper', of the religion of Muhammad, a title which evoked his own name of Nasir Muhammad.¹⁹ According to his son, 'Andalib was himself that 'helper';²⁰ indeed, he was no less than 'the *qiblah* of the two worlds', the person to whom all beings, in heaven and on earth, should direct their prayers, for his spiritual proximity to the Prophet had made him, like the Mujaddidi *qayyum*, God's representative on earth.²¹

Mir Dard, whose name means 'pain' in Persian – denoting the pain felt by the mystic lover on being separated from the divine beloved – is best known as a pioneer of mystical verse in Urdu and a Sufi musician. The poetry sessions and mystical concerts which he held in Delhi were famous; the Mughal Emperor Shah 'Alam II (r. 1759–1806) is said to have been among the participants. Yet he was also a mystical philosopher and the theorist of the Pure Muhammadan Path. Evoking Sirhindi, he thought of his work as an exercise in cyclical renewal.²² 'In every age,' he writes, 'a precious person appears from among the saints of this blessed community to undertake the revival and renewal of this clear religion.'²³ That person, he believed, was himself, and the renewal of the faith lay not in the established Sufi orders or books on theology or law, but in the Pure Muhammadan Path, which is the 'cream, quintessence, harvest and culmination' of all the existing spiritual ways and so has 'abrogated' other Sufi orders just as the religion of Muhammad had abrogated other religions.[24]

Dard entered that path at the feet of his father. His knowledge of mystical truths, he explains, did not come from reading classical manuals of the Sufi path, like the *Knowers of Mystical Truths*, a much-studied mystical handbook written by the thirteenth-century Sufi shaykh of Baghdad 'Umar al-Suhrawardi (d. 1234), or works on philosophical Sufism like *The Ringstones of Wisdom* of Ibn 'Arabi; rather, 'it is only from the abundant grace of the book *The Nightingale's Lament* that the door of all realities and subtleties was opened for my ignorant heart'.[25] Equally formative was the experience of having been there when his father had encountered Hasan, at which Dard submitted to 'Andalib's spiritual path and so became 'the first of the Pure Muhammadans'.[26]

Like his father, Dard was inspired by mystical visions. His own magnum opus, *The Knowledge of the Book*, completed in Persian in 1766/7, is an explanation of the 111 mystical 'inrushings' that he received from God between his entry to the path and his father's death in 1758.[27] Much as Ibn 'Arabi had claimed to receive *The Ringstones of Wisdom* in a vision of the Prophet, Dard claimed that his book had been given directly to him by God; indeed, he writes, 'the True Speaker [of the book] is always God'.[28] That being the case, the book is patterned on the Qur'an: Dard describes his text as *kitab-i mubin*, a 'clear' or 'clarifying' book, a term that the Qur'an uses about itself. In this way, he implied the existence of what Homayra Ziad has referred to as 'a type of continuing revelation' after the prophethood of Muhammad, an idea with roots in Ibn 'Arabi and Ahmad Sirhindi, and which, as we shall see, would later be developed by the Ahmadiyyah movement.[29]

The central topic of *The Knowledge of the Book* is what

Dard calls 'Muhammadan metaphysics'.[30] While heavily indebted to Ibn 'Arabi, Dard's metaphysical vision, or what he refers to as *tawhid-i muhammadi* or 'Muhammadan monotheism', professes to surpass both the theory of the 'unity of existence' associated with Ibn 'Arabi and the theory of the 'unity of witnessing' associated with Sirhindi; indeed, even more than his father, Dard is harshly critical of the *wujudis*, accusing them of relying too much on reason and of interpreting the Qur'an in accordance with their pre-existing ideas.[31] Nevertheless, for Dard like for Ibn 'Arabi and his interpreters, the phenomenal world is a self-manifestation or 'delimitation' of God's being, which reveals itself through a series of hierarchical 'descents'. Within this framework, a key role is allotted to the spiritual reality or 'light' of Muhammad. A Hadith often cited by the Sufis says that the first thing that God created was the light of His Prophet, and, in the writings of Ibn 'Arabi and his commentators, the 'Muhammadan Light' or 'Muhammadan Reality' is presented as both the first delimitation of God's being and the source of all other existent beings, similar to how Jesus as God's 'Word' or *logos* is presented in the prologue to the Gospel of John.[32] Dard describes the spiritual reality of Muhammad in much the same way: 'The reality of Muhammad,' he writes, '[is] the first manifestation of the sun of existence breathed into all existing entities [and] the reason that creation came into being.'[33]

This spiritual reality of the Prophet, Dard taught, is accessible to those who have traversed the Pure Muhammadan Path. 'Andalib, 'the Prince of the Muhammadans', is described by his son as a locus of manifestation of the Muhammadan Light.[34] Those who follow him earn the title of 'Pure Muhammadans', a status that Mir Dard restricts to *sayyids*, that is, to those, like himself, who are descended from the Prophet through 'Ali and his daughter Fatimah – an indication of the limits on the democratizing tendency in eighteenth-century Islamic thought.[35]

Since the light of Muhammad is the cause of created beings, these Pure Muhammadans recognize all things as a manifestation of the divine being, unencumbered by the limitations of particular perspectives.[36] They know God 'through presence' – a concept derived from the twelfth-century 'philosopher of illumination' Yahya Suhrawardi (d. 1191) – meaning that the distinction between the knower (the mystic) and the object of knowledge (God) disappears, the mystic knowing God not through reason but through passionate love or *'ishq*.[37]

But mystical absorption in God or His Prophet is not, as Dard saw it, the ultimate aim of the Muhammadan Path. Developing the classical Sufi distinction between *fana'* and *baqa'*, or the 'annihilation' and 'endurance' of the self, Dard teaches that the path consists of two three-stage cycles of annihilation and endurance: first, the mystic progresses from annihilation in the shaykh, through annihilation in the Prophet, to annihilation in God; then he or she passes from endurance in God, through endurance in the Prophet, to endurance in the shaykh.[38] This last concept, of the endurance of the mystic's self in the Sufi guide, was original to Dard, and seems to be related to the extremely close connection he felt to his father. Yet it also reflects a focus on activity in this world – as opposed to passing away into the realm of the spirit – which is characteristic not only of the Mujaddidi-Naqshbandi tradition out of which 'Andalib and Dard emerged, but also of other teachers of the Muhammadan Path in this period.

One of those teachers was Muhammad 'Abd al-Karim al-Samman (d. 1775). Born in Medina in 1720, a year before Mir Dard, al-Samman, whose name means 'the butter merchant', was an initiate of multiple Sufi orders, as was common in this period. His most famous teacher was Mustafa al-Bakri (d. 1748/9), a student of 'Abd al-Ghani al-Nabulusi and shaykh of the Khalwatiyyah order (so named because of its commitment to *khalwah*, the spiritual retreat), who like his teacher was an exponent of the Sufi metaphysics of Ibn 'Arabi and had claimed to have had no fewer than nineteen visions of the Prophet.[39] In 1760 al-Samman was in Cairo, where he earned a reputation for the *dhikr* sessions (Sufi gatherings at which the name of God and other pious formulae are repeatedly recited) that he held at the mosque and mausoleum of the Prophet's grandson Husayn.[40]

Most of his life, however, was spent in Medina. Indeed, al-Samman's life and thought were dedicated to the Prophet and his city. He lived near to al-Rawdah – 'The Garden' – the open space in the mosque of Medina near to where the Prophet is buried, which a Hadith calls 'one of the gardens of Paradise', and served as guardian of Muhammad's tomb.[41] When he died in 1775, he was buried near to the Prophet's wives in the revered Baqi' cemetery, which the Wahhabis would vandalise when they took Medina less than three decades later.[42]

Al-Samman's thought and piety hinged on the concept of the Muhammadan Light, the pre-existent spiritual reality of the Prophet out of which all things were created. Muhammad, al-Samman asserts in a short treatise on the celebration of the Prophet's birthday, is 'the light of being and the cause of all beings'.[43] In another treatise, *The Divine Revelations*, he explains that the Prophet 'is emanated from the light of the divine essence' and so encompasses 'all divine attributes, all divine actions, all divine effects, all divine names'.[44] Because he both embodies the divine names and attributes and is fully human, the Prophet is the 'isthmus' or *barzakh* – a Qur'anic term often used by Ibn 'Arabi and his interpreters – between God and creation.[45]

In contrast to the Wahhabis, who sought to eradicate any practices that placed human intermediaries between man and God, al-Samman built his vision of Islam around the idea of prophetic mediation. Whereas the followers of Ibn 'Abd al-Wahhab argued that worshipping and obeying God meant loving Him alone, al-Samman stressed the love of the Prophet above all others. 'I feel a strong love for the Prophet even in my bones, my spirit, my hair and my eyes,' al-Samman writes, 'like cold water refreshes in terribly hot temperatures.'[46] Just as Jesus, according to Matthew 10:37, had instructed his disciples to love him more than their own parents and children, so too did the Hadith of the Prophet indicate that true believers would love Muhammad more than they loved themselves, their wealth and their family. Through exclusive love of Muhammad, al-Samman taught, the believer could achieve *fana'* or annihilation in the Messenger. The ensuing stage of endurance – *baqa'* – in the Prophet is the prelude to an actual waking vision of Muhammad, an experience that all Muslims should strive to attain.[47] Al-Samman himself claimed to have met the Prophet while sitting near to the pulpit from which Muhammad had preached in the mosque of Medina.[48] Through visions such as this, he held, mystics could effectively become one of Muhammad's Companions, taking their knowledge of Islam directly from the Prophet just as the historical Companions did.[49]

These mystical experiences went hand in hand with a Prophet-centred practical piety. Like many Muslims of the post-classical period, al-Samman places special emphasis on prayers for the Prophet, like those collected in al-Jazuli's *Proofs of Good Deeds*, copies of which the Wahhabis would burn after their conquest of the Hijaz. Such prayers, al-Samman asserts, should be recited as often as possible. Other pious practices commended by al-Samman naturally include the visitation of the Prophet's tomb, as well as the celebration of the *mawlid* or birthday of the Prophet, another custom that the Wahhabis would outlaw following their conquest of the Hijaz, but which was deeply embedded in popular Islamic piety. The Dutch orientalist Snouck Hurgronje, who was in Mecca in 1884–5 (when the holy city was no longer under

Wahhabi control), reports that Muhammad's birthday was marked by recitations from the Prophet's biography, and that an unusually large number of women and children would come in their finest clothes to the mosque.⁵⁰ Hurgronje, who went on to serve as a professor and colonial official in the Dutch East Indies, also relates that al-Samman's followers in Indonesia were known for practising an especially boisterous and popular form of *dhikr* (also known as *ratib*) that had been introduced by al-Samman himself.⁵¹

Al-Samman's position as keeper of Muhammad's tomb meant that he received visitors from across the Muslim world; among those who came to pay homage to him were West Africans, Eritreans, Yemenis, Afghans and Indonesians.⁵² Some of them, like Ahmad al-Tijani (d. 1815), a Sufi from the oasis of 'Ayn Madi in south-western Algeria who met al-Samman while on pilgrimage in 1773/4, would themselves prove influential exponents of the Muhammadan Path. Under pressure from the Ottoman Turks, al-Tijani left Algeria in 1798 for the Moroccan city of Fez, where he remained until his death in 1815. He was on good terms with the 'Alawi sultan of Morocco Mawlay Sulayman (r. 1792–1822), who gave him a house, helped him build a *zawiyah* or Sufi lodge and appointed him to his council of religious scholars. Mawlay Sulayman and his father, Mawlay Muhammad (r. 1757–90), were traditionalist religious reformers who, possibly under Wahhabi influence, sought to revitalize Moroccan Islam by encouraging the direct study of the Hadith collections instead of the manuals of Maliki law (which enjoyed almost total dominance over North African Islam) at Fez's famous Qarawiyyin mosque-school and banning practices associated with popular Sufism, such as the celebration of saints' birthdays and the construction of domes over their graves.⁵³

Al-Tijani, who like other reformers felt that he was living in an age of unmatched impiety, was a supporter of these reforms.[54] His own vision of renewal, which is set out most clearly in *The Jewels of Spiritual Meanings*, a text completed by his disciple 'Ali Harazim (d. 1804) in the year he arrived in Fez, contains all the classic features of the Muhammadan Path. That path, he claimed, had been given to him directly by the Prophet. In 1782, while living in the oasis of Abu Samghun in the Algerian desert, al-Tijani experienced what his followers referred to as 'the greatest illumination'. The Prophet appeared to him while he was awake and told him that he should leave behind all spiritual paths and Sufi saints, for it was through his prophetic mediation and support that al-Tijani would achieve *tahqiq* or verified knowledge.[55] Nor was this a one-off; according to al-Tijani's disciples, many of whom also claimed to have received visions of the Prophet, Muhammad was a constant presence in the life of their shaykh, teaching him special prayers and answering his questions on religious matters.[56] Al-Tijani even claimed that *The Jewels of Spiritual Meanings* had been authored by the Prophet himself.[57]

These visions were possible because al-Tijani was in touch with the Muhammadan Reality, the light which al-Tijani described as the 'source' and 'sustenance' of all beings.[58] Verified knowledge – the *tahqiq* that the Prophet had promised al-Tijani in that first vision – meant actualizing this Muhammadan Reality within oneself, through exercises such as praying for the Prophet and the recitation of special litanies.[59] Al-Tijani, his followers believed, was a perfect mirror of the Muhammadan Reality. This being the case, following his path was the only way to Muhammad, which meant in turn that it was the only way to spiritual realization and salvation.[60] 'Anybody who loves you,' the Prophet is reported to have said to al-Tijani, 'is the beloved of the Prophet.'[61] By the same token, 'whoever disparages you, will die as an unbeliever, unless he is of my family'.[62] Just as Muhammad was the Seal of Prophets, so al-Tijani was the 'Seal of Saints', as Ibn 'Arabi had claimed to be, and as al-Nabulusi's and al-Samman's disciples had believed them to be.[63] He was the 'hidden' or 'supreme' pole around which the universe turned (a status, al-Tijani claimed, which conferred infallibility upon him) and his path – the Tijaniyyah *tariqah* – encompassed and abrogated all other spiritual paths, one consequence of which was that members of the Tijaniyyah order were forbidden from visiting other saints, both living and deceased.[64]

Following this path meant following the divine law. In al-Tijani's view, those who claimed to be Sufis but neglected the Shari'ah were what the Qur'an called 'the party of Satan' (Q. 58:19), and one of the chief signs of the corruption of the age was the improper performance of the ritual prayer. Adhering to the law, however, did not simply mean applying the manuals of Maliki jurisprudence that were taught in the Qarawiyyin and other madrasahs in the Maghreb. Though al-Tijani did not reject the *madhhab* tradition entirely, he thought that where possible the law should be taken directly from the Qur'an and Hadith, which needed to be interpreted by scholars with *basirah* or 'inner vision'. He declared smoking forbidden, for instance, on the grounds that the Prophet had said, 'Everything that saps the strength is forbidden.'[65]

Al-Tijani's Sufi order, the Tijaniyyah, would eventually become the leading *tariqah* in West Africa, while also winning numerous followers in the Maghreb, the Middle East and Southeast Asia. In part this success was down to the order's exclusivist insistence that Muslims should not follow any other spiritual paths. Perhaps even more important, however, was the fact that al-Tijani's interpretation of the Muhammadan Path tapped into a broader current of ideas that were circulating in West and North Africa at the time, such as the possibility – and desirability – of unrestricted *ijtihad* and of meeting the Prophet Muhammad in a waking state.

These ideas are expressed in *The Book of Pure Gold*, a text that was widely read in Tijani and other Sufi circles in the Maghreb. Compiled in Fez around 1720 by Ahmad ibn Mubarak al-Lamati (d. 1743), a scholar originally from the Saharan trading post of Sijilmasa who claimed unrestricted *ijtihad* for himself, *The Book of Pure Gold* records the teachings of al-Lamati's teacher 'Abd al-'Aziz al-Dabbagh (d. 1720).[66] Among the insights of this illiterate Sufi shaykh of Fez is that those who experience a mystical 'illumination' of the Prophet while awake attain a level of knowledge that far surpasses that of the ordinary religious scholars, and so are not bound by any of the schools of law. 'If all the schools of law were nullified', al-Lamati writes, the saint or 'friend of God' would 'be able to bring the divine law back to life'.[67]

Al-Dabbagh's teachings were carried forward by a follower of one of his disciples, Ahmad ibn Idris (d. 1837). A descendant of the Prophet through his grandson Hasan, Ibn Idris came to Fez around 1770, when he was about twenty, to study at the Qarawiyyin mosque, and remained there for roughly thirty years, overlapping with al-Tijani (though we do not know if they ever met). This was the period in which the 'Alawi sultans Mawlay Muhammad and Mawlay Sulayman were pushing through their traditionalist religious reforms at the Qarawiyyin, and Ibn Idris took eagerly to the study of Hadith, poring over the six canonical Sunni collections under the guidance of his teacher, the Hadith scholar Ibn Sudah (d. 1795). Having established himself as a teacher in his own right, Ibn Idris seems to have aroused the enmity of the Maliki jurists of Fez on account of his traditionalist commitment to deriving the law directly from the Qur'an and Hadith and his claim to have had visions of the Prophet. In 1798 he left Fez on pilgrimage, travelling through Egypt, where he is said to have taught at al-Azhar, the leading centre of Sunni orthodoxy in the Middle East, before settling in Mecca in 1799. He remained in the holy city following the Wahhabi conquest of the Hijaz in 1803, only leaving in 1813, when the Wahhabis were expelled by Muhammad 'Ali, the ruler of Egypt. He then spent some time at Luxor, before finally settling at Sabya, in 'Asir, a prosperous agricultural region in northern Yemen, for the final seven years of his life.[68]

Besides being, like his Zaydi contemporary al-Shawkani, a traditionalist in law, Ibn Idris was also a Sufi in the tradition of Ibn 'Arabi. In Sabya he would give two public lectures a day on Hadith and law, one after sunrise and the other after the afternoon prayer, while also teaching the *Ringstones of Wisdom* of Ibn 'Arabi and the Egyptian poet Ibn al-Farid's mystical *Poem of the Way* to a select few. His views on the law, Sufism and the Muhammadan Path are encapsulated in two texts, the first a treatise he wrote against the schools of law, and the second the record of a debate that he held with some Wahhabi scholars in Yemen in late 1832.[69]

In the first text, titled *An Epistle Refuting the Partisans of Opinion* – 'opinion', or *ra'y*, denoting fallible human judgement as opposed to the inerrant divine word – Ibn Idris stresses the importance of following revelation alone when trying to work out God's law.[70] The Qur'an and Sunnah, he explains, contain all legal rulings that are needed; whenever the scriptural sources are silent about something – such as the permissibility of singing, or of swaying and chanting during Sufi *dhikr* sessions – that act should not be interpreted using analogical reasoning, but should simply be declared permitted or 'forgiven'.[71] Like Ibn 'Arabi, whose approach to the law pervades his legal thinking, and Ibn 'Arabi's later interpreter al-Nabulusi, Ibn Idris stresses that the 'original permissibility' of things is part of the divine mercy that underlies the Shari'ah.[72] To issue a ruling on something that is not covered by the Qur'an or Sunnah is to claim divinity or 'lordship' for oneself and is a great sin – indeed, it is rank unbelief – and those who blindly emulate scholars who rely on their own opinion are guilty of *shirk* or polytheism.⁷³ Religious scholars who are unable to derive the law directly from scripture suffer from a lack of *taqwa*, a central Qur'anic term denoting the fear of God. *Taqwa*, Ibn Idris asserts, is the key to understanding the Qur'an, for the godfearing are given a special kind of 'discernment' – Ibn Idris uses the Qur'anic term *furqan* – enabling them to know the law in a direct, mystical way.⁷⁴

Here Ibn Idris' attack on the schools of law and advocacy of unrestricted *ijtihad* are interwoven with a Sufi belief in the possibility of acquiring knowledge directly from God and His Prophet. This mystical dimension of his thought meant that his relationship with the Wahhabis, whose traditionalism he shared, was necessarily marked by a certain ambivalence. As we have seen, Ibn Idris stayed in Mecca during the Saudi-Wahhabi occupation of the holy city, indicating a degree of mutual toleration between the two parties. In 1832, however, after he had moved to Sabya, a series of accusations were made against him by one of the Wahhabi 'volunteers' or *mutawwi'ah*, a kind of religious police, leading to a debate between Ibn Idris and some of the Wahhabi scholars of 'Asir. The Wahhabis were led by one Nasir ibn Muhammad al-Kubaybi, who opened the debate by extolling 'the preaching of the Najdi' (meaning Muhammad ibn 'Abd al-Wahhab) and claiming that the Wahhabi mission had rescued people from a state of *jahiliyyah* – that is, pre-Islamic barbarism and ignorance – in which they worshipped idols and permitted what was forbidden. Ahmad ibn Idris agreed with this proposition, but, when Kubaybi then declared that Ibn 'Abd al-Wahhab was the *mujaddid* or 'renewer' of the age, he protested that the Wahhabi movement was guilty of extremism and had erred in condemning as unbelievers and killing those who believed only in God – a criticism of the Wahhabis that we have also seen made by the Zaydi traditionalists of Yemen Ibn al-Amir and al-Shawkani.[75] Far from having recovered the original spirit of Islam, the Wahhabis, he asserted, were 'miserable wretches who are bound inflexibly to the externalities of the Law'.[76]

The debate then turned to the charges levelled against Ibn Idris. The first and foremost of these was his attachment to the 'unbelieving sect' of Ibn 'Arabi and his commitment to the doctrine of the unity of being, which, the Wahhabis declared, was unbelief, and, insofar as it assumed that God unites with His creation, was comparable to the Christian doctrine of the Incarnation.[77] In response, Ibn Idris resorted to arguments that we have seen employed by al-Nabulusi: even if some passages in Ibn 'Arabi's writings struck the Wahhabis as blasphemous, he asserts, it was wrong to label Ibn 'Arabi and his followers as unbelievers, since, it being impossible to look into another person's heart, there was no way to prove with the certainty required by the divine law that this was the case. 'The best way, in our opinion,' he declared, 'is to think well of people.' In any case, it was possible that the problematic passages in Ibn 'Arabi's writings were later interpolations.[78] Ibn Idris dealt similarly with the accusation that his own disciples had sinned by mixing with handsome young boys and women, thereby opening the door to fornication and other abominations. This accusation had no legal basis, he argued, because Islamic law requires four witnesses to prove a charge of sexual immorality, and no such witnesses were forthcoming. More fundamentally, it overlooked the metaphysical reality that all humans, save the prophets, are sinners, since humans must sin in order for God's mercy to be made manifest – a point that again echoes Ibn 'Arabi's approach to the law.[79] Elsewhere in his writings, Ibn Idris systematizes this charitable approach into four basic principles that should guide a Muslim's approach to everyday life:

(1) to remember, before every word or action, that God will question one concerning that action;
(2) to perform every word and action for God alone;
(3) to make one's heart a home for mercy toward all Muslims, great or small; and
(4) to treat one's family and household and all Muslims kindly and gently.[80]

Evidently, it was not only in his mysticism that Ibn Idris differed from the Wahhabis.

Nevertheless, mysticism remained central to Ibn Idris' Islam. In practical terms, his conception of the Muhammadan Path centred around the practice of *tawajjuh*, a term which had traditionally been used in Sufism (particularly within the Naqshbandi order) for the disciple's 'visualisation' of his Sufi guide as a means to obtaining mystical experiences, but which Ibn Idris applied to the visualization of the Prophet himself.[81] Ibn Idris' leading disciple, Muhammad ibn 'Ali al-Sanusi (d. 1859), explains the practice in the following way: if you imitate the Prophet in your words and deeds and continuously invoke God's blessings on him, he wrote, 'the vision of him takes hold of your heart and you see his form before your inner eye'. This, according to al-Sanusi, is the basis of the Muhammadan Path.[82]

Al-Sanusi was an Algerian *sayyid* who, like Ibn Idris, had studied in Fez before departing for the Islamic heartlands. In Fez he associated with Ahmad al-Tijani, from whom, al-Sanusi reported, he 'took' the Qur'an – meaning that he learnt its true meaning – just as al-Tijani had 'taken' the Qur'an directly from the Prophet in a mystical vision.[83] He was also connected, like al-Tijani and Ibn Idris, to the reforming 'Alawi sultans of Morocco, sharing their belief in the importance of studying Hadith and not being limited to the compendiums of the Maliki school of law. It was his desire to study the jurisprudence of the other schools of law, in fact, which seems to have motivated al-Sanusi's departure for the Middle East.[84] After visiting Mecca on pilgrimage in 1815 and returning to Fez and Algeria, he spent time at al-Azhar in Cairo before settling in 1826 in Mecca, where he became a disciple of Ibn Idris, his 'long-sought goal', with whom he studied the Qur'an, the six canonical books of Hadith and other major Sunni collections of prophetic reports.[85] When Ibn Idris left the Hijaz the following year, he appointed al-Sanusi as his *khalifah*, or representative, in Mecca. By the summer of 1828, al-Sanusi had built a large *zawiyah*, or Sufi lodge, on Jabal Abu Qubays, a hill next to Mecca, as a place of residence for the followers of Ibn Idris in the holy city. He would frequently travel back and forth between Mecca and Sabya, maintaining close contact with Ibn Idris until his master's death in 1837.[86]

Seeing himself as a *mujtahid* within the Maliki school (just as Shah Wali Allah had regarded himself as a *mujtahid* within his own Hanafi school), al-Sanusi was not as radical as his teacher in his critique of the *madhhab* tradition. He was initially hesitant to study with Ibn Idris because the latter did not follow any of the schools of law, a position that al-Sanusi compared to that of the Kharijites, the paradigmatic extremists of early Islamic history who recognized no authority except that of God. It was only the intervention of the Prophet, who, he believed, had come to him in a series of dreams, that persuaded him to follow Ibn Idris.[87]

Like his teacher and other eighteenth- and nineteenth-century reformers, al-Sanusi condemned *taqlid* and fanatical attachment to one's own school of law, advocating *ijtihad* in their place. His major work on legal theory, *Waking the Somnolent to Act upon the Qur'an and Hadith*, quotes liberally from Ibn Idris' treatise against the partisans of *ra'y* or fallible opinion and from the writings of both Ibn Taymiyyah and Ibn 'Arabi.[88] According to al-Sanusi, *taqlid* in the sense of emulating a scholar who responds to a legal question simply by declaring, 'This is my opinion or the opinion of my Imam or school', is forbidden; ordinary Muslims should only follow a scholar's opinion when it is backed up by proofs from the scriptural sources.[89] Like the Zaydi traditionalist al-Shawkani, whose ideas he may have been exposed to while in the Hijaz, al-Sanusi translated this emphasis on *ijtihad* into a rethinking of how the ritual prayer should be performed. Among his writings is a treatise on ten issues connected to ritual devotion in which he diverged from the authoritative Maliki opinion, including the issue of when to raise the hands during prayer that was so contentious in Zaydi Yemen. In challenging the traditional Maliki view on these issues, however, al-Sanusi was not declaring his departure from the Maliki school so much as claiming to have identified the correct Maliki position through his own *ijtihad*.[90]

Ibn Idris did not himself establish an organized Sufi order. That task would be left to his disciples, of whom the three most important were al-Sanusi, founder of the Sanusiyyah *tariqah*, which would become particularly strong in Cyrenaica in eastern Libya; the Meccan scholar Muhammad 'Uthman al-Mirghani (d. 1852), whose order, the Khatmiyyah, which found success in Sudan, was so named because, like al-Tijani, he claimed that his path was the culmination or 'seal' – *khatm* – of all spiritual paths; and Ibrahim al-Rashid (d. 1874), the initiator of the Rashidiyyah *tariqah*, which spread through Upper Egypt and northern Sudan into the Middle East and Southeast Asia.[91] They professed to carry on Ibn Idris' interpretation of the Muhammadan Path, which was exemplified in special prayers such as the 'Azimiyyah – so called because of the repetition of the divine name *al-'azim*, 'the Great One' – and in practices such as the visualization of the Prophet. At the same time, they added new elements to Ibn Idris' teaching.

In the case of the Sanusiyyah, one of those new elements

was millenarianism, the expectation of the imminent appearance of a messianic figure. Millenarian thinking in Islam is connected to traditions about the Mahdi, the messianic saviour whose coming will herald the end of time. The English explorer Richard Burton, visiting Mecca and Medina in 1854, found that some of al-Sanusi's disciples 'look upon him as the Mahdi'.[92] Inspired by a vision of the Prophet, al-Sanusi named his first son Muhammad al-Mahdi, which according to Islamic tradition will be the name of the Mahdi.[93] Muhammad al-Mahdi, who, having succeeded his father as shaykh of the Sanusiyyah, led the order from 1859 to 1902, did not himself claim to be the Mahdi, but the idea seems to have taken hold among his followers.[94]

Millenarian thinking was in fact a prominent feature of Islamic thought in the nineteenth century, particularly among Sufis connected to the Muhammadan Path movement. Often, such thinking was tied to a commitment to armed jihad and the establishment of an ideal Islamic polity. Islamic Africa was particularly fertile ground for this militant kind of millenarianism. A contemporary of Ahmad al-Tijani and Ahmad Ibn Idris, the Fulani scholar Muslim Usman dan Fodio (d. 1817) – known as 'the Shehu', or shaykh, to his followers – was a follower of the Maliki school of law and the Qadiri Sufi order who inspired a jihad in Hausaland (today's northern Nigeria) at the beginning of the nineteenth century. Islam had been established in Hausaland, a region divided into several kingdoms led by nominally Muslim rulers, in the fourteenth or fifteenth century, but its practice was often mixed with animist rites and customs.[95]

Usman dan Fodio's career was driven by hostility to this 'mixed' type of Islam. From his youth, his own piety centred on the figure of the Prophet. Inspired by *The Mantle Ode* of al-Busiri, which the Wahhabis had condemned as unbelief, among his earliest compositions were poems in Arabic and

Fulfulde – the native language of the Fulani people – in praise of the Prophet. 'I swear by the Merciful God,' he declares in a poem written in 1774, 'nothing graces me / Save my desire to love the Prophet Muhammad ... The sun of the forenoon, crown of right guidance, sea of generosity, / There is no other good than following Muhammad.'[96]

In the same year as he wrote this poem, Dan Fodio turned to missionary activity, travelling through the kingdoms of Hausaland preaching an Islam purified of pagan customs. In this concern for combatting the mixing of true monotheism and local paganism, Dan Fodio echoed the preaching of Muhammad ibn 'Abd al-Wahhab. Indeed, one of Usman's early teachers, the Berber scholar Jibril ibn 'Umar, who held the radical Kharijite position that sin made one an unbeliever, had been exposed to Wahhabi ideas while on the pilgrimage to Mecca. Yet Dan Fodio had also studied *The Meccan Revelations* of Ibn 'Arabi in his youth, and in the first part of his career he tempered this reforming zeal with the Ibn 'Arabi tradition's emphasis on charity towards one's fellow Muslims.[97]

His first major prose work, *The Revival of the Muhammadan Sunnah and the Extinguishing of Innovations*, which he completed before 1793, was written to instruct the Muslims of Hausaland in how to follow the practice of the Prophet and his Companions and avoid 'Satanic innovations' in their daily lives, covering such topics as how they should pray, what clothes they should wear and what they should eat and drink. The stress of this work, however, is more on the spiritual and moral benefits of following the path of Muhammad than on the condemnation of ordinary Muslims. Usman begins the treatise by citing a statement recorded in *The Well-Trodden Path* of Malik, the founding father of his legal school: 'Do not look into the faults of people as if you were lords, but look into your own faults, as if you were slaves.' Diverging from the Kharijism of his teacher, Jibril ibn ʿUmar, Dan Fodio asserts that it is not permitted to loathe any sinner who has uttered the Islamic testimony of faith. One should loathe them for their sin, he writes, echoing Augustine of Hippo, but love them for their faith.[98]

This sentiment was later repeated by Usman's daughter, Nana Asmaʾu (d. 1864), a scholar and Sufi who founded a successful educational movement – called the Yan Taru, meaning 'the Collective' in the Hausa language – for training female teachers. In her first work, *A Warning to the Ignorant and Reminder to the Rational of the Ways of the Pious*, written in Arabic in 1820, she explains that the 'remedy' for divine judgement is 'loving what is good for all Muslims, and loathing what is evil for them, and leaving aside three things, namely envy, hatred, and hypocrisy'. 'Enmity and opposition towards the believer', she likewise writes, is the first of the nine 'habits which cause one to perish'.[99]

Yet, as relations with the Hausa kings soured in the wake of their failure to heed his preaching and persecution of their Muslim subjects, Usman's own thinking became angrier and more militant. In a book on *The Difference between the Rule of the Muslims and the Rule of the Unbelievers*, he outlines the various ways in which the Hausa rulers had failed to uphold the Shariʿah. These include their imposition of un-Islamic taxes, their consumption of food and drink forbidden in God's law, marrying women without an Islamic marriage contract, their refusal to enact the scriptural penalties for crimes such as adultery and theft, their prohibition of veils and turbans and their indulgence in pastimes such as beating kettle drums on occasions not prescribed by the Shariʿah.[100]

Since preaching had failed to reform these abuses, more radical means were required. In 1794, Dan Fodio experienced the kind of mystical vision that was characteristic of reformers in the Muhammadan Path tradition, albeit with a militant twist. 'Abd al-Qadir al-Jilani, the twelfth-century founder of the Qadiri Sufi order, appeared to him on behalf of the prophets and saints and presented him with a green cloak embroidered with the Islamic testimony of faith, and a turban on which was inscribed the first verse of the 112th surah of the Qur'an: 'Say, He is God, One.' Addressing him as 'Imam of the saints', 'Abd al-Qadir then gave Dan Fodio the 'sword of truth' to use against the enemies of God.[101]

Ten years later, the sword of truth was unsheathed. In late 1803, Usman wrote *Important Issues*. In terms typically used to describe the actions of the Prophet and his Companions in the face of the persecution of the pagans of Mecca, he declares it an obligation to practise *hijrah* – emigration – away from pagan states and to wage jihad against them. At the beginning of the following year, he was elected Imam of the Muslim community of Degel, the settlement in which he had grown up and begun his preaching, and took the caliphal title of *amir al-mu'minin*, Commander of the Believers.[102] Apparently inspired by another vision of 'Abd al-Qadir al-Jilani, Usman and his followers then made *hijrah* to Gudu, located some thirty miles from Degel on the border of the Kingdom of Gobir, one of the major Hausa states.[103] For the next four years, Usman's followers, led by his son Muhammad Bello (d. 1837) and his brother 'Abd Allah ibn Muhammad (d. 1828), fought a jihad against the Hausa kingdoms. The result was the foundation of the Sokoto Caliphate, so named after the capital city built in 1809 by Muhammad Bello, who eventually succeeded his father as caliph.

In the aftermath of the jihad, Usman devoted himself once more to teaching and scholarship. Among the important works which date to this period is *An Explanation of God's Servants' Obligation to Emigrate*, in which he further develops his theory of *hijrah* and jihad and outlines how the Islamic state should be run.[104] Also indicative of his thinking at this time is the 1811 text, *The Lamp Guiding the Brethren to the Most Important Things Needed at this Time*. Departing from the tolerant attitude of *The Revival of the Sunnah*, he argues that those who merely utter the Islamic testimony of faith but do not practise the ritual devotions prescribed by the Shari'ah deserve to be fought. Like the Wahhabis, he further justifies fighting Muslims on the grounds that the helpers of the unbelievers – meaning, in this case, those who fail to support the jihad against the Hausa kingdoms – are themselves unbelievers who should be killed.[105]

Like other reformers of this period, Usman presented his campaign to purify Islam and establish an Islamic state in Hausaland as an exercise in renewal. In *The Lamp Guiding the Brethren*, he quotes al-Maghili (d. 1504), an influential Maliki scholar who had led an assault on 'mixed' Islam in West Africa at the turn of the fifteenth/sixteenth century and argued for the legitimacy of jihad against Muslims whose religion was contaminated with paganism.[106] The *mujaddid* sent by God at the beginning of every century, al-Maghili had written, 'commands what is right and forbids what is wrong' – a Qur'anic principle often cited by Muslim reformers – 'and reforms the affairs of the people, and judges between them, and assists the truth against vanity, and the oppressed against the oppressors'.[107]

This is how Usman dan Fodio saw himself and how he was seen by his followers. His daughter Nana Asma'u opens her book *A Warning to the Ignorant* by describing herself as 'the daughter of the renewer of the faith',[108] while her brother Muhammad Bello likewise describes their father as 'the renewer of the turn of this century'.[109] More than that, influenced by a prophecy that the Mahdi would appear at the beginning of the thirteenth Islamic century – about 1785 AD – some of his supporters regarded him as the messiah of the last days. While Usman denied this, he did draw a connection between his role as *mujaddid* and what he saw as the imminent advent of the Mahdi. 'By God, I swear that I am not the Awaited Mahdi,' he declares in one poem, 'But I am the one who comes to give good tidings about the Mahdi.' In another poem, written in 1814, he explains that the Mahdi would govern all corners of earth, join with Jesus in combatting Dajjal, the anti-Christ of Islamic tradition, and 'unravel ... the confusion that is involved in the tangle of the times'.[110] When combined with this kind of millenarian thinking, the concept of *tajdid* provided Usman with what Mervyn Hiskett has described as a 'ready-made rationale for revolution'.[111]

Throughout his work, Usman dan Fodio repeatedly cited the opinions of medieval authorities from his Maliki school, and most of his thinking was carried out within the bounds of Maliki tradition. Nevertheless, like other reformers, he was critical of *taqlid*, especially on questions of theology, and, under the influence of 'Abd al-Wahhab al-Sha'rani (d. 1565), a sixteenth-century Egyptian interpreter of the thought of Ibn 'Arabi, eventually came to adopt the position of Shah Wali Allah in arguing for breaking down the boundaries between the schools of law.[112] In a late work, *Guidance for Students*, he observes that Muhammad had brought not a school of law but the divine law: 'Does God in His Book or His Prophet in the Sunnah,' he asks rhetorically, 'make it necessary to rely on a single school of law or one *mujtahid* in particular?'[113]

An even stronger attitude towards the schools of law – closer, that is, to the stance of al-Shawkani and Ahmad ibn Idris – is discernible in another Sufi leader of jihad in nineteenth-century West Africa, the Tijani scholar al-Hajj 'Umar Tal (d. 1864). A Fulani, like Usman, and a native of Futa-Toro in the Senegal river basin, al-Hajj 'Umar had spent six years in Sokoto between 1831 and 1837 on his return from the pilgrimage to Mecca, where he had become a disciple and representative of Ahmad al-Tijani's deputy in the

Hijaz.[114] In Sokoto, 'Umar befriended and fought alongside Usman's son, Muhammad Bello, whom he seems to have initiated into the Tijaniyyah. Having imbibed from Bello the idea that nominal Muslims whose Islam was mixed with paganism ought to be fought, in August 1852 al-Hajj 'Umar announced that he had been instructed by a 'divine voice' to commence a jihad.[115] The resulting wars in the Senegal and Niger river basins brought him into conflict both with the non-Muslim Bambara states of Mali and the French colonizers, and with the king of Masina, who was a Fulani Muslim and follower of the Qadiri order. Al-Hajj 'Umar justified the jihad against him, as Usman had justified his own wars against Muslim rulers, on the grounds that, in aiding the unbelieving Bambara against him, the king of Masina had himself become an unbeliever.[116] This justification was rooted in the Kharijite principle that sin made a Muslim an unbeliever, though it may also have owed something to the exclusivism of the Tijani order. Adopting Ahmad al-Tijani's view of his order as the 'seal' of all spiritual paths, al-Hajj 'Umar, who was strongly opposed to the Qadiriyyah, declared that no other Sufi order would emerge after the Tijaniyyah.[117]

Al-Hajj 'Umar's jihad resulted in the establishment of an empire that stretched from Senegal to Timbuktu, and which would last until 1897. His conquests were crucial in spreading the Tijaniyyah in West Africa, where it became the dominant Sufi order. To his followers, al-Hajj 'Umar was the renewer of Islam in his time.[118] Reflecting the millenarian thinking circulating in this period, some regarded him as the Mahdi's minister, or perhaps as the Mahdi himself, though, like Usman dan Fodio, 'Umar did not claim to be the messiah.[119] A scholar as well as a military leader, al-Hajj 'Umar's major text, *The Lances of the Party of the All-Merciful against the Throats of the Party of the Accursed Satan*, which he completed in 1845, is regarded as one of the two most important texts of the Tijaniyyah, alongside *The Jewels of Spiritual Meanings* by Ahmad al-Tijani's disciple 'Ali Harazim.[120]

Drawing, like Usman dan Fodio, on Ibn 'Arabi's interpreter al-Sha'rani, in that work 'Umar argues forcefully against exclusive reliance on a single school of law. The only proper basis for legal judgements, he asserts, is the Qur'an and Sunnah, which are to be understood through the direct application of reason. The so-called founders of the four *madhhabs* had not, in fact, wished to establish a school of law or for people to emulate their legal judgements, since they knew that these were fallible. This being the case, diversity between the schools of law is to be accepted, and they should all be recognized as equally valid. Citing *The Book of Pure Gold*, the record of the teachings of the illiterate Moroccan mystic 'Abd al-'Aziz al-Dabbagh that had also influenced Ahmad ibn Idris and his followers, al-Hajj 'Umar further explains that the mystically inspired 'friend of God' or saint is not bound to any single school of law, and that, should the schools of law disappear, he would be able to recover the entire Shari'ah thanks to his spiritual connection with the Prophet.[121]

Besides these reflections on law and mysticism, which closely echo the ideas of other reformers in the Muhammadan Path tradition, al-Hajj 'Umar, who like Usman dan Fodio consciously sought to emulate the career of the Prophet, also devoted a chapter of *The Lances of the Party of the All-Merciful* to *hijrah* and jihad. According to a Hadith often cited in Sufi literature, the Prophet Muhammad, on returning from battle, is said to have declared that he had come back from the 'lesser jihad' (meaning armed struggle) to undertake the 'greater jihad' (which was interpreted to mean the struggle against the passions of the lower self).[122] For al-Hajj 'Umar, the greater jihad, meaning purifying one's soul, is a prerequisite for fighting in the way of God, though he still insists that dying in God's cause is the most meritorious way to die.[123]

Furthermore, 'Umar transposed the classical distinction between the two kinds of jihad onto his theory of *hijrah*. *Hijrah* – in this case meaning physical migration – is necessary, he declares, 'where disobedience to God is openly practised without any concern for it', meaning that faithful Muslims must abandon the 'land of the unbelievers' in preparation for armed struggle against it. Yet there is also a 'greater' *hijrah*, involving the abandonment of worldly attachments.[124] This second form of *hijrah* is linked to *zuhd*, the renunciation of the world, an important concept in Sufi piety, which in al-Hajj 'Umar's thought denotes not the renunciation of material comforts so much as 'detaching the heart' from the world while remaining involved in it.[125] Like the other Sufi reformers of the eighteenth and nineteenth centuries that we have encountered, al-Hajj 'Umar represents what the sociologist Max Weber called 'inner-worldly asceticism', in which the ascetic seeks, in Weber's words, 'to transform the world in accordance with his ascetic ideals' rather than abandoning it as a lost cause.[126]

According to Weber's theory, this desire to transform the world sometimes leads the ascetic to become a revolutionary. That was the case with two nineteenth-century Sufis connected to the Muhammadan Path tradition who were more explicit in claiming the title of Mahdi. The more famous of the two, at least in Europe, was Muhammad Ahmad (d. 1885), the so-called 'Sudanese Mahdi'. An initiate of the Sammaniyyah order – whose founder, Muhammad al-Samman, was one of the original theorists of the Muhammadan Path – he declared himself Mahdi in 1881 and became a household name in Britain following his conquest of Khartoum and the killing of General Gordon in 1885. Drawing on the Muhammadan Path tradition, Muhammad Ahmad claimed to have been invested as the Mahdi in a mystical vision of the Prophet in which Muhammad had placed him on his chair, designated him as his *khalifah* or viceregent and commissioned him to wage jihad against the unbelievers.[127] Constructing an Islamic state in the Sudan, he did away with the schools of law, asserting that the only three sources of the law were the Qur'an, the Hadith and his own mystical inspiration from the Prophet.[128]

More influential in the wider Islamic world, however, was the millenarian movement led by the Indian mystic Sayyid Ahmad Barelwi (d. 1831), and theorized by his disciple, Shah Muhammad Isma'il (d. 1831), the grandson of Shah Wali Allah, in the early decades of the nineteenth century. Having little formal education in Islamic theology and law, Sayyid Ahmad was a soldier and mystic who came aged eighteen to Delhi, where he was initiated into the Naqshbandi, Qadiri and Chishti orders by Shah 'Abd al-'Aziz, the son of Shah Wali Allah. Having been inducted in this way into what Shah Muhammad Isma'il called the 'path of sainthood', Sayyid Ahmad was also initiated into the 'path of prophethood' in a series of visions of the Prophet, the Prophet's daughter Fatimah and her husband 'Ali and ultimately of God Himself, at the Akbarabadi Mosque in Delhi in 1807.[129]

The son of Shah Wali Allah's youngest son, Shah Muhammad Isma'il had been raised by another of Wali Allah's sons, Shah 'Abd al-Qadir, who was famous for his translation of the Qur'an into the Hindi-Urdu vernacular. Trained, unlike his master Sayyid Ahmad, in the traditional Islamic sciences, Shah Muhammad Isma'il was known for his unusual fondness for athletic pursuits such as swimming, archery, riding and fencing, and for his fearless condemnation of innovations from the Sunnah of the Prophet.[130] Having been initiated by Sayyid Ahmad in 1811, Isma'il devoted himself to public preaching and missionary work. He would go to the brothels of Delhi to warn the patrons of their impeding judgement, and preached on the permissibility of widow remarriage – an issue which, under Hindu influence, was hotly debated in

South Asian Islam – at the city's Jami' mosque. Indeed, having been persuaded by Sayyid Ahmad that the prohibition on widow remarriage was a Hindu custom that contradicted the prophetic Sunnah, he not only arranged the marriage of his widowed sister, but went round the villages of northern India seeking out Muslim widows who might be remarried.[131]

Isma'il was also the theorist of Sayyid Ahmad's version of the Muhammadan Path. In *The Straight Path*, the 'manifesto' of the movement which he completed in 1819, he defines the distinction between the 'path of sainthood' and the 'path of prophethood', explaining that, while the former leads the mystic to the divine mysteries through saintly intermediaries, the latter grants direct access to God and His Prophet. The path of prophethood – the 'straight path' of the book's title, also known as the Muhammadan Path – involves scrupulous observance of the divine law that God revealed to His Prophet, hence the book also attacks innovations connected to Sufism, including the doctrine of the unity of existence (which Isma'il had earlier upheld, but which he seems to have rejected under Sayyid Ahmad's influence), and practices such as the visualization of the Sufi guide.[132]

Some of these ideas had already been voiced in *The Strengthening of Faith*, a text that was even more important for spreading the teachings of Shah Muhammad Isma'il and Sayyid Ahmad Barelwi. Written in a form of Hindi-Urdu that was intended, Isma'il declares, to be 'easy for the masses', *The Strengthening of Faith* was heir to the popularizing tradition represented by the Qur'an translations and commentaries of his famous grandfather and uncles.[133] One of the most pernicious and baseless myths current among ordinary people, Isma'il writes, is the idea that religion is difficult to understand, and hence that knowledge is restricted to scholars and saints. In fact, God has told us that the verses of His Book are 'explicit and conspicuously clear' – *saf saf* in Urdu – and so it is the religious duty of all Muslims, whether commoners or elite, to seek *tahqiq* or 'verified knowledge' of the Qur'an and Sunnah, to act upon that knowledge and to 'mould their faith within its framework'.[134] Facilitating that task, and the process of popularizing religious knowledge, was the rise of print in the Muslim world in this period. Sayyid Ahmad had his own printing press, enabling the wide circulation of Isma'il's works.[135]

The clear teaching that Isma'il wanted his readers to find in scripture, and which he stresses in his own work, is the distinction between *tawhid* and *shirk*, that is, between true monotheism, which Isma'il deemed to be 'in scarcity' in the India of his day, and polytheism, which he thought was widespread.[136] In Isma'il's view, polytheism did not simply mean believing in or worshipping other deities than God; it meant anything that undermined the unrestricted sovereignty of God. Indeed, so committed was Isma'il to God's absolute sovereignty that he insisted, controversially, that, if He wished, God could create a million Muhammads. To the objection of his opponents that God's ability to create more prophets would mean that God had lied when He declared in the Qur'an that Muhammad was the 'Seal of Prophets', Isma'il further insisted that God was capable of lying.[137]

These contentious views, which would go on to be major points of controversy between the differing ideological orientations of late nineteenth- and early twentieth-century Muslim India, were part of a larger assault made by Isma'il on the beliefs and practices of his Indian Muslim contemporaries. According to Isma'il, practices that undermine God's sovereignty include calling on prophets, saints, Imams or angels for assistance or thinking that those intermediaries have some role to play in one's destiny.[138] Specifically, Isma'il identifies four kinds of *shirk*. First, there is polytheism pertaining to knowledge – *'ilm main shirk* – which means imagining that another being shares in God's perfect and all-encompassing knowledge. Second, there is polytheism pertaining to the capacity to act – *tasarruf main shirk* – which means imagining that another being shares in God's perfect control over the affairs of the universe. Third, there is polytheism pertaining to worship – *'ibadat main shirk* – which means rendering any form of devotion to a being other than God. (Here Isma'il displays a special concern for the infiltration of polytheism into the rites associated with the Hajj, a ritual obligation on which he placed particular importance.) Finally, there is polytheism pertaining to customs – *'ibadat main 'adat* – as examples of which Isma'il gives performing an action in the name of someone other than God, or giving one's child a name such as 'Abd al-Nabi, 'the Servant of the Prophet', instead of 'Abd Allah, 'the Servant of God'.[139]

In seeking to purge Islamic monotheism of any hint of polytheism, Isma'il, as both his Sufi and Shi'i opponents and the British never tired of pointing out, echoed the preaching of the Wahhabis. Yet the similarity with the message of Ibn 'Abd al-Wahhab was most likely due to a common source – namely, Ibn Taymiyyah, to whose ideas Isma'il was exposed through the work of his grandfather, Shah Wali Allah, and especially through the influence of the Zaydi traditionalist al-Shawkani, to whom he wrote in 1822 asking for a copy of a work the Yemeni scholar had written on apocryphal Hadiths.[140]

Similar to the Wahhabis and al-Shawkani, as well as other reformers such as Usman dan Fodio and al-Hajj 'Umar Tal, Isma'il and his teacher recognized that the recovery of true monotheism could most easily be carried out from a position of political power. After the British conquest of Delhi in 1803, Sayyid Ahmad's teacher Shah 'Abd al-'Aziz had issued a fatwa declaring India to be *dar al-harb*, 'the abode of war' where unbelief reigned. Shah 'Abd al-'Aziz did not, however, recommend emigration from India, and in practice his ruling meant that dispensations could be made for certain acts – such as the charging of interest on loans – that were forbidden in territories under Muslim rule.[141] Sayyid Ahmad and Shah Muhammad Isma'il, however, seem to have gradually reached the conclusion – as Usman dan Fodio and al-Hajj 'Umar likewise did – that emigration from the abode of unbelief was obligatory. In 1826, Sayyid Ahmad and his followers left British India for the North-Western Frontier region, which was dominated by Pashtun tribes. From there they waged a jihad against the Sikh empire that had been established in the Punjab by Ranjit Singh in 1799, apparently with the eventual aim of confronting the British.

The theory of *hijrah* and jihad that motivated these actions is outlined in *The Rank of the Imamate*, a work composed by Shah Muhammad Isma'il in Persian in 1827. If *The Strengthening of Faith* was written to restore God's sovereignty in the realm of everyday practice and belief, *The Rank of the Imamate* was concerned with the recognition of divine sovereignty in the political realm.[142] So, while the crucial distinction in the earlier text had been between monotheism and polytheism, here the key dichotomy is between what Isma'il calls 'the politics of belief' (*siyasat-i imani*) and what he terms 'the politics of power' (*siyasat-i sultani*). 'The politics of belief' denotes the kind of political community founded by the prophets, whose politics were motivated by 'abundant love' for their people and aimed at their moral reform. 'The politics of power', by contrast, signifies a political system that is set up to serve the interests of the ruler, and which is driven by the desires of his *nafs* or base self.[143] The worst kind of power-based politics, Isma'il further states, is what he calls 'the kingdom of unbelief' – *saltanat-i kufr*. Crucially, the ruler of such a kingdom might or might not be a Muslim; what defines his polity as a kingdom of unbelief is that God's law is suppressed. 'Resisting and killing this ruler,' Isma'il writes, 'is the essence of Islam', and it was the religious duty of all Muslims living in his realm either to migrate away from it or to wage jihad against it.[144]

At the opposite end of the spectrum from the kingdom of unbelief is the 'rightly guided' caliphate, the archetypal form of the politics of belief. Within Sunni Islam, this term is conventionally applied to the viceregency of the first four caliphs – Abu Bakr, 'Umar, 'Uthman and 'Ali – whose rule is held to constitute a golden age of Islamic politics. While recognizing the first four caliphs as examples of 'the most perfect Imam', however, Isma'il did not regard the rightly guided caliphate as a thing of the past.[145] The Prophet, he says, had predicted the appearance of another rightly guided caliph who would be a type of Mahdi – not the 'awaited Mahdi' who heralded the end of time, but what he calls *mahdi ul-wasat*, a 'Mahdi of the middle period', whose task was to reform the world.[146] The implication, of course, was that this intermediate Mahdi was Sayyid Ahmad.

In May 1831, Sayyid Ahmad Barelwi was killed, together with his chief disciple and theorist Shah Muhammad Isma'il, by the Sikhs at Balakot. Henceforth, both men were known to their supporters by the title *shahid* – 'the martyr'. For many, Sayyid Ahmad's martyrdom only reinforced his messianic status; some of his supporters believed, as the Shi'ah did of their twelfth Imam, that he had not died but gone into *ghaybah* or 'occultation', in preparation for his victorious return as the Mahdi.[147] Yet it was not the millenarianism that surrounded his career, but the example of Sayyid Ahmad's armed struggle, and his disciple Isma'il's reformist preaching and writing, that would leave the deepest imprint on South Asian Islam in the nineteenth and twentieth centuries.

Islamic thought in the Sunni world in the eighteenth and early nineteenth centuries was marked by the appearance of several concurrent visions of renewal. Though each of these visions was unique, they shared a number of common characteristics. In practically all cases, the recovery of true Islam was linked to a call for a return to the revealed sources of the religion – the Qur'an and especially the Hadith. This call was often expressed, at least in a legal context, in terms of the desirability of *ijtihad* and the reprehensibility of *taqlid* and fanatical attachment to a single school of law. For many theorists of renewal, particularly those with links to Sufism, this act of going back to the fundamental texts was reinforced by a belief that they were directly connected to God and His Prophet through mystical experiences. These experiences enabled them to claim the exalted status of Companions of the Prophet and, in some cases, to assert that they were the 'Seal of Saints' of Sufi tradition. While the history of the Wahhabi reform movement, which looked critically on the more ecstatic and theoretical kinds of Sufi mysticism, is well known, it is in fact this mystical kind of renewal that is the more prominent in early modern Islamic thought. Even the Wahhabis were open to a 'sober' kind of Sufism, and portrayed Ibn 'Abd al-Wahhab as a divinely inspired reformer, just as the followers of the Sufi proponents of renewal did.

Often inspired by the Sufi metaphysics of Ibn 'Arabi, the Sufi renewers were typically advocates of a charitable attitude towards other Muslims and, in some cases, towards non-Muslims. In this regard, they were again different from the Wahhabis, who took little persuading to declare other Muslims to be unbelievers who were worse than the followers of other religions, and from the intolerant attitude of the Zaydi traditionalists, whose thought would prove influential within twentieth-century Salafism. Nevertheless, none of the Sufi thinkers we have met in these chapters was an unqualified pluralist, and in some cases their mysticism was connected to a millenarianism that manifested itself in a commitment to separation from the unbelievers and violent jihad against them.

Another defining feature of the visions of renewal put forward in the eighteenth and nineteenth centuries – by both Sufis and non-Sufis – is their egalitarian tendency. This tendency, a departure from the hierarchical orientation of much premodern Islamic thought, is a corollary of the call for a return to the scriptural sources, the implication being that those sources – and the divine knowledge contained within them – are equally available and accessible to all, and that their meaning does not need to be expounded by specialist interpreters. Again, however, theirs was a qualified egalitarianism. Many of the Sufi renewers, coming as they did from *sayyid* backgrounds, and inspired as they were by visions of Muhammad and his family, were of the view that certain forms of knowledge could only be attained by descendants of the Prophet. And while the Wahhabis and the Zaydi traditionalists railed against the notion of saintly intermediaries standing between man and God, the Sufis often claimed that the path to God went through the mystic guide in his capacity as 'God's helper', 'the perfect human' or 'the Imam of the saints'.

Islamic reform of the early modern period can be characterized as 'renewal from within', in two senses. First, the visions of renewal articulated in this period were a response not so much to external challenges to the *ummah* as to a sense that Islamic society was disintegrating from within, owing to the corruption of Islamic practice and belief as Muslims lost sight of the fundamental sources of their religion. Second, for the thinkers whom we've met in these chapters, the reform of society had to be preceded by a renewal that took place within the human person. It was by remoulding the practices and beliefs of individual believers, in the first instance, that Islam would be renewed at the wider societal level. As al-Hajj 'Umar

Tal put it, a prerequisite for the jihad against the unbelievers was a jihad against unbelief in one's own soul, just as, in the view of Ahmad ibn Idris, understanding the Qur'an and Hadith was dependent on *taqwa* – the fear of God – being present in the interpreter's heart. In this as in their emphasis on the direct study of scripture and the vernacularization of religious knowledge, the Islamic reformers of the eighteenth and early nineteenth centuries echoed those Protestant Reformers in sixteenth-century Europe who, quoting Paul's Letter to the Ephesians, urged their followers to first 'be renewed in the spirit of your mind'.[148]

Unlike the movements of renewal discussed in these chapters, Islamic reform in the later nineteenth and twentieth centuries *was* carried out under the shadow of European colonialism and the rise of the West. Yet, as we shall see in subsequent chapters, the later reformers would repeat and develop many of the same ideas that we find in the works of their eighteenth- and early nineteenth-century predecessors. Not all of these ideas, it is true, immediately took hold: most Sunni Muslim intellectuals remained wedded to one of the four schools of law, to the Ash'ari or Maturidi schools of theology and to the Sufism of the orders, into the twentieth century, as many still are today. Yet, in attacking blind emulation and zealous devotion to the schools of law, opening up Islamic theology, mysticism and law to ordinary Muslims, and calling on their followers to follow the path of Muhammad, the renewers of this period paved the way for the development of Islam in the era of colonization and globalization. Before we turn fully to that era, however, let us first consider the developments that were taking place within Shi'i Islam in the eighteenth and nineteenth centuries.

5

Following the Imams: Shi'ism in the Eighteenth and Nineteenth Centuries

Shi'ism, a minority branch of Islam whose adherents are estimated to constitute around 10 per cent of the world's Muslims today, is distinguished from Sunnism by its position on religious authority. For the Shi'ah, authority in religious matters is vested in the Imams, descendants of the Prophet endowed with a special insight into questions of theology and religious law. 'After His Prophet,' writes Ibn Babawayh (d. 991), the compiler of a major collection of the sayings of the Imams and author of an early Shi'i creed, 'the proofs of God for the people are the Twelve Imams', using a term – *hujaj* or 'proofs' – commonly used for a source of divine law.[1] The Imams provide for a continuous channel of communication between God and His creation after the era of prophecy has ended. In this respect, they are crucial for the ongoing guidance of humanity. 'If creation were to be without a proof' – that is, a *hujjah* – 'even for an instant,' runs one often-cited Shi'i Hadith, 'it would cease to exist.'[2]

The presence of a living guide to the will of God means that, theoretically at least, the Shi'ah should have no need for the kind of rational methods for answering questions of theology and law that were developed by Sunni scholars. 'The Imams, peace be upon them,' writes the Isma'ili Shi'i jurist al-Qadi al-Nu'man (d. 974), in a work criticizing Sunni legal theory, 'commanded us to act in accordance with the Book of God and the Practice of His Messenger Muhammad regarding that which was clear and obvious to appointed officials and to refer to the Imams that which was unclear to them, just as God commanded us to do in His Book and in the utterances of His Messenger. They did not command us to resort to analogy, speculative reason, preference, personal judgement, legal interpretation, or anything else that the Sunnis have professed, commanded, and adopted.'[3]

In the minority Isma'ili branch of Shi'ism, in which al-Qadi al-Nu'man's work remains a major point of reference, this theory has continued to hold true in practice. Within the Nizari sub-branch of Isma'ili Shi'ism, direct and accessible divine guidance has been maintained through the Aga Khan, the title adopted by the Nizari Isma'ili Imam in the first half of the nineteenth century. Among the Bohra Isma'ili communities of India, meanwhile, access to the Imam, who they believe to be hidden, is mediated through his representative, who is titled *al-da'i al-mutlaq* or 'the missionary with unrestricted authority'.[4]

In the case of the Twelver or Imami Shi'ah, the largest branch within Shi'ism, the situation is rather different. In 874, their eleventh Imam, Hasan al-'Askari, died, apparently without leaving an heir. Since the Shi'ah held that the world could not be without an Imam – and since, for the Imamis, it was expected that an Imam would be succeeded by his son in an unbroken chain of succession – a period of crisis and uncertainty ensued in which several competing models of the Imamate were put forward. The model that eventually won out was the doctrine of *ghaybah* or 'occultation'. Hasan al-'Askari, the Twelvers came to believe, *had* had a son, who was in hiding. Initially, the Twelfth Imam was thought to be in communication with his followers through a series of agents – later called 'envoys' – who continued to perform the tasks associated with the Imamate. In 941, however, the fourth envoy announced, shortly before his death, that no one would succeed him as intermediary with the Hidden Imam.[5] This marked the beginning of what the Twelvers call 'the greater occultation', a period in which ordinary communication with the Imam can no longer take place (except, that is, in dreams). It will be brought to an end only when the 'Awaited Imam' returns as Mahdi to usher in a reign of perfect justice on earth.[6]

The occultation of the Imam begged the question of how the Shi'ah were to be guided now that God's 'proof' was no longer among them. The solution favoured by most Shi'i scholars in the century following the occultation was to turn to traditionalism, that is, to cling in the first instance to Hadith, which in the Shi'i case means the *akhbar* or 'reports' of the Imams alongside the sayings of the Prophet. A tradition began to circulate according to which those who transmitted the sayings of the Imams were the 'proofs' of the Imams, just as the Imams were the proofs of God, and Shi'i scholars began to put together collections of Shi'i Hadith just as the Sunnis had done.[7] In time, four such books, collected between the early tenth and mid-eleventh centuries, came to be considered canonical within Twelver Shi'ism, similar to *The Authentic Collections* of Bukhari and Muslim and the other four Hadith collections deemed canonical by the Sunnis. The title of one of them, *The Book for Those Who Do Not Have a Jurist with Them*, by the aforementioned Ibn Babawayh, implies the traditionalist view that to be a specialist in the law means to know Hadith.[8]

Consistent with this attitude, the earliest works of Twelver

Shi'i legal theory, written in Baghdad in the eleventh century, echo the Isma'ili scholar al-Qadi al-Nu'man's attack on the rational procedures of Sunni jurisprudence. The authors of these works, who are among the most revered scholars in Twelver Shi'i history, attack *qiyas*, or analogical reasoning, regarded as one of the four sources of the law in Sunni legal theory, as well as *ijtihad*, by which they mean the derivation of the law through *ra'y* or personal opinion. Because these rational procedures are subjective, the Shi'ah argue, they lead only to probable or 'conjectural' knowledge – in Arabic, *zann* – as opposed to true or certain knowledge of God's law, which is termed *'ilm*. 'Conjecture (*zann*) has no place in the law,' writes al-Sharif al-Murtada (d. 1044), one of the first Twelver legal theorists, 'and it is not valid that the juristic status of a thing (i.e. whether it is forbidden or permitted) should be established by opinion.'[9]

Like al-Qadi al-Nu'man, whose critique of Sunni legal theory is pointedly titled *The Disagreements of the Jurists*, the Twelver scholars worried that the use of subjective reasoning would produce *khilaf* – differences of opinion regarding the content of God's law – and that, as a result, the Shi'i community, which had previously benefited from the clear and certain guidance of the Imam, would split apart. Nevertheless, the attack on *ijtihad* was partly a rhetorical move in the Shi'i polemic against Sunnis. This polemic had become especially heated in the period in which the first Twelver legal theorists were writing, in the wake of the rise to power in Baghdad of the Buyids, a dynasty from northern Iran who adhered to Shi'ism and enabled the public celebration of Shi'i festivals in the capital of the 'Abbasid caliphate.

Partly as a reaction to Sunni criticisms, the Twelvers, whose traditionalism had always been qualified by a willingness to use reason to make their case, increasingly came to accept the application of reason to the scriptural sources.[10] The appearance of works of legal theory, the rational explanation of the structure of the divine law, is after all itself an indicator of a tendency towards rationalism. So too is the fact that, while the earliest of the four canonical books of Shi'i Hadith is simply a collection of sayings of the Prophet and Imams ordered by topic, the later books, especially the two written by Shaykh al-Ta'ifah al-Tusi (d. 1067), who was also one of the pioneers of Shi'i legal theory, feature exegetical commentary and an attempt to harmonize those Hadith that appear to contradict one another. Whereas, in the decades following the occultation of the Twelfth Imam, it was thought that the Hadith *were* the law, now the reports of the Imams were seen as the starting point for rationally working out the law.[11] Accordingly, the Twelvers developed their own *madhhab* or school of law – named the Ja'fari school after the sixth Imam, Ja'far al-Sadiq (d. 765) – to parallel those of the Sunnis.[12] They also accepted, like the Sunni jurists, that there were four sources of the law: the Qur'an, Hadith, consensus and 'the evidence of reason', the last replacing analogical reasoning in the Sunni scheme.[13] In their approach to theology, similarly, the Twelver scholars of Baghdad opened the door to human reason, adopting many of the positions of the rationalist Mu'tazili school.[14]

The rationalization of Twelver theology and law reached its culmination in the thirteenth and fourteenth centuries in the work of al-Muhaqqiq al-Hilli (d. 1277), who acknowledged that Shi'i jurists in fact used *ijtihad*, and especially of his nephew, al-'Allamah al-Hilli (d. 1325), who, in the words of the historian of Islamic law Norman Calder, made *ijtihad* the 'central principle' of Shi'i legal theory.[15] Whereas the earliest Twelver legal theorists had rejected *ijtihad* on the grounds that it led only to probable knowledge, al-'Allamah accepted that a substantial part of the jurist's knowledge of God's law was merely conjectural, based as it was on Hadith reports for which there was only one or at most a few chains of transmission.[16] This being the case, ordinary Shi'ah – that is, those without the scholarly training required to undertake *ijtihad* themselves – should follow the opinions of those who were qualified to practise *ijtihad*, and should treat these opinions as if they constituted certain knowledge – that is, as *'ilm* rather than *zann*. To do otherwise, in fact, was a sin.[17]

Al-'Allamah al-Hilli was here developing al-Sharif al-Murtada's view that laymen should be encouraged – or even obliged – to emulate the opinion of qualified scholars.[18] In making *ijtihad* a key component of Shi'i legal theory, al-'Allamah was trying to account for the diversity of Shi'i interpretations of the law both in the past and in his own time, and to allow for the development of Shi'i law to account for changes in circumstances.[19] Perhaps most of all, he was reflecting the influence on his thinking of Sunni jurisprudence, in which he'd been trained while studying Shafi'i legal theory in Baghdad.[20] The result was that, from the fourteenth century, the Twelver Shi'i community was divided between scholars who were tasked with interpreting the law, and hence were known as *mujtahids*, 'those who practise *ijtihad*', and laypeople who were tasked with emulating the scholars' interpretations, and hence were known as *muqallids*, 'those who practise *taqlid*'.

The model developed by al-'Allamah al-Hilli became known as Usulism, because the *mujtahids* applied their reasoning to the *usul* or 'sources' of the law. In the centuries after al-'Allamah wrote, Usulism became the dominant approach to the law within Twelver Shi'ism, particularly in Iran, where Shi'ism was established as the official religion after the rise of the Safavid dynasty in 1501. It was a model that allotted significant authority to the Twelver jurists. In 1532/3, the Safavid ruler Shah Tahmasp issued an edict recognizing 'Ali al-Karaki (d. 1534), one of several Twelver scholars who had come to Safavid Iran from Jabal 'Amil in modern Lebanon to help propagate the correct interpretation of Shi'ism, as *na'ib al-imam*, the deputy or 'viceregent' of the Twelfth Imam.[21] All Safavid subjects, declared the Shah, ought to consider al-Karaki 'their guide and leader'; 'whatever he commands is to be enforced and whatever he prohibits, to be banned'. Notwithstanding such rhetoric, 'the viceregency of the Imamate' in fact only applied to the religious sphere. In employing the concept, al-Karaki seems to have meant that jurists had the right to act as judges in courts of Islamic law and to lead the Friday congregational prayer (a religious duty which the Shi'ah had generally considered to be in abeyance during the occultation, owing to the absence of their rightful leader), not that they should assume the Imam's rightful function as *political* leader (as Ayatollah Khomeini would later argue).[22]

Nevertheless, the extension of the jurist's authority within Usulism eventually provoked a backlash from those who felt that the Shi'ah had travelled too far from their traditionalist roots. In 1606, Muhammad Amin al-Astarabadi (d. 1625/6), a Twelver scholar of northern Iranian origin who had studied in Shiraz and in the Shi'i shrine city of Najaf in Iraq, arrived in Mecca. There he came under the guidance of a Shi'i Hadith scholar who also hailed from the northern Iranian province of Astarabad and who was known as Sahib al-Rijal (d. 1619), 'the master of the study of narrators of Hadith'. Having taught him the various sub-disciplines relating to the study of Hadith, Sahib al-Rijal instructed al-Astarabadi to 'revive the way of the Akhbaris'. 'Dispel the doubts of those who oppose this way,' he continued. 'These ideas may have been lost to their minds, but God has decreed that these ideas flow from your pen!'[23]

This is al-Astarabadi's account of how he came to write his most important work, *The Useful Lessons of Medina*. Completed in 1622, it has been described as a 'manifesto' of

Akhbarism, the traditionalist movement founded – or, as he and his followers saw it, 'revived' – by al-Astarabadi.[24] Above all, the text is an attack on the Usuli approach to the law that dominated Twelver jurisprudence in al-Astarabadi's time.[25] Al-Astarabadi argues against the use of what he calls 'conjectural derivations' in working out God's law – that is, the rational procedures grouped under *ijtihad*, which only produce *zann* – probable or conjectural knowledge of the divine law.[26] For al-Astarabadi, it is possible – and obligatory – to obtain certain knowledge, if not of God's will in itself (for that would require a kind of mystical union with God's essence, which is impossible), then at least of the duties that God has imposed on His servants.[27] God, he writes, has given us a specific command for every eventuality, along with a 'certain guide' to what that command is.[28] That certain guide is scripture, meaning the Qur'an and Sunnah of the Prophet, and the only way to understand those revealed sources is through the *akhbar* or sayings of the Imams, who possessed a divinely inspired knowledge of the meaning of scripture.[29]

Here we come back to the traditionalist principle that the Hadith or *akhbar are* the law.[30] In light of his commitment to this principle, al-Astarabadi rejects the Usuli division of the Shiʻi community into experts on legal reasoning (the *mujtahids*) and laypeople who must emulate them (the *muqallids*). Instead, he proposes that it is experts in Hadith – known as *muhaddithun* – who should serve as muftis (those who issue fatwas or opinions on the content of the law) and Islamic judges.[31] While the Usuli *mutjahids*, as the historian of Shiʻism Juan Cole has observed, 'come very close to being clergy' in the Christian sense of 'a body of persons specially ordained to perform sacraments', Akhbari scholars like al-Astarabadi, by contrast, 'resembled Pentecostalist ministers, who rejected priesthood and whose training emphasized scriptural knowledge, eschewing rationalist theology'.[32]

In creating a clerical class, just as in their adoption of juristic mechanisms such as analogical reasoning and consensus, al-Astarabadi argues, the Usulis have made the mistake of imitating Sunni 'innovations', out of a misplaced desire to prove to their Sunni opponents that the Shi'ah, too, possess a rationally grounded legal theory.[33] Claiming that Akhbarism was consistent with the traditionalist approach of the earliest Twelver scholars, al-Astarabadi lays the blame for the Sunnification of Shi'i thought at the door of al-'Allamah al-Hilli, whose widely used textbook on legal theory betrayed the influence of his Sunni training. Like al-Qadi al-Nu'man, al-Astarabadi holds that the use of *ijtihad* inevitably leads to disagreements, which he describes as a 'defect or evil'. 'Every path except holding to the speech of the Imams,' he writes, 'leads to conflicting legal opinions and blasphemy.'[34]

As a result of al-Astarabadi's arguments, Akhbarism quickly won many supporters, particularly in the Shi'i shrine cities of Najaf and Karbala in Iraq and at al-Ahsa in eastern Arabia, but also in Safavid Iran. '[Al-Astarabadi] knew the way of the companions of the holy, sinless Imams,' wrote Muhammad Taqi Majlisi (d. 1659/60), an Akhbari scholar with links to the Safavid court, 'and wrote *The Useful Lessons of Medina*, and sent it to this land. Most of the people of Najaf and the holy shrine cities approved of his method and returned to the *akhbar*.'[35] The revival of 'the way of the Akhbaris' inspired a new wave of Hadith collection among the Twelver Shi'ah. In the seventeenth century, three massive collections of sayings of the Imams – compiled by the Akhbari al-Hurr al-'Amili (d. 1708/9), the Akhbari and mystical philosopher Muhsin Fayd al-Kashani (d. 1680), and Muhammad Baqir Majlisi (d. 1699/1700), the son of Muhammad Taqi Majlisi and the chief religious scholar of Safavid Iran in his day – were produced to supplement the Four Books of earlier times.

Yet though Akhbarism had gained the upper hand, Usulism

continued to have prominent adherents, especially among those religious scholars connected to the royal court in the Safavid capital of Isfahan. In the early eighteenth century, a list of forty points of disagreement between the Usulis and Akhbaris – or, as they are described in the text, between the *mujtahids* and *muhaddiths* – was compiled by an Akhbari scholar from eastern Arabia called 'Abd Allah al-Samahiji (d. 1723). His text not only indicates that the dispute between the Usulis and Akhbaris was still going on in his day, but also highlights the presence of internal differences within the two camps as well as the existence of a third, hybrid camp of *mujtahid-muhaddiths* who possessed the qualifications to undertake *ijtihad* but based their rulings entirely on transmitted sources.[36]

Most importantly, Usulism soon found a reviver to compare to al-Astarabadi. In 1722, Isfahan fell to the Ghilzai Afghans, eventually leading to the demise of the Safavid empire and the rise to power of Nader Shah, who, ruling Iran between 1736 and 1747, attempted an ecumenical rapprochement between Sunnis and Shi'ah and undermined the authority of the Shi'i scholarly establishment. As a consequence, hundreds of Iranian scholars migrated to the Shi'i shrine cities in Iraq, which at that time were bastions of Akhbarism.[37] Among them was Muhammad Baqir Bihbahani (d. 1791/2), the scholar widely recognized as the reviver of Usulism in the eighteenth and nineteenth centuries. Revered by his students as the *mujaddid* or 'renewer' of Islam in his century, among the other titles by which he is known are *wahid*, 'the unique one', and *murawwij al-madhhab*, 'the propagator of the true religion', a title (more common in the Shi'i tradition than the Sunni, just as *mujaddid* is used more often by the Sunnis) which had earlier been applied to the powerful Safavid cleric 'Ali al-Karaki and by the Akhbaris to al-Astarabadi.[38]

Born in Isfahan at the beginning of the eighteenth century,

in his youth Bihbahani was taken by his father to study in the shrine city of Karbala. Having finished his studies, he is said to have been prompted by a dream of Imam Husayn, whose death at Karbala in 680 is one of the focal points in Shi'i sacred history, to stay in the city and propagate Usulism.[39] Nevertheless, in the early 1730s, he moved to Bihbahan, the town in south-western Iran from which he derived his name. Over the course of his three decades in the town, which at the time of his arrival was dominated by Akhbaris of eastern Arabian origin, Bihbahani won a reputation as a teacher of Usuli jurisprudence and a vigorous polemicist against the Akhbaris.

At the beginning of the 1760s, Bihbahani returned to the Iraqi shrine cities. The Akhbaris of Najaf and Karbala were at that time led by the eastern Arabian scholar Yusuf al-Bahrani (d. 1772), best known as the author of a work of substantive law titled *The Rare Gardens*. Though he is sometimes characterized as a 'moderate' Akhbari, owing, among other things, to his unease at the harshness of al-Astarabadi's attack on the Usulis, al-Bahrani's approach to the law nevertheless bears all the hallmarks of the Akhbari movement. He rejects consensus and reason as sources of the law on the grounds that they provide only *zann* or conjectural knowledge; argues that the law should in the first instance be sought in the sayings of the Imams; and criticizes any attempt to undertake rational analysis of those sayings – for instance, by applying analogical reasoning to them. *Ijtihad* is rarely mentioned in his work, and then only in negative terms.[40]

At the time of Bihbahani's return to the shrine cities, adherence to these Akhbari ideas was strictly enforced. It is said that anyone carrying books of Usuli jurisprudence would have to cover them up to avoid being beaten.[41] According to another tradition, al-Bahrani and his Akhbari students would only touch Usuli texts through a cloth to avoid being contaminated by their ritual impurity.⁴² Not to be deterred, Bihbahani is reported to have begun teaching Usuli books in his cellar to an increasingly large gathering of students, many of them former disciples of al-Bahrani. Soon he had acquired enough supporters to be able to teach Usulism out in the open. After al-Bahrani died in 1772, more of his students went over to the Usuli cause, and the Akhbari hold over the shrine cities was further loosened by the plague that struck Iraq in the same year, wiping out thousands of Akhbari scholars. In the following decades, Bihbahani's students, many of whom were of Iranian origin and so better placed than their Arab Akhbari counterparts to flee the plague, helped revive Usulism in the scholarly centres of Iran. When the Qajar dynasty came to power in Iran in 1794, the Usuli scholars, who were willing to acknowledge the temporal authority of the new rulers in exchange for autonomy in the religious sphere, were able to further entrench their position.⁴³

Much like al-Astarabadi's revival of Akhbarism in the previous century, Bihbahani's revival of Usulism owed much to his ability to point out the flaws in his opponents' position. His critique of Akhbarism hones in on what he sees as the Akhbaris' errors in epistemology, and in particular their mistaken understanding of *zann*, probable or 'conjectural' knowledge. The Akhbaris are wrong, Bihbahani argues, to regard *zann* as mere subjective opinion; in fact, *zann* is the result of the jurist's systematic and disciplined analysis of the scriptural texts – that is, of his *ijtihad*. The Hadith themselves (along with reason and consensus) indicate that *ijtihad* and its corollary – the layperson's emulation of a scholar's opinion – are necessary and have always been a part of Shi'ism.⁴⁴ *Zann* is only a proof of the law, then, when it is the carefully reached conclusion of a *mujtahid*. Once a scholar has exhausted his mental effort in working out the law from the sources (the definition of *ijtihad*), he is obliged to act on this conclusion as if it constituted certain knowledge, just as those who have chosen to emulate him (that is, his *muqallids*) are obliged to put his conclusion into practice.⁴⁵ 'Whoever has not reached the rank of *ijtihad*,' he writes in a treatise on *ijtihad* and the reports of the Imams, 'his only recourse is *taqlid*.'⁴⁶

While Bihbihani located the Usuli-Akhbari dispute in their different theories of knowledge, in practice the revival of Usulism meant the strengthening of the religious authority of the jurists. According to Bihbahani, once a non-scholar has chosen to follow a particular *mujtahid*, he or she must follow the opinion of that *mujtahid* alone. In choosing which scholar to follow, the layperson should attempt to find the most learned jurist among the Shi'ah. 'When the most learned and most knowledgeable is found,' he writes, 'following him is an individual duty, and if they are all equal, then one must choose.'⁴⁷ In the mid-nineteenth century, this principle was institutionalized through the creation of the office of *marja' al-taqlid*, 'the source of emulation'. The holder of this office, as Devin Stewart observes, carries out three functions: 'he is a mufti who grants legal opinions, a *mudarris* or professor of law, and a *ra'is* or head of the legal establishment'.⁴⁸ While there is no formal process for electing a jurist as *marja'*, the defining characteristic is said to be *a'lamiyyat* – being the 'most learned' of the Shi'ah – a quality defined by Murtada Ansari (d. 1864), the second holder of the office, as being 'more skilful [than others] in deducing God's law and comprehending it from the revealed evidence'.⁴⁹ At least in theory, the *marja'* is regarded as the supreme source of scholarly authority over the entire Shi'i community. In the view of Ansari, a Najaf-based scholar whose authority is said to have been acknowledged among the Shi'ah in Ottoman Anatolia and India as well as Iran and the Arab lands, it is an 'absolute duty' to emulate the most learned jurist.⁵⁰

The creation of the office of *marja' al-taqlid* reflects the consolidation of the authority of Twelver jurists – and the development of a more formal hierarchy within their ranks – following the triumph of Usulism. The same goes for the emergence of the title of *hujjat al-islam* – 'the proof of Islam' – which was first applied to the leading jurist of early nineteenth-century Isfahan, Muhammad Baqir Shafti (d. 1844). In the early twentieth century, that title was superseded by *ayat Allah* – 'the sign of God'. It seems to have been applied to Shafti as a way of reflecting his role in imposing true Islam in Isfahani society, and so is indicative of the debate that was held at this time over the extent to which the jurists' authority extended into the political sphere.[51]

An important catalyst for this debate was the first Persian–Russian war of 1810–13, during which the Qajar government requested fatwas from leading Shi'i jurists to legitimize the war effort as a jihad. Among those who responded favourably was Shaykh Ja'far Kashif al-Ghita' (d. 1812/13), who was widely acknowledged as the leading *mujtahid* of the time. He authorized the jihad on the grounds that, as 'deputies of the Imam' (the status that had been claimed by al-Karaki in the sixteenth century), the jurists were obliged to undertake the Imam's duty to defend Islam.[52] This idea was echoed by his student, Muhammad Hasan Najafi (d. 1850), the first jurist to be recognized as *marja' al-taqlid*. In *The Jewels of Theology*, a major work on Shi'i jurisprudence that he began early in the nineteenth century, Najafi asserts the *wilayah 'ammah* or 'general authority' of the jurists during the occultation. Though he criticizes those jurists who aspire to 'leadership and dominion' and recognizes that there are limits to juristic authority (for instance, in the waging of aggressive jihad), Najafi nonetheless holds, like his teacher, that this authority extends to the political and military domains.[53] Najafi's student and successor as *marja'*, Murtada Ansari, by contrast, took a more quietist position. To transfer the general authority possessed by the Prophet and the Imams to the jurists, he asserts, is to 'strip the tragacanth tree [a particularly thorny species] of its thorns' – that is, to do something absurd.⁵⁴ His own designation as *marjaʿ al-taqlid*, it is reported, was thanks to his reputation as an otherworldly scholar, in contrast to his contemporaries who spent more time on mundane affairs than on deepening their knowledge of Shiʿi law.⁵⁵

The most sustained reflection on juristic authority articulated in this period was that of Ahmad Naraqi (d. 1828/9), a former student of Najafi, director of the royal madrasah in the city of Kashan and another jurist who supported the Qajars' war against the Russians. His major legal work, *The Profits of Days*, contains a long section devoted to *wilayat al-faqih*, the authority or 'guardianship' of the jurist. As we shall see in chapter eight, this phrase was adopted by Ayatollah Khomeini, who credits Naraqi's theory as the model for his theory of an 'Islamic government' led by the supreme Shiʿi jurist.⁵⁶ However, while Naraqi asserts that the authority of the jurist is inherited directly from the Prophet and Imams and covers many areas of life, his emphasis is very much on the traditional functions of the Usuli scholar. The longest part of the section concerns the authority of the jurist to issue fatwas or legal opinions, in the course of which Naraqi rehearses the Usuli position that in the period of occultation the community is divided into *mujtahids*, who possess the ability to identify the most probable answer to legal questions from the scriptural evidence, and *muqallids*, who are obliged to identify the most learned jurist and emulate him. Other examples of the jurist's *wilayah* include his duty to act as judge in a court of Islamic law, to impose the *hudud*, that is, the penalties fixed by scripture for certain crimes, to manage the property of orphans, the insane and men who are absent, to supervise marriages, and to collect and spend the religious taxes that the Shiʿah are obliged to pay to the Imam.⁵⁷ While Naraqi does mention in passing that the jurist should investigate the performance of the sultan, it would be anachronistic, as the sociologist of Islam Saïd Amir Arjomand argues, to read his text as an anticipation of Khomeini's theory of the jurist's right to political leadership.[58]

While Ahmad Naraqi's analysis of the authority of the jurist is indicative of the triumph of Usulism within Twelver Shi'i jurisprudence, the career of his father, Mulla Muhammad Mahdi Naraqi (d. 1794), illustrates another important feature of Shi'i thought in the Qajar period, namely, the revival and development of philosophy. In the post-classical Islamic period, philosophy, which was generally known as *hikmah* or 'wisdom', was dominated by three intellectual traditions: the Aristotelian philosophy of Ibn Sina, known in the West as Avicenna, the Sufi metaphysics of Ibn 'Arabi and the Illuminationist philosophy of Suhrawardi.[59] One of the most important interpreters and defenders of Avicennian philosophy was a Shi'i, Nasir al-Din al-Tusi (d. 1274). Described by the scholar of Islamic philosophy Jon McGinnis as 'arguably the most important and influential Shi'i scholar of the Middle Ages', al-Tusi's works include a commentary on Ibn Sina's *Pointers and Reminders* in which he responds to criticisms of Avicenna made by the prominent Sunni Ash'ari theologian Fakhr al-Din al-Razi (d. 1210), as well as a highly influential treatise on Shi'i theology and a work on Aristotelian ethics that became the best-known book on the subject in the post-classical Islamic world.[60] A century after al-Tusi, the northern Iranian scholar Haydar Amuli (d. after 1385), who had studied with al-'Allamah al-Hilli's son in Baghdad and eventually settled in Najaf, argued that Shi'ism and Sufism were identical and interpreted Ibn 'Arabi's thought in accordance with Twelver Shi'i beliefs. He upheld the doctrine of the unity of existence and designated 'Ali, the first Imam, as the 'Seal of Universal Sainthood' (a status which Ibn ʿArabi had allotted to Jesus) and the Twelfth Imam as the 'Seal of Muhammadan Sainthood' (a title which Ibn ʿArabi had claimed for himself).[61] A century or so after him, the eastern Arabian Shiʿi scholar Ibn Abi Jumhur al-Ahsaʾi (d. after 1491) attempted, in his major work, *Burnishing the Mirror of the One Who Saves Regarding Theology, the Two Philosophies, and Sufism,* to reconcile Muʿtazili and Ashʿari theology, Aristotelian and Illuminationist philosophy, and the mystical philosophy of Ibn ʿArabi.[62]

The harmonization of Avicennian philosophy, the monistic metaphysics of Ibn ʿArabi and the Illuminationist wisdom of Suhrawardi – as well as the coming together of Shiʿism and philosophy more generally – had reached its high point in the Safavid period in the work of Mulla Sadra (d. *c.* 1635/6). Born in Shiraz, Sadra studied in Isfahan with Mir Damad (d. 1631), the grandson of ʿAli al-Karaki and a prominent philosopher who was close to the Safavid court, and Shaykh Bahaʾi (d. 1620/1), the leading Twelver jurist in the age of the great Safavid ruler Shah ʿAbbas I (r. 1588–1629). He later taught in Qom, where his students included the Akhbari scholar Fayd al-Kashani (the collector of one of the three new compilations of the sayings of the Imams), and, for the last few years of his life, at a madrasah in his native Shiraz that had been specially endowed by the Safavid governor for the teaching of philosophy.[63]

Sadra's philosophy, which is set out in *The Transcendent Philosophy in the Four Journeys of the Intellect* and other lesser works, seeks to bring together the mysticism of Ibn ʿArabi with the rationalism of Ibn Sina, while also engaging with the philosophy of the Neoplatonists Plotinus and Proclus, whose work he accessed directly in Arabic translation. For Sadra, philosophy is, as it was for the ancient Greeks, a way of life.[64] 'Philosophy,' he writes, 'is the perfection of the human soul through acquiring knowledge of things as they really are.' Such knowledge is acquired through rational proofs, not – and here Sadra seems to take a swipe at his Usuli contemporaries – through *zann* and *taqlid*. By ordering the world rationally in his mind, the philosopher – as both the Greeks and the Islamic philosophers of the classical period had claimed – comes to resemble God, and his soul becomes a perfect image of existence.[65]

In his analysis of 'things as they really are', Mulla Sadra introduced three innovative metaphysical ideas.[66] Ibn Sina had famously distinguished between existence and essence – that is, between being and that which makes a thing what it is – a distinction which raises the question of which of the two is primary. Responding to the Illuminationist philosopher Suhrawardi's view that essence precedes existence, Mulla Sadra instead asserted *asalat al-wujud*, 'the primacy of existence'. For him, 'nothing is real except existence'. Like Ibn 'Arabi, he identifies pure, unrestricted existence with God Himself, and holds that God's absolute being is manifested in various forms that he calls 'modes of existence'. The essences of these modes, he thinks, have no concrete objective reality, but exist only in the mind. It is only in this sense that things are distinct from God, who is, as the Neoplatonist philosopher Plotinus had indicated, *basit al-haqiqah* – 'simple reality' – and 'the simple reality,' Mulla Sadra declares, 'is all things'.[67]

Yet while God's existence is the only reality, Mulla Sadra must still account for the apparent diversity that we see in creation. In response to this old philosophical problem of 'the one and the many' Mulla Sadra, drawing on earlier philosophers such as Nasir al-Din al-Tusi, developed his second, and perhaps most fundamental, doctrine, the concept of *tashkik al-wujud* or 'the gradation of existence'. Existence, he explains, is qualified by varying degrees of intensity. 'Know that the reality of being,' he writes, 'is graded in levels, and the higher comprehends all under it in a real sense.'[68] Some modes of being are closer than others to the pure existence of God. Put another way, if being, as the 'philosopher of illumination' Suhrawardi had said, is light, then some things are more luminous than others.

In this way, Mulla Sadra introduces a hierarchy of existence. Within creation, the most intense form of being or light is that of 'the perfect human', whom Mulla Sadra, in accordance with the Shi'i interpretation of Ibn 'Arabi, identifies with the Imam.[69] Yet, this hierarchy is not fixed, for things – and here we come to Sadra's third key doctrine – are in a constant process of movement, or what he calls *harakah jawhariyyah*, 'substantial motion'. 'Being permits intensification and debilitation,' he writes, 'meaning that it permits intensifying motion. Substance in its substantiality, that is its substantial being, allows for essential change.'[70] Drawing, again, on Ibn 'Arabi, Sadra holds that substances are not stable, for God 'renews' their existence at every moment.[71] This doctrine allows him to solve the debate between the Islamic theologians and philosophers over whether the world is eternal or created in time, for God, as he sees it, creates existence anew in every instant, that is, within time.[72]

Mulla Sadra's thought – and philosophy more generally – were controversial in Iran and the wider Shi'i world, both in his own time and after. In the introduction to his major work, *The Four Journeys of the Intellect*, Sadra laments his persecution at the hands of those 'whose eyes are blind to the lights of philosophy and its mysteries', which they regard as an illicit 'innovation'.[73] While his students enjoyed the protection and patronage of the Safavid court under Shah 'Abbas II (r. 1642–66), in the latter part of the seventeenth century both philosophy and Sufism were virulently attacked by Muhammad Baqir Majlisi and other leading clerics.[74] The study of philosophy in Iran is said to have suffered another blow with the Afghan sack of Isfahan in 1722 (though the historicity of that account has been called into question).⁷⁵ Later in the eighteenth century, Muhammad 'Ali Bihbahani (d. 1801), the son of the reviver of Usulism, declared that philosophy had been brought into Islam through the instigation of Satan and subsequently borrowed from the Sunnis by ignorant Shi'ah.⁷⁶ The younger Bihbahani was known as 'the Sufi killer' owing to his role in the persecution of the mystics.⁷⁷

Nevertheless, philosophy continued to be taught in the madrasahs of Iran throughout the eighteenth century, with the Iranian cities of Qom, Mashhad and Hamadan emerging as new centres for philosophical study, and the teaching of *hikmah* recovering in Isfahan soon after the Afghan conquest.⁷⁸ Philosophy subsequently flourished under the Qajars, particularly during the long reigns of Fath 'Ali Shah (r. 1797–1834) and Nasir al-Din Shah (r. 1848–96), who were notable patrons of philosophers. Under Nasir al-Din, the Qajar capital of Tehran became another new centre of philosophical output.⁷⁹

As the scholar of Islamic philosophy Sajjad Rizvi has shown, Shi'i philosophy in Iran in this period was characterized by a close engagement with the thought of Mulla Sadra, in whose shadow almost all philosophical activity was carried out, and a tendency to combine rational philosophical activity with mystical theorizing, a combination which ultimately produced a new intellectual tradition called *'irfan* or 'gnosis'.⁸⁰ Though one or both of these tendencies are discernible in a number of thinkers of this period, three philosophers of the late eighteenth and nineteenth centuries are especially important in the history of Shi'i thought.

Rizvi identifies Mulla Muhammad Mahdi Naraqi, the father of the theorist of juristic authority Ahmad Naraqi, as 'the most important philosopher of the 18ᵗʰ century' in Iran.⁸¹ Born near Kashan, in Isfahan province, Naraqi senior studied in Isfahan with Isma'il Khwaju'i (d. 1759), a philosopher and theologian who wrote a treatise against Ibn 'Arabi's doctrine of the unity of existence and is said to have learnt Ibn Sina's philosophical compendium *The Healing* by heart.[82] In the middle of the eighteenth century, Mahdi Naraqi went to Karbala, where he studied under the Akhbari scholar Yusuf Bahrani, before switching his allegiance to the Usuli jurist Muhammad Baqir Bihbahani.[83] In 1766, he returned to Kashan, where he remained for the last three decades of his life, founding and directing a madrasah with the support of the ruling Zand dynasty, and writing a treatise in Persian on commercial law (Kashan was a centre for the production of Persian carpets and silks) and an exposition and defence of Usulism.[84]

Mahdi Naraqi's most important writings, however, are on philosophy. They include a commentary on the metaphysical section of *The Healing* of Ibn Sina, a work in the Illuminationist tradition of Suhrawardi, and a huge text on ethics in the Aristotelian tradition of Nasir al-Din al-Tusi.[85] Naraqi's metaphysics and epistemology are marked by an often-critical engagement with Mulla Sadra. On the one hand, he accepts Mulla Sadra's theory of the primacy of existence, and adopts from Mulla Sadra the Illuminationist concept of direct and intuitive knowledge 'through presence' (which we earlier met in our analysis of the Indian Sufi Mir Dard). On the other, he does not think that Sadra's notion of the 'gradation of existence' is a description of actual reality, rejects the idea of 'substantial motion' as an explanation for God's creation of the world in time and, like his lifelong mentor Isma'il Khwaju'i, regards the notion of the unity of existence, which Mulla Sadra had taken from Ibn 'Arabi, as incompatible with the fundamental Islamic doctrine of the unity of God.[86]

Significant as his metaphysical writings are, it is ethics which Naraqi regards – innovatively – as the highest part of philosophy. Knowledge of the qualities that lead to salvation, and those which lead to perdition, he asserts at the beginning of his encyclopaedic work on ethics, *The Compendium of Happiness*, is 'the true philosophy', about which no one is permitted to be ignorant, for it leads to 'true life' and 'eternal happiness'. The book, which Naraqi wrote in Arabic – though a Persian version was later made by his son Ahmad for the benefit of ordinary Shi'ah – is an attempt to gather together the ethical wisdom of the scriptures, the mystics and the philosophers in a single, comprehensive 'textbook' of ethics.[87] Besides the Aristotelian ethics of Nasir al-Din al-Tusi and his predecessor Ibn Miskawayh (d. 1030), it draws heavily on a Shi'i reworking of the (Sunni) Sufi al-Ghazali's *Revival of the Religious Sciences* by Mulla Sadra's son-in-law and student, the Akhbari mystic Fayd al-Kashani. For the philosophers, Naraqi observes, true happiness consists in the acquisition of knowledge and the perfection of the intellect; for the mystics, it consists in love of God; and for the jurists, in renunciation of the world. Seeking to harmonize these various traditions, Naraqi declares that each of these perspectives is true.[88] As an Aristotelian, Naraqi lays particular emphasis on the principle of '*adalah* or *i'tidal* – 'balance' or 'moderation' – advocating the middle course between extremes in the exercise of human faculties such as reason, irascibility, appetite and cunning, each of which, he thinks, has its place in the right circumstances. (For instance, irascibility is essential to the waging of jihad against the unbelievers.)[89] In keeping with his description of the highest good of the jurists, his ethical philosophy stresses the rejection of the world: in his treatment of pride, for instance, Naraqi sharply condemns the hypocrisy of the wealthy and the arrogance of men of noble rank or lineage.[90]

While Naraqi was a critical reader of Mulla Sadra who drew on a wide range of philosophical sources, the next major Shi'i philosopher of this period, Mulla 'Ali Nuri (d. 1831), was a much more committed Sadrian. A professor at the Kasagaran madrasah in Isfahan, where he is said to have had no fewer than five hundred students in philosophy, Nuri played a major role both in the consolidation of philosophy in the early Qajar period and in putting the works of Mulla Sadra at the centre of the philosophical curriculum in Iran.[91] In his own writings, which include glosses on the most important works of Mulla Sadra as well as a *Treatise on the Simple Reality*, Nuri defends the three key Sadrian doctrines of the primacy of existence, the gradation of being and substantial motion, arguing that God is the only true being, and that other things possess only 'shadowy existence' by virtue of the 'expansion' or manifestation of the divine existence within them.[92]

Though, like Muhammad Baqir Majlisi and Muhammad 'Ali Bihbahani, Nuri was a vociferous critic of the Sufi orders, describing them as 'a Satanic group of heretics who in their ignorance and ability to misguide are like Christian missionaries', he was also committed to the metaphysical monism of Ibn 'Arabi, and so can be considered a contributor to the development of *'irfan* or gnostic Shi'ism.[93] Following Mulla Sadra and earlier Shi'i Sufis such as Haydar Amuli, he identifies the Imams as the true 'perfect humans' and 'Ali and the Twelfth Imam as the two 'Seals of Sainthood'.[94] Such identifications were common among the practitioners of *'irfan* in this period: Nuri's student 'Ali Mudarris Zunuzi (d. 1889), for instance, holds that the Twelfth Imam is the perfect human, the 'pole' of existence, and the manifestation of the Muhammadan Reality, while Muhammad Rida Qumsha'i (d. 1888), who had studied under Nuri's son, considered 'Ali to be the 'Seal of Saints' on account of his being 'the closest of all human beings to the Seal of Prophets [that is, Muhammad]'.[95]

Nuri's most significant contribution to the development of Shi'i philosophy was through the impact he had on his students and successors. Both Zunuzi and Qumsha'i, for example, played a key role in establishing the Qajar capital of Tehran as a major centre of philosophical study during the reign of Nasir al-Din Shah. Nuri's most important student, however, was Mulla Hadi Sabzavari (d. 1878). Certainly, the English orientalist Edward Granville Browne, who spent a year living in Iran between 1887 and 1888, expresses a commonly held view when he describes the 'Sage of Sabzavar' as 'the greatest philosopher whom Persia has produced during the present [that is, the nineteenth] century'.[96]

Born in Sabzavar, in the north-eastern Iranian province of Khorasan, in 1797 or 1798, at the age of ten Sabzavari left his hometown for Mashhad, the site of the shrine of the eighth Shi'i Imam and therefore a major destination for Shi'i pilgrims, which lies about 150 miles to the east of Sabzavar. He remained in the shrine city for ten years, studying Arabic, Islamic law and legal theory, before making the long journey south to Isfahan, the historic centre of philosophical studies in Iran, where, he relates in his autobiography, 'I spent most of my time studying the philosophy of the Illuminationist school' of Suhrawardi, along with the philosophy of Mulla Sadra.[97] It was during his eight years in Isfahan that he studied with Mulla 'Ali Nuri, as well as with one of Nuri's students known as 'the One-Eyed'. After a period back in Khorasan, during which he deepened his knowledge of Illuminationist philosophy, he went on pilgrimage to Mecca, before finally returning to his hometown around 1837.[98]

Once settled in Sabzavar, he taught philosophy at the Fasihiyyah madrasah – also known as *dar al-mu'minin*, the 'House of the Believers' – for some three decades. Browne, who studied with one of Sabzavari's students during his stay in Tehran, reports that Sabzavari would give two lectures every day, each lasting two hours, and both devoted to metaphysics, 'taking as his text either some of the writings of Mulla Sadra, or his own notes'. Before enrolling in this course of study, prospective students, who came from all over Iran to study under the Sage of Sabzavar, were required to demonstrate proficiency in grammar and rhetoric, logic, mathematics and astronomy, law and theology. Sabzvari's course on metaphysics lasted some seven years, and nearly a thousand students are said to have completed it.[99]

Embodying the ethical principle of world-rejection that had been advocated by Mahdi Naraqi, Sabzavari is said to have lived a life of renunciation, giving most of the property that he inherited from his father (a merchant and landowner who died when Sabzavari was only eight) to students and the poor, eating only a piece of bread for lunch (and never touching spices or onions), and limiting himself to four hours of sleep (for which he used a cloak as a mattress and a stone for a pillow) so as to have more time for study and devotions.[100] Unlike Nuri, a regular smoker who, on once being brought a water-pipe that did not work, declared in jest, 'The water-pipe that the Akhbaris forbid is none other than this one!' Sabzavari never smoked, though he did reportedly take his tea with twelve sugars.[101] Like other renunciants, he was believed to be a worker of miracles. Browne relates a story according to which, after his death, he appeared to a paralyzed girl in a dream and instructed her (like Christ at Capernaum) to get up, after which she was able to walk.[102]

Sabzavari's fame in his own lifetime was such that, besides the hundreds of students who came to study with him, the Qajar ruler Nasir al-Din Shah twice visited him at his humble home in Sabzavar on his way to the shrine of the eighth Imam at Mashhad. On one of these occasions, the Shah asked the philosopher if he would write a book on theology in Persian, in response to which Sabzavari wrote *The Secrets of Wisdom*, a treatise 'in an easy style' of Farsi, as Browne puts it.[103] Other works of his include a commentary on *The Spiritual Couplets*, a long and celebrated mystical poem in Persian by Jalal al-Din Rumi, which Sabzavari regarded as a kind of esoteric verse commentary on the Qur'an, as well as glosses on *The Four Journeys* and other works by Mulla Sadra.[104] Sabzavari's most important written work, however, is the commentary that he wrote on a philosophical poem that he himself had composed. Covering logic, physics, theology and metaphysics, *The Commentary on a Philosophical Poem* was completed in 1845, about two decades after the composition of the original poem. Like Sabzavari's other works, it was printed in his own lifetime, and remains, as the scholars of Islamic philosophy Mahdi Muhaqqiq and Toshihiko Izutsu have observed, 'the most popular textbook of scholastic philosophy' in the Shi'i seminaries of Iran.[105]

Though, like Mahdi Naraqi, he does criticize Mulla Sadra on certain points (for instance, at some points in his work Sabzavari takes issue with Sadra's epistemological claim that knowledge consists in the union of the knower and the object of knowledge), Sabzavari's metaphysics are firmly rooted in Sadra's philosophy.[106] The Sadrian formulation of Ibn 'Arabi's concept of the unity of existence is, as Muhaqqiq and Izutsu put it, 'the very basis on which stands the whole of his metaphysics'.[107] 'Being,' Browne quotes his teacher as saying, 'is a single simple reality' – a reference to Sadra's view of God as *basit al-haqiqah*, 'the simple reality' – 'and it has different degrees in excellence'.[108] For Sabzavari, the unity and simplicity of existence are a consequence of its primacy – what Mulla Sadra had termed *asalat al-wujud* – for it is essences, which are only real in the mind, that create the appearance of multiplicity.[109] Existence, moreover, is graded in levels of intensity – the principle of *tashkik al-wujud* – just as light is more or less luminous depending on how far removed it is from its source.[110]

In accordance with this principle, and the connected Sadrian principle of 'substantial motion', Browne reports that Sabzavari professed the existence of two complementary 'arcs' of being – one descending from God to the most material kind of existence, the other ascending in the opposite direction. Each of these arcs has seven principal levels or grades, and the purpose of philosophy is to enable a person to climb the levels of the 'arc of ascent'. The individual who completes all the levels of ascent is the perfect human, 'who', Sabzavari writes, 'has been created for God and for whose sake all things are created'. It is through the perfect human – who in the Shi'i philosophical tradition is identified with the Imam – that phenomenal multiplicity is resolved into its original existential unity.[111]

Sabzavari represents the culmination of the Sadrian tradition of philosophical Shi'ism. That tradition would survive into the twentieth century through the work of notable scholars such as Muhammad Husayn Tabataba'i (d. 1981), the author of a widely studied commentary on the Qur'an who held that mysticism and philosophy were 'two of the major pillars of the sacred religion', having been taught by the Imams themselves.[112] While Sadrian philosophy was largely accepted as a component of the dominant Usuli form of Twelver Shi'ism, other variants of Shi'i mystical philosophy took a different course. Among those under whom Sabzavari had studied in Isfahan was Shaykh Ahmad al-Ahsa'i (d. 1826), a scholar who, while not representative of the mainstream tradition of Sadrian philosophy, would nevertheless have a major impact on the subsequent religious history of Iran through the Shaykhi school of Twelver Shi'ism that took inspiration from his thought, and subsequently through the Babi and Baha'i religions that emerged out of Shaykhism.

Al-Ahsa'i was born in 1741 or 1742 in the oasis of al-Ahsa in eastern Arabia, traditionally a stronghold of Akhbarism. It was also the native region of the mystical philosopher Ibn Abi Jumhur al-Ahsa'i, whose library he is said to have used as a young man.[113] In the course of his education, Ahmad al-Ahsa'i received instruction in the Sufi metaphysics of Ibn 'Arabi, whom he would later criticize while also adopting some of his key ideas.[114] In his youth al-Ahsa'i claimed to have received mystical visions of the Prophet and Imams reminiscent of the visions of the Sufi affiliates of the Muhammadan Path in the same period. On one occasion al-Ahsa'i had a strange dream that suggested a kind of initiation into the hidden wisdom of the Prophet and Imams. Hasan – the grandson of the Prophet whom Shah Wali Allah had seen in Mecca and 'Andalib had met in Delhi – appeared to him and stuck his tongue in his mouth, mixing his saliva, which was 'burning hot', with his. Later he was visited by Muhammad, and he too gave al-Ahsa'i his saliva, which was 'icy cold', to drink. From these initiatory visions, his leading disciple, Sayyid Kazim Rashti (d. 1844), reports, al-Ahsa'i drew 'knowledge and enigmas', for which he subsequently found corroborating evidence in the Qur'an and the Hadith of the Prophet and the Imams.[115]

After briefly visiting the shrine cities of Iraq around the time of the plague of 1772, al-Ahsa'i finally departed for Iraq sometime in the early 1790s, probably in the wake of Wahhabi incursions into al-Ahsa. In Najaf and Karbala he received licenses to teach jurisprudence from some of the leading students of Muhammad Baqir Bihbahani, the reviver of Usulism, including the Usuli jurist widely acknowledged as Bibahani's successor, Sayyid Muhammad Mahdi Tabataba'i (d. 1798). Known as Bahr al-'Ulum, 'the Ocean of Knowledge', he was known for his success in converting Sunnis and non-Muslims to Shi'ism and for constructing a loosely organized hierarchy of scholars under his direction (an informal precursor of the office of *marja' al-taqlid*). As well as being a leading *mujtahid*, Bahr al-'Ulum was also a mystic who, like al-Ahsa'i, claimed to have received esoteric knowledge from the Twelfth Imam in mystical visions.[116] Al-Ahsa'i's decision to study under him and other leading Usulis indicates that, though he claimed that his own knowledge was mystically inspired, he did not see this mystical wisdom as incompatible with orthodox Twelver Shi'ism in its Usuli form.[117] Indeed, while he has sometimes been characterized as an Akhbari, al-Ahsa'i in fact wrote in defence of the acceptability of *zann* – conjectural knowledge acquired through rational analysis of the legal sources – observing against the Akhbaris that a literalist reading of scripture is not possible in those instances where the meaning of the Qur'an or Hadith is ambiguous.[118]

From 1806 until his death while on the Hajj some twenty years later, al-Ahsa'i led a peripatetic life, spending several years at a time in the major cities of Iran. In 1806, he went to Yazd, the central Iranian city known for its large Zoroastrian population and celebrated as *dar al-'ibadah* – 'the abode of worship'. Having been warmly welcomed by the leading Twelver jurists of the town, many of whom were also former students of Bahr al-'Ulum, al-Ahsa'i was reportedly prevented from leaving by the populace, who recognized the prestige and protection from government interference that accompanied the presence of a famous religious scholar in their city. Yet soon the Qajar monarch Fath 'Ali Shah, a pious ruler known for his patronage of Shi'i scholars, shrines and mosques, heard of al-Ahsa'i's reputation and invited him to Tehran. 'We desire to meet you,' the Shah wrote, 'as the one fasting desires the new moon, as the thirsty longs for pure waters, as the husband is eager for his wife, and the destitute for wealth.'[119] According to one source, in fact, 'the Shah was convinced that obedience to the Shaykh was obligatory, and that opposition to him constituted unbelief'.[120] Anxious not to become embroiled in politics, al-Ahsa'i did his best to turn down the invitation, writing back to the Shah with answers to some of his theological questions. Eventually, however, he was persuaded to go to the Qajar capital, where he lived for a few short months at the end of 1808 and the beginning of 1809, spending much of his time discussing metaphysics with the monarch. Having convinced Fath 'Ali Shah to let him leave with the argument that his growing religious authority would sooner or later inevitably clash with the Shah's political authority, al-Ahsa'i returned for five years to Yazd, before going in 1814 to Kirmanshah in western Iran.[121]

It was in Kirmanshah, and during the eight-month period that he spent in the Iraqi shrine cities on his way back from the pilgrimage to Mecca in 1818, that Shaykh Ahmad al-Ahsa'i wrote some of his most important works. These include a voluminous commentary on a key text of Shi'i devotional piety attributed to the tenth Imam, *The Greatest and All-Comprehensive Visitation*, in which al-Ahsa'i lays out his understanding of the status and function of the Imams, as well as critical commentaries on key works by the philosopher Mulla Sadra and his student Fayd al-Kashani.[122] In the mid-nineteenth century, the Shaykhis of Tabriz, in north-western Iran, would publish his collected works, which come to more than 130 titles, under the title *The All-Comprehensive Words*, alluding to a Hadith in which the Prophet declares that he was given 'the all-comprehensive words'.[123]

Al-Ahsa'i criticized the fundamental tenets of Sadrian metaphysics, vigorously attacking Sadra's doctrines of the primacy and gradation of being. Existence and essence, he holds, are both equally real, and are created and renewed simultaneously by God, a position that drew a sharp reaction from the philosopher Hadi Sabzavari, who, though he had briefly studied with al-Ahsa'i and considered him 'unrivalled in his ascetic ways', was much more committed to the metaphysics of Mulla Sadra.[124] Ibn 'Arabi's concept of the unity of existence, which had been adopted by Sadra and his followers, was likewise subjected to trenchant critique. In his commentary on a treatise on divine knowledge written by Fayd al-Kashani, Mulla

Sadra's son-in-law and student and a leading Shi'i follower of Ibn 'Arabi, al-Ahsa'i asserts that those Sufis and philosophers who profess such doctrines as the unity of existence or the simplicity of reality represent the 'way of falsehood', in contrast to 'the way of the Infallibles', meaning true Shi'ism.[125] Elsewhere he describes Ibn 'Arabi – who was known to his admirers as Muhyi al-Din, 'the reviver of religion' – as 'the murderer of religion', and takes issue with Ibn 'Arabi's claim that the Sufi saints are the hidden 'poles' governing the universe, a role, al-Ahsa'i asserts, that belongs rightfully only to the Imams.[126]

Nevertheless, though al-Ahsa'i is critical of Ibn 'Arabi, Mulla Sadra and their followers, he remained under their influence, while also drawing extensively on the Illuminationist philosophy of Suhrawardi.[127] Similar to the Shi'i followers of Ibn 'Arabi, al-Ahsa'i identifies the twelve Imams, Muhammad and the Prophet's daughter Fatimah with the cosmic 'intellect', the divine names and attributes and the Muhammadan Reality. These fourteen 'infallibles' are, he says, the 'cause of creation' and the 'place' or 'locus' in which God's will is fulfilled. 'If it were not for the Imams,' he writes, 'God would not have created anything.'[128] Using a term of apparently Syriac origin that had been introduced to Islamic philosophy by Suhrawardi, al-Ahsa'i located the Imams in *hurqalya*, an intermediary world of 'images' existing between the divine realm and the physical world.[129] Though it is accessed by means of the imagination, this world, al-Ahsa'i believed, is in fact more 'real' than the world of senses.[130] Following al-Suhrawardi, al-Ahsa'i held that it is in *hurqalya* that visionary encounters with the Prophet and the Imams take place.[131] His own visions of the Imams, he believed, provided him with certain knowledge on questions of theology, and gave him the ability to determine whether a saying that had been attributed to the Prophet or the Imams was authentic. Ibn 'Arabi, and his successors in the Muhammadan Path tradition, had claimed the same ability on the basis of their own mystical experiences.[132] Though he defended the *ijtihad* of the Usulis, therefore, for al-Ahsa'i the ideal jurist was a mystic who acquired his knowledge through visionary encounters in the world of images.

It was in connection with the idea of the intermediary world of images that al-Ahsa'i developed his most innovative and controversial theory. Arabic has two common words for 'body' – *jism* and *jasad*. According to al-Ahsa'i, human beings have four kinds of body – two kinds of *jism*, or 'subtle body', and two kinds of *jasad*, or 'fleshly body'. The two kinds of *jasad* are a body of earthly flesh, which perishes when a person dies, and a body of 'spiritual flesh', which will be resurrected after a person's earthly death in the intermediary world of *hurqalya*. Though this theory of resurrection was a development of the views of Mulla Sadra and other thinkers in the Illuminationist tradition, al-Ahsa'i was sailing very close to the wind of acceptable Islamic opinion.[133] Anticipating the charge of heterodoxy, he claimed that his view was, despite appearances, 'exactly what the Muslims profess' about the resurrection of the body.[134] His opponents, however, were not convinced. In the early 1820s, al-Ahsa'i passed through Qazvin, in north-central Iran, on his way to visit the shrine of the eighth Imam at Mashhad. There he clashed with Mulla Muhammad Taqi al-Baraghani (d. 1847), the leader of the Friday congregational prayer in Qazvin. A known controversialist, al-Baraghani declared al-Ahsa'i an unbeliever on the grounds of his denial of the resurrection of the body and other fundamental Islamic doctrines, and went to some trouble to circulate the declaration throughout Iran and the Iraqi shrine cities.[135] Though al-Ahsa'i retained the support of some of the leading ulema of Iran, including, in the intellectual centre of Isfahan, the philosopher Mulla 'Ali Nuri and 'the proof of

Islam' Muhammad Baqir Shafti, the charge of infidelity was the first step towards the creation of 'Shaykhism' – so called after al-Ahsa'i's title Shaykh Ahmad – as a separate school or 'sect' of Shi'ism, replacing Akhbarism as the common enemy of the Usuli jurists.[136]

In 1824, after spells in Isfahan and Kermanshah, al-Ahsa'i was back in the Iraqi shrine city of Karbala. Before leaving for a final pilgrimage to the Hijaz, he designated as his 'qualified representative' his leading student, Sayyid Kazim Rashti.[137] A descendant of the Prophet, Rashti was a silk merchant from Gilan, in northern Iran, who had first met al-Ahsa'i in Yazd after being instructed to go to the Shaykh by a vision of Fatimah.[138] After that, barring his own pilgrimages, Rashti went almost everywhere with al-Ahsa'i; one source refers to him as the 'shirt on the body' of the Shaykh as a mark of how close they were.[139] Though al-Ahsa'i does not appear to have intended to create a new *madhhab*, by designating Rashti as his deputy and successor – an unusual act for an Usuli jurist – he took another step towards the formation of a Shaykhi school.[140] When al-Ahsa'i died, just outside Medina, in 1826, Rashti consolidated his followers into a *firqah* or 'group' calling themselves the Kashfiyyah, on account of the importance which their founder attached to *kashf* or mystical experience.[141]

Rashti continued, however, to uphold his teacher's position that the Shaykhis – a name given to them by their opponents which they progressively 'reclaimed' – were not a separate *madhhab*, and tried, through his writings and participation in public debates with leading clerics, to demonstrate the compatibility of Shaykhism and Usuli orthodoxy. Some of this may have been *taqiyyah* – the dissimulation or concealment of one's true beliefs to avoid persecution – an important and legitimate principle within Shi'i Islam. In one of his works, Rashti states that the Islamic era is divided into two ages, 'an age of outward observances and an age of inward realities', and that the second age had just begun, with al-Ahsa'i as its *murawwij* or 'propagator', a title used as the equivalent of *mujaddid* in the Shi'i tradition – an indication that he was committed to an esoteric interpretation of Shi'i doctrine in which the messianic age was believed to be imminent.[142] Regardless, it was after Rashti's death in 1844, and the division of the Shaykhi school into at least two regional branches, one in the north-western Iranian city of Tabriz and the other in Kirman in the south-east of the country, that the fundamental doctrines of Shaykhism were openly and systematically developed.

It was in Kirman, the historic centre of the Ni'matullahiyyah, the leading Shi'i Sufi order in Iran, and also the home of a sizeable Nizari Isma'ili community, that the more radical implications of al-Ahsa'i's teachings were worked out. The leader of the Kirmani branch of Shaykhism, al-Hajj Muhammad Karim Khan (d. 1871), was the son of a Qajar prince, Zahir al-Dawlah (d. 1825). A cousin of Fath 'Ali Shah and himself a follower of Sayyid Kazim Rashti, Zahir al-Dawlah had built an important madrasah, called the Ibrahimiyyah, near the Kirman bazaar in 1817. After studying with Rashti in Karbala, in 1834 Muhammad Karim Khan returned to Kirman as Rashti's representative. There he taught at his father's madrasah, for which he built up a splendid library, and wrote the numerous works – some 278 are attributed to him in total – in which he outlines his interpretation of Shaykhi doctrine.

Central to that doctrine is the notion of a hidden hierarchy of saintly figures – termed *rijal al-ghayb*, 'the men of the unseen realm' – who provide access to the Twelfth Imam. These hidden saints consist of two groups. The first are the *nuqaba'* or 'chiefs', rulers who perfectly implement the Imam's commands. At their head stands an individual called *natiq-i wahid* ('the single speaker'), the Bab (that is, the 'gate' to the Imam), or *shi'ah-yi kamil* ('the perfect Shi'ah'), who communicates directly with the hidden Imam. The second group are the *nujaba'* or 'nobles', teachers who share in the Imam's knowledge through their encounters with him in the intermediary world of images. Knowledge of these hidden saints, Karim Khan asserts, is the 'fourth pillar' of Shi'ism after knowledge of God, knowledge of the Prophet and knowledge of the Imams. Submitting to them is a condition of salvation, and the true Shi'ah are those who love them and hate their enemies.[143]

In Karim Khan's view (though he was not always consistent on this point), al-Ahsa'i had been the 'perfect Shi'ah' of his time, and Rashti had inherited that status from his teacher.[144] Al-Ahsa'i's mystically inspired knowledge, he asserts, 'takes the place of the ulema's consensus' and so 'to refute him is to refute the Imams'.[145] Furthermore, Karim Khan portrayed himself as the heir to Rashti, stating that he had come to 'reveal more' than his predecessors had done, and claiming in one passage that the book he was writing was a 'dictation' and 'copy' of God's eternal 'Book of knowledge'.[146] This claim to possess a mystical connection with the Awaited Imam and divinely inspired and infallible knowledge was evidently a challenge to the religious authority of the Usuli jurists. Karim Khan was accordingly barred from the mosques of Yazd when he stopped in the 'abode of worship' on his way to Mashhad, and his disciples were declared unbelievers.[147] For his part, Karim Khan declared that 'our religion has fallen into the hands of Satan', by which he meant the Usuli *mujtahids*.[148]

At the same time, the nascent Shaykhi school was splitting, not only between Karim Khan's more radical Kirmani branch and a Tabrizi branch that hewed more closely to orthodox Twelver Shi'ism, but also through the emergence at the time of Rashti's death of an even more radical movement known as Babism. This movement took its name from the claim initially made by its leader, a *sayyid* and merchant from Shiraz called Muhammad 'Ali (d. 1850), to be the Bab or 'gate' to the Twelfth Imam. This title had earlier been applied to the 'envoys' of the hidden Imam in the period preceding the announcement of the 'greater occultation'. Some Shaykhis ascribed the function of 'gate' to al-Ahsa'i and Rashti and, as we have seen, it was one of the names that Muhammad Karim Khan gave to the figure at the summit of the hidden hierarchy of saints.

Sayyid Muhammad 'Ali announced himself as the Bab in 1844 – a millennium, in the Islamic lunar calendar, after the occultation of the Awaited Imam, and therefore a time of great messianic expectation among the Shi'ah, particularly within the Shaykhi school. Having himself briefly studied with Rashti in Karbala, Sayyid Muhammad 'Ali succeeded in winning a small group of Shaykhis to his cause. He called this core group *huruf-i hayy*, 'the Living Letters'. Numbering eighteen, Sayyid Muhammad 'Ali identified them as incarnations of the Prophet Muhammad, his daughter Fatimah, the twelve Imams and the four original envoys or gates of the Twelfth Imam.[149] A leading figure among them was a female religious scholar and poet, Qurrat al-'Ayn (d. 1852), who claimed to be the incarnation of Fatimah, and to whom the Bab allotted the name Tahirah, 'the Pure'. Ironically, she was the niece and step-daughter of Muhammad Taqi al-Baraghani, the Qazvini scholar who had declared Ahmad al-Ahsa'i an unbeliever. A qualified jurist in her own right (there has historically been more scope for women to become jurists within the Shi'i tradition than the Sunni),[150] she became the leading teacher of the new doctrine in Karbala, instructing men as well as women, and led the development of that doctrine in a more radical direction. Developing the Shaykhi idea that the period of 'outward observances' was giving way to the age of 'inward realities', by 1846 Qurrat al-'Ayn was calling on her followers to abandon Islamic law, which the Bab had initially encouraged his disciples to uphold. Leading by example, she took to appearing in public without a veil.[151] In the ensuing scandal, she was expelled to Baghdad, while Sayyid Muhammad ʿAli himself, who had earlier been placed under house arrest in his hometown of Shiraz, was imprisoned at Maku in the province of Azerbaijan in north-western Iran.

By 1848, the Bab had begun to make ever more expansive claims for his own spiritual station. Identifying himself as the *qaʾim*, a traditional title of the Twelfth Imam meaning 'he who shall rise up', he first claimed to be the hidden Imam himself. 'Anyone who has seen me has seen the Father,' Jesus says in the Gospel of John (14:9). Likewise, in *The Everlasting of the Names*, an unusual commentary on the Qurʾanic story of Joseph written in the style of the Qurʾan itself, Sayyid Muhammad ʿAli, who was deeply influenced by his reading of the Gospels, says that whoever follows, loves and sees him has followed, loved and seen the Imam.[152] 'We are he and he is we,' he has the Imam say about him.[153] Soon he was claiming to be a *mazhar* – or 'locus of manifestation' – of God Himself. In *The Exposition*, a work written in Persian between 1847 and 1848 (an incomplete Arabic version soon followed) he expounded a new set of laws to substitute the laws of Islam. Subsequently, in the summer of 1848, a meeting of the Bab's leading followers at the village of Badasht in north-eastern Iran, in which Qurrat al-ʿAyn played a leading role, concluded with the announcement that the Islamic Shariʿah had been abrogated and a new religious dispensation had begun.[154]

Such a view was anathema both to the mainstream Twelver Shiʿah and the Shaykhis of Kirman, whose leader, Hajj Muhammad Karim Khan, attacked the Bab as an impostor and blasphemer and ridiculed him as the 'gate to hell', while also issuing a fatwa permitting the killing of Babi missionaries.[155] Violence between the Babis and the Shiʿah ensued, most notoriously with the siege and massacre of hundreds of Babis at the shrine of Shaykh Tabarsi in the very north of Iran in 1848–9, which the Babis regarded as a re-enactment of the slaughter of Husayn and his companions at Karbala in 680.[156] Finally, in 1850, Sayyid Muhammad 'Ali was executed on the orders of the Qajar government.

Yet the movement he inspired did not die with him. In the Persian *Exposition*, Sayyid Muhammad 'Ali had pointed towards the coming of a messianic individual called 'He whom God shall make manifest'. In 1863, one of his followers, Baha' Allah (d. 1892), who had participated in the meeting at Badasht and had since been sent into exile in Ottoman Baghdad, claimed to be this messiah. Having been sent first to Edirne (in the north-west of modern Turkey) and then to Acre in Palestine, Baha' Allah went on to identify himself as the return of the Bab and as a locus of divine manifestation. This status, he asserted, was shared by all the prophets, each of whom had brought a new system of revelation that improved upon that of their predecessor. The evolution of revealed religion culminated, Baha' Allah explained, in his own revelation, which he set out in a Persian scripture titled *The Most Holy Book*. The religion that he founded, Baha'ism, preaches such modern values as the unity of humanity, the equality of all human beings, the education of women and the harmony of science and religion.[157] Its followers have been subjected to significant persecution within Iran, Baha'ism, along with its predecessor Babism, being generally considered the 'arch-heresy' within Twelver Shi'ism.[158]

In breaking with Islam, the Bab and his successors provide a counterpoint to those thinkers, from both the Sunni and Shi'i traditions, who sought the renewal of the Islamic religion in the same period. It is instructive in this respect to compare a vision that the Bab experienced early in his mission with the dream of 'Abd al-Ghani al-Nabulusi with which this book opened. Al-Nabulusi, it will be remembered, had a vision of the sacred Ka'bah in a state of ruin, and saw it as his mission, as the renewer of Islam, to rebuild it. Sayyid Muhammad 'Ali likewise reported that he had seen the Shi'i shrine cities of Iraq 'fallen in pieces', yet took this as a sign that the Islamic era had come to an end.[159] Committed to the view that religion progresses through a series of evolutionary cycles, the Babis and their Baha'i successors believed that the Islamic cycle was over, and a new, culminating cycle of universal religion had begun. The Islamic renewers, by contrast, in seeking to recover the original religion of Muhammad, aimed to return to the beginning of that cycle, clinging to the notion of Islam as the final, perfect and universal religion. For them, the golden age of true religion was not merely something that lay in the distant past; it was also a hope for the future. As we shall see in the next chapter, with the rise of Western power and influence in the Muslim world, the urge to return to that golden age would be felt in an even more pressing way.

6

Engaging with Modernity I: Islamic Renewal in Colonial India

'In Ramadan 1273 A.H. [May 1857], such turmoil erupted that the mere thought of it would cause one's hair to stand on end.'¹ So wrote 'Ashiq Ilahi Miruti (d. 1941) in a biography of his teacher, the Sufi scholar Rashid Ahmad Gangohi (d. 1905), published between 1908 and 1910. The reference was to the events traditionally known as the Indian Mutiny, an uprising of Indian soldiers and civilians against the rule of the East India Company that began in the author's native town of Meerut, spread within a day to nearby Delhi, and soon took in other major cities of northern India such as Lucknow, Kanpur, Allahabad and Bareilly. Famously, the Mutiny was said to have been sparked by the introduction of the new Enfield rifle, the cartridges of which were rumoured to be lubricated with a mixture of pig and cow fat, making them impure to both Hindu and Muslim soldiers in the service of the East India Company. But at the root of the Mutiny were what the historian of British India Lawrence James has described as 'a tangle of grievances: economic, religious, political, tangible and intangible'.²

According to Sir Sayyid Ahmad Khan (d. 1898), whom we

will meet later in this chapter as a pioneer of Islamic modernism, the root cause of the Mutiny was the exclusion of Indians from the government of their own country. From this injustice, he explains in *The Causes of the Indian Revolt*, sprang other causes, the chief of which were widespread (and, in the loyalist Ahmad Khan's view, mistaken) fears regarding British intentions, particularly in matters of religion. 'There is not the smallest doubt,' he writes, 'that all men whether ignorant, or well-informed, whether high or low, felt a firm conviction that the English Government was bent on interfering with their religion and with their old established customs. They believed that Government intended to force the Christian Religion and foreign customs upon Hindu and Mussulman alike.'³ A similar view was expressed by Fazl-i Haqq Khayrabadi (d. 1861), a prominent religious scholar and critic of the reformist vision of Shah Muhammad Isma'il. The British, he explains in his memoirs, were widely believed to be 'planning to destroy the culture and civilization of India and so reduce all classes and communities to the same level'.⁴

Some of the Muslim rebels seem to have believed that, in rising up against non-Muslim rule, they were engaging in jihad. When the rebels took Delhi on 11 May 1857, they chose the Mughal Emperor, Bahadur Shah II, an eighty-two-year-old opium addict and poet with no effective power, as their nominal leader, the implication being that the rebellion was about restoring Islamic rule. In July 1857, Islamic missionaries, including a religious scholar from Bareilly, the native town of Sayyid Ahmad Barelwi, the founder of the Tariqah-yi Muhammadiyyah, were found preaching jihad in the North-Western Frontier region, where Sayyid Ahmad and Shah Muhammad Isma'il had waged their own holy war against the Sikhs four decades previously.⁵ Many of the British, James observes, likewise believed that God was 'on their side' and saw their ultimate victory, as a result of which the British

Crown assumed direct rule over India, as a 'manifestation of Divine justice'.[6] From the Islamic side, as the scholar of South Asian Islam SherAli Tareen has written, the failure of the Mutiny and final demise of the Mughal Empire 'dealt a fatal blow to any possibility of resurrecting Muslim political sovereignty' in India.[7] Yet, as psychologically devastating as it was, the loss of political power produced not despair among Muslim thinkers, but a determination to strengthen and renew Islam by other means. The result was the emergence, in the post-1857 period, of several new *masalik* – *maslak* in the singular form – 'methods' for the revival of Islamic piety, thought and society. Since Delhi, the historic centre of the reformist tradition of Shah Wali Allah and his family, had become the capital of the British Raj, these revivalist movements tended to be centred in north Indian *qasbahs*, smaller towns with large Muslim populations and longstanding traditions of Islamic scholarship, which, with the establishment of the telegraph, the postal service and the railway, were becoming increasingly interconnected and important in this period.

Among those caught up in the turmoil of the Mutiny were three religious scholars who played a key role in the formation of one of the most influential ideological orientations in modern Islam, in both South Asia and the wider world. These scholars were the aforementioned Rashid Ahmad Gangohi, his collaborator Muhammad Qasim Nanautvi (d. 1880) and their shared teacher Hajji Imdad Allah (d. 1899). The *maslak* founded by them is known as Deobandi Islam, after the *qasbah* of Deoband where Gangohi and Nanautvi established a madrasah in 1866. The events pertaining to their alleged involvement in the Mutiny took place in Thana Bhawan, a *qasbah* situated fifty miles north of Delhi, and are recorded by Gangohi's biographer Miruti.[8]

After Delhi had fallen to the rebels, Miruti reports, the headman of Thana Bhawan was arrested and subsequently hanged on the charge of sending elephants to the Mughal capital to support the Mutiny. The people of Thana Bhawan then went to Hajji Imdad Allah, a Sufi in the tradition of Shah Wali Allah and Sayyid Ahmad Barelwi, to ask him, as the leading religious scholar of Thana Bhawan, to manage their worldly affairs as *amir al-mu'minin*, 'Commander of the Believers', a historic title of the caliph. Imdad Allah accepted their request and sat as an Islamic judge in civil and criminal cases, employing his student Gangohi to assist him on account of his knowledge of the divine law. 'This issue,' Miruti writes, 'enabled certain people to accuse him of joining the ranks of the insurgents and gave some spies the opportunity to spread false information', though in actual fact, the biographer claims, they were steadfastly opposed to the Mutiny. When 'cowardly troublemakers' informed the government that Imdad Allah and his students Gangohi and Nanautvi were the ringleaders of the rebellion in Thana Bhawan, a warrant was issued for their arrest. Imdad Allah fled to Mecca, where he would remain until his death in 1899. Gangohi was not so fortunate, spending six months in jail until, Miruti reports, 'his innocence was proven as clear as the sun at midday'.[9]

In the 1920s, a narrative developed among Deobandi scholars seeking to justify their own involvement in nationalist politics, retrospectively casting Imdad Allah, Gangohi and Nanautvi as active participants in the Mutiny.[10] Though the extent of their actual involvement in the uprising remains unclear, the primary interest of these three scholars was not political resistance but religious reform and renewal. Like other movements of Islamic reform, the Deobandis referred to these activities by the terms *islah* and *tajdid*. Some identified Gangohi as the *mujaddid* of the century. Gangohi himself, while using *tajdid* in the usual sense of reviving the Sunnah of Muhammad and extirpating illicit innovations from prophetic practice, also developed an innovative conception of *tajdid* as a collective endeavour. For him, renewal was not just the responsibility of one divinely chosen individual but the shared responsibility of religious scholars. The idea of *tajdid* as both an individual and collective activity was adopted by Ashraf 'Ali Thanawi (d. 1942), another of Hajji Imdad Allah's students and a graduate of the seminary at Deoband, aptly described by the historian of South Asian Islam Brannon Ingram as 'the most influential Deobandi scholar in the history of the movement'.[11] Thanawi and other Deobandis often spoke of the need for *islah*, the 'reformation' or 'correction' of ritual practice and belief. Several of his works – *The Reformation of Customs* (published in 1893), *The Reformation of Thought* (1901) and *The Reformation of the Vicissitudes of the Muslim Community* (1928) – have *islah* in the title, and, like the early modern reformers we encountered earlier in this book, he argues that the reform of society needs to be rooted in the reform of the individual person. 'The reformation of one's actions,' he writes, 'is obligatory.'[12]

For the founders of the seminary at Deoband, the principal means of achieving religious renewal was education. Situated roughly ninety miles north-east of Delhi, and connected to other towns and cities of north India by the Northwest Railway line that was completed a year after the foundation of the madrasah, Deoband had a population of about 20,000, over half of whom were Muslim.[13] The choice of location is evidence of the Deobandi movement's connections to the longer tradition of Islamic reform in South Asia, as well as the belief, which they shared with other members of that tradition, that their vision of renewal was divinely inspired. It was reported that not only the 'renewer' of the second Islamic millennium Ahmad Sirhindi, but also Sayyid Ahmad Barelwi, the leader of the Muhammadan Path movement, had remarked upon the 'odour of learning' emanating from the soil of Deoband. What was more, Rafi' al-Din

Dihlawi, the son of Shah Wali Allah famous for his literal translation of the Qur'an into Urdu, was said to have dreamt that the Ka'bah had come to Deoband, that the Prophet's son-in-law 'Ali had founded a school whose students turned out to be those of Deoband, and that the Prophet himself had served milk to those students.[14]

Known as Dar al-'Ulum, 'the House of Sciences', the madrasah's curriculum harked back to the reformist tradition of Shah Wali Allah. The study of Hadith was, in the words of the historian Barbara Metcalf, 'the crowning subject' of the Deobandi curriculum, and the most important teacher at the school was the *shaykh* of Hadith.[15] Instead of the compendiums of selected Hadith that had become common fare at other madrasahs in post-classical Islam, students at Deoband studied – as Shah Wali Allah had encouraged – the canonical books of Sunni Hadith compiled in the late ninth century AD.[16] 'The study of the six canonical collections of hadith,' writes Muhammad Qasim Zaman, another historian of South Asian Islam, 'was, as it remains to this day, the culmination of a madrasa education at Deoband.'[17] The Deobandis, however, were not unqualified fundamentalists. Adherents of the Hanafi school of law, one of their aims was to show that the rules of the Hanafi *madhhab* (which is sometimes accused by followers of other schools of giving too much scope to human reasoning) were supported by Hadith.[18] A similar exercise had been undertaken a century earlier by the famous Arabic lexicographer, Sufi and Hadith scholar Murtada al-Zabidi (d. 1791). A student of Shah Wali Allah of Indian origin who eventually settled in Cairo, he wrote a book in 1782 attempting to show that Abu Hanifah's legal opinions were based on Hadith like those found in the six canonical collections.[19] Consistent with their commitment to the Hanafi legal tradition, the Deobandis did not attack *taqlid* – the emulation of juristic authority – with the same zeal as the more radical traditionalists. In the 1930s, a Deobandi scholar named Habib Ahmad Kiranwi wrote a treatise attacking those who condemned *taqlid*: 'In the worst of times,' he writes, 'a misguided group arose – insulting the Imams [of the four legal schools], condemning *taqlid*, and calling on others to do the same, even though most of their criticisms and all their proofs are based on *taqlid* of their predecessors.' 'The father of this group', according to Kiranwi, was Ibn Taymiyyah's leading student Ibn Qayyim al-Jawziyyah, indicating the Deobandis' divergence from those Hanbali scholars' ultra-traditionalist position.[20]

Still, like the Rahimiyyah madrasah founded by Shah Wali Allah's father, the seminary at Deoband put more weight on the study of Hadith than on the teaching of rationalist disciplines such as theology and logic. Muhammad Qasim Nanautvi, it is true, hoped that a student at Deoband would 'attain proficiency in all the rational and transmitted [that is, revealed] sciences', and was even open to them studying the 'new philosophy' coming from the West.[21] Yet Gangohi, who after Nanautvi's death in 1879 was more easily able to impose his vision on the curriculum at Deoband, was not so taken by knowledge rooted in unaided reason. Serving as an examiner at the affiliated Deobandi seminary at nearby Saharanpur in 1880, Gangohi lamented that one of the classes had not made sufficient progress in the study of Hadith, which was 'the goal of founding these [Deobandi] madrasahs and nothing else', because they had spent too much time on philosophy and other rational sciences.[22] 'Philosophy,' he wrote in a letter of 1884, 'is a useless thing'; hence it had been taken off the Deoband curriculum. Indeed, it was a 'wicked art' as well as a useless one, for it was liable to lead students into *shirk* and *kufr* – polytheism and unbelief.[23] In his emphasis on Hadith, his biographer Miruti writes, he was 'the true successor of Shah Wali Allah'.[24]

While the Deobandis' emphasis on Hadith was consistent with a longer tradition of reformist scholarship, the institutional organization of the school was conspicuously modern. A medieval madrasah was a charitable foundation, or *waqf*, founded by a private individual as an act of piety.[25] Though the founder would typically determine what was taught in his or her madrasah (the main subject was always law) and how the school was organized, teaching activities, as the historian Jonathan P. Berkey has observed, 'remained personal and informal'. 'No medieval madrasa,' Berkey explains, 'had anything approaching a set curriculum, and no system of degrees was ever established.'[26] The Dar al-'Ulum at Deoband was a much more formal affair. The founders borrowed many features of modern schooling, including classrooms, a central library, a set curriculum (taught in Urdu), yearly exams (following which school prizes could be obtained) and professional administrators and lecturers.[27] In introducing these innovations they were inspired by the example of Delhi College, an institution founded by the British, where the curriculum included the natural sciences, mathematics, natural philosophy, economics, ethics and history alongside the Arabic and Persian texts of the *dars-i nizami*, the curriculum of the rationalist Farangi Mahall tradition at Lucknow.[28] Both Rashid Ahmad Gangohi and Muhammad Qasim Nanautvi had studied with Mamluk 'Ali (d. 1851), the Arabic lecturer at the college, as young men in Delhi.

One of the Deobandis' most important institutional innovations involved the funding of the college. The Dar al-'Ulum was not a charitable foundation in the classical sense; instead of *waqf*, it was funded through what today would be called crowdsourcing, its finances deriving from charitable donations given by members of the Muslim community. Many of the donors were ordinary Muslims of relatively modest means, who were encouraged to regard their donations as *zakat*, the almsgiving that is one of the five pillars of Sunni Islam.²⁹ This system of funding ensured that the school at Deoband was embedded in the community, and that it survived when other madrasahs that relied on the patronage of the landed Muslim gentry, such as Farangi Mahall, died out.³⁰ It also enabled the emergence of a growing network of madrasahs across the Indian subcontinent that were modelled on Dar al-'Ulum at Deoband. Less than six months after the founding of the original seminary, a second madrasah, the Mazahir al-'Ulum, was established at the nearby *qasbah* of Saharanpur.³¹ Within fifteen years, there were more than a dozen Deobandi schools; by 1900, there were at least forty, including in places as far removed as Chittagong in Bengal, Madras in southern India and Peshawar in the North-Western Frontier region. When the Dar al-'Ulum celebrated its centenary in 1967, there were reportedly 8,934 schools in the network.³² Today, the number is somewhere between 50,000 and 60,000 schools in the Indian subcontinent, with other schools in South Africa, the UK and the USA.³³

The aim of the schools was to prepare a class of ulema capable of disseminating the true interpretation of Islam among lay Muslims.³⁴ Though the Deobandis were inspired by the reformist legacy of Shah Muhammad Isma'il and the Tariqah-yi Muhammadiyyah, they did not share what Brannon Ingram describes as Isma'il's 'hermeneutical populism' – that is, 'the notion that the Qur'an and the Sunna are "easy" to understand and, therefore, do not require the mediation of the 'ulama.'³⁵ 'It is absurd,' writes the leading second-generation Deobandi scholar Ashraf 'Ali Thanawi, 'to think that Muslims can dispense with the ulema.'³⁶ In their role as guardians and propagators of the faith, the Deobandis saw themselves as heirs to a scholarly tradition that went right back to the first centuries of Islam, and regarded their schools – as the annual report of the Mazahir al-'Ulum madrasah at Saharanpur put it in 1904 – as the 'deputies' or representatives of the Prophet.[37]

In stressing the role of the religious scholarly class, the Deobandis were responding not just to the populist tendencies in eighteenth- and early nineteenth-century Islamic thought, but also to the ruptures in the legal domain brought about by British rule in India. In 1772, the East India Company claimed jurisdiction over civil and criminal affairs and decreed that, in matters of personal status such as marriage, divorce and inheritance, Muslims and Hindus would be governed by their respective religious laws. This intervention marked the inception of a hybrid legal system known as Anglo–Muhammadan Law, according to which officials of the East India Company applied the concepts and principles of English Common Law to the interpretation of Islamic law. Initially, Company judges were advised by religious scholars known as *mawlawis* – much as the traditional *qadi* or Islamic judge received advice from a mufti (a scholar qualified to issue legal opinions) – but in 1864 this post was abolished, on the assumption that Islamic law was embodied not in the reasoning of individual scholars but in English translations of classic Hanafi legal texts.[38] This side-lining of the ulema class went hand in hand with the restriction of Islamic law to matters of personal status following the Indian Penal Code of 1860, which abolished any remaining role for Islamic law in the regulation of criminal affairs.[39]

The Deobandi ulema responded to this assault on their authority by turning with gusto to the issuing of fatwas, opinions issued in response to a petition for legal or theological guidance.[40] In 1893, they established a special department for issuing fatwas. In the first hundred years of the Deobandi movement, no fewer than 269,215 fatwas were issued by Deobandi scholars, mainly on questions of Islamic ritual and belief and the laws of personal status, and the opinions of eminent Deobandis such as Rashid Ahmad Gangohi, who jointly served as one of the first directors of the fatwa department, and Ashraf 'Ali Thanawi were collected into multi-volume works of reference.[41]

One of the major concerns of the Deobandi fatwa literature is the eradication of *bida'*, innovations from the Sunnah of the Prophet.[42] Gangohi, his biographer Miruti tells us, 'abhorred *bida*'', and he rejected the distinction that was traditionally made by Islamic jurists between 'reprehensible' and 'praiseworthy' innovations.[43] In particular, the Deobandis were concerned with innovations in the domain of *'ibadat* or ritual devotion. Gangohi adopted the definition of *bid'a* given by a grandson of Shah Wali Allah, the Hadith scholar Shah Muhammad Ishaq (d. 1846): 'Any practice which is not reported as an act of devotion practised by the *salaf*,' that is, the 'pious predecessors' who made up the earliest generations of Islam, the latter explains, 'if performed as an act of devotion is *bid'a*.'[44] Acts connected with the Sufi orders and popular religion – such as *ziyarah* (the visitation of saints' shrines) or the celebration of the *urs* (the anniversary of a saint's death) and the *mawlid* (the birthday of the Prophet) – were seen as especially fertile breeding ground for innovations.[45] While not necessarily forbidden in themselves, the danger was that these acts could be elevated, in the minds of ordinary Muslims, to the level of religious obligations equivalent to the ritual prayer, fasting in Ramadan and the pilgrimage to Mecca. Echoing Hajji Imdad Allah's view that a permissible action becomes an act of disobedience when it is insisted upon as if it were a religious obligation, the Deobandis worried that a kind of 'faux-Shari'ah' was being created, as innovations came to wear what SherAli Tareen has called 'the mask of religion'.[46]

Especially suspect in this respect – at least in the eyes of Gangohi – was the *mawlid*, the celebration of the Prophet's birthday, on which he issued numerous fatwas.[47] 'This festival,' one of them concludes, 'did not exist in the era of the Prophet Muhammad, in the era of the pious Companions, in the era of the Followers [that is, the generation succeeding the Companions], or the Followers of the Followers [the generation after them], or in the era of the founders of the Islamic legal schools. It was invented some four hundred years later by a king whom most historians regard as immoral.' Hence, he asserts, 'holding a *mawlud* gathering [another name for the *mawlid*] is not permissible under any condition'.⁴⁸ The feature of the *mawlid* celebration that most troubled Deobandis like Gangohi and his student, the Hadith scholar Khalil Ahmad Saharanpuri (d. 1927), was the *qiyam* – the act of standing to greet the Prophet during the *mawlid* – for it implied the heretical idea that the Prophet was spiritually present during the gathering.⁴⁹ Such ideas were widely held among the Sufis of South Asia: a poem by Amir Khusraw (d. 1325), the most celebrated Persian poet of medieval India, which was often recited at Sufi gatherings, identified Muhamamd as the 'candle illuminating the assembly'.⁵⁰

Besides having no precedent in the customary practice of the pious predecessors, many of the innovations found in popular religion were condemned as borrowings from Hinduism and other religious traditions. Inspired by the Hadith, 'Whoever imitates a people becomes one of them', the Deobandis attacked those Indian Muslims who engaged in *tashabbuh bi-l-kuffar*, 'the imitation of unbelievers'. Gangohi and Saharanpuri condemned the *mawlid* of the Prophet, for instance, on the grounds that it emulated Krishna Janmashtami, the Hindu festival commemorating the birth of Krishna, and the Deobandis more generally encouraged Muslims to distinguish themselves from unbelievers in their appearance and daily habits.

While the practices attacked by the Deobandis were associated with popular Sufism, the leaders of the Deobandi movement were not opposed to Sufism itself. Hajji Imdad Allah was affiliated to all four of the major Sufi orders of India – meaning the Naqshbandi, Chishti, Qadiri and Suhrawardi *tariqas* – and claimed to have been initiated into the Naqshbandiyyah through a mystical vision of the Prophet and Sayyid Ahmad Barelwi, whose understanding of *bidaʿ* was very close to the Deobandis' own.[51] After his migration to Mecca, he gave classes on *The Spiritual Couplets* of Rumi, one of the great works of Persian mystical literature. Among his own works are a marginal commentary on *The Spiritual Couplets*, an Urdu poem written in the same style and metre as Rumi's and a *Treatise Explaining the Unity of Existence*, a doctrine which, according to his disciple Thanawi, Imdad Allah had understood and accepted in the wake of a mystical experience brought on by hearing Qur'an 20:8: 'There is no god but Him! He has the most beautiful names.'[52]

Under Imdad Allah's guidance, Gangohi, Nanautvi and Thanawi all entered the mystical path. As a young man, Nanautvi reputedly spent six or seven hours at a time on mystical devotions, while Gangohi, who was affiliated to the Chishti order, describes 'the knowledge of Sufism' as equivalent to the knowledge of the Shariʿah and of Islam itself.[53] Ashraf ʿAli Thanawi was probably the most committed mystic of the three; indeed, according to Metcalf he is 'widely considered the preeminent Sufi of modern India'.[54] While studying under Hajji Imdad Allah in Mecca he embraced Ibn ʿArabi's doctrine of the unity of existence and wrote a text defending it, as well as a commentary on Ibn ʿArabi's *The Ringstones of Wisdom*.[55] Later he became the spiritual director of Hajji Imdad Allah's old Sufi lodge in Thana Bhawan and wrote a long commentary on Rumi's *Spiritual Couplets*. In keeping with the central theme of Rumi's work, Thanawi identifies '*ishq* or 'passionate love' as 'the human being's true distinguishing quality'. In his view, belief and love were coterminous: 'Belief,' he writes, 'involves passionate love. When you say, "we believe", you in fact state, "we adore and love".'[56] Like other Sufis, Thanawi stresses that divine mysteries can be revealed to people through mystical 'unveiling' or 'inspiration', mystical experience being a complementary source of religious knowledge to the study of Qur'an, Hadith and law.[57]

For the Deobandis, Sufism only goes wrong when it is set up as an alternative to the divine law. Like al-Ghazali and many other classical Sufi authorities, they insist on the unity of the Shari'ah and the *tariqah*, the sacred law and the mystical path.[58] 'Both [the Shari'ah and the *tariqah*],' writes Gangohi, are one ... Both are derived from the rules of the Qur'an and the Hadith.'[59] Gangohi and his followers regard Sufism as being primarily about the cultivation of ethical virtues or what is called *tazkiyah-yi nafs*, 'the purification of the self'.[60] As they see it, crucial to the process of character formation is *suhbat*, 'companionship' with a Sufi guide, who should be chosen and emulated not on account of an ability to work miracles, as some pseudo-Sufis believe, but for his religious knowledge and upright character.[61] The virtues exemplified by the Sufi shaykh, they hold, are a model for all Muslims, not just a mystical elite. While the Deobandis uphold the traditional role of the ulema as guardians and disseminators of religious knowledge, they open up Sufism to ordinary Muslims. 'Deobandi works,' Ingram informs us, 'are replete with the idea that any Muslim can be a "saint" (*wali*)', an idea reminiscent of certain Protestant interpretations of sainthood, and one which diverges markedly from the hierarchical understanding of sanctity prevalent in the premodern Sufi tradition.[62] In fact, since in their view Sufism means the refinement of character and following the Shari'ah, the Deobandis sometimes go so far as to assert that Sufism is *obligatory* for all Muslims.[63]

This concern for disseminating true Islam among all

Muslims was extended to women as well as men. In 1902/3 Ashraf 'Ali Thanawi began a compendium of Islamic law aimed specifically at a female readership. Titled *Heavenly Ornaments* – because, Thanawi explains, women are generally fond of ornaments, and the real ornaments are 'none other than those perfections of religion thanks to which one shall receive ornaments to wear in heaven' – and written in an Urdu 'whose style', he asserts, is 'very simple', the resulting text is a massive book that comes to somewhere between 800 and 1,000 pages depending on the edition.[64] According to the leading scholars of the Deobandi movement, it became 'one of the most influential texts of the scripturalist reform movements characteristic of Muslim societies in the past century', 'one of the most widely printed books in South Asia' and 'a classic gift for Muslim brides, who [in the words of the scholar of Urdu literature C.M. Naim] "entered their husband's home with the Holy Qur'an in one hand and [*The Heavenly Ornaments*] in the other."'[65]

In the book's introduction, Thanawi laments the 'ruination' of the religion of Muslim women in India, the cause of which he identifies as 'women's ignorance of the religious sciences'. This ignorance, he goes on, 'corrupts their beliefs, their deeds, their dealings with other people, their character, and the whole manner of their social life', and also has a corrupting effect on the children 'whom they nurture in their very laps'. Furthermore, when a woman's husband is similarly ignorant, 'the two together grow more corrupt'. Applying the traditional medical principle that 'the cure of each thing is its opposite', Thanawi therefore resolved to save Indian Muslim women by teaching them Islamic theology and law, with a concentration on those legal issues that particularly pertain to women.[66]

The notion of gender relations outlined here is undoubtedly patriarchal and hierarchical. It is necessary to teach women the religious sciences, Thanawi declares in the opening lines of the book, in order to 'manage' them. 'It is required of men,' he writes a few pages later, 'that they set their wives and daughters to study this work.' While Thanawi offers his female readers the hope that, after three years of studying the text, they would 'join the ranks of the ulema' and be qualified to issue fatwas and teach children Arabic, he qualifies that offer by stating that those who read the book would become 'middling' religious scholars who would still require the guidance of 'expert' scholars.[67] 'In reality,' he says, 'Muslims can never become independent of their religious authorities.'[68]

Heavenly Ornaments is divided into ten parts, the first of which includes a list of the fundamental beliefs to which a Muslim must adhere. Thanawi identifies forty-nine such beliefs, which he explains in a simple Hindi-Urdu, avoiding the Arabic terminology of formal Islamic theology. As Barbara Metcalf notes, these beliefs are implicitly contrasted with the false beliefs of other groups.[69] The first beliefs outlined in the list, which include the doctrine that the world was created from nothing by God, who is One, has always existed, gave birth to no one, and is unlike all things in His power and knowledge and all other attributes, distinguish the Muslims from atheists (who deny the existence of God), Aristotelian philosophers (who hold that the world is eternal), Hindus (who believe in many gods) and Christians (who believe that Jesus was 'begotten of the Father'), among other erroneous groups. Next come those beliefs that differentiate true Muslims from 'false Sufis'. Starting from the Deobandis' equalizing principle that all Muslims who 'worship faithfully, avoid sin, do not love the world and obey the Messenger in every way' are saints, Thanawi asserts that no saint is the equal of a prophet, that saints are always bound to follow the sacred law, that apparent miracles performed by those who neglect the ritual duties of the law are in fact either magic or the work of Satan, and that divine mysteries revealed to the saints in dreams or visions should only be accepted if they are in keeping with the law. These assertions are followed by two points that, in celebrating the Companions of the Prophet, particularly the first four caliphs (the first two of whom, Abu Bakr and 'Umar, are reviled by the Shi'ah for having denied 'Ali the caliphate), distinguish Sunni Muslims from their Shi'i counterparts. Another fundamental belief – that 'no one other than Almighty God knows the unknown' – is directed against the Ahl-i Sunnat or Barelwi movement, which, as we shall see, asserted that the Prophet Muhammad shared in God's knowledge of the unseen. Finally, Thanawi turns to Islamic beliefs concerning the world to come and the Day of Judgement, emphasizing that it is correct belief that will determine a person's salvation.[70]

Correct belief, as Thanawi and the Deobandis see it, is manifested in correct actions, while false belief is manifested in – and strengthened by – wrong actions. Having listed the fundamental beliefs to which a Muslim woman must adhere, Thanawi goes on to outline the sins, innovations and bad customs – signified by the term *rusum*, which like *bida'* denotes a kind of 'anti-Sunnah' – that have dreadful consequences in this life and the next. Building upon Shah Muhammad Isma'il's understanding of innovation, Thanawi identifies among the most grievous sins actions that put some other individual in a position that rightfully belongs only to God. It is, for example, a sin for someone 'to call on some holy person from afar and to believe that person will hear', 'to believe that someone other than God is responsible for all your profit and loss', 'to demand fulfilment of your wishes from someone other than God' or 'to ask that person to grant you livelihood or offspring'. Fasts, acts of prostration, sacrifices or vows to holy people are also sinful, and so is – and here Thanawi takes directly from Shah Muhammad Isma'il's *The Strengthening of*

Faith – giving children names such as 'Ali Bakhsh (meaning 'Granted by 'Ali'), Husayn Bakhsh ('Granted by Husayn') or 'Abd al-Nabi ('the Servant of the Prophet').[71]

Thanawi's list of innovations is likewise inspired by the reformist vision of Shah Muhammad Isma'il. Stirred by Isma'il's campaign for widow remarriage, he insists that it is a reprehensible innovation 'to regard a second marriage for a woman as a fault, despite there being a need for it'.[72] Other innovations generally fall into three categories. First, there are the illegitimate practices that take place at the graves of holy men: lighting candles at the graves, putting shawls over them, kissing them or making offerings of sweets to the saint are all evil customs, and it is reprehensible, he says, for women to go to graves at all. Second, there are the frivolous activities and expressions of excitability (many of them particularly associated with women) that Islam had always sought to control: singing while bringing pitchers of water from the river, spending unseemly amounts of money on a wedding or excessive amounts of time decorating one's home, wailing uncontrollably when someone dies. Third, there are acts of *tashabbuh* – the 'emulation' of unbelievers that the Prophet had warned against – such as celebrating the Hindu festivals of Holi or Diwali or adopting Hindu wedding practices.[73] 'To like the customs of the unbelievers,' in fact, is included in Thanawi's 'very grievous sins'.[74]

When Deobandis such as Thanawi attacked the emulation of unbelievers, their aim was not so much to attack other religions as to commend Sunnah instead of *bid'ah* and in so doing to define true Islam. Though they did engage in public debates with representatives of other faiths – most famous is Nanautvi's participation in the Festival of Deciding the True God at Shajahanpur in 1877, when he debated the founder of the revivalist Hindu movement the Arya Samaj, Dayananda Sarasvati (d. 1883), and a Methodist missionary called Samuel Knowles – their principal opponents were other *Islamic* movements of renewal, who differed with them in some way over what 'true Islam' meant.[75]

Though the Deobandi curriculum was traditionalist in the sense that it emphasized the study of Hadith over the rationalist sciences, the Deobandis, as we have seen, were not radical traditionalists or fundamentalists in the sense of rejecting the schools of law. Indeed, they were committed to showing that the Hadith corpus supported the doctrine of the Hanafi school of law. Much purer in their traditionalism were the Ahl-i Hadith, 'the people of prophetic traditions', a name which harked back to the movement of traditionalist jurisprudents in early Islamic history who, in contrast to *ahl al-ra'y*, 'the people of opinion', argued that the law should entirely be derived from the Qur'an and Hadith without recourse to speculative reasoning.

The founding fathers of the Ahl-i Hadith were two scholars hailing from the Muslim aristocracy of northern India, Nazir Husayn of Delhi (d. 1922) and Siddiq Hasan Khan (d. 1900), the Nawab of Bhopal. Like other Indian reformers, their intellectual genealogies tied them, on the one hand, to the scholarly tradition of Shah Wali Allah mediated through the Tariqah-yi Muhamamdiyyah of Sayyid Ahmad Barelwi and Shah Muhammad Isma'il, and on the other to the traditionalism of the Yemeni scholar al-Shawkani. Insofar as al-Shawkani was the major source of inspiration to Shah Muhammad Isma'il, these channels of influence were complementary, and both led back to the writings of the iconoclastic Hanbali traditionalist of thirteenth-fourteenth-century Damascus, Ibn Taymiyyah.

Born in Bihar in the east of India in 1805, at sixteen Nazir Husayn moved to the village of Sadiqpur, a centre of reformist scholarship, where he lived with one of Shah Muhammad Isma'il's associates, before moving to Delhi, the home of the scholarly tradition of Shah Wali Allah. In Delhi he studied at the Aurangabadi Mosque with Shah Muhammad Ishaq (d. 1846) – known as Muhajir-i Makki, 'the emigrant to Mecca' – the grandson and successor of Shah 'Abd al-'Aziz, the son of Shah Wali Allah who had famously declared India to be part of 'the abode of war' following the British conquest of Delhi in 1803. Succeeding Muhammad Ishaq as teacher of Hadith at the Aurangabadi Mosque, before moving to the mosque by the Ethiopian Gate of Delhi, Nazir Husayn was known as *shaykh al-kull*, 'the master of all', since almost all the major Hadith scholars of turn-of-the-century India studied with him. In 1897, the Earl of Elgin, the British viceroy of India, conferred on him the title of *shams al-'ulama'*, 'the sun of scholars', which had been created ten years previously to mark the golden jubilee of Queen Victoria.[76]

Nazir Husayn's major work, *The Criterion of Truth*, was an apology for the writings of Shah Muhammad Isma'il. Written in 1865 or 1866 in response to a book attacking the ideologue of the Tariqah-yi Muhammadiyyah, *The Criterion of Truth* marshals various arguments against *taqlid* or blind emulation of a single school of law. The influence of al-Shawkani is palpable throughout: for instance, Nazir Husayn rejects the common view that it is harder for Muslims to understand the Qur'an and Sunnah than in times past; in fact, he says, echoing the Zaydi traditionalist, the wider availability of books of Hadith makes it *easier* for contemporary Muslims to know the Sunnah of the Prophet. Al-Shawkani had begun his treatise on the proofs for *ijtihad* and *taqlid* by criticizing the proponents of the legitimacy of *taqlid* for using Qur'an 21:7 – 'Ask the people of remembrance if you do not know' – as one of their proof texts. Nazir Husayn likewise focuses on this verse and rejects it as a Qur'anic justification for *taqlid*.[77]

Siddiq Hasan Khan, the second major figure of the Indian Ahl-i Hadith, was similarly embedded in an intellectual network that connected al-Shawkani and the Zaydi traditionalists to the Tariqah-yi Muhammadiyyah movement of Shah Muhammad Isma'il. He was born in Bareilly, the hometown of Sayyid Ahmad Barelwi, in 1834. His father had studied with three of Shah Wali Allah's sons, converted from Shi'ism to Sunni Islam and accompanied Sayyid Ahmad Barelwi to Afghanistan, where he acted as a missionary for Sayyid Ahmad's purified form of Islam.[78]

Though his father died when he was only five years old, Siddiq Hasan Khan continued in the tradition of reformist scholarship. He went to Delhi, where he studied logic, law, Hadith and Qur'anic exegesis with Sadr al-Din Azurdah (d. 1868), a prominent poet and religious scholar who had himself studied with Shah Wali Allah's sons Shah 'Abd al-'Aziz and Shah 'Abd al-Qadir and held the post of *sadr al-sudur*, the top judicial office in the administration of the East India Company attainable by Indians.[79] Towards the end of 1854 Siddiq Hasan Khan arrived at the princely state of Bhopal, one of the largest Muslim principalities in British India. The prime minister of Bhopal, Munshi Jamaluddin (d. 1881), himself followed the scholarly tradition of Shah Wali Allah, and in 1863 he invited to the princely court two Yemeni scholars who had studied under al-Shawkani's son Ahmad, one of whom became the chief judge of Bhopal and a firm friend of Siddiq Hasan Khan's.[80] Siddiq Hasan Khan took the opportunity afforded by these connections to immerse himself in the writings of al-Shawkani and his predecessor Ibn Taymiyyah. While travelling through Yemen and the Hijaz on pilgrimage in 1869, he sought out and purchased manuscripts of the writings of these two great traditionalist scholars, including a copy of Ibn Taymiyyah's *Refutation of the Logicians* in the author's own hand.[81]

Under the influence of al-Shawkani, Siddiq Hasan Khan turned against the schools of law. 'After his return to Bhopal,' writes his biographer, Saeedullah, 'he was no more a *muqallid* [that is, someone who practises *taqlid*]; on the contrary, he started writing books against *taqlid* and the followers of Abu Hanifah who, according to him, were chiefly responsible for the intellectual stagnation of Muslim India.'[82] Abu Hanifah, from whom the Hanafi school of law followed by the majority of South Asian Muslims took its name, was one of *ahl al-ra'y*, 'the people of opinion' of early Islamic history against whom the original *ahl al-hadith* had struggled. For Siddiq Hasan Khan, as for al-Shawkani, there was no room for personal opinion of any kind – including analogical reasoning – in the working out of the law. As Saeedullah puts it, 'He believed that the Qur'an and the Hadith encompassed all political, social, economic and legal matters and there was no need for further development.'[83]

In 1871, Siddiq Hasan Khan married Shah Jahan Begum, the widowed ruler of Bhopal. As a result, Saeedullah reports, he acquired 'a handsome *jagir* [or land grant] worth 75,000 rupees a year, a free press, and an efficient team of ulema of the royal court of Bhopal'.[84] He was also given the princely title of *nawab*. With money, status and staff, Siddiq Hasan Khan was able to produce a continuous stream of books and treatises, in Arabic, Persian and Urdu, to advance the traditionalist teachings of the Ahl-i Hadith. More than any Muslim reformer before him, Siddiq Hasan Khan used the new medium of print to propagate his message of renewal.[85] Printed in India, Cairo and Constantinople, his books found a readership in the Arab Middle East as well as in South Asia, and in so doing contributed to the emergence of the Salafi current of Islamic reform which we shall meet in the next chapter.[86]

Many of these books were commentaries, abridgements or supplements to works by Siddiq Hasan Khan's heroes. In one, a Persian commentary on a Shafi'i text in which Siddiq Hasan Khan claims to be the *mujaddid*, he attacks the harmful innovations associated with shrine religion and Muslim women's imitation of Hindu and Western dress in terms reminiscent of the Deobandis.[87] In another, he criticizes the idea of Sufi guides or saints as mediators between God and man, the only true mediators being the Qur'an and Sunnah; condemns as *bid'ah* the celebration of the Prophet's birthday and the death anniversary of saints, the popular Sufi songs known in South Asia as *qawwali* and giving children names such as 'Servant of the Prophet'; and advances the same view as the Deobandis that anyone who believes in God and follows the divine law is a saint or 'friend of God'.[88] In the same text he also identifies the theory of the unity of existence as an innovation, though in another work – a series of biographies of traditionalist scholars, including Ibn 'Arabi's chief opponent Ibn Taymiyyah, taken from al-Shawkani's biographical dictionary of ulema – Siddiq Hasan Khan praises Ibn 'Arabi for going back to the scriptural sources instead of relying on *taqlid* and advises withholding judgement on the question of whether the Andalusian Sufi was a heretic.[89] He also directed a collaborative, multi-volume Urdu translation of the Qur'an that relies heavily on the translation made by Shah Wali Allah's son Shah 'Abd al-Qadir and on the Qur'an commentaries of al-Shawkani and Ibn Kathir (d. 1373), a leading follower of Ibn Taymiyyah, reflecting his view that the Qur'an ought to be understood with reference to itself and to Hadith, rather than interpreted through the lens of the later traditions of Islamic theology, mysticism and jurisprudence.[90]

Siddiq Hasan Khan also expressed his traditionalist commitments in Persian verse. 'The Hadiths of the Prophet shine everywhere,' he declares in one couplet. 'There are a hundred easts for the face of this Sun' – a statement of the comprehensiveness of the Hadith corpus.[91] In another poem, he warns that blind emulation of others will not avail them on the Day of Judgement, 'when you and I will be asked about the Qur'an and the Sunnah'.[92] In his most important work of poetry,

The Pleasant Breeze, the Nawab of Bhopal reworks the celebrated Persian verse of Hafiz (d. 1390) and Rumi in order to attack *taqlid*: to cling unthinkingly to a single school of law, he says, is to abandon the beauty of the beloved – that is, the Messenger of God. The poem was written as a contribution to a debate initiated by a leading Hanafi scholar from the rationalist Farangi Mahall tradition, Mawlana 'Abd al-Hayy (d. 1886), who had written articles defending *taqlid* in Urdu journals. As Barbara Metcalf has observed, while this Hanafi scholar saw emulation as a guarantor of the stability, predictability and unity of the law, Siddiq Hasan Khan and the Ahl-i Hadith, by contrast, regarded it as a path to reprehensible innovation.[93]

They saw the corpus of Hadith not only as the way to certain knowledge of legal and theological issues, but also – and here their Sufi background is discernible – as a way for Muslims to fashion themselves according to the prophetic example and attain salvation. A major Ahl-i Hadith work, a commentary by 'Abd al-Rahman Mubarakpuri (d. 1935) on the collection of prophetic Hadith compiled by al-Tirmidhi – one of the six canonical books of Hadith in Sunni Islam – explains that the subject of the science of Hadith is the 'essence of the Messenger of God'; its definition is 'the science through which the words, deeds and states of the Messenger of God are known'; and its aim is 'the achievement of bliss' in this life and the next. The discipline, Mubarakpuri goes on to say, is divided into the study of the transmission of the reports, which is the means to establish their authenticity, and the study of the content of the reports, the aim of which is 'to adorn oneself with prophetic traits' and 'to avoid what [the Prophet] disliked and forbade'. The science of Hadith is therefore 'the foremost part of the religious sciences and the key to them' and 'the basis and foundation of the laws of Islam'. In practice, this meant that, like other traditionalists, the Ahl-i Hadith differed from the followers of the legal schools on certain issues. For example, like al-Shawkani and al-Sanusi, they advocated raising the hands repeatedly during the ritual prayer, a distinctive marker of difference from rival ideological orientations.

In their emphasis on scripture as the path to individual salvation and the democratization of scriptural knowledge through print, the Ahl-i Hadith are an almost perfect example of what the historian of Islam in South Asia Francis Robinson calls 'Muslim Protestants'.[94] This tendency, as Nile Green, another scholar of Indian Islam, has shown, was catalyzed by the encounter with Protestant Christian missionaries, who had been evangelizing Muslims in South Asia since the 1830s.[95] A pioneer of Protestant missionary activity in India was the German Pietist missionary Carl Gottlieb Pfander (d. 1865). Beginning in the late seventeenth century, Pietism was a movement of renewal within Lutheran Protestantism, which, in the words of the scholar of Christianity Ulriche Gleixner, 'advocated the education of all classes, promoted individual responsibility and self-improvement, and also applied itself to the study of nature'.[96] Pfander had been a missionary in Georgia and Iran between 1825 and 1835, during which time he wrote his major work, *The Balance of Truth*, in which he attempted to demonstrate that the Christian Gospels, not the Qur'an, are 'the true revelation and divine word'.[97] In 1839, he was sent to Calcutta, where *The Balance of Truth*, which had already been translated from German into Persian and Armenian, was translated into Urdu, before settling in 1841 in the northern Indian city of Agra. Pfander's missionary work, and the diffusion of his book, required a response from the ulema. The eventual leader of this Muslim counterattack was Rahmat Allah Kairanawi (d. 1891), who held a public debate with Pfander at Agra in 1854 and authored a series of books in Persian and Urdu attempting to refute Christianity.

In conducting this counter-polemic against Christianity,

Kairanawi focused on two arguments: first, the irrationality of the Trinity, and second, the corruption of the Biblical text. Of the two, it was the latter argument that was the more effective: while the charge of *tahrif al-lafz*, the alteration of the words of the Bible, was an age-old theme of Islamic anti-Christian polemic, Kairanawi gave it new meaning and greater force by incorporating the results of the historical or 'higher' criticism of the Bible that had been developed in Germany in the late eighteenth and early nineteenth centuries. (He also cited European religious sceptics such as Spinoza, John Toland, Jean-Jacques Rousseau and Thomas Paine.) Pfander, whose education had not included the historical-critical approach to the Bible, was unable to respond convincingly to these arguments, which Kairanawi summarized in a multi-volume work that he wrote in Arabic in 1864 while living in Constantinople.[98]

The controversy between Pfander and Kairanawi not only set the terms of the later Muslim–Christian debate in India; it also left a deep mark on the founder of another of the major ideological orientations of late nineteenth-century India. This was Sayyid Ahmad Khan, the founder of the Aligarh movement of Islamic modernism, which sought to demonstrate Islam's essential compatibility with modernity. A descendant of the Prophet, Sayyid Ahmad was born in Delhi in 1817 into a family with connections to the Mughals, the East India Company and the Sufism of the Shah Wali Allah and the Muhammadan Path traditions. His maternal grandfather, in whose house he was raised, served as an ambassador for the East India Company in Iran and Burma, taught mathematics and astronomy at the Calcutta Madrasah founded by Warren Hastings, the first British Governor General of India, and had connections with Shah Wali Allah's son Shah 'Abd al-'Aziz.[99] His mother, whom he regarded as an embodiment of the Sufi virtue of *tawakkul*, complete trust in God, was related to Mir

Dard, the theorist of the 'Pure Muhammadan Path'.[100] Sayyid Ahmad Khan was himself taught Hadith by another of Shah Wali Allah's sons, Shah Rafi' al-Din, and identified Mir Dard's father, the poet 'Andalib, as the spiritual pole of his time.[101] Following in his grandfather's footsteps, he also entered the service of the East India Company, rising to become a magistrate in Delhi and the chief judicial officer of the city of Bijnor.[102]

Looking back on his intellectual journey later in life, Sayyid Ahmad Khan described how he had progressed from a Wahhabi kind of worldview to a Mu'tazili one, the Mu'tazilah being the archetypal rationalists of the Islamic theological tradition.[103] By 'Wahhabi', Sayyid Ahmad Khan, like many Indian authors of this period, meant the reformist Islam of Sayyid Ahmad Barelwi and Shah Muhammad Isma'il. His first work, an Urdu text titled *The Polishing of Hearts*, which he completed in 1842, was a biography of Muhammad intended to purge the prophetic biographies commonly used at *mawlid* gatherings of their more fantastical elements.[104] Soon, Ahmad Khan turned against the very celebration of the Prophet's birthday. 'When I became stricter in terms of religious matters and leaned more towards those doctrines which are called Wahhabism,' he later wrote, 'I began to perceive *mawlud*-gatherings as *bid'at*.'[105] In keeping with this reformist tendency, his second major work, *The Word of Truth* (1849), sets out the limits on devotion to a Sufi shaykh or *pir* (the Persian term for a Sufi shaykh). 'There are no grounds [in the Sunnah],' Sayyid Ahmad Khan concludes, 'for becoming a disciple in a certain [Sufi] order.'[106] Muhammad is 'the one true *pir*', and the 'only sign of a saint,' he writes, prefiguring the definition of the *wali* common to the Deobandis and Ahl-i Hadith, 'is whether he follows the Sunnah and Shari'ah of the Messenger of God.'[107] A third early work, *The Sunnah and the Rejection of Innovations*, which was completed the next year, adopts

Shah Muhammad Isma'il's definition of *bid'ah*, and concludes that 'only those customs, habits and religious services which were prevalent among [Muhammad's Companions and their successors] are meritorious and the remaining [are] futile'.[108]

Though he never entirely moved on from these 'Wahhabi' commitments, Sayyid Ahmad Khan's religious views seem to have begun to shift around the time of the Mutiny, of the causes of which, as we saw at the beginning of this chapter, he wrote an influential analysis that aimed to bring about a reconciliation between the British and the Muslims of India.[109] At the same time, his religious horizons were enlarged by the debate conducted by Pfander and Kairanawi at Agra. In the wake of both these events, Sayyid Ahmad Khan set to work on an unusual – though not totally unprecedented – project for a Muslim writer: a commentary on the Bible. His motives in undertaking it were mixed. On one level, the commentary can be read as part of a conciliatory attempt to highlight the commonalities between Islam and Christianity and in so doing to promote mutual understanding between the British rulers of India and their Muslim subjects in the aftermath of the Mutiny.[110] At another level, however, as Sayyid Ahmad's biographer, the Urdu poet Hali (d. 1914) highlighted, the commentary aims to explain the Christian scriptures from the perspective of Islamic doctrine, and so uses the Bible – which evangelical missionaries like Pfander regarded as the fundamental source of Christian doctrine – to prove the truth of Islam in the face of the Protestant missionary challenge.[111]

Written in Urdu with an accompanying English paraphrase, the commentary was issued in three volumes, the first two of which were published in 1862 and 1865, the last volume appearing only in a later collection of Ahmad Khan's writings. In the first volume, Ahmad Khan considers the question of the authenticity of the Biblical text, which had been so central to the debate between Pfander and Kairanawi. In classical exegesis of the Qur'an, the Qur'anic charge of *tahrif*, the People of the Book's distortion of their scriptures, was taken to refer either to their actual corruption of the Biblical text or to their mistaken interpretation of the revealed books. Kairanawi, as we have seen, used European Biblical criticism to put forward the charge of textual corruption. Ahmad Khan, by contrast, upholds the integrity of the Christian scriptures, arguing only that Christians had distorted the *meaning* of those scriptures by introducing such erroneous doctrines as the Trinity and Original Sin.[112] In keeping with this position, he also departs from the traditional interpretation of *naskh*, the idea that the Qur'an 'abrogated' or annulled the Gospel, asserting instead that the revelation given to Muhammad is a *renewal* of the message of Christ that accounts for the social developments that had taken place in the intervening centuries.[113] These interpretations enabled Muslims like himself to cite the Bible as an authoritative book; hence in his *Causes of the Indian Revolt* Ahmad Khan quotes liberally from the letters of Paul, particularly on the theme of love for one's fellow men.[114]

The second and third volumes of the Bible commentary are devoted, respectively, to Genesis 1–11 and Matthew 1–5. In the introduction to the commentary on the Gospel of Matthew, Sayyid Ahmad Khan cites the chapter on Jesus from Ibn 'Arabi's *The Ringstones of Wisdom* to make the point that, on account of his being 'born of the spirit only and not through any external cause' – a reference to the Virgin Birth (which is accepted in Islam) – Jesus was a paragon of 'spiritual holiness'.[115] Jesus came to 'teach spiritual holiness and spiritual light', he explains, at a time 'when no spiritual holiness remained', due to the corruption of the Pharisees, Sadducees, Essenes and Samaritans, who 'had introduced numerous harmful innovations [*bid'at*] into the Law of Moses'.[116] Jesus, in other words, was a model for the renewal of religion in the face of the spread of innovations.

As well as reinterpreting the Christian scriptures from his

own reformed Islamic perspective, Sayyid Ahmad Khan was concerned with refuting European criticisms of Islam and the Prophet Muhammad. Again, this concern was partly a response to the legacy of Pfander. At the beginning of 1857, the year of the Mutiny, William Muir of the Bengal Civil Service – who was later the Lieutenant-Governor of the North-Western Provinces and Principal of the University of Edinburgh – brought out the first volume of his four-volume *Life of Mahomet*. This work, Muir acknowledged in the preface, had been undertaken 'at the insistence of the Rev. C. G. Pfander ... who urged that that a biography of the Prophet of Islam, suitable for the perusal of his followers, should be compiled in the Hindoostanee language, from the early sources acknowledged by themselves to be authentic and authoritative'.[117] According to his biographer Hali, Ahmad Khan was 'visibly agitated' by the appearance of this work.[118] While recognizing it to be 'the best of all the biographies of Mohammed from the pen of foreign authors', he felt chastened by Muir's 'animus' towards Islam and the Prophet, and criticized the Scottish orientalist's use of unreliable sources, such as the historian of early Islam al-Waqidi (d. 822), whose reports were widely considered to be untrustworthy by scholars of Hadith.[119]

Sayyid Ahmad Khan resolved to write a life of the Prophet based only on sources that Muslim scholars considered 'trustworthy, genuine, and authoritative'.[120] While he was unable to fulfil this intention, he did write twelve essays that were published in 1870 in Urdu as *The Sermons of Ahmad* and in English translation as *A Series of Essays on the Life of Muhammad and Subjects Subsidiary Thereto*. The main research for this work was carried out in the libraries of London, where Sayyid Ahmad stayed for eighteen months between 1869 and 1870, renting a room in Bloomsbury in a house later occupied by the Christian socialist writer R. H. Tawney, attending Charles Dickens' last public reading and meeting the Scottish essayist and historian Thomas Carlyle, whose favourable depiction of the Prophet Muhammad in *On Heroes, Hero-Worship, and the Heroic in History* (1841) Ahmad Khan cites with approval in his *Essays*.[121]

Sayyid Ahmad's introduction to the *Essays* reveals his increasingly modernist understanding of Islam. Religion, he contends, is essentially a system of moral values, teaching 'that true principle to which all the ideas and actions of man should be conformable'. This 'true principle' is none other than 'Nature' – true religion being in perfect harmony with the laws of nature. The religion which most perfectly corresponds to the laws of nature, he asserts, is Islam. This, at least, is true of the 'real principles' of Islam, which Ahmad Khan distinguishes from 'those that are solely the productions of those persons whom we designate as learned men, divines, doctors and lawyers'. Reliance on the latter was the definition of *taqlid*, which was the cause of present Muslim weakness.[122] 'I state it unambiguously,' Ahmad Khan writes, '– if people do not break with *taqlid* and do not seek (especially) that light which is gained from Qur'an and Hadith and if they are going to prove unable to confront religion with present-day scholarship and science, then Islam will disappear from India.'[123] In exhorting his readers to move beyond blind emulation of their religious authorities, he claimed to be inspired by the same 'love of monotheism' that motivated Shah Muhammad Isma'il to write *The Strengthening of Faith*. Like Isma'il, he advocates the egalitarian view that the Qur'an is accessible to everyone: 'In the religion of Islam,' he states, 'the Glorious Qur'an is in reach of everyone and every person is free to search in it for the truth.'[124]

Abandoning *taqlid* meant applying a critical eye to the Hadith corpus. Even the reports collected in the *Two Authentic Collections* of al-Bukhari and Muslim should not be blindly accepted.[125] While pre-modern Hadith scholars had largely judged the authenticity of a report by analyzing its *isnad* or chain of transmitters, Ahmad Khan turned his attention to the content of the reports. Hadith reports, he argues, should be weighed against the Qur'an, well-attested historical facts and knowledge acquired through sense perception and reason to determine whether they are genuine.[126] For questioning the authenticity of much of the Hadith canon, Sayyid Ahmad Khan was attacked by the Ahl-i Hadith scholar Siddiq Hasan Khan, who declared that the modernist and his followers 'can scarcely be called Muslim'.[127]

In the conclusion to the fourth volume of his *Life of Mahomet*, William Muir had opined that three 'radical evils' flowed from Islam: namely, the perpetuation of polygamy, divorce and slavery, the suppression of freedom of religion, and the prevention of the spread of Christianity.[128] Ahmad Khan sought to refute these charges by critically reviewing both the Islamic and the Biblical traditions. Polygamy, he observes, is in keeping with the laws of nature and society and is not prohibited by the Jewish and Christian scriptures. 'Truly pious and religious persons do not indulge in it', however, realizing that the Qur'an in fact advises against polygamy and allows it only in special cases. Similarly, he argues that 'the indulgence of divorce by Islam ... is greatly conducive to its health, prosperity, and welfare', and cites John Milton's argument for the legality of divorce from a Christian perspective in the 'Treatise on Christian Doctrine'. As for slavery, in contrast to both the Old and New Testaments, which assume its legality, 'the Prophet did almost entirely abolish slavery', permitting the enslavement only of prisoners of war unable to pay a ransom. Nor, he argues, is it true that Islam has been imposed by the sword. While Moses had been permitted to use the sword 'to extirpate all idolaters and infidels', 'Islam inculcates and demands a hearty and sincere belief in all that it teaches; and that genuine faith which proceeds from a person's heart cannot be obtained by force or violence.'[129]

These arguments, which turned the charges commonly levelled against Islam against its critics' own Christian religion, were later developed by Sayyid Ahmad Khan's more radical associate, the Indian modernist author Chiragh 'Ali (d. 1895), in *A Critical Exposition of the Popular "Jihad"*, which was published in Calcutta in 1883 and dedicated to Ahmad Khan. Observing that many of the criticisms made of Islam applied to 'the untenable theories of the Mohammadan Common Law' – that is, to the juristic tradition of the ulema – rather than to the Qur'an itself, he argues that all of Muhammad's wars were defensive, that the Qur'an prohibits aggressive warfare and forced conversion, and that the true meaning of the term 'jihad' is 'striving' or 'toil'. Muhammad, he further argues, 'raised the moral standard of his countrymen, ameliorated the condition of women, curtailed and mitigated polygamy and slavery, and virtually abolished them as well as infanticide'.[130]

Another who went further than Ahmad Khan was the Muslim modernist Sayyid Amir 'Ali (d. 1928). Born into a Shi'i family in Bengal, Amir 'Ali was called to the bar at London's Inner Temple in 1873, and later served as a judge at the Calcutta High Court and as the first Indian on the Judicial Committee of the Privy Council of the United Kingdom. While a student in London, he began work on a life of the Prophet that was ultimately incorporated into a book titled *The Spirit of Islam* (first published in 1891 and reissued in an expanded form in 1922). Under the influence of Western scholars of religion such as Max Müller, an Oxford professor who sought to uncover the evolutionary development of religion, Amir 'Ali aimed to prove that Islam was not a barrier to, but the *culmination* of, the religious development of mankind. Drawing on Edward Gibbon's *History of the Decline and Fall of the Roman Empire* (1776–89), 'Ali contrasts the sectarianism, fanaticism, irrationalism, authoritarianism and immorality of the early Christian Church with the adaptability and rationality of the message of Muhammad, whose mind,' he writes, was 'in its intellectualism and progressive ideals, essentially modern'.[131] In a classic statement of Islamic modernism, 'Ali exclaims, 'The wonderful adaptability of Islamic precepts to all ages and nations; their entire concordance with the light of reason; the absence of all mysterious doctrines to cast a shade of sentimental ignorance round the primal truths implanted in the human breast – all prove that Islam represents the latest development of the religious faculties of our being.'[132]

That these modernist ideas were able to take hold owed something not just to Sayyid Ahmad Khan's writing, but also to his efforts to modernize the education of Indian Muslims. In addition to writing his riposte to Muir, Ahmad Khan used his time in England to investigate the British education system, visiting Cambridge to study the governance structure and curriculum of the university and its colleges.[133] On his return to India, in 1872 he led an educational commission that called for the establishment of Muslim schools where 'useful knowledge might be taught along with religion'. Madrasahs of the 'old system' – in which category the commission rather inaccurately placed the recently established seminary at Deoband – were 'altogether useless to the nation at large, and ... no good can be expected from them'.[134]

To remedy this situation, in 1875 Sayyid Ahmad Khan founded the Anglo–Muhammadan Oriental College at Aligarh, a quiet town roughly eighty miles south of Delhi. Partially funded by the British government, the college was modelled on a Cambridge college: 'Sayyid Ahmad,' writes the historian David Lelyveld, 'called for the building of boarding-house quadrangles, each a world unto itself with dining room, mosque, library and reading room, debating club, garden, and playground.' Like students at Oxford and Cambridge or the English public schools, students 'would all eat, play, and study together at fixed times'.[135] The curriculum, as he originally conceived it, would cover religion, literature, mathematics and the natural sciences, and would be taught in Urdu or English. Students would learn Latin and English as well as Arabic, Persian or Urdu.[136] The school was open to both Sunni and Shi'i Muslims, as well as to Hindus, and was a male-only affair: although, as Gail Minault has shown, the Aligarh movement initiated a 'lively debate' about the education of women and girls, Ahmad Khan believed that reforms to the education of Muslim men should precede the introduction of female education.[137] Students wore black gowns and a Turkish fez (then a symbol of modernity), and were taught by a combination of Indians (both Hindus and Muslims) and Englishmen. The Europeans included Theodore Beck, a Cambridge graduate and Quaker who served as the second principal of the college from 1883 to 1889. A former president of the Cambridge Union and member of the secret society known as the 'Cambridge Apostles', Beck was reportedly attracted to the college on account of its being the 'Muslim Eton' and having a well-known cricket team.[138] Also on the staff were the orientalist Thomas W. Arnold, whose 1896 book *The Preaching of Islam* detailed how Islam had been spread by missionary activity more than by force, and, from 1907 to 1914, the German–Jewish scholar of the Qur'an and early Arabic literature Josef Horovitz, who encouraged students to engage with the Arabic literary revival then taking place in Egypt and introduced the teaching of Hebrew at the college.[139]

Among the Muslim teachers at Aligarh, the outstanding figure was Shibli Nu'mani (d. 1914), who served as professor of Arabic and Persian at the college from 1883. With the encouragement of Sayyid Ahmad Khan, Shibli authored a widely read series of Urdu biographies on the 'heroes of Islam' – his subjects included the 'Abbasid caliph al-Ma'mun (a key figure in the establishment of the Greek-into-Arabic translation movement), the second caliph 'Umar, the jurist

Abu Hanifah, the Sufi and theologian al-Ghazali, the Persian mystical poet Jalal al-Din Rumi, and the freethinking poet and philosopher 'Umar Khayyam. He aimed to introduce his readers both to the Arabic sources on which his biographies were based and to modern developments in Western historiography, while also evoking the historical richness of Islamic history in the face of contemporary Western criticism.[140] Shibli's wide learning in Islamic history was commended by Thomas Arnold, who thanks his Aligarh colleague in the preface to *The Preaching of Islam* for having assisted him 'most generously out of the abundance of his knowledge of early Muhammadan history'.[141] In Shibli's view, it was religious knowledge, *'ilm*, that determined a person's standing as a Muslim. What mattered, he said, was not whether one was 'a *sayyid*, shaykh, or Arab', but whether one possessed knowledge, and all Muslims with knowledge were equal.[142]

This egalitarian statement was made at the first general meeting of Nadwat al-'Ulama' – 'The Council of Religious Scholars' – a reformist movement founded by a group of fourteen scholars who met at the graduation ceremony of the Fayz-i 'Amm Madrasah in Kanpur in 1892. The Fayz-i 'Amm had been established earlier in the century by Mufti Inayat Ahmad (d. 1865), who had studied with Shah Wali Allah's grandson Shah Muhammad Ishaq and been exiled to the Andaman Islands for his role in the Mutiny of 1857, and counted the Deobandi scholar Ashraf 'Ali Thanawi among its teachers. Of the fourteen scholars who launched the Nadwat al-'Ulama', several had studied under Shah Fazl-i Rahman Muradabadi (d. 1895/6), who had also been a student of Shah Muhammad Ishaq and had taught Hadith to Thanawi, and half of them were disciples of Hajji Imdad Allah, the spiritual guide of the founders of the seminary at Deoband.[143] Like the Deobandis, the Nadwat al-'Ulama' aimed to strengthen Islam in India by reforming the madrasah education given to aspiring religious scholars. In 1894 they founded an important madrasah at Lucknow, to which Shibli moved from Aligarh. Like Sayyid Ahmad Khan, however, they sanctioned the use of the English language in their teaching, and saw their madrasah as a kind of bridge between the Deobandi and modernist models. Their overall aim was to achieve unity among the ulema of different denominations and ideologies – Shi'i as well as Sunni, and Deobandi as well as Ahl-i Hadith scholars were initially involved – with the hope of re-establishing the role of the religious scholars in public life and countering Western influence.[144] In keeping with the views of Shibli, who had argued at the first meeting of the Mohammedan Educational Congress founded by Sayyid Ahmad Khan in 1886 that the Muslims of India should study Arabic and Persian as well as Western sciences and literature, the curriculum of the Nadwat al-'Ulama''s madrasah at Lucknow was founded on the study of Arabic and the Qur'an.[145] Like the seminary at Deoband, the school, whose graduates were styled 'Nadwi', would go on to produce some of the leading South Asian ulema of the twentieth century.

Alongside his activities as an educational reformer, after his return from England Sayyid Ahmad Khan continued to spread his modernist interpretation of Islam through his writings. From 1870 he published a journal, *The Refinement of Morals*, the title of which was taken from a famous ethical treatise from the medieval Arabic Aristotelian tradition by Ibn Miskawayh. The journal was aimed at the growing Muslim middle class of north India and was modelled on English magazines like the *Spectator* and *Tatler*. Ahmad Khan hoped that it would support *islah u-taraqqi*, the 'reform and progress' of Muslims in India, on the pattern of the 'refinement and civilization of Europe'.[146] Combining Shah Muhammad Isma'il's and the Deobandis' attack on innovations with a modernist yearning for development and progress, he wrote in the first issue of the journal, 'If we want to elevate our own ways of life and civilization to the highest level of refinement, so that those nations that are more refined than ours may not look upon us with scorn, we must critically examine all our customs and habits, cast off those that are bad, and reform those that are worthy of reform.'[147]

The most important intellectual contribution made by Sayyid Ahmad Khan in the latter half of his career was his attempt to work out what he called *'ilm al-kalam-i jadid*, a new Islamic theology.[148] To carry out this endeavour, he turned to the exegesis of the Qur'an, and tried to show that the divine revelation (God's word) was in perfect concordance with the laws of nature (what he called 'God's work') as expounded in the modern sciences – for, as the medieval Andalusian philosopher Ibn Rushd had put it when arguing for the harmony of the Qur'an and Aristotelian philosophy, 'truth cannot contradict truth'.[149] From John H. Pratt, Archdeacon of Calcutta, mathematician and astronomer, and (like Theodore Beck) Cambridge Apostle, Ahmad Khan adopted the idea that – as Pratt put it in an 1856 book on the harmony of scripture and science – 'it is impossible that Scripture can, when rightly interpreted, be at variance with the works of Divine Hand,' for the 'Book of Nature and the Word of God emanate from the same infallible Author, and therefore cannot be at variance'.[150] Under Pratt's influence, in 1874 Ahmad Khan wrote a long essay titled 'The Interpretation of the Heavens', in which he seeks to disentangle the cosmology of the Qur'an from the Ptolemaic model of the universe that had been accepted by medieval Muslim astronomers, and instead to reconcile the Qur'anic view of the cosmos with Copernican astronomy.[151] Between 1880 and his death in 1898, he published six volumes of a commentary on the Qur'an in which he advances naturalistic interpretations of supernatural phenomena such as miracles, Satan and the angels, and heaven and hell. Miracles

THE RENEWAL OF ISLAM

are a particular focus for creative reinterpretations – Ahmad Khan denies the Virgin Birth of Jesus and that Jonah had been swallowed by a fish, claims that the prophet Joseph was able to predict the years of famine and plenty in Egypt because of his knowledge of the Nile's flooding patterns, and asserts that Moses led the Children of Israel over a ford in the Red Sea.[152]

In the view of Sayyid Ahmad Khan's critics, this naturalistic exegesis of scripture was tantamount to apostasy. The Deobandi Muhammad Qasim Nanautvi declared that, having 'stretched the Word of God to correspond to his own vague reason', Ahmad Khan was an unbeliever.[153] In an 1887 fatwa, his Deobandi colleague Ashraf 'Ali Thanawi opined that the *naichariyyah* – the 'naturalist sect', as Sayyid Ahmad Khan and his followers were known to their opponents – 'refute all genuine scholars of Islam and adulterate the divine norms'. It was the task of the *mujaddid*, the renewer of the faith, Thanawi said, to refute such heresy.[154] Indeed, Thanawi blamed the Muslim modernists for having opened up a space in which even graver forms of religious deviancy could flourish.

Thanawi singled out the Ahmadiyyah – or what he derisively called the 'Qadiyan sect', in reference to the Punjabi town in which the movement's founder, Mirza Ghulam Ahmad (d. 1908), had been born – as one of the heretical movements that had branched off from the *naichariyyah*.[155] Ghulam Ahmad had burst onto the Indian religious scene in 1880 with the publication of the first two volumes of *The Proofs of Ahmad*, a book eventually published in four volumes by a Christian press at Amritsar. Like other modern Muslim reformers, his starting point in this book is the decrepit state of contemporary Islam and the need to demonstrate the truth of the religion – when it is understood authentically – in the face of non-Muslim attacks.[156] Lamenting the 'widespread corruption and chaos prevalent in this age', he explains that he has 'made the truth of Islam more evident than the shining sun' by bringing forward three hundred 'incontrovertible rational arguments' in its favour.[157]

Following the appearance of the first two volumes of *The Proofs of Ahmad*, Ghulam Ahmad made a name for himself in polemical debates with Christian missionaries and the Hindu revivalists of the Arya Samaj, earning notoriety for his insistence on the practice of *mubahalah*, a procedure by which the participants in a debate invoked a divine curse on the person whose views were incorrect.[158] Much more controversial were the claims that Mirza Ghulam Ahmad made about his own spiritual station. He had written *The Proofs of Ahmad*, he explained, in response to a vision of the Prophet that he had experienced in 1864/5, and many parts of the text were divinely inspired.[159] He claimed to be the *mujaddid*, in which capacity he deemed himself responsible for responding to the 'poisonous teaching' of the Christian missionaries and for revealing the secrets of the Qur'an.[160] He described himself as a *muhaddath*, a person who is 'spoken to' by the angels, a status that the Twelver Shi'ah ascribe to their Imams, and which in Sunni Islam is traditionally associated with the second caliph 'Umar. (Indeed, evoking 'Umar's title *al-faruq* – which originally seems to have denoted the caliph's status as eschatological redeemer – Ghulam Ahmad claimed to possess a *'faruqi* substance'.[161]) He was *al-insan al-kamil*, the 'perfect human', who, in the thought of Ibn 'Arabi and his interpreters, is a perfect manifestation of the divine names and attributes.[162] He was a 'likeness' and 'representative' of Jesus, the Mahdi and 'promised messiah' who would fulfil the eschatological functions traditionally allotted by the Sunni tradition to Jesus.[163]

In making these claims, Mirza Ghulam Ahmad came close to presenting himself as a prophet. He expanded, for instance, the notion of the renewal of the faith to connect it more closely to prophecy: the renewers, he says, are 'like the prophets' in that they are sent to reveal the divine secrets.[164] In claiming to be a *muhaddath*, likewise, he draws on the early mystic al-Hakim al-Tirmidhi's (d. 910) idea that the *muhaddath* receives *wahy* or prophetic revelation, and claims that the station of *muhaddath* 'potentially' includes all the elements of prophecy.[165] By the beginning of the twentieth century, he was openly claiming to be a prophet. 'As I have explained time and again,' he wrote in 1902, 'the words which I say are certainly the words of God, like those of the Qur'an and of the Old Testament. In a "shadowy" and "manifestational" manner I am a prophet of God. Every Muslim must obey me in religious matters.'[166] By 'shadowy' and 'manifestational' he meant that his prophecy was a continuation of – and entirely indebted to – that of Muhammad. Under the influence of Ibn 'Arabi's theory that, while 'legislative prophecy' – the kind of prophethood that involves the revelation of a scripture or law – had concluded with Muhammad, a non-legislative or 'general' kind of prophecy continues after Muhammad's death, Mirza Ghulam Ahmad interprets the Qur'an's description of Muhammad as the 'seal of prophets' to mean not that Muhammad was the *last* prophet, but that all prophets subsequent to him derive their prophetic perfections from him and are confirmed by him.[167]

This claim, like Ghulam Ahmad's claim to be a likeness of Jesus, was part of his larger attempt to demonstrate the superiority of Islam over Christianity and other faiths, for 'a religion that lacks prophecy,' he said, 'is lifeless'.[168] Also explicable in terms of the polemical context is his reinterpretation of jihad. The jihad enjoined by the Qur'an, he says, echoing the Muslim modernists, was a purely defensive form of warfare, and the command to engage in it is only valid when Islam is under mortal threat.[169] Today, when the Muslims of British India are free to practise their religion, he writes in a treatise titled *The British Government and Jihad*, 'religious wars involving armed combat, killing and bloodshed' should be avoided.[170] Islam is under intellectual, rather than physical, attack, and so the 'jihad of the sword' should be replaced with the 'jihad of the pen', that is, 'the sword of arguments and proofs'.[171]

The Ahmadiyyah began as a religious movement in March 1889, in the Punjabi city of Ludhiana, when Ghulam Ahmad held a ceremony of initiation into his new interpretation of Islam.[172] In 1914, the movement split into two factions, a Qadiyani branch led by Mirza Ghulam Ahmad's son Mahmud Ahmad (d. 1965), and a Lahori branch which downplayed Ghulam Ahmad's claim to prophecy. Both branches conducted 'the jihad of the pen' through engaging in extensive missionary activity, within and beyond the Muslim world. The Ahmadi mission has seen particular success in England, where, in 1924, Mahmud Ahmad, leader of the Qadiyani Ahmadiyyah, laid the foundation stone of the London Mosque, while the Lahori branch took over the running of the Shah Jahan Mosque in Woking, Surrey, which had been built in 1889 as the first purpose-built mosque in the United Kingdom.[173]

The relative success of the Ahmadiyyah in a traditionally Christian country like England is appropriate insofar as Mirza Ghulam Ahmad's ideas were, like those of the Muslim modernists, forged in reaction to Christian criticisms of Islam. Christianity, Mirza Ghulam Ahmad declared, is 'the most perfect manifestation of Satan', and Jesus had not died on the cross, as the Christians believe, or been taken up to heaven alive, as the Sunnis think, but had gone to live in India, where he died in the Kashmiri city of Srinagar at the age of 120. 'In the death of the son of Mary,' he said, 'there is life for Islam.'[174]

Yet the most vociferous opponents of the Ahmadiyyah were not Christian missionaries, but other Muslims, for Mirza Ghulam Ahmad's claim to be a prophet – like the Bab's claim to have been given a new religious law – appeared to undermine one of the most fundamental tenets of Islam, the finality of Muhammad's prophecy. The Deobandi Ashraf ʿAli Thanawi, for instance, wrote a treatise titled *The Leader of Qadiyan* in which he declared Ghulam Ahmad an unbeliever, and identified the Ahmadiyyah as 'the first prey' of Sayyid Ahmad Khan's naturalist heresy.[175] Even more hostile to the Ahmadiyyah has been a movement known for its similarly fierce opposition to Deobandi Islam and the other reformist currents of nineteenth-century India. They call themselves Ahl-i Sunnat wa-Jamaʿat – after the Arabic name for the followers of Sunni Islam – but are known to outsiders as Barelwis, after their leading figure, and the scholar they recognize as the *mujaddid* of his time, Ahmad Riza Khan Barelwi (d. 1921).

Ahmad Riza Khan was born in Bareilly, also the native town of Sayyid Ahmad Barelwi, yet he stood opposed to almost everything represented by Sayyid Ahmad and the Tariqah-yi Muhammadiyyah. He inherited this attitude from his father, who had written treatises attacking Wahhabism and Shah Muhammad Ismaʿil's *The Strengthening of Faith* and defending controversial practices like the celebration of the Prophet's birthday and standing to honour the prophetic presence.[176] Ahmad Riza Khan did not attend a madrasah, but, having reputedly read the entire Qur'an by the age of four and first preached in the mosque at the age of six, by his early teens he was issuing fatwas.[177] Throughout his career, fatwas were the principal means he used to spread his ideas, and the collection of his opinions comes to twelve volumes that collectively add up to roughly a thousand pages.[178]

At the centre of Ahmad Riza Khan's thought is an insistence on the necessity of intermediaries between man and God, an idea which had come under sustained assault from reformist movements ranging from the Wahhabis and the Zaydi traditionalists through to the Deobandis, the Ahl-i Hadith, the modernists at Aligarh and the Nadwat al-'ulama'. Against the egalitarian instincts of these movements, Ahmad Riza Khan insisted that no one could know God without the mediation of the Prophet, for only the Prophet was perfect, and to claim that his mediation was not needed was to arrogantly assume that you could attain salvation through your own effort.[179] 'The true servant of God,' he writes in a fatwa directed against the Deobandis, 'is he who is a servant of Mustafa [one of the names of the Prophet]; if not, he will be the servant of Satan'.[180] Drawing on classical Sufi ideas, Ahmad Riza Khan asserted that Muhammad was God's beloved, to whom He had granted knowledge of the unseen, and for whom He had created the world; without the existence of the Prophet – who, like the other prophets and saints, was still alive in his grave – the world would cease to exist. Muhammad was pure light, and so cast no shadow.[181] At the *mawlid*, the celebration of his birthday, he was spiritually present and would watch over the ceremony. The Barelwis accordingly practised *qiyam*, the act of standing up to greet the Prophet at the *mawlid*, and adopted the phrase, *ya rasul Allah*, 'O Messenger of God', as 'a sort of emblem of identification' (in the apt phrase of Usha Sanyal, a leading scholar of their thought).[182] In response, their Deobandi opponents accused the Barelwis of deifying the Prophet. 'They turn the Prophet into a God but a defective one,' wrote 'Ashraf 'Ali Thanawi. 'We understand him to be a servant [of God] but a perfect one.'[183]

For Ahmad Riza Khan, the mediation of the Prophet itself presupposed the mediation of Sufi guides – that is, the shaykh, by which he meant the founder of the Sufi order, and the *pir* or living Sufi master. Though he was initiated – as was common practice – into all the major Sufi orders of India, Ahmad Riza Khan was particularly committed to the Qadiri order and its founder, the twelfth-century mystic 'Abd al-Qadir al-Jilani. 'Except for divinity and prophethood / You encompass all perfections, O Helper,' he declared to al-Jilani in one of his poems.[184] In his view, Sufi guides were an indispensable means to reach the Prophet, who in turn was an indispensable means to reach God, meaning that 'without a *pir* one cannot reach God'.[185]

While rooted in classical Sufism, these ideas were developed and expressed in a deeply reactionary way. Many of Ahmad Riza Khan's fatwas were explicit denunciations of the rival ideological orientations of nineteenth-century India, against all of which he directed his ire. In a series of fatwas written in 1896, which received approval from the leading ulema of the Hijaz in 1900, he wrote against the modernists, the Shi'ah, the Ahl-i Hadith, the Deobandis and the Nadwat al-'ulama'. On account of their critical attitude towards the Qur'an and Hadith, he asserts, Sayyid Ahmad Khan and the *naichariyyah* 'have no relation to Islam'; they are unbelievers and apostates, and anyone who considers them a Muslim is likewise an unbeliever.[186] Against the Ahl-i Hadith, he argues for the necessity of following a school of law: 'the salvation-attaining group,' he says, 'is today divided into four madhhabs: the Hanafi, Shafi'i, Maliki, and Hanbali. Whoever is outside these four is an innovator and destined for hell.'[187] He condemns the Nadwat al-'ulama', meanwhile, against which he wrote some two hundred fatwas in all, for refusing to declare the Ahmadiyyah unbelievers. From 1900, the Barelwis held an annual gathering at Patna whose 'sole purpose,' Sanyal explains, 'was opposition to the Nadwa'.[188] It was at the first such gathering that they declared Ahmad Riza Khan the *mujaddid*, in succession to Shah 'Abd al-'Aziz, the eldest son of Shah Wali Allah.[189]

Part of the renewer's task was to expose unbelief within the *ummah*. In a 1902/3 fatwa, Ahmad Riza Khan explained that Mirza Ghulam Ahmad, the founder of the Ahmadiyyah, was an unbeliever on ten counts (the most egregious of which was his claim to prophecy), and declared that the wife of an Ahmadi convert was released from her marriage on the grounds that her husband had become an unbeliever (to whom, in Islamic law, a Muslim woman cannot be married).[190] Later, in 1906, he attempted to establish a consensus on the apostasy and unbelief of both the Ahmadiyyah and the leading Deobandis in a work that he presented to the leading ulema of Mecca and Medina titled *The Sword of the Two Sanctuaries upon the Throat of Unbelief and Falsehood*. Describing Mirza Ghulam Ahmad as 'the anti-Christ inspired by Satan' (thereby inverting Ghulam Ahmad's claim to be a likeness of Jesus) and the Deobandis Rashid Ahmad Gangohi, Muhammad Qasim Nanautwi and Ashraf 'Ali Thanawi as 'Wahhabis' and 'leaders of heresy', he attacks the Deobandis for reputedly questioning the superiority and finality of Muhammad's prophethood, for claiming that God can lie, and – most of all – for denying that the Prophet knows the unseen.[191]

In this way, Ahmad Riza Khan carried into the twentieth century the debate about the Prophet's role in the relationship between God and His creation that had been inaugurated in the early nineteenth century by Shah Muhammad Isma'il. In condemning the positions of the reformers as unbelief and arguing for the renewal of an Islam that was centred on the mediation of the Prophet, Ahmad Riza Khan and the Barelwis preached an Islamic revivalism which, though rooted in classical Sufi ideas and practices, was decidedly modern. In the religious marketplace of colonial India, they called on individual Muslims to consciously choose to practise a Prophet-centred Islam.[192] In so doing, they, like the other reformers we have met in this chapter, claimed the reformist legacy of Shah Wali Allah and his family for themselves. While that legacy had, by the late nineteenth century, splintered into irreconcilable and opposing factions, those factions were united by the agency that they gave to individual

Muslims, who were now much freer to choose the form of Islam that appealed to them, and by their concern for recovering 'true Islam' in a context where Muslims, having failed to properly understand and implement their religion, were being left behind by the West.

7

Engaging with Modernity II: Islamic Renewal in the Modern Middle East

Over a murderous eight-day period in July 1860 – two years after the Indian Mutiny had rocked the Muslims of South Asia – Damascus experienced what the historian Eugene Rogan has called a 'genocidal moment'. In the wake of the massacre of some ten thousand Maronite Christians in Mount Lebanon at the hands of Druze forces earlier in the summer, a Muslim mob slaughtered an estimated 5,000 Christians in Damascus. Many Christian men who were not killed were forced to convert to Islam, while many young women were abducted and raped, in a massacre that came to be euphemistically known as 'the Damascus Events'.[1]

The causes of the Events, like the causes of the Indian Mutiny, were complex. At their root was the widespread (and not incorrect) perception among the Muslims of Syria that what they regarded as the natural state of affairs – that, in accordance with the Pact of 'Umar, Christians and Jews should live under Muslim rule as protected but second-class subjects – was being overturned. In the 1830s – the same decade that India was opened up to Protestant missionary activity – Western powers began to open consulates in Damascus, facilitating the introduction of European manufactured goods into the previously closed Syrian market. The Western consulates and trading houses employed local Christians and Jews, who enjoyed special legal privileges in keeping with the Capitulations, a set of treaties going back to the sixteenth century that exempted Europeans and those under the protection of European consulates from Ottoman criminal law. Most humiliating of all was the Ottoman reform decree of 1856 – part of a series of nineteenth-century Ottoman reforms known as the Tanzimat – which, in violation of the *dhimmi* regulations of Islamic law, gave full legal equality to the Ottomans' non-Muslim subjects.[2] In 'conferring equality and freedom [on non-Muslims] and other [provisions] that clash with the pure Shariʿah,' wrote Muhammad Saʿid al-Ustuwani (d. 1888), the preacher at Damascus' famous Umayyad Mosque, the decree 'was ashes upon all Muslims'.[3]

Some of the ulema of Damascus, it seems, justified the bloodshed on the grounds that, in claiming the equality afforded to them by the Tanzimat, the Christians of Damascus had flouted the *dhimmi* restrictions. Others, however, came out strongly against the wanton taking of human life. A sermon written by the religious scholar Mahmud Efendi Hamza (d. 1887), which the Ottoman Foreign Minister Fuad Pasha ordered to be read out throughout the mosques of Damascus following the massacre, declared that, by shedding Muslim and *dhimmi* blood, raping Christian women, stealing their property and destroying their homes, the mob had 'pull[ed] down one foundation of religion'.[4] Most important was the role played by the exiled Algerian resistance leader and mystic ʿAbd al-Qadir al-Jazaʾiri (d. 1883), whose heroism in protecting Christian lives during the Events prevented the slaughter from turning into an outright genocide. With just over a thousand North

African troops at his disposal, 'Abd al-Qadir offered shelter to the beleaguered Christians of Damascus. By the third day of the massacre, no fewer than 4,000 Christians were under his protection.[5] When the mob came to his home, baying for Christian blood, he quoted Qur'an 5:32 ('Whoever kills another soul – unless [in retaliation] for murder or for spreading corruption on earth – it is as if he killed the whole of mankind'), as well as the Qur'an's injunction that there should be 'no compulsion in religion' (Q. 2:256).[6] Just as murder could be justified in the name of religion, so too could the saving of innocent life; indeed, 'Abd al-Qadir would later write that, in protecting the Christians of Damascus, he had been motivated by 'nothing other than obedience to our sacred law and the principles of humanity'.[7]

Even before he distinguished himself in the Damascus Events, 'Abd al-Qadir al-Jaza'iri was already, as Rogan puts it, 'the world's most famous Arab', renowned in both the Muslim world and the West for leading the resistance to the French occupation of Algeria between 1832 and 1847.[8] He was also a religious scholar of the Maliki school of jurisprudence and a Sufi in the intellectual tradition of Ibn 'Arabi, whose life and thought provide a window into a number of key issues in Islamic thought in the late nineteenth and early twentieth centuries, including the response to European colonialism and scientific developments in the West, the relationship between reason and revelation, the role of religion in politics, the status of women in Islam, Islam's relationship with other faiths, the meaning and relevance of jihad and the place of Sufism in the modern world.

Born near Mascara, in north-western Algeria, in about 1807, like many of the other thinkers we have encountered in this book 'Abd al-Qadir was a descendant of the Prophet, tracing his lineage to Muhammad through the Prophet's grandson Hasan. Like other renewers, as well, he and his family were immersed in Sufism. His grandfather had been initiated in Cairo into Ibn 'Arabi's chain of spiritual transmission by the famous Indian scholar Murtada al-Zabidi, a former student of Shah Wali Allah.[9] 'Abd al-Qadir's father, who like Ibn 'Arabi was called Muhyi al-Din – 'the reviver of the religion' – succeeded his own father as shaykh of a local branch of the Qadiri Sufi order. 'Abd al-Qadir received his early education, which included the memorization of the canonical Hadith collection of al-Bukhari, at his father's Sufi lodge. In 1826, father and son set off together on the Hajj. In Mecca they visited their fellow Algerian, the Sufi traditionalist Muhammad ibn 'Ali al-Sanusi, who is said to have served them couscous and predicted that 'Abd al-Qadir would 'make the sacred lands of Islam expand and raise the banner of jihad'.[10] In Medina, 'Abd al-Qadir, still only nineteen or twenty, felt that he experienced visions in which he had been vouchsafed the 'Muhammadan inheritance'.[11] Returning with the Damascus caravan, they met the Naqshbandi Sufi Shaykh Khalid (d. 1827). Of Kurdish origin, Khalid was a renowned miracle worker – he claimed to be able to foretell the future, protect the living from harm and converse with the dead – who founded an important branch of the Naqshbandiyyah-Mujaddiyyah order known as the Khalidiyyah. Having settled in Damascus, he was widely recognized there as the renewer of the century and, seeking the reform of Islam in an age of decline, preached 'perfect following of the Prophet' alongside 'perfect love of the shaykh'.[12] 'Abd al-Qadir was initiated into the Naqshbandi order at the hands of one of Khalid's leading disciples before he returned to Algeria.

In 1830, France occupied Algiers. 'The end of time has come,' wrote the Algerian notable Ahmad Sharif Zahhar (d. 1872), who witnessed the fall of the Regency of Algiers, a semi-autonomous state within the Ottoman Empire.[13] When the French forces then took the city of Oran in the north-west, the notables of the region looked for support to Mawlay 'Abd al-Rahman, the 'Alawi sultan of Morocco, who sent a deputy to assert his sovereignty over the region. When that deputy was forced to withdraw under pressure from the French and mutiny within the 'Alawi army, he left in his place 'Abd al-Qadir's father Muhyi al-Din, who commanded allegiance as leader of the Qadiri order in the area. In November 1832, shortly before his death, Muhyi al-Din passed the mantle of leadership onto his son, supposedly following a dream in which 'Abd al-Qadir al-Jilani, the founding father of the Qadiri order (who had also, as we've seen, appeared to 'Uthman dan Fodio), had said to him, 'Your son, or you, must be sultan of the Arabs. If you accept power for yourself, your son will die; if you accept it for him, you will die soon.'[14] The tribal leaders subsequently made an oath of allegiance, or *bay'ah*, to 'Abd al-Qadir that was modelled on the pledge that the Prophet had received from his Companions – 'Those who pledge allegiance to you,' the Qur'an says, addressing Muhammad, 'pledge allegiance to God' (Q. 48:10). The young Sufi – again like 'Uthman dan Fodio before him – took the caliphal title *amir al-mu'minin*, 'the Commander of the Believers', and a council of ulema that he convened declared him 'our *amir* and guarantor of the upholding of the bounds of God's law'.[15] Invoking the example of the Prophet and the 'rightly guided' caliphs, he sought to impose the public performance of the five mandatory prayers in the territory under his control and to eradicate un-Islamic vices such as gambling, drinking and smoking.[16]

In keeping with this Shari'ah-minded vision, 'Abd al-Qadir regarded his resistance to the French as a jihad and condemned those Muslims who opposed the anti-colonial struggle as renegades from Islam. In a treatise titled *The Sword of Religion for Cutting the False Claims of the Apostates*, which he wrote in 1842–3, 'Abd al-Qadir attempted to show that it was a religious duty for all able-bodied Muslims whose lands had fallen to non-Muslim conquerors to make *hijrah* – that is, to emigrate – to Muslim-ruled territory. In making this argument, which again echoed the position of 'Uthman dan Fodio, 'Abd al-Qadir drew on earlier Maliki authorities, including dan Fodio's hero, the fifteenth-century North African scholar al-Maghili. If a person is able to emigrate, 'yet remains under the rule of the believers,' 'Abd al-Qadir writes, 'it shall not be said of him that he is a Muslim'. Indeed, such a person was one of the *munafiqun*, the 'hypocrites' condemned by the Qur'an for saying 'We believe' with their tongues while not having faith in their hearts. In apostatizing from Islam, 'Abd al-Qadir asserts, those who submit to French rule render themselves liable to be fought.[17]

In making this argument, 'Abd al-Qadir specifically had in mind the Tijani Sufis of 'Ayn Madi, the oasis town in which the founder of their order had been born. 'Abd al-Qadir had led an unsuccessful siege against the town in 1838 after the head of the Tijani order obtained a fatwa from the Tunisian city of Qayrawan allowing them to remain under French rule so long as they were allowed to practise Islam. Nevertheless, 'Abd al-Qadir's commitment to the principles of *hijrah* and jihad was not just born from the needs of the moment. Later in his career, after he had settled in Damascus, he would continue to insist that jihad was obligatory until 'the enemies of Islam' submitted to Muslim rule and agreed to pay the *jizyah* poll tax. 'The religion is jihad', he declares at one point in his writings, and God has a 'special affection' for those who wage it.[18]

At the same time, both during and after his jihad against the French, 'Abd al-Qadir maintained cordial relations with French military leaders, sometimes discussing religious questions with them. In 1840, Eugène Daumas, a French general stationed in Algeria who had learned Arabic and would later collaborate with 'Abd al-Qadir on a book on Arabian horses, posed a series of twenty written questions on the status of women in Islam – a topic which, as we saw in the debate between William Muir and Sayyid Ahmad Khan, was a major point of contention in the Muslim–European encounter in this period, as it would be in later times. 'Abd al-Qadir wrote a detailed response to each of these questions, attempting both to refute what he saw as Western misconceptions and to highlight the wisdom of the Islamic approach to managing relations between the sexes.

Daumas' questions focused on Islamic laws and customs relating to marriage. He began by asking how it was possible for a Muslim man to marry a woman without having previously seen her, a practice which would surely lead to unhappy marriages. 'Abd al-Qadir replied that Islamic law *did* allow a man to look at the face, hands and feet of his intended bride – and for the woman to look at her prospective husband – and that this was in fact the practice of all Muslims. When the French general went on to ask whether the common practice of Muslim men marrying four wives and taking concubines caused problems in the family, 'Abd al-Qadir responded that God had not made it a duty for men to take four wives. Those men who were able to avoid fornication while marrying only one woman were better than those who required multiple wives. He also observed, as Sayyid Ahmad Khan would likewise do in his response to Muir, that the Old Testament patriarchs had practised polygamy and taken concubines. In the next question, Daumas noted that Muslim Arabs were often criticized in the West for beating their wives. Adopting and developing the classic interpretation of Qur'an 4:34 – which permits men to hit their disobedient wives after they have tried other forms of punishment – 'Abd al-Qadir asserted that, while the law of Islam permits a light hit that leaves no mark on the skin and draws no blood, it prohibits the beating of women, for the Prophet had said, 'Only evil men beat women.'

Though he sought, like many Muslim modernists, to deny that Islam was hostile to women, 'Abd al-Qadir was no feminist. In his reply to Daumas' question about polygamy, he declared that women had been created for procreation and, evoking the mental and physical benefits of sex, boasted that he rarely went twenty-four hours (and only then when he was travelling or had some other reason) without sleeping with one of his wives. His views on gender relations, as on all questions, were rooted in Islamic jurisprudence and Sufism. In his seventh question, for instance, Daumas contrasted the Christians' custom of admiring women for their 'praiseworthy qualities and beautiful deeds' with the Muslims' supposed focus on a woman's beauty and lineage. 'Abd al-Qadir confirmed that Muslim men do love a beautiful woman, but only if her beauty is accompanied by piety; indeed, he went on, physical beauty usually goes hand in hand with moral excellence, because (and here he resorted to Sufi language) 'the outward', or *zahir*, 'is a sign of the inward', the *batin*. Similarly, responding to Daumas' allegation that the veiling of Muslim women was an indicator of their husbands' 'excessive jealousy', 'Abd al-Qadir asserted that Muslims' jealousy was moderate and beneficial. The veiling and seclusion of women, he explained, was a means for preserving lineages from corruption – the 'preservation of lineages' being of the five essential *maqasid* or 'aims' of the Shari'ah.[19]

This insistence on the essential moderation and rationality of Islam was also in evidence in another work that 'Abd al-Qadir addressed to a Western readership. Having finally surrendered to the French in 1847, 'Abd al-Qadir was taken – contrary to the terms of his surrender agreement – to France. There he and his entourage of about a hundred family members and followers were kept under house arrest at Château d'Amboise, the royal château in the Loire valley where Leonardo da Vinci is buried, while a public campaign for his release was conducted by, among others, the amateur artist and dandy the comte d'Orsay, Alexandre Dumas, Victor Hugo, William Makepeace Thackeray and the Duke of Wellington.[20] 'Abd al-Qadir devoted his time to teaching, taking his followers through a creedal work written by the fifteenth-century Ash'ari theologian Muhammad ibn Yusuf al-Sanusi (whom we met in chapter one as a major influence on Islamic thought in the seventeenth century and afterwards) and a major tenth-century epistle on Maliki law.[21] When, in late 1852, Napoleon III, the last Emperor of France, finally agreed to his release, 'Abd al-Qadir travelled to Paris, where he sought admittance into the Société Asiatique, the first orientalist scientific society founded in Europe. After leaving France for the Ottoman city of Bursa in north-western Anatolia, he composed an essay on the relationship between reason and revelation in Islam that was sent to the society and translated into French by one of its members.

Titled *A Reminder to the Intelligent and a Warning to the Ignorant*, the essay argues for the superiority of *nazar* and *dalil* – rational contemplation and proof – over *taqlid* or unthinking emulation of authority, while at the same time asserting the limits of reason and the need for divine revelation. The perfection of man, 'Abd al-Qadir asserts, adopting an idea that had made its way into later Ash'ari theology from the Arabic Aristotelian tradition, consists in the acquisition of knowledge – and specifically in the knowledge of God. The *'aql*, or intellect, is the noblest part of man, because it is through the intellect that man acquires such knowledge. *Taqlid*, by contrast, does not lead to genuine knowledge – a position consistent with the view of the rationalist theologian Muhammad ibn Yusuf al-Sanusi, whose work 'Abd al-Qadir had taught at Amboise, that those who rely on the opinions of others in theological matters are sinners or unbelievers. The intelligent person, 'Abd al-Qadir says, citing the great theologian and Sufi al-Ghazali, should consider *what* is said, not who says it. Such a person judges men according to the truth, not the truth according to men. That said, according to 'Abd al-Qadir there are some forms of knowledge that are beyond the powers of the intellect to acquire on its own. In these matters, people must first assent to the truths brought by the prophets and then interpret those truths using their reason. All the prophets, he further asserts, brought the same fundamental truths: that God is one and without cause; that He is the creator of the world and all that is in it; that life, reason, progeny and wealth should be preserved (as in the theory of the *maqasid* of the law). This being the case, Judaism, Christianity and Islam, in 'Abd al-Qadir's view, are sister religions that are in fundamental agreement. The abrogation of an earlier prophet's message by a later prophet does not mean that the earlier message is annulled, but rather that it is perfected or – as Jesus said about the Mosaic law – fulfilled. This perfecting of the divine message culminated in Islam: while the Torah contains laws pertaining to the physical world and the Gospel is oriented towards the spiritual realm, the revelation vouchsafed to Muhammad, 'Abd al-Qadir asserts, unites the two.[22]

By drawing on the rationalist tradition within pre-modern Islamic theology while also emphasizing Islam's close relationship to Judaism and Christianity, 'Abd al-Qadir aimed to prove to his learned French contemporaries that Islam was suitable to the modern world of science, religious tolerance and reason. Indeed, he celebrates in the essay the 'wondrous crafts and marvellous benefits' derived by French scientists who have embraced the use of practical reason. 'Abd al-Qadir was able to witness these technical innovations up close when, on a return visit to Paris, he visited the 1855 international exhibition at the newly built Palais de l'Industrie.[23]

This stress on the pre-modern Islamic rationalist tradition and openness to Western scientific progress are also evident in the work of one of 'Abd al-Qadir's Egyptian contemporaries, the religious scholar, translator and educational reformer Rifa'ah Rafi' al-Tahtawi (d. 1873), who had a similarly first-hand experience of modern France. Born in Upper Egypt into a family of religious scholars in 1803, al-Tahtawi was educated at Cairo's al-Azhar, the leading seminary in the Sunni world. His teachers included Hasan al-'Attar (d. 1835), who in the last four years of his life would hold the post of Shaykh al-Azhar or head of the seminary. Al-'Attar had been on intimate terms with the French scholars who accompanied Napoleon's occupation of Egypt in 1798, 'learning from them the arts practised in their country and teaching them Arabic', as his son later recalled.[24] He was also known for his teaching and writing on theology, philosophy and logic, adopting some of the arguments and views of the Maturidi school of theology dominant among Turkish, Central Asian and South Asian Muslims, and introducing into Egypt the study of several Indo-Islamic texts on logic that he had encountered through his contacts with Ottoman scholars.[25]

In 1826, al-Tahtawi was chosen to serve as the religious guide to a group of forty-four Egyptian students that the modernizing ruler of Egypt Muhammad 'Ali was sending to France. During his five-year stay in Paris, al-Tahtawi developed a lasting admiration for European philosophy, literature, science, education and industry, reading Enlightenment philosophers like Voltaire, Rousseau and Montesquieu, conversing with French orientalists, and studying French mores and the country's political and legal institutions in the heady days of the 1830 Revolution. In 1834, with the encouragement of his former teacher al-'Attar, he published an account of his experiences in France, *The Extraction of Gold in the Distillation of Paris*, the aim of which, he wrote, was 'to urge

Islamic countries to examine the foreign sciences, the arts and crafts'.[26] The following year, he became the founding director of Egypt's first School of Languages, in which capacity he supervised the translation of over 2,000 European scientific, philosophical, historical and literary works into Arabic.[27] At the same time, in his own writings al-Tahtawi drew extensively on the classical Islamic philosophical tradition, marshalling extracts from medieval texts such as Ibn Miskawayh's *The Refinement of Morals* (the text from which the Indian modernist Sayyid Ahmad Khan took the title of his Urdu journal) to make the point that acquiring modern scientific knowledge and technical expertise was a religious duty.[28]

This marrying of the Islamic tradition to modern knowledge was institutionalized through the School of Languages, where students studied Arabic and Islamic jurisprudence as well as modern European languages and geography, history and mathematics.[29] In his own writing on Islamic law, al-Tahtawi argued that *taqlid* was responsible for the stagnation of the Arab-Muslim world, and challenged what he took to be the widespread view that the gate of *ijtihad* had been closed, showing in an essay on *ijtihad* and *taqlid* that there had never been a consensus on this matter and that no age had been entirely devoid of *mujtahids* of some kind.[30] Though he belonged to the Shafi'i school, the dominant *madhhab* in Egypt, al-Tahtawi was happy to borrow rulings from the Hanafi school, the official *madhhab* of the Ottoman Empire, when he felt that their position on a certain issue – for instance, taxation – fitted better with the needs of the age.[31] Through *ijtihad*, he came to the conclusion that polygamy was only permitted if a husband could treat each of his wives equally – a Qur'anic principle that later Muslim modernists took to mean that polygamy was prohibited in practice if not in principle – and that the Christians and Jews of Egypt should enjoy total freedom of religion.[32] Together with the Egyptian educational reformer 'Ali Mubarak (d. 1893), he also advocated the education of girls, observing in his travelogue that in the strongest nations girls were given the same education as their male counterparts.[33] In 1871, two years before the Egyptian government established the first state primary school for girls, he published, at the behest of the Ministry of Education, a book arguing that the education of girls would foster marital harmony, save women from a life of gossip and prepare them to 'to take up occupations that men take up, to the limit of their strength and ability'.[34]

From Ibn Miskawayh, al-Tahtawi adopted the Aristotelian view of ethical virtue as the mean between two extremes. Ibn Miskawayh, for instance, had contrasted the person who acquires wealth through just means with those who disdain their good fortune, on the one hand, and those who care not how their wealth comes about, on the other.[35] Al-Tahtawi took this position as the basis for his own argument for the goodness of wealth and his critique of Sufis who go to an extreme in their renunciation of the world.[36]

'Abd al-Qadir al-Jaza'iri, who boasted of his sexual exploits, and received large pensions from both the French and Ottoman governments after settling in Syria, was likewise no advocate of renunciation. Unlike al-Tahtawi, however, his thought was saturated with Sufi ideas. Similar to al-Nabulusi, Shah Wali Allah and Ibn Idris, 'Abd al-Qadir was a devotee of the Sufi metaphysics of Ibn 'Arabi. During his years in Bursa, he worked on the first modern edition of Ibn 'Arabi's encyclopaedic work *The Meccan Revelations*.[37] When he arrived in Damascus, he headed straight for Ibn 'Arabi's tomb in the Salihiyyah district, where al-Nabulusi had spent the final decades of his life.[38] Having settled in the Syrian capital he gave a daily series of lectures on the Qur'an and Hadith, which he interpreted from his particular Sufi perspective. These lectures were collected after 'Abd al-Qadir's death into what is widely recognized as his major work, *The Book of Spiritual Stations*, a work that recalls the Prophet-centred piety, the emphasis on dreams and visions and the Ibn 'Arabi-inspired metaphysics of the Muhammadan Path tradition. There is, 'Abd al-Qadir declares, only one existence, that of God, 'the True One Existence', of whom created things are limited reflections.[39] The spirits of created things derive from the spirit of Muhammad, who is the *barzakh* or 'isthmus' connecting God and creation and the perfect model for the Sufi.[40] 'Abd al-Qadir claims to have realized these truths through 'intimate conversation' with the divine, for God, he says, 'cast' the meaning of the Qur'an into his heart. Such mystical experiences, he claims, are signs of the 'Muhammadan inheritance', which is acquired by those Sufis who have conformed themselves to the prophetic model.[41] According to 'Abd al-Qadir, Ibn 'Arabi, whose claim to be 'the Seal of Muhammadan sainthood' the Algerian Sufi recognized, was the greatest of these heirs of the Prophet. 'He is our treasure, from which we draw what we write, whether it be from his spiritual form or from what he has himself written in his works,' 'Abd al-Qadir says of the Andalusian shaykh, next to whom he was to be buried in Salihiyyah (though his remains were returned to Algeria following Algerian independence).[42]

At the same time as 'Abd al-Qadir was giving the lectures that would make up *The Book of Spiritual Stations*, Muhammad 'Abduh, an Egyptian religious scholar who was to become the leading proponent of Islamic modernism in the late nineteenth and early twentieth centuries, was working on a treatise that was similarly indebted to the Sufi metaphysics of Ibn 'Arabi and his interpreters. Born into a family of Egyptian peasants in 1849, as a teenager 'Abduh was sent to the school attached to the Ahmadi Mosque in Tanta, an institution named after the famous Sufi saint Ahmad al-Badawi, whose *mawlid* attracted hundreds of thousands of pilgrims from across Egypt every year. In the account of his life that he later told to his chief disciple, Muhammad Rashid Rida (d. 1935), 'Abduh recalled how he had learnt next to nothing at the school on account of the deficient teaching methods employed there. 'The teachers,' he remembered, 'confronted us with grammatical and legal technical terms which we did not understand', without explaining their meaning.[43] Resigned to the futility of education, 'Abduh ran away from school. His life was transformed, however, by an encounter with his great uncle, Shaykh Darwish Khadir, a Sufi who may have been influenced by the reformist Sufism of the Muhammadan Path tradition. In an account that echoes *The Deliverer from Error*, the autobiography of al-Ghazali in which the great theologian recalled how his doubts about reason and sense perception were cured by a mystical light that God had cast into his heart, 'Abduh explained how, by teaching him the meaning of certain Sufi books, Shaykh Darwish 'came to free me from the prison of ignorance and opened before me the gates of knowledge'.[44]

In 1866, now aged seventeen, 'Abduh headed to Cairo to study at al-Azhar, only to find himself bitterly disappointed once again by what he described as 'the restricted mentality' of his teachers, who, he recalled, 'only repeat mechanically what has been transmitted to them', without explaining the deeper meaning or relevance of the texts they were teaching.[45] Once again, however, 'Abduh was lifted out of his despair by an encounter with an inspirational teacher. Eager to study philosophy and Sufism, but conscious that the scholars of al-Azhar looked dimly upon such pursuits, 'Abduh's doubts were dispelled by the arrival of the man whom he called 'the sun of realities' and 'the perfect sage' – 'our teacher, Jamal al-Din al-Afghani'.[46]

Claiming to be from Afghanistan so as to conceal his Shi'i background, al-Afghani was in fact born at Asadabad, near

Hamadan, in western Iran. As a young man he was exposed to the major intellectual and religious currents of nineteenth-century Iran and the Shi'i shrine cities of Iraq, including philosophy in the tradition of Mulla Sadra and Shaykhism and its Babi offshoot. At Qazvin, in north-central Iran, he is reported to have studied philosophy with a student of Mulla 'Ali Nuri, one of the great representatives of Sadrian philosophy in this period.[47] In Baghdad, he copied a treatise by Ahmad al-Ahsa'i, the founder of the Shaykhi school, and would later serve as the major source for the entry on Babism in the pioneering Arabic encyclopaedia compiled by the Syrian Christian intellectual Butrus al-Bustani (d. 1883).[48]

Turning up at various points in a chequered career in India, Afghanistan, Istanbul, Egypt, Paris, London, Russia and Iran, al-Afghani was a charismatic if deeply controversial figure who devoted his career to the unification of the Muslim world and the renewal of Islam with the aim of overcoming European – and specifically British – imperialism. The English anti-imperialist Wilfrid Scawen Blunt, who was a friend of 'Abduh's and an advocate of Egyptian independence, referred to him as 'a wild man of genius'.[49] E. G. Browne, who also knew 'Abduh and al-Afghani, described him in similarly gushing terms as 'a man of enormous force of character, prodigious learning, untiring activity, dauntless courage, extraordinary eloquence both in speech and writing, and an appearance equally striking and majestic'.[50] In the eyes of 'Abduh, he was the 'perfect human' of the Sufi tradition of Ibn 'Arabi, 'the sage of the East' who inspired him, as Rashid Rida put it, with 'the transcendent prophetic spirit'.[51] In the view of his enemies, on the other hand, al-Afghani was a political and religious subversive – 'a dangerous agitator' who was prepared to be all things to all men.[52]

True to his training in the Shi'i philosophical tradition, al-Afghani's interpretation of Islam was essentially a philosophical one. In his famous *Decisive Treatise on the Connection between Religion and Philosophy*, the Muslim Aristotelian Ibn Rushd – known in the West as Averroes – had argued that the study of philosophy had been made obligatory by the Qur'an, for it was only through demonstrative reasoning that the Qur'an's ambiguous verses could correctly be explained. Rational interpretation of scripture was the task, Ibn Rushd said, of those people whom the Qur'an refers to as 'those firmly-established in knowledge' (Q. 3:7). For people without philosophical training, the Qur'an spoke in poetic images – the flowing rivers of paradise, for instance, or the burning fires of hell – that were not literal depictions of reality so much as means of convincing ordinary people to follow the religion. This was important, because religion, by giving people legal and moral guidance, created stability in society. While philosophers interpreted the Qur'an in terms of Greek philosophy and science, therefore, they concealed these deeper truths from ordinary people to prevent them from falling into confusion and error and disrupting the balance of society. Prophets, meanwhile, were a kind of philosopher, possessing both perfect intellects, which enabled them to know the true nature of things, and perfect imaginations, which enabled them to convey those truths in poetic symbols fit for the masses.[53]

The first sign of al-Afghani's commitment to this way of viewing the relationship between religion and reason was a lecture that he gave in Istanbul in 1870. Following his arrival in the Ottoman capital the previous year, al-Afghani began to associate with the political leaders behind the Ottoman Empire's Westernizing Tanzimat reforms. In February 1870, al-Afghani was invited to give one of the speeches at the opening ceremony of Dar al-Funun, a modern university consisting of faculties of philosophy and letters, law, and the mathematical and physical sciences, at which instruction was to be in French or, failing that, Turkish.⁵⁴ Later in the same year, he was again invited to speak at the new university, this time on the importance of developing modern industries. According to Rashid Rida's account, during his speech al-Afghani likened human society to a living body. Each industry, he said, is like a limb of the body and brings a corresponding *manfaʿah*, or benefit – a term which the Egyptian reformer al-Tahtawi had earlier adapted from Islamic legal theory to denote the 'social benefits' of modern industries.⁵⁵ While the king is like the brain of the body, iron working is like the upper arm, agriculture is like the liver, sailing is like the legs, and so on and so forth. Moreover, he said, without a spirit, a body has no life, and the spirit of the social body is either prophecy or philosophy. This statement seemed not only to place philosophy on a par with prophecy, but also to suggest that, when a society has philosophers, it no longer needs prophets. Though al-Afghani did go on to highlight the differences between philosophy and prophecy, the damage had been done. Accused of teaching that prophecy itself was an industry or craft, he was forced to leave Istanbul, arriving in Cairo in the spring of 1871.⁵⁶

In Cairo, al-Afghani gathered round him a circle of talented and ambitious followers, some of them, like ʿAbduh, students at al-Azhar, others government officials or notables. They came for private lessons in philosophy, theology, legal theory and astronomy at al-Afghani's home in Khan al-Khalili, the old Cairo bazaar adjacent to al-Azhar. 'His madrasah,' says Rida, 'was his home.'⁵⁷ The 'curriculum' included texts that were part of the Shiʿi philosophical tradition of Iran, such as the *Pointers and Reminders* – Ibn Sina's famously allusive summary of philosophy – and works from the Illuminationist tradition of Suhrawardi. Al-Afghani also taught a theological text by the Central Asian Maturidi theologian al-Taftazani (d. 1390) – a staple of the madrasah curriculum in the central

Ottoman lands – which displayed the characteristic interest of post-Avicennian theologians in philosophical questions such as the nature of being, as well as a work on legal theory by the same author that pointedly opened with a description of legal theory as the science that combines rational and revealed knowledge.[58]

Al-Afghani, in other words, was inducting his disciples into the rationalist tradition of post-classical Islam, with an added dose of mysticism that was typical of later Shi'i philosophy. Muhammad 'Abduh's first written works reflect his immersion in these traditions under al-Afghani's guidance. The first, *The Treatise on Mystical Inspirations*, written in 1874, brings together the philosophy of Ibn Sina, the Illuminationist wisdom of Suhrawardi and the Sufi metaphysics of Ibn 'Arabi – a synthesis which was the hallmark of the Sadrian philosophical tradition of Shi'i Iran. 'Abduh rehearses three classic philosophical proofs for the existence of God, including Ibn Sina's famous argument based on the distinction between necessary and contingent existence, according to which the contingent beings that make up the universe require a being that is 'necessary in itself' in order to exist. He commits himself – without actually using the term – to the theory of 'the unity of existence' that typifies the Sufi metaphysical tradition of Ibn 'Arabi. 'There is no existence (*wujūd*) apart from His [that is, God's] existence,' writes the young 'Abduh, 'and no attribute apart from His attribute'. Reflecting his teacher's Shi'i philosophical background, he alludes to Mulla Sadra's theory of 'substantial motion'. And, again following al-Afghani, he advances a philosophical view of prophecy, describing Muhammad as 'the divine sage' and 'the perfect man', and in so doing blurring the distinction, as his teacher had done in his infamous Istanbul lecture, between the philosopher and the prophet. Overall, the treatise aims to show how the questions contested by the philosophers and theologians – on whether God's knowledge includes particulars as well as universals, or whether the bodies of human beings will be resurrected as well as their souls – are resolved by the Sufi perspective, in keeping with the view advanced by the fifteenth-century Persian poet and commentator on Ibn 'Arabi, 'Abd al-Rahman Jami, in his treatise *The Precious Pearl*.[59]

'Abduh's second written work was a series of marginal glosses on the commentary by the fifteenth-century Sunni Iranian theologian Jalal al-Din al-Dawani (d. 1502) on the creed of 'Adud al-Din al-Iji (d. 1356). He finished the work, which was based on al-Afghani's lectures on the two medieval texts, in 1876. Al-Iji, who was the teacher of the Maturidi theologian al-Taftazani, was an Ash'ari theologian whose manual of theology, like that of his student, was much studied in the Sunni madrasahs and displays a heavy Avicennian influence. Al-Dawani's works, including the commentary on al-Iji's creed, were a major part of the philosophical training of theologians and philosophers in the Ottoman and Mughal empires in the seventeenth and eighteenth centuries. As in *The Treatise on Mystical Inspirations*, 'Abduh uses the *Glosses* to try to resolve questions that had historically been points of contention between the philosophers and theologians. These questions include the relationship between existence and essence, whether good and evil can be known through reason and whether the Qur'an is created, as well as the three philosophical doctrines that al-Ghazali had condemned as *kufr* or 'unbelief' in *The Incoherence of the Philosophers*, namely, the eternity of the world, God's knowledge of particulars 'in a universal way' and the resurrection of the soul but not the body. Notably, 'Abduh's sympathies on all these issues appear to lie with the more rationalist position. For instance, he suggests – in keeping with the position of the Mu'tazili and Maturidi schools of theology – that moral categories can be known through reason independent of revelation, tries to reconcile Ibn Sina's position that existence and essence are identical in God with the position of the Ash'ari school, and appears to endorse the philosophers' view that the Qur'an's description of bodily resurrection was intended only for the masses.[60]

Eager to spread the spirit of rationalism among the students at al-Azhar, 'Abduh began to teach the theological text by the Maturidi theologian al-Taftazani that he had studied with al-Afghani. When one of the conservative ulema of al-Azhar accused him of being a Mu'tazili, his prospects of graduating from al-Azhar were briefly threatened, but in 1877 he received his licence to teach. Like al-Afghani, he subsequently acquired a group of disciples who came to his home, where he taught them Ibn Miskawayh's *The Refinement of Morals* – a philosophical text which, as we have seen, was also admired by Sayyid Ahmad Khan and Rifa'ah al-Tahtawi – and the French politician François Guizot's *General History of Civilization in Europe: From the Fall of the Roman Empire to the French Revolution*. Originally published in 1828, Guizot's work had been translated into Arabic by another of al-Afghani's Egyptian disciples in the same year that 'Abduh graduated from al-Azhar. Reform-minded Arab intellectuals – both Muslim and Christian – drew from it a conceptual vocabulary of 'decline', 'stagnation' and 'progress', as well as a general picture of how, through the Renaissance, Reformation and Enlightenment, the 'barbarism' of the European Middle Ages had given way to the rationalism and liberal pluralism of modern 'civilization'.[61] Guizot wrote contemptuously of the 'stationary state' into which Islamic civilization had everywhere fallen – a judgement shared by 'Abduh and al-Afghani, who often wrote of the *jumud* or 'stagnation' of the Muslim world – and their reading of the late French Prime Minister's work convinced them that Islam, too, needed a reformation.⁶² At the same time, like other modern reformers, 'Abduh also discovered an indigenous Arab-Islamic counterpart to Guizot's account of the rise and fall of civilization in the *Introduction to History* of the fourteenth-century North African historian Ibn Khaldun, which had been published in Cairo at the instigation of al-Tahtawi – for whom Ibn Khaldun was 'the Montesquieu of Islam' – in 1857.⁶³ 'Abduh taught Ibn Khaldun's text, which appealed to reformers like him on account of its interpretation of Islamic history in terms of universal rational laws, at the Dar al-'Ulum, a college for training teachers in the modern sciences, after he joined the faculty in 1878.⁶⁴ His lectures on Guizot and Ibn Khaldun likely formed the basis of his unpublished book, now lost, on *The Philosophy of Society and History*.⁶⁵

Alongside his teaching activities in this period, 'Abduh also contributed to the popular press, which he saw as a vehicle both for the moral education of the Egyptian public and for the development of a clear and unencumbered Arabic prose style that was suitable for the modern age.⁶⁶ In late 1880 he was appointed editor-in-chief of *The Egyptian Events*, the official journal of the Egyptian government. He used this platform to call for reform along three main lines. First, 'Abduh's experiences at the mosque school in Tanta and at al-Azhar had convinced him of the sorry state of education in Egypt, and many of his articles were devoted to educational reform, a concern which he shared with other Muslim reformers of this period such as Sayyid Ahmad Khan and the founders of the seminary at Deoband. Second, like those South Asian reformers, 'Abduh also sought to reform what he saw as outdated customs. In an article on 'The Regulations of the Shari'ah regarding Polygamy', for example, he used the same argument employed by Sayyid Ahmad Khan and al-Tahtawi, namely that the Qur'an's injunction that men should only marry multiple wives if they could treat each of them equally amounted to an effective prohibition of the practice. He also, finally, wrote on political reform, arguing that the laws of a country must be adapted to the circumstances of the time, and that representative government was perfectly in keeping with Islamic principles.[67] In making that last point, he referred to the Qur'anic concept of *shura*, or 'consultation'. Al-Tahtawi had used a term from the same root to describe the processes of the upper house of the French parliament, while the Tunisian political reformer and Islamic modernist Khayr al-Din al-Tunisi (d. 1890) argued for a parliamentary system of government on the basis that consultation was a *sunnah* or normative custom of the Prophet.[68] 'Abduh regarded it, as Malcolm Kerr observes, 'as a genuine restriction on the ruler's power', and following him Muslim modernists have continued to invoke it as an 'indigenous principle of representative or constitutional government in Islam'.[69]

In line with his commitment to representative government, 'Abduh supported the so-called 'Urabi revolt, the 1882 uprising led by Colonel Ahmad 'Urabi against foreign interference in Egypt. When the revolt was defeated following Britain's invasion of Egypt in that same year, 'Abduh was sent into exile. He went first to Beirut, where he associated with members of 'Abd al-Qadir al-Jaza'iri's circle, before heading in 1884 to Paris to join his old teacher al-Afghani. Al-Afghani had himself been deported from Egypt at the instigation of the British in 1879. From Egypt al-Afghani had returned to India. Settling in the princely state of Hyderabad, he wrote articles advocating Indian nationalism and the study of the modern sciences and philosophy, and in 1881 published an attack on Sayyid Ahmad Khan and the modernists of Aligarh. Originally written in al-Afghani's native Persian, the book was quickly translated into Urdu, and in 1886 'Abduh produced an Arabic version titled *The Refutation of the Materialists*, using a term, *al-dahriyyin*, which was used in medieval Islamic heresiography for atheists and those who believed only in *dahr* – 'time' or 'eternity'.[70] By contrast, al-Afghani's original title, *The Truth of the Naichari Sect and an Explanation of the Condition of the Naichariyyah*, employed the pejorative term for Ahmad Khan's 'naturalistic' interpretation of Islam that had been coined by the latter's Indian Muslim opponents, leaving no doubt as to his principal target.

Though Ahmad Khan was a fellow Muslim modernist, his great sin, in the eyes of the anti-imperialist al-Afghani, was his loyalty to the British. Al-Afghani, whose own orthodoxy was deemed suspect by many, seized the opportunity to portray himself as a defender of Islam against the Aligarh modernists' insidious 'naturalism', which, he alleged, had been introduced into the Muslim world by the British.[71] His defence of Islam, however, was an essentially utilitarian one. Like the Aristotelian philosophers of medieval Islamic history, al-Afghani was less interested in the truth of Islamic doctrine than in its usefulness as a means of creating and preserving social order.[72] The flourishing of nations, he declares, calling to mind Shah Wali Allah's notion of the *irtifaqat* or 'civilizational supports', depends on four things, each of which is uniquely to be found in Islam. First, the minds of the populace must be cleansed of superstitions and delusions. 'The first pillar upon which the Islamic religion is built,' he writes, 'is the polishing of rational minds with the polish of monotheism and the purifying of them from the dirt of delusions.' Second, each and every member of a society should be encouraged to recognize their essential worth as human beings and to strive to perfect themselves. This will lead to competition between people in acquiring virtues and performing good deeds. According to al-Afghani, whose position here is reminiscent of the democratizing tendency discernible in Shah Muhammad Isma'il and other reformers of the eighteenth and early nineteenth centuries, Islam is again uniquely placed among the great religions to instil this egalitarian attitude. Other religions, al-Afghani alleges, are built on the principle of hierarchy: Hinduism has its caste system, Judaism has the idea of the chosen people, while Christianity has a priesthood that intercedes between people and God. Islam, by contrast, came to 'wipe away the privileges of races and the hierarchy of classes', and teaches that people are only distinguished according to reason and virtue, which all human beings are, in principle, capable of attaining. The third thing that supports civilization, in al-Afghani's view, is for people's beliefs to be based on rational proof rather than conjecture and blind submission to authority – that is, *zann* and *taqlid*, in his critique of which al-Afghani echoes the Akhbari movement in seventeenth- and eighteenth-century Shi'ism. Once again, he asserts, 'the Islamic religion is practically unique among the religions in censuring those who believe without proof and scolding those who follow conjecture'. Finally, successful nations require a group of people who devote themselves to teaching others, and in Islam it is a religious duty to identify teachers to teach the faith and carry out the Qur'anic principle of 'commanding right and forbidding wrong'.[73]

This was an idealized picture of Islam. What al-Afghani thought of Islam as it had actually been practised in history comes out in the debate that he conducted after his arrival in Paris with the historian of religion Ernest Renan (d. 1892). One of the most famous public intellectuals in France, Renan was a religious sceptic who had been suspended from his post as Professor of Hebrew at the Collège de France for implying that Jesus, though an 'incomparable man', was not divine, a view that underlay his demythologizing 1863 book on *The Life of Jesus*. In March 1883, Renan, who had written his doctoral thesis on the medieval Muslim Aristotelian philosopher Ibn Rushd, gave a lecture at the Sorbonne titled 'Islam and Science', in which he explained that the present 'inferiority' and 'decadence' of Muslim societies was the result of Islam's supposed hostility to science and education. Though he conceded that the Muslim world had made great contributions to science and philosophy in the medieval period, Renan alleged that this was in spite of Islam, not because of it. Islam, he said, had in fact 'always harassed science and philosophy'; 'it is the reign of dogma, it is the heaviest chain that humanity has ever borne', a 'fact' which Renan, alleging that the Arabs are essentially irrational, put down to Islam having been born among the Arabs.[74]

Renan's lecture was published in the *Journal des Débats*, one of the leading daily newspapers in France. A few weeks later, the same journal published al-Afghani's response. While he rejected Renan's racist claim that the Arabs are naturally hostile to science, al-Afghani conceded the main point, acknowledging that 'the Muslim religion has tried to stifle science and stop its progress' – though 'a similar attempt', he pointed out, had been made by the Christian religion, and was still being made by the Catholic Church. Echoing the evolutionary view of religion advanced by the Shaykhis and Babis, he attributed Islam's history of hostility to science to the fact that it was at a less advanced stage of historical development than Christianity – for 'no nation at its origin is capable of letting itself be guided by pure reason'. Just as Christian Europe had managed to overcome Christianity's innate hostility to science, he proposed, so too might Muslim society one day succeed 'in breaking its bonds and marching resolutely in the path of civilization'.[75]

Among the 'bonds' that needed to be broken, in al-Afghani's view, was the bond of European imperialism. Between March and October 1884, al-Afghani and 'Abduh published *The Firmest Handle*, a journal advocating Muslim unity as the way to counter Western dominance. Taking its title from the Qur'an – which declares that whoever believes in and submits to God, rejects evil, and does good 'has grasped the firmest handle' (Q. 2:256, 31:22) – its stated goals included instilling a sense of hope into the souls of its readers, refuting the charge that 'Eastern' peoples were incapable of progressing towards civilization, and strengthening the connections between Eastern nations.[76] A recurring refrain of the journal was a Qur'anic verse that al-Afghani had already cited at the end of *The Refutation of the Materialists*, and which 'Abduh, too, would make his own: 'God will not change the condition of a people until they change what is in their souls' (Q. 13:11).[77]

The Firmest Handle, as E. G. Browne observed, was 'mainly political and strongly anti-English'.[78] Calling for pan-Islamic 'unity, solidarity and cooperation', al-Afghani and 'Abduh reminded their readers that Islam did not simply address man's spiritual side; it also regulated social interactions, established a system of rights and obligations, and defined the functions of government.[79] Banned in both India and Egypt, the journal was forced to close, probably owing to lack of funds, after just eighteen issues. 'Abduh subsequently went to Tunis, and then back to Beirut, where his home became a magnet for Syrians of all religious communities – Sunnis and Shi'ah, Druze, Christians and Jews. Together with the English clergyman Isaac Taylor, he established a society for harmony and reconciliation between Judaism, Christianity and Islam.[80] To those who came to his home he lectured from the biography of the Prophet compiled by the Shafi'i mufti of Mecca, Ahmad ibn Zayni Dahlan (d. 1886), a strong critic of Wahhabism whose account of Muhammad's life was extremely popular at that time.[81] At the Sultaniyyah Madrasah, meanwhile, which was located near to the recently established Christian missionary schools in one of the newer quarters of Beirut, 'Abduh gave a series of lectures that would later be collected into his most important work on theology, *The Epistle on Monotheism*.[82]

The lectures aimed to give students with little background

an overview of some of the fundamental topics of Islamic theology, including the different kinds of existence (here 'Abduh again drew on Ibn Sina's fundamental distinction between necessary and contingent being), the existence of God, God's attributes and actions, the nature of human action (that is, whether it is freely willed or determined), the function of prophecy and the nature of the Qur'an. In the published treatise, 'Abduh announces that he has kept close to the method of the *salaf*, or predecessors (here meaning early Muslim theologians such as al-Ash'ari, who gives his name to one of the two orthodox schools of Sunni theology) while not impugning the views of their successors (meaning later theological writers such as al-Iji, al-Taftazani and al-Dawani, whose work he had taught and written on as a young man).[83]

At the same time – and more importantly – the lectures are also an argument for a certain way of viewing Islam. Their overriding message is the modernist claim that Islam, in its original, Qur'anic form, is the religion of reason. In the introductory preliminaries, 'Abduh draws a contrast between the pre-Islamic religions, which were often 'the enemy of reason', and the Qur'an, which, rather than commanding blind acceptance, offers 'arguments and evidence' and speaks to the rational mind. 'For the first time,' he declares, 'reason and religion became brothers in a sacred book.'[84] Adopting, like al-Afghani, an evolutionary view of religious development, in a later chapter he argues that the progress of humanity reached its culmination in Islam, insofar as it addressed the intellect, obliged man to look after both his body and soul and to care for this life as well as the next, laid down rights for the followers of other religions living under Muslim rule, did away with distinctions of race, and enjoined rituals that were rationally explicable.[85]

Like al-Afghani, however, 'Abduh acknowledges that actual Islam has failed to live up to this ideal. The history of

Islamic theology that he offers at the beginning of the treatise is a narrative of decline, detailing the Muslim community's descent from rationality to blind emulation, knowledge to conjecture and ignorance, unity to disunity, and moderation to extremism.[86] Throughout the lectures, he displays a deep impatience with what he calls 'the barren wrangles' of the schools of theology.[87] While reason, he asserts, can establish the existence of God and enables humans to know the essential divine attributes, those who exhaust their mental energy on unsolvable questions such as whether God is required to act in the best interest of mankind – a key doctrine of the Mu'tazili school of theology – or the relationship between human free will and divine determinism cause only division within the Muslim community, while the misguided among them fall into extremism.[88] The way to renewal – and *The Epistle on Monotheism*, its English translators observe, could equally be called *The Epistle on Renewal* – is to return to the Qur'an.[89] 'It is necessary to limit one's belief,' 'Abduh writes towards the end of the treatise, 'to what is explicitly stated in revelation, and it is not permitted to add conjectural knowledge to certain knowledge.'[90]

Having been pardoned by Tawfiq, the Egyptian viceroy, in 1888, 'Abduh was permitted to return to Egypt. He was appointed a judge in the Courts of Native Tribunals, a new type of court that administered a form of law based on the Napoleonic Code. According to Rashid Rida, 'Abduh was a *qadi mujtahid* – that is, a judge who based his decisions on his own independent interpretation of the sources rather than on *taqlid*.[91] Remembering his own unhappy experiences as a student, 'Abduh also worked towards the reform of al-Azhar, acting as 'the moving spirit' within a committee tasked with improving that venerable institution. Besides the rationalization of teachers' salaries and improvements to the students' living conditions and the administration of the seminary, the committee recommended reforms to the curriculum, advocating the inclusion of mathematics, geography, Islamic history and classical Arabic literature, and that students, instead of spending years studying commentaries and glosses on theological and legal texts, should first concentrate on mastering the fundamentals of the religion.[92] Anxious that students should have access to classic texts, 'Abduh established a proper library at al-Azhar and its newly affiliated mosque schools – 'If you are looking for a rare book, a fine collection, a valuable reference, or a useful item from our tradition of learning,' he once lamented, 'you will find it in the libraries of European countries such as the one in Cambridge, in England' – and in 1899 he founded the Society for the Revival of the Arabic Sciences, whose remit was 'to edit and finance the publication of forgotten classical works'.[93] In 'Abduh's view, classical Arabic literature was a vehicle for the moral formation of readers and a means for training them in correct and eloquent Arabic, activities which he saw as closely related.[94]

A teacher at heart, 'Abduh also began lecturing again, giving classes at al-Azhar on theology, rhetoric, logic and the Qur'an.[95] Among the attendees at his Qur'an lectures was the orientalist E. G. Browne, who was in Cairo to improve his Arabic. Browne reported to Wilfrid Blunt that the lectures were 'admirable and very fearless', observing that 'Abduh had 'a ready facility in answering objections made to him by the old-fashioned interpreters of the Koran'.[96] From 1900, the lectures were published by 'Abduh's closest disciple, Rashid Rida, who added his own remarks and continued the commentary after his teacher's death. The resulting work, known as *The Commentary of the Lighthouse* after the title of the journal published by Rida, became a model for modern Qur'anic exegesis.

The guiding principle of the commentary is that the Qur'an should be approached primarily as a source of 'guidance' – the

Arabic terms *hidayah* and *irshad* are both used – which, if properly understood and implemented, would lead Muslims to flourish in both this world and the next. This fundamental goal of the Qur'an, 'Abduh and Rida allege, has been obscured by pre-modern commentators, who have focused too much on specific linguistic or theological issues arising from the text, or, much worse, have read into the text legendary stories taken from Jewish tradition – the so-called *Isra'iliyyat* – or the metaphysical speculations of Sufis such as Ibn 'Arabi, which 'Abduh had so admired in his youth, but which Rida in particular loathed. Insofar as the Qur'an refines the souls of its readers, lifts them from the pit of ignorance to the pinnacle of knowledge and guides them on the path of social life, it – and not the scholarly tradition of the schools of law – deserves to be called 'true jurisprudence', and it is necessary for everyone to try to understand it as far as his or her capacity allows. 'Abduh and Rida further explain that there are many levels of Qur'anic exegesis, the highest of which involves an understanding of the distinctive terminology and style employed by the Qur'an, the condition of the human race, the nature of the Qur'an's guidance to all of humanity and the biography of the Prophet.[97]

Like other modern exegetes, 'Abduh and Rida stress the connections between phrases and verses of the holy book and try to identify within each surah major thematic units. They encourage using the Qur'an to interpret itself, and adopt the interpretative rule of the Aristotelian philosophers that, when the Qur'an seems to conflict with science or reason, it should be interpreted in accordance with what science and reason tell us is true.[98] 'God,' we read in the commentary, 'has sent down two books: one created, which is nature, and one revealed, which is the Qur'an', a statement that echoes Sayyid Ahmad Khan's insistence on the harmony between 'God's work' and 'God's word'. 'The Qur'an itself,' they likewise insist, 'is too elevated in character to be in opposition to science.'[99] The commentators accordingly interpret the Qur'anic jinn as microbes, refer to modern inventions like the telephone, airplane and radio, and, most controversially, attempt to read the key concepts of Darwinian evolutionary theory – 'natural selection', 'the struggle for survival' and 'the survival of the fittest' – into the sacred book.[100] 'Abduh was a reader of *The Selection*, the journal which had been the first to publish extracts from the *Origins of the Species* in Arabic, and in 1903 he went to England specifically to meet the social Darwinist Herbert Spencer, from whom Darwin had taken the phrase 'the survival of the fittest'.[101]

Hand in hand with this commitment to showing the Qur'an's compatibility with modern science, 'Abduh also responded – as Sayyid Ahmad Khan, 'Abd al-Qadir al-Jaza'iri and al-Afghani had responded before him – to the common charge that Islam was hostile to rationality and science. In March 1900, Gabriel Hanotaux, a former foreign minister of France, published a two-part article in the Parisian newspaper *Le Journal* in which he argued that it was the moral duty of France to bring modern, French-style civilization to the Muslim world. Modern civilization, Hanotaux asserts, is derived from Christianity, which is an essentially Aryan religion. The Christian doctrine of the Incarnation, he says, by making God immanent within humanity, encourages people to view themselves as fundamentally valuable, while Christianity's emphasis on human free will encourages people to be active. By contrast, Islam, as an essentially Semitic religion, stresses God's transcendence and His determination of events, and so Muslims do not possess those same natural impulses that drove European Christians to attain modern civilization.[102]

Hanotaux's article was translated into Arabic and published on the front page of the leading Egyptian newspaper

The Support in April of the same year. It immediately caused a stir, and more than fifty articles were written in response to it in the Arabic and French press.[103] 'Abduh read it on his train ride home from al-Azhar, and immediately fired off a response. Observing that the former foreign minister had relied on blind emulation – *taqlid* – of stereotypical images of Islam and Christianity, 'Abduh begins his response by turning Hanotaux's racist, pseudo-historical account of the development of modern civilization on its head. Anyone who has studied the history of Christian Europe, he observes, knows that, at the time of the rise of Islam, the sciences were unknown in Europe, and it was only under Islamic influence – specifically, through their contact with Muslims in al-Andalus – that European Christians discovered science, which the Church subsequently tried to suppress. There is no connection, 'Abduh further argues, between contemporary European civilization and Christianity. While the Gospels teach renunciation and non-violence, the 'Aryan' civilization of modern Europe, by contrast, is a civilization of power and dominion, of silver and gold, of showiness and ostentation and of deception and hypocrisy, the highest authority being the guinea or the lira. 'Abduh then turns to the two theological issues cited by Hanotaux. Contesting the French author's characterization of Islam as a religion of predestination, he states that the *salaf* – the pious predecessors from early Islamic history – were a model of activism, and alleges that it was only under the influence of non-Arab converts to Islam and corrupt Sufis that the heresy of predestination and an attitude of passive resignation were introduced into Islam. The Islamic doctrine of *tanzih* or divine transcendence, meanwhile, far from separating man from the divine, as Hanotaux alleged, in fact makes the relationship between the individual and God *more* direct by removing intermediaries – a task, 'Abduh notes in passing, that the Protestant Reformers had also pursued. It was also more rational than the Christian Trinity, which Christians acknowledged to be beyond logical explanation. While here, too, the Muslims had deviated from the fundamental principles of their faith by adopting the notion of *tashbih* or divine immanence, were they to return to the message of their scripture, 'Abduh insists, they would be able to attain modern civilization without European tutelage.[104]

Two years later, that same conviction drove 'Abduh to get involved in another polemical exchange – this time with the Syrian Christian intellectual Farah Antun (d. 1922). Antun was the founder and editor of the prominent journal *The Unifier* and an old associate of 'Abduh's disciple Rashid Rida, with whom he had emigrated to Egypt. A secularist influenced by Ernest Renan, in 1902 Antun published an article arguing that Christianity had historically been more tolerant of philosophers and scientists than Islam – the example he gives is Ibn Rushd, who was widely read in Christian Europe but virtually ignored in the Islamic world – on account of the Christian separation of church and state. 'Abduh was urged to write a response by Rashid Rida, who published his teacher's reply in *The Lighthouse*. Repeating some of the points he had made in his response to Hanotaux, 'Abduh argued that, of the two religions, it was in fact Christianity that was less compatible with science, that contemporary European civilization was the product of Europe having departed from its Christian heritage and not a consequence of that heritage, and that the present state of Muslim societies was the result of Muslims' failure to put into practice the original principles of their faith, rather than the innate hostility of Islam to science. Rejecting Antun's premise that religion was a barrier to science and civilization, 'Abduh asserts that 'Islam will never be an obstacle on the road to civilization'; rather, he says, Islam and civilization will eventually support one another.[105]

When 'Abduh wrote his responses to Hanoteaux and Antun,

he was serving as the Grand Mufti of Egypt, a position to which he had been appointed in June 1899. In this role he was responsible for giving legal opinions according to the Hanafi school of law – the official *madhhab* of the Ottoman Empire – in response to queries from government departments. Like the Deobandis Rashid Ahmad Gangohi and Ashraf 'Ali Thanawi or the Barewli Ahmad Riza Khan, 'Abduh was a prolific writer of fatwas, issuing some 1,000 legal opinions during his six years as Mufti.[106] Ever the reformer, he diverged from the practice of his predecessors in refusing to sign off opinions without first reviewing the evidence – particularly in cases involving the death sentence, which required the Grand Mufti's signature – and in being more willing to issue fatwas in response to questions on Islamic law received from private individuals, including Muslims living abroad.[107]

His most famous and controversial fatwa, dated 3 October 1903, was an opinion that he gave on three questions received from a Muslim living in the South African province of Transvaal. Was it permissible, the questioner asked, for Muslims living in Transvaal to wear European hats when conducting their business? Were they allowed to eat meat that had been slaughtered by Christians, who, contrary to Islamic requirements, first strike the animal with an axe before cutting its throat, and do not slaughter it in the name of Allah? And was it permitted for South African Muslims who follow the Shafi'i school of law to pray behind a Hanafi imam, even though the two schools differ on minor points of detail in how they pray?[108]

In response to the first question, 'Abduh, echoing a theme that we came across in al-Nabulusi's defence of music and smoking, declared that what mattered was the intention of the Muslim who chose to wear a European-style hat, an act which in itself did not make one an unbeliever. If the intention was to achieve some clear *maslahah*, or benefit, or to ward off some definite harm, then wearing a European hat was not even reprehensible, 'because the idea of conformity to another religion has disappeared entirely' – a position which both evokes Shah Wali Allah's emphasis on the 'universal benefits' of the law and separates 'Abduh from those modern reformers, including the Deobandis, who worried about *tashabbuh bi-l-kuffar*, 'the emulation of unbelievers'.

Consistent with this position, 'Abduh also allowed the Transvaal Muslims to eat meat slaughtered by their Christian compatriots. This was the most controversial of the three opinions issued in the Transvaal fatwa. As Jakob Skovgaard-Peterson observes, eating meat slaughtered by non-Muslims 'was not customary in Egypt' and Islamic jurists 'had before almost invariably answered [the question of whether it was permissible] in the negative'.[109] 'Abduh's reasoning, too, was daringly innovative. Practising unrestricted *ijtihad*, he bypassed the accumulated legal tradition, which had devoted considerable attention to the issue, and went back to scripture. The Muslims of Transvaal, he declared, should follow Qur'an 5:5 – 'the food of those who were given the Book is permitted to you' – which, 'Abduh reasoned, is an explicit declaration of the lawfulness of meat slaughtered by Christians. The one classical jurist whose opinion he cited, moreover, was not a follower of his own Hanafi school but a famous judge of the Maliki *madhhab*. In calling on a Maliki authority, 'Abduh was practising what in Islamic legal theory is known as *takhayyur* or *talfiq* – 'choosing' between the opinions of the four schools, or 'patching' them together.[110]

Openness to the opinions of other legal schools had been a theme of Islamic reform going back at least to Shah Wali Allah. Like Wali Allah, 'Abduh had little time for *madhhab* zealotry, and it was this concern for what united Sunni Muslims rather than what set them apart that guided his answer to the third question raised by the Muslim of Transvaal. 'In regard to the prayer of the Shafi'i behind the Hanafi,' he wrote, 'there is no doubt in my mind concerning its correctness, so long as the prayer of the Hanafi is correct according to his own rite; for the religion of Islam is one.'

These declarations, like 'Abduh's whole project of modernist reform, were deeply controversial. In December 1903, the Egyptian newspaper *The Manifest* published an article titled 'How can that be declared lawful which God has declared unlawful?', the first in a series of ten articles attacking the Transvaal fatwa. In the view of the newspaper's editor, by failing to practise *taqlid* within the Hanafi madhhab, 'Abduh showed himself to be unfit to be Grand Mufti, a view for which the editor claimed the support of the scholars of al-Azhar.[111] Others criticized the Mufti's reforms to al-Azhar's curriculum. 'Abd al-Rahman al-Shirbini (d. 1908), the rector of the seminary, lamented that 'Abduh had turned al-Azhar 'into a school of philosophy and literature that wages war on religion and extinguishes its light'.[112] One of 'Abduh's successors as Grand Mufti, Muhammad Bakhit al-Muti'i (d. 1935), was likewise reported to have told a student that no one had 'corrupted the beliefs of the Muslims and introduced misguidance to al-Azhar' to the same extent as 'Abduh.[113] Later, Mustafa Sabri (d. 1954), the last Shaykh al-Islam or chief mufti of the Ottoman empire, wrote of how, following his arrival in Egypt in 1922, he 'found the cultural atmosphere in Egypt poisoned by the Western cultural trend'. A defender of the post-classical *kalam* tradition of Islamic rational theology, Sabri attributed this poisoning of the Egyptian mind to the pernicious influence of 'Abduh, whose debate with Farah Antun was evidence, as Sabri saw it, of his religious scepticism and capitulation to Western rationalism and empiricism.[114]

One of the reasons that these conservative scholars feared 'Abduh's influence was that his call for a fresh reading of the fundamental sources could be taken as the basis for socially liberalizing reforms. In fatwas published in his widely read journal *The Lighthouse*, for instance, 'Abduh's disciple Rashid Rida advocated a laissez-faire attitude to new Western commodities such as toilet paper, or the use of the gramophone to listen to recitals of the Qur'an.[115] More significant were the reforms proposed by 'Abduh's followers and associates to the status of women in Muslim society, an issue that generated significant discussion in Egypt in the last decade of the nineteenth century.

The improvement of the position of women in Muslim society was an important element of 'Abduh's own programme of modernist reform. In his view, just as Islam was *the* religion of reason and science, so too was it the paradigmatic religion of gender equality. Yet just as the essential rationality of original Islam had been obscured by *taqlid*, so too, he thought, had the egalitarianism of the Qur'an been obscured by patriarchal social practices that were cultural rather than religious in origin. Commenting on Q. 3:195, in which God declares that He will not allow the labour of anyone – male or female – to be in vain, 'Abduh observes that Islam promises that pious men and women will be equally rewarded by God. 'Moreover,' he continues, '... the claim of the Europeans to have been the first to honour woman and grant her equality, is false. For Islam was before them in this matter'.[116] Yet in this as in other respects, 'Abduh acknowledged, Muslims had 'failed to follow the guidance of [their] religion'. Specifically, they had failed, as al-Tahtawi had earlier observed, to give girls a proper education – a failing which 'Abduh sought to correct by founding Islamic charities whose purpose was to set up schools for the education of girls as well as boys.[117]

Polygamy, too, was contrary to the egalitarian spirit of the Qur'an. Like Sayyid Ahmad Khan and al-Tahtawi, in his Qur'an commentary 'Abduh argued that the Shari'ah held up monogamy as the ideal form of marriage and had only permitted polygamy as a concession to the conditions prevailing in Arabia in Muhammad's day.[118] Similarly, 'Abduh introduced a new explanation for the Qur'an's stipulations on testimony. Qur'an 2:282 instructs believers to call on two men, or, failing that, on one man and two women, to act as witnesses to financial contracts. Invoking the so-called 'deficiency Hadith', in which women are said to be deficient in both reason and religion, Qur'an commentators had traditionally explained this injunction in terms of women's supposed tendency to be more error-prone or forgetful. In his Qur'an commentary, 'Abduh declares this explanation 'unconvincing'. Women's testimony in financial cases counts for less, he suggests, simply because women tend not to work outside the home. In those areas in which they have more experience, their testimony should be weighted equally.[119]

In denying that women were inherently deficient, 'Abduh was echoing a point that had already been made by Zaynab Fawwaz (d. 1914), a Shi'i Muslim woman from southern Lebanon who emigrated to Egypt and became an important contributor to the Cairo press in the 1890s. Going further than modernists like al-Tahtawi and 'Abduh, Fawwaz advocated the education of girls not so much to make them better mothers and housewives as to help them understand the basis of their oppression and to take on more active roles outside the home.[120] She attacked the assumptions that underlay the patriarchy, particularly the notion that women were less capable than their male counterparts.[121] In response to a series of articles by a male Egyptian author who upheld 'women's essential corruptibility [and] lesser intelligence', Fawwaz argued that the idea of female deficiency in religion and reason conflicted with both the egalitarian message of the Qur'an and the Prophet's treatment of women. 'We came to be here in this life, possessors of complete minds, of ideas, perceptions, and feelings, just as the men have, and we are not deficient, lower than them, in anything,' she wrote.[122] On the question of women's testimony, she argued that it was men, in fact, who were the more forgetful sex, because they were more involved in worldly affairs. Far from making them inferior to men, Fawwaz said, 'God charged women to be the originating cause for the world's existence' – a statement that echoes the way in which Sufi authors spoke of the Prophet Muhammad.[123]

Fawwaz made these radical arguments some years before the appearance of the treatise generally regarded as the first major landmark of Islamic feminism. This was *The Liberation of Woman* by Qasim Amin (d. 1908). An Egyptian lawyer trained in France, Qasim Amin was a friend of 'Abduh's who served as a judge in the Courts of the Native Tribunals. *The Liberation of Woman*, which appeared in Arabic in 1899, was premised on the assumption that there was a close correlation between civilizational progress and the condition of women.[124] Echoing 'Abduh, Amin asserted that Islam was the first religion to establish complete equality between men and women.[125] The cause of the degraded status of women in Muslim societies was not Islam, therefore, but customs which Muslims had borrowed from other nations, and in particular the long history of oppressive government in Muslim countries, which had provided a model for Muslim men's oppressive treatment of women.[126] To call for the liberation of women, then, was not to introduce a *bid'ah* or illicit innovation into Islam; rather, it was to return to fundamental Islamic principles.[127]

Following the example of al-Tahtawi, the first of the social reforms advocated by Amin was the improvement of women's education. Education, Amin observes, is the first requirement of any civilized nation, and in Western countries, he argues with some exaggeration, the education of women actually exceeds that of men.[128] In Islam, contrary to what some think, the education of women is a religious duty.[129] The obligations imposed on women by the Shari'ah indicate that God gave them the same intellects as men, but women have been prevented from achieving their intellectual potential by being denied a proper education.[130] The resulting ignorance of Egyptian women, Amin argues, has had dire consequences for the family and society, for women are largely responsible for the early education of their children. Ignorant mothers have failed to inculcate moral virtues in their children and have passed on to them superstitions such as the fear of jinn and demons and belief in the protective power of amulets and the graves of holy men.[131] To improve women's education would not only be to return to the Prophet's example – for had not Muhammad instructed believers to take half their religion from his wife 'A'ishah, a prolific transmitter of Hadith? It would also be a cure for the 'sickness' diagnosed by Western observers of Muslim societies.[132]

Coming several decades after the establishment of the first girls' schools in Egypt, these proposals for improvements to women's education, which were governed by the assumption that a woman's primary role was as a mother and homemaker, were relatively modest. More radical and controversial were his remarks on veiling. Though Amin did not reject the hijab *per se*, he condemned the practice of forcing women to cover their faces and hands as a cultural custom that predated Islam and has no basis in a scriptural text.[133] Islam, he writes, is a religion of ease rather than difficulty, for women as well as men, and this principle applies to the rules on veiling.[134] Furthermore, extreme veiling deprives women of the social rights that Islam gives them, by preventing them from engaging in business and crafts or from fulfilling their legal duties such as appearing as witnesses in court.[135] To those who claim that the unveiling of women will lead to *fitnah* or temptation – a justification often given by jurists for restricting women's access to the mosque or preventing them from taking on roles in public life – Amin asks rhetorically why men are not also commanded to veil themselves to ward off temptation.[136]

The Liberation of Woman, which also includes an argument for monogamy as the ideal form of Islamic marriage and a condemnation of easy divorce, evoked a storm of protest. At least thirty books were written attacking Amin, who responded by writing another book, *The New Woman*, in which he took an even more liberal position. Others defended him and carried forward his arguments. The female writer Malak Hifni Nasif (d. 1918), who took the pen name Bahithat al-Badiyah or 'the Seeker of the Desert', was the daughter of a leading member of 'Abduh's circle. She gave lectures to female audiences on Fridays at the Egyptian University, the first modern university in Egypt, which Qasim Amin had helped establish in 1908. These lectures were collected along with some essays she wrote into a volume titled *Women's Matters* that was published in 1910. Hifni Nasif was a proponent of better education for girls, the relaxation of customs around betrothal and marriage and the more moderate form of veiling practised by the women of Istanbul. In response to those who said that women had been created for the home, Hifni Nasif, employing a kind of *ijtihad*, pointed out that neither the Qur'an nor any other holy book had stated this explicitly. At the same time, she cautioned against the emulation – or *tashabbuh* – of European gender norms, condemning the 'excessive' freedom that allowed women and men to dance together in public or women to perform on stage with their breasts showing. Advocating a 'moderate' and authentically Islamic form of feminism, her models were the early female religious scholars and descendants of the Prophet Sayyidah Nafisah and Sayyidah Sukaynah – both of whom were buried in Cairo – and Khawlah bint al-Azwar al-Kindi, a companion of the Prophet who had gone to Syria to fight the Byzantines and free her brother from captivity.[137]

Another pioneer of an indigenous Islamic feminism was the Lebanese author of Druze background Nazirah Zayn al-Din (d. 1976), whose book *Unveiling and the Hijab* was published in Beirut in 1928. Like Amin and Hifni Nasif, she adopted 'Abduh's back-to-the-Qur'an approach, criticizing those who 'look at Islam through the narrow vision of commentaries and interpretations which interpret Islam in ways they want to see it'. The Qur'an, she argued, does not mandate the segregation of the sexes, nor does it indicate that women are mentally or spiritually inferior to men. 'God,' she writes, 'dislikes slavery. He dislikes polygamy and any violation of women's rights. God loathes divorce.' Those Qur'anic verses – on inheritance, testimony and marriage – which apparently give men greater rights than women are to be understood not as a statement of male superiority, but as the imposition of a greater burden on men. Since giving testimony, for instance, is a 'bothersome obligation', it was an act of divine kindness to women to place the burden of testifying on men.[138]

As editor of *The Lighthouse* and the author of *An Invitation to the Gentle Sex: Women's Rights in Islam and their Share of the Universal Muhammadan Reform* (1932), Rashid Rida was an important contributor to the gender debate. Rida supported Qasim Amin's call for the emancipation of women and said that he wished Amin's treatise had been published in *The Lighthouse*.[139] Among the rights of women in Islam that he identifies are the right to pray in the mosque, to go on pilgrimage without covering their hands and face, to engage in trade and to teach and study with men.[140] At the same time, Rida was a fierce critic of the emulation of Western gender norms, praising Malak Hifni Nasif for her condemnation of this kind of *tashabbuh*, and became increasingly conservative in his later years.[141] His *Invitation to the Gentle Sex* ends by calling on Muslim women not to emulate their Western counterparts – the word he uses is *taqlid* – by demanding equality with men, a status, Rida says, which will afford them no good.[142]

This more conservative stance on the gender question is indicative of the role that Rida played in the emergence of Salafism, a socially conservative form of Islam that rejected the post-classical traditions of law, theology and Sufism and claimed to return to the 'pure' Islam of *al-salaf al-salih*, the 'pious ancestors' who lived in the first generations of Islam. Though, as Henri Lauzière has shown, the Arabic term *salafiyyah* was not used as a proper noun until the 1920s, the roots of this phenomenon lie in the rehabilitation of Ibn Taymiyyah – who refers to his own theological position as *madhhab al-salaf*, 'the doctrine of the ancestors' – and the critique of the legal *madhhabs* by eighteenth- and nineteenth-century reformers such as the Yemeni traditionalist al-Shawkani and the Indian Ahl-i Hadith scholar Siddiq Hasan Khan. At the turn of the nineteenth/twentieth century, their ideas circulated in the major cities of the Arab Middle East through the work of reformist scholars such as Nuʿman Khayr al-Din al-Alusi (d. 1899) and his nephew Mahmud Shukri al-Alusi (d. 1924) in Baghdad, Tahir al-Jazaʾiri, ʿAbd al-Razzaq al-Bitar (d. 1917) and Jamal al-Din al-Qasimi (d. 1914) in Damascus, and Rashid Rida in Cairo.[143]

Under the influence of the Ahl-i Hadith leader Siddiq Hasan Khan, with whom Nuʿman al-Alusi struck up a correspondence, these scholars sought out and published the writings of Ibn Taymiyyah, seeing the Hanbali traditionalist as a model of critical reasoning and objective scholarship who had been unfairly marginalized by the post-classical tradition.[144] In a long 1882 treatise defending Ibn Taymiyyah against the criticisms of a prominent sixteenth-century Shafiʿi scholar, Nuʿman al-Alusi put forward al-Shakwani's view that no age could be devoid of a *mujtahid*, someone who derives the law directly from the scriptural sources using their independent reasoning.[145] Al-Qasimi, who was impressed by that treatise, was a leading member of 'the *mujtahids*' club', a group of like-minded scholars who met at each other's homes in Damascus to read Hadith and texts advocating innovative legal methods. The group also included Ignaz Goldziher's friend Tahir al-Jaza'iri, and 'Abd al-Razzaq al-Bitar, a follower of 'Abd al-Qadir al-Jaza'iri who had been in close contact with 'Abduh since the latter's exile in Beirut. In 1896, they were accused of abandoning the *madhhabs* and basing the law on their own opinions, in what became known as 'the *mujtahids*' incident'.[146] Al-Qasimi responded with a poem that recalls the Persian verses of Siddiq Hasan Khan:

The truth is that I am of the Salafi creed.
My school is that which is in the Book of God ...
Then that which is sound of the Hadith reports,
Not disputable opinions.[147]

In the view of al-Qasimi, *taqlid* was a 'leprosy' that not only acted as a barrier to critical reasoning, but also created disunity within the ummah by breeding fanatical attachment to the schools of law – a point which he took directly from Shah Wali Allah.[148] Besides *taqlid*, he and other turn-of-the century reformers also condemned aspects of popular Sufism, particularly the veneration of saints' shrines, this being another feature of Ibn Taymiyyah's programme of reform. In his treatise defending Ibn Taymiyyah, Nu'man al-Alusi quotes the Qur'an commentary of his father Shihab al-Din al-Alusi (d. 1854), who observed that the cult of saints 'has no shred of basis in revelation or the sayings of the early Muslims'.[149] Having been converted to this way of seeing things, 'Abd al-Razzaq al-Bitar stopped working on the biographical dictionary he was compiling because it featured accounts of popular saints and their miracles.[150]

Though as a follower of 'Abduh he was more concerned than the reformers of Baghdad and Damascus to highlight Islam's compatibility with modernity, Rashid Rida, who published al-Qasimi's writings in *The Lighthouse* and celebrated al-Bitar as 'the reviver of the Salafi school in Damascus', shared their traditionalist commitments.[151] Already as a young man in the Lebanese city of Tripoli, Rida had reacted harshly to the Sufi rituals of the Mevlevi order, condemning the whirling dervishes for having – in the words of the Qur'an (Q. 6:70, 7:51) – 'made their religion a joke and a plaything'.[152] As 'Abduh's biographer and editor, Rida downplayed his teacher's youthful involvement with Sufism, removing his *Treatise on Mystical Inspirations* from the second edition of his biography of 'Abduh, and changing the title to make it sound as if 'Abduh did not identify with the Sufi position.[153] Though he was not himself averse to citing rationalist theologians and philosophers when it suited him, Rida also moved away from 'Abduh's openness to the *kalam* tradition of rational theology.[154] He removed a passage from the second edition of 'Abduh's *Epistle on Monotheism* that seemed to endorse the view of the rationalist Mu'tazili school that the Qur'an had been created in time, and stated that *The Lighthouse* was committed to following *madhhab al-salaf*, the doctrine of the pious ancestors, on questions of theological doctrine – by which he meant a literal understanding of the scriptural text.[155] Rida also supplied readers of *The Lighthouse* with a genealogy of *mujtahids* who had contributed to the reform of Islam in their own time and provided an example for reformers today. This reformist lineage was populated by traditionalist scholars, including the Zahiri literalist Ibn Hazm, Ibn Taymiyyah – whom Rida identified as the *mujaddid* of the seventh Islamic century – and al-Shawkani.[156]

Among Rida's collaborators was Muhibb al-Din ibn al-Khatib (d. 1969), a writer and publisher from Damascus who had studied with 'the Muhammad 'Abduh of Syria' Tahir al-Jaza'iri. After moving to Cairo, he co-founded the Salafiyyah Bookshop and Publishing House, which printed books by Ibn Taymiyyah, his student Ibn Qayyim al-Jawziyyah and their modern disciple Muhammad ibn 'Abd al-Wahhab, and popularized the name 'Salafiyyah'.¹⁵⁷ Like Ibn al-Khatib, Rida was increasingly sympathetic to the Wahhabi movement, which had returned to prominence following the Saudi ruler 'Abd al-'Aziz Al Sa'ud's conquest of the Hijaz in 1925. Rida was strongly opposed to 'Abd al-'Aziz's chief rival, Sharif Husayn of Mecca, whom he regarded as a British stooge, and saw the Saudi ruler as the only person capable of maintaining Muslim sovereignty over the sanctuaries of Mecca and Medina.¹⁵⁸ Shortly after 'Abd al-'Aziz's victory over Husayn, Rida published *The Wahhabis and the Hijaz*, in which he defended the Wahhabis against their many detractors and presented them as the heirs to Ibn Taymiyyah. Evoking the *mujaddid* Hadith, in the introduction Rida asserts that in every age there is a group of Muslims who proclaim the truth, from among whom God sends out 'reforming renewers' to weed out blind emulation and illicit innovation. In the Middle Ages, he goes on to say, the greatest of these renewers was Ibn Taymiyyah, who refuted Christians and innovators and sought to establish the supremacy of *madhhab al-salaf* over the opinions of the rational theologians and Sufis. Nevertheless, those who practised *taqlid* prevented people from accessing Ibn Taymiyyah's books, until a *mujaddid* appeared in central Arabia by the name of Muhammad ibn 'Abd al-Wahhab, who brought his people from polytheism back to monotheism and from innovations back to the Sunnah. Along with his children and grandchildren, Rida says, Muhammad ibn 'Abd al-Wahhab revived the method of Ibn Taymiyyah, a process that was continued by what he calls 'the new awakening of reform' in Egypt, India and other Islamic lands.¹⁵⁹

In this way, Rida incorporated Wahhabism into the genealogy of the modernist reform project that was associated with al-Afghani and 'Abduh. At 'Abd al-'Aziz's request, several of Rida's disciples went to the Hijaz, where, coming under the influence of Wahhabi scholars, they drifted further towards a more puritanical brand of Salafism. In 1926, one of these disciples, Muhammad Hamid al-Fiqi (d. 1959), founded Ansar al-Sunnah al-Muhammadiyyah, 'The Helpers of the Muhammadan Sunnah', which became one of the most important Salafi organizations in Egypt.¹⁶⁰ Closely resembling the Wahhabis of Saudi Arabia, twentieth-century Salafis stress purity of creed and ritual practice. In theology, they adopt Ibn Taymiyyah's distinction between *tawhid al-rububiyyah*, the monotheism of God's lordship, and *tawhid al-uluhiyyah*, the monotheism of God's divinity; claim that the only valid sources of doctrine are the Qur'an, the canonical Hadith and the consensus of the Prophet's Companions, which provide certain knowledge and ought to be interpreted literally; and strive to eradicate any trace of polytheism or innovation from their fellow Muslims' belief and practice through preaching and education. In their interpretation of the law, they adopt the stance of *la-madhhabiyyah* – 'no-madhhabism' – following al-Shawkani in arguing that even ordinary Muslims should avoid *taqlid*.¹⁶¹ Salafis also set themselves apart from other Muslims through distinctive forms of piety and dress which, so they claim, go back to the Prophet and his Companions. Distinctive practices advocated by Ansar al-Sunnah al-Muhammadiyyah include praying in shoes, strict gender segregation, growing one's beard to the length of a fist and wearing a robe that doesn't go below the ankle.¹⁶²

The leading scholarly representative of twentieth-century Salafism was the Hadith scholar Nasir al-Din al-Albani

(d. 1999). Born in Albania but brought up in Syria, he was inspired to turn to Hadith scholarship by reading an article by Rida in *The Lighthouse* criticizing al-Ghazali's *Revival of the Religious Sciences* for its dependence on unreliable Hadith and dubious Sufi ideas. Al-Albani subsequently attended the reformist circle of one of the students of Jamal al-Din al-Qasimi, and taught himself Hadith scholarship by reading through manuscripts in the Zahiriyyah library in Damascus founded by Tahir al-Jaza'iri. Rejecting the authority of the *madhhabs*, he proposed that the law should be taken directly from Hadith reports. Proclaiming his task to be 'bringing the Sunnah within reach of the *ummah*', he focused his efforts on sifting authentic Hadith reports from spurious ones by analyzing their *isnads* or chains of transmission (as pre-modern Hadith critics had done). This led him to reject reports that were found in the canonical Sunni books of Hadith (even, on occasion, in the *Authentic Collections* of al-Bukhari and Muslim) and to arrive at some idiosyncratic and controversial legal opinions – for instance, that women were not required to veil their faces and were prohibited from wearing gold bracelets, or that a Muslim wasn't required to fast during Ramadan if he or she couldn't see sunlight.[163]

In a comment recorded by Rashid Rida, Muhammad 'Abduh recalled that, besides the reform of the Arabic language, the major cause to which he had devoted his career was 'freeing rational thought from the chains of *taqlid*, understanding the religion in keeping with the way of the forefathers of the community before disagreement arose, returning to the original sources for the acquisition of religious knowledge, and weighing it in the scales of human reason'.[164] In inviting individual Muslims, as his eighteenth- and early nineteenth-century predecessors had done, to go back to the sources and interpret them for themselves, 'Abduh helped to open the door both for a liberal form of Islam that was at ease with the values of Western modernity and for a fundamentalist Salafism that was concerned with doctrinal and ritual purity and abhorred emulation of the West. As we shall see in our final chapter, as the twentieth century progressed, both of these tendencies would continue to grow in strength.

8

Defending God's Sovereignty

In May 1925, a book appeared that shook the foundations of the Egyptian religious establishment. Written by 'Ali 'Abd al-Raziq (d. 1966), an Azhar-educated judge in the Egyptian Shari'ah courts, *Islam and the Fundamental Principles of Government* was a revolutionary statement of Islamic secularism. Muhammad, 'Abd al-Raziq argued, was a divine messenger, not a king. Though the Prophet had founded a state in Medina, his divine mission was not political.[1] The caliphate, too, was not part of the Islamic message. Reviewing the scriptural evidence, 'Abd al-Raziq found that the caliphate was mandated neither by the Qur'an nor by the Sunnah. The claim that its necessity had been established by the consensus of the community, he argued, was likewise invalid.[2] In actual fact, the caliphate was a kind of 'kingship' that rested solely on brute force, and this was true even for the supposedly 'rightly guided' caliphate of Abu Bakr, the first caliph, and his three successors.[3] In short, Islam was *risalah la hukm* ('a divine message, not a system of government') and *din la dawlah* ('a religion, not a state'). While the jurists had traditionally maintained that the caliphate was necessary to protect Islam and the welfare of the community, these aims,

'Abd al-Raziq concluded, could be undertaken by any form of government – 'absolute or limited, personal or republican, oppressive, constitutional, or consultative, democratic, socialist or Bolshevik'.[4] If Muslims wished to catch up with other societies, then they should do away with the caliphate and establish a system of government based on 'the latest discoveries of the human intellect and the experience of nations'.[5]

In addition to the Islamic education that he had received at al-Azhar, 'Ali 'Abd al-Raziq had studied philosophy and economics for a year at Oxford, and his book – as his critics pointed out – featured references to the English political philosophers Thomas Hobbes and John Locke.[6] 'Abd al-Raziq also made use of a then recently published book on the caliphate by the orientalist Thomas W. Arnold, whom we met in chapter six as a member of the faculty at Sayyid Ahmad Khan's college at Aligarh, and whose book anticipates some of the major themes of 'Abd al-Raziq's treatise, including the absence of a Qur'anic basis for the caliphate and the essentially autocratic character of the institution.[7] The main thesis of *Islam and the Fundamental Principles of Government* also echoes Ahmad Khan's view that political matters were never considered 'revelatory in character' in Islam.[8]

A more important and direct influence on 'Abd al-Raziq, however, was Muhammad 'Abduh. Like the feminist writer Malak Hifni Nasif, 'Ali 'Abd al-Raziq's father was close to 'Abduh, with whom he founded an Islamic charitable organization. 'Ali's brother, Mustafa (d. 1947), who later served as a liberal-minded professor of philosophy at Cairo University (formerly the Egyptian University) and as rector of al-Azhar, was a student and biographer of 'Abduh and co-authored a French translation of 'Abduh's *Epistle on Monotheism*, which 'Ali cites in *Islam and the Fundamental Principles of Government*.[9] 'Ali 'Abd al-Raziq's reconsideration of the scriptural evidence for the necessity of the caliphate can be read as a response to 'Abduh's call to return to the original sources of the religion and weigh them in the scales of human reason, just as his use of Ibn Khaldun's analysis of the transformation of the caliphate into kingship echoes 'Abduh's use of the great North African scholar's *Introduction to History* in his teaching. For 'Abd al-Raziq, as for 'Abduh and other modernists, Islam is essentially a religion of equality and rationality, and his call for the abolition of the caliphate, which he thinks is based on armed force, reflects a desire to renew Islam along these lines.

Even more than Qasim Amin's *The Liberation of Woman*, *Islam and the Fundamental Principles of Government* was deeply controversial. In August 1925, the Council of Senior Scholars at al-Azhar stripped 'Abd al-Raziq of his degree and barred him from holding any post in the religious courts. In the same year, the former Grand Mufti Muhammad Bakhit al-Muti'i, whom we met in the last chapter as a critic of 'Abduh, published *The Truth about Islam and the Principles of Government*, declaring that everything in 'Abd al-Raziq's book constituted 'a clear denial of what the Muslims have unanimously agreed upon, or of what has been stated explicitly in the Mighty Book or the Prophetic Sunnah'.[10]

The vehemence of the criticism that 'Abd al-Raziq received owed something to the historical context, and specifically to what the historian of Islamic political theory Andrew March has called 'the crisis of the caliphate'.[11] On 1 November 1922, the Turkish Grand National Assembly had voted to abolish the Ottoman sultanate, leaving the caliphate (which the Ottoman sultans had long claimed for themselves) as a purely 'spiritual' office. On 3 March 1924, the caliphate itself was abolished, as part of the Turkish President Mustafa Kemal's wider programme of secularization. Later that same month, Mustafa al-Sabri, the last Ottoman Shaykh al-Islam, and another critic of 'Abduh and the modernists, brought out *The Disavowal of*

Those Who Disavow the Blessings of Religion, Caliphate, and Community. In 1925, al-Sabri went to the Vatican to plea for the papacy's aid in restoring the caliphate and 'combatting the atheist-nationalist destruction of the social-religious order'.[12]

Of more fundamental significance than the immediate historical context, however, was the sense that 'Abd al-Raziq's argument, in restricting the Prophet's mission to the religious realm, somehow diminished that mission, and with it Islam itself. Contrasting the worldliness of Muhammad's message with the spirituality of Jesus's prophecy, Bakhit insisted that 'the Islamic religion is based on the pursuit of domination and power and strength and might, and the refusal of any law which is contrary to its divine law'.[13] In the view of Rashid Rida, who, though he was a fellow follower of 'Abduh, was among 'Abd al-Raziq's leading critics, *Islam and the Fundamental Principles of Government* violated the very 'essence and character of the Muslim community' in the service of Western colonialism. 'The enemies of Islam,' he wrote in a review of 'Abd al-Raziq's book published in *The Lighthouse*, 'continue to endeavour to topple its throne, destroy its dominion, invalidate its laws and enslave the peoples that worship God through its teachings.'[14]

Rida had published his own book on the caliphate in 1923, after the separation of the caliphate from the Ottoman sultanate, but before its actual abolition. Positioning himself as a sympathetic if not uncritical advisor to the new Turkish government, Rida begins by affirming that Islam is both 'spiritual guidance' and 'the politics of civil society' and by setting down the classical legal arguments for the necessity of the caliphate – the foremost of which is that it has been established by *ijma'* or the consensus of the community.[15] His main aim in the treatise is to counteract the argument of 'Europeanized Muslims' such as Mustafa Kemal that the way for Muslim societies to recover their former glory is to separate politics from religion.[16] For Rida, by contrast, the 'medicine' that will cure the diseases afflicting Muslim societies – which include Muslims' loss of sovereignty to foreign aggressors, factionalism and illicit innovations in religious practice and belief – is 'the revival of the institution of the caliphate'.[17] The caliphate, he thinks, will re-establish the unity and sovereignty of the Muslim community, safeguard its *maslahah*, or welfare, and spearhead religious and moral reform.[18] Crucially, its revival will go hand in hand with the revival of *ijtihad*, which, according to Rida, is the only way to achieve 'the renaissance of the Muslims' and the renewal of Islam, for it demonstrates the flexible and progressive character of Islamic law and enables the adaptation of the law to changing needs and conditions.[19] In line with the classical theory of the caliphate, Rida holds that the caliph himself must be a *mujtahid*.[20] So must the representatives of the community known in the classical theory as *ahl al-hall wa-al-'aqd* – 'the people who loose and bind' – whose task it is to elect the caliph, engage in consultation, or *shura*, with him and to interpret and administer the Shari'ah on behalf of the Muslim *ummah*.[21] Rida conceived the idea of establishing an 'advanced madrasah' for training *mutjahids* who could go on to assume the roles of caliph and the people who loose and bind.[22] His overall vision, as Andrew March has described it, was of a 'living Shari'ah', forged through consultation and *ijtihad* on the part of the caliph and the representatives of the community.[23]

Though Rida's writing on the topic was stimulated by events in Turkey, his vision of the caliphate was not embodied in the Ottoman sultan. One of the qualifications for the caliphate identified by the classical theorists was membership of the Quraysh, the Arab tribe to which the Prophet Muhammad had belonged. Those who disputed this criterion, Rida observed, did so merely to legitimize the caliphate of the Ottoman sultans, which in fact was based purely on brute force.[24] Here

Rida was thinking of the Khilafat Movement, an organization of Indian Muslims who campaigned for the preservation of the Ottoman Empire following the First World War. One of the intellectual leaders of that movement, the religious scholar-turned-journalist Abu l-Kalam Azad (d. 1958), had published his own book on *The Problem of the Caliphate* in Urdu in 1920. The book was based on an address that he had given to a meeting of the Bengal Provincial Khilafat Conference in Calcutta in February of that year, and an Arabic translation was serialized by Rida in *The Lighthouse*.[25] Establishing and defending the caliphate, Azad argued, was a religious duty of all Muslims, whatever their nationality, for it was the caliph who ensured that the Muslim community was on the straight path, that justice and peace were established in Muslim lands, and that the word of God was spread throughout the world.[26] For Azad as for the other leaders of the Khilafat Movement, therefore, any threat to the caliphate was, as Muhammad Qasim Zaman has put it, 'a threat to Islam itself'.[27] In Azad's view, the Ottomans' legitimacy derived from the fact that, over the long centuries of their rule, they had shown themselves capable of fulfilling the functions of the caliphate. Azad rejected the stipulation of Qurayshi lineage on the grounds of the basic egalitarianism of the Qur'anic message. 'It would be a hard exercise of faith,' he wrote, 'to believe that Islam which came to level all distinctions of family or race and establish the unfettered and universal dignity of man ... should advocate any policy of tribal or racial superiority.'[28]

When the Khilafat Movement was founded in 1919, Abu l-Kalam Azad already enjoyed a reputation as an Urdu prose stylist, anti-colonial activist and advocate of religious reform. Educated in the rationalist tradition of Farangi Mahall, as a young man he had read with eagerness the writings of Sayyid Ahmad Khan – though he later turned against Aligarh modernism – as well as the work of al-Afghani, 'Abduh and

Rida.[29] Inspired by his reading of *The Firmest Handle*, the short-lived periodical that al-Afghani and 'Abduh had produced during their exile in Paris, in 1912 Azad founded *The Crescent*, an Urdu journal published in Calcutta. Like Rida, Azad was a keen admirer of Ibn Taymiyyah, and he used *The Crescent* to call for religious reform based on a return to the Qur'an. His message, as the historian Gail Minault has written, was that 'the Qur'an offered solutions for all the political, intellectual, and social problems of contemporary life'.[30] One of the significant implications of that message was that authority over the political sphere properly belonged to God. In an article published in *The Crescent* in July 1913, Azad wrote of how an 'intense war' was taking place between what he called 'the government of God' and 'human kingdoms'. Writing in the aftermath of France's occupation of Morocco, Italy's conquest of Ottoman Libya and the Ottomans' loss of their Balkan territories, Azad lamented that 'Satanic kingdoms' were seeking 'to utterly destroy God's government'.[31]

Other leaders of the Khilafat Movement would speak in similar terms. At the centre of the movement were the brothers Shawkat (d. 1938) and Muhammad 'Ali Jawhar (d. 1931). The 'Ali brothers were graduates of Sayyid Ahmad Khan's college at Aligarh: Shawkat captained the college cricket team and both brothers later played a key role in the school's old boys' network. Like 'Ali 'Abd al-Raziq, Muhammad 'Ali also studied at Oxford, reading history at Lincoln College. Like Abu l-Kalam Azad, they were journalists: in 1911, Muhammad founded *Comrade*, an English-language journal whose stated aim was to enable Muslims to make 'their proper contribution to territorial patriotism', meaning the Indian independence movement, in which the leaders of the Khilafat Movement played an important role, 'without abating a jot of the fervour of their extraterritorial sympathies which is the quintessence of Islam', meaning loyalty to the Ottoman caliphate.³² During the First World War, the 'Ali brothers were confined, on account of their pro-Turkish stance, to the small town of Chhindwara in central India. There Muhammad 'Ali devoted himself to reading the Qur'an and fell under the spell of the poetry of Muhammad Iqbal (d. 1938).³³

A lawyer, philosopher and poet, Iqbal had studied under Thomas W. Arnold – the orientalist who taught at Aligarh and whose work on the caliphate was cited by 'Abd al-Raziq – in Lahore, before going in 1905 to England, where he studied neo-Hegelian philosophy in Cambridge and was called to the bar at Lincoln's Inn. In 1908, he submitted a doctoral thesis to the University of Munich on *The Development of Metaphysics in Persia*, which introduced English readers to the Illuminationist wisdom of Suhrawardi, the Sufi metaphysics of Ibn 'Arabi as developed by his later interpreter 'Abd al-Karim al-Jili and the metaphysics of the Shi'i philosophers Mulla Sadra and Hadi Sabzawari.³⁴ He also writes enthusiastically about Shaykhism, Babism and Baha'ism, which he sees as a culmination of Persian thought and interprets through the prism of neo-Hegelianism and Schopenhauer's philosophy of will.³⁵

On his return to India later that year Iqbal established his reputation as a poet in Urdu and Persian. An admirer of al-Afghani, Iqbal regarded *ijtihad* as 'the principle of movement in the structure of Islam' and often quoted Qur'an 13:11 – 'God will not change the condition of a people until they change what is in their souls.'³⁶ In his poetry, he preached the strengthening of the Muslim self and the unity of the Islamic community. In *The Complaint*, a 1909 Urdu poem, he asks God why He has made the unbelievers rich and powerful while the Muslims have been denied His blessings. The reason, revealed four years later in *The Response to the Complaint*, is that Muslims have failed to put their faith into practice by neglecting to love the Prophet and replacing the divinely instituted principle of Islamic unity with man-made ethnic nationalism.[37] In *The Secrets of the Self*, a Persian poem of 1915 whose form is modelled on *The Spiritual Couplets* of Jalal al-Din Rumi, he laments how, under the influence of a Platonized Sufism, Muslims have embraced the doctrine of the renunciation of the self.[38] In its place, Iqbal preaches *khudi*, or 'selfhood'. The strengthening of the Muslim self, he says, is a three-step process involving obedience to 'the statutes of Muhammad', achieving self-control by practising the five pillars of Islam, and attaining 'divine viceregency' – the literal meaning of the term 'caliphate' – which Iqbal interprets in keeping with the Sufi idea of the perfect human.[39] In *The Mysteries of Selflessness* (1917), Iqbal puts these ideas into a sociopolitical context. The ideal community is not the nation but the community of Islam. This community is not bounded by space or time; its founding principle is the covenant which man made with God at the beginning of creation, recognizing him as Lord of all – and its law is the Qur'an.[40]

Inspired by this vision of Muslim self-assertiveness, the Khilafat leader Muhammad 'Ali came to recognize that 'the main theme of the Qur'an and … of the sayings of the Prophet as perceived in authentic Traditions is the Kinghood of God and the Service of Man as His Agent and vicegerent'.[41] Standing trial in the port city of Karachi on the charge of inciting Indian Muslims to refuse to serve in the British army in 1921, Muhammad 'Ali pointed out to the Christian colonizers that while they prayed, 'Thy kingdom come', in fact, 'God's kingdom has come'. Significantly, he expressed this in terms of the principle of divine sovereignty: 'Islam,' Muhammad 'Ali declared at the trial, 'recognises one sovereignty alone, the sovereignty of God, which is supreme and unconditional, indivisible and inalienable.'[42]

An echo of one of the key ideas of the early nineteenth-century reformer Shah Muhammad Isma'il, this notion of the sovereignty of God was to become the core concept of Islamism, the movement to renew Islam through political means. Its chief theorist and popularizer was Abu l-'Ala' Mawdudi (d. 1979), an Indian scholar and journalist who was involved in the Khilafat movement as a young man and later became the founder of the Jama'at-i Islami, the leading Islamist organization in South Asia. Born in Aurangabad, in the princely state of Hyderabad, in 1903, Mawdudi came from a family which, he said, had 'provided [Muslims] with spiritual guidance and lived ascetic lives for thirteen hundred years' – that is, since the time of the Prophet, from whom the family claimed descent.[43] His father had briefly attended Sayyid Ahmad Khan's modernist college at Aligarh, but was withdrawn from the school when his father learnt that he was playing cricket wearing *'kafir'* clothes, and, after a career as a solicitor, later turned towards a world-denying form of Sufism.[44] Abu l-'Ala' was himself educated at a modern school, studying history, philosophy, politics, economics, religious studies and sociology.[45] In his teens, Mawdudi, whose father had read Abu l-Kalam Azad's articles to him when he was still a boy, became a sympathizer of the Khilafat Movement. 'We disliked Western culture and Western domination right from the beginning,' he later recalled, 'and, naturally, we were prepared to support any movement that strove for freeing India from this domination, [especially] as it appealed to religious sentiments too.'[46] In 1919 or 1920 he moved to Delhi, where he studied the traditional religious disciplines with Deobandi scholars at the Fathpuri Mosque and became the editor of the newspaper of the Jam'iyyat-i 'ulama-i Hind (The Association of the Scholars of India), a Deoband-linked organization which, like the Khilafat Movement, had been founded in 1919 to campaign against the breakup of the Ottoman Empire. Among the articles he wrote for this paper was a series on jihad in which, reacting against the interpretations of the modernists and the Ahmadiyyah, he argued for the permissibility of offensive warfare for the sake of the common good.[47] The articles were collected into his first book, which was published in 1929. Three years later, Mawdudi acquired the journal *The Interpreter of the Qur'an*, which became the platform for his vision of a renewed Islam, just as *The Lighthouse* was for Rashid Rida. In 1937, he was invited by Muhammad Iqbal to come to the Punjab to collaborate on the 'reconstruction and codification' of Islamic law and to direct a centre for Islamic research.[48] Iqbal was an admirer of Mawdudi's work on jihad, while Mawdudi, for his part, credited the poet for having identified 'the real *malaise* of the Western culture', namely that Western political ideologies were based on 'hate, suspicion and resentment'.[49] When Iqbal died shortly afterwards, Mawdudi went to Lahore, where, in 1941, he founded the Jama'at-i Islami as a vehicle for transforming society in accordance with his ideological vision.[50]

That vision was based on four conceptual pillars that would prop up most twentieth-century Islamist thinking. First, there was the notion of the comprehensiveness of Islam in its original Qur'anic form that had been advanced by Abu l-Kalam Azad. The Prophet, Mawdudi asserts in *Towards Understanding Islam* (1940), brought 'a complete system of individual as well as collective life of man', formulating laws about 'morality, social life, domestic economy, civil polity and the common matters of human life'.[51] Islam is therefore, as he puts it in *The Four Fundamental Concepts of the Qur'an*, a complete *nizam-i zindagi* or 'system of life', which includes all of life's 'faith-related, intellectual, moral, and practical aspects'.[52] While the idea that the Shari'ah covers all areas of human existence was an age-old one, Mawdudi gave it an explicitly political meaning. As he explains in *The Political Theory of Islam* (1939), it is not just Islam but the Islamic *state* which 'seeks to mould every aspect of life and activity in consonance with its moral norms and program of social reform'. In this respect, he acknowledges, Islam is a political ideology analogous to Fascism or Communism.[53]

Second, in Mawdudi's theory, the sovereign of the Islamic state is none other than God Himself. 'In principle,' he writes, in his 1941 treatise *How is an Islamic State Established?*, '"Islam" is the name of a movement that strives to erect the entire building of human existence on the concept of the sovereignty of the one God.'[54] Just as for the early twentieth-century Dutch neo-Calvinist Abraham Kuyper 'there is not a square inch in the whole domain of our human existence over which Christ, who is Sovereign over *all*, does not cry, "Mine!"', so too, for Mawdudi, the *hakimiyyah* or sovereignty of God extends over the whole of human existence.[55] The *rububiyyah* or lordship which the Qur'an ascribes to God, he explains in *The Four Fundamental Concepts of the Qur'an* (one of which is *rabb* or 'lord'), means that 'He is the supreme sultan of the universe and its sole king and ruler.'[56] Human beings, he says, must therefore seek to apply the 'rules and regulations' that God has communicated to them in His Book. In practice, this would mean such things as the prohibition of usury, the imposition of gender segregation and the patriarchal ordering of family life, restricting non-Muslims' religious freedom and their participation in public life (here Mawdudi drew on the Qur'an commentary of the Zaydi traditionalist al-Shawkani), and the enforcement of the death penalty for apostates.[57]

An implication of the exclusive sovereignty of God is that it is illicit for human beings to legislate. 'The Qur'an establishes that obedience must be rendered to God alone and that only His law must be followed,' Mawdudi writes in a 1966 work on *The Caliphate and Kingship*. 'It is forbidden for man to neglect or abandon this law and follow the laws of others, or his own law or whims.'[58] Human beings, then, are not legislators but caliphs or viceregents of God – the third conceptual pillar of Mawdudi's Islamist ideology. Islam, he tells us in *The Political Theory of Islam*, 'rears its polity on the foundations of the sovereignty of God and on the viceregency of man'.[59] Overturning the classical theory of the caliphate, Mawdudi, who may have been influenced by Iqbal as well as by the Deobandi notion of the sainthood of all believers, argues that the caliphate belongs to all believing Muslims. 'Every believer is a caliph of God in his particular place,' he writes in *The Political Theory of Islam*, explaining his theory of 'popular viceregency'. 'As caliph, he is individually answerable to God.'[60] Though at some points in his writings Mawdudi indicates that the religious scholars will assume a special role in the Islamic state as guardians and interpreters of the divine law, *The Political Theory of Islam* advances the populist argument that 'the entire Muslim population [should run] the state in accordance with the Book of God and the practice of His Prophet' – a system of government which Mawdudi calls 'theo-democracy' or 'divine democractic government'.[61]

This is not democracy in the secular, Western sense, however. For Mawdudi (and here we reach the fourth and final pillar of his thought) any political system that fails to acknowledge the sovereignty of God is a form of polytheism, for it puts some human beings in a position of dominion or lordship over others – a position that rightfully belongs only to God. Nationalism, imperialism, capitalism and Marxist class struggle, he asserts, are not merely erroneous or sinful; they are forms of *jahiliyyah*, a term traditionally used to describe the pre-Islamic era of pagan barbarity and ignorance, which Mawdudi turned into a transhistorical phenomenon representing the polar opposite of everything truly Islamic.[62] 'The meaning of "*jahiliyyah*" in Islam,' he wrote in the Qur'an commentary that he published between 1949 and 1972, 'comprises every course of action which runs counter to the Islamic culture, Islamic morals and conduct, or Islamic mentality.'[63] The history of Islam, Mawdudi explained in a 1940 book on *The Renewal and Revival of Religion*, was a story of perpetual struggle between Islam and *jahiliyyah*, in which the great 'renewers' of the past – including al-Ghazali, Ibn Taymiyyah, Sirhindi, Shah Wali Allah and Sayyid Ahmad Barelwi – had struggled (and rarely with complete success) to purify Islam of *jahili* elements. What was needed today, therefore, was a *mujaddid-i kamil* or 'perfect renewer' – a concept, again, which was indebted to Iqbal – who would 'establish a caliphate on the prophetic pattern' and impose the sovereignty of God throughout the world.[64]

Mawdudi initially refused to support the foundation of Pakistan on the grounds that the basis of the new state was popular rather than divine sovereignty. In 1949, however, the country's Constituent Assembly passed the Objectives Resolution, the preamble of which recognized that 'sovereignty over the entire universe belongs to God Almighty alone'. Under Mawdudi's influence, the idea of the sovereignty of God became a commonplace in Pakistan, including among traditionally educated ulema, modernist intellectuals and even the Ahmadiyyah, despite the prominent role played by Mawdudi and the Jama'at-i Islami in the anti-Ahmadi riots in the Punjab in 1953.[65]

Even more significantly, Mawdudi's ideas were taken up by Islamist ideologues in the Middle East, including the Egyptian Sayyid Qutb (d. 1966), one of the leading theoreticians of the Muslim Brotherhood. Jama'at al-Ikhwan al-Muslimin, 'The Society of the Muslim Brothers', had been founded in 1928 by the Egyptian primary school teacher Hasan al-Banna (d. 1949). A graduate of Dar al-'Ulum, the teacher training college where 'Abduh had once taught, a Sufi of the Hasafiyyah order, and a sometime associate of Rashid Rida and Muhibb al-Din ibn al-Khatib, the proprietor of the Salafiyyah Bookshop, al-Banna thought of the Muslim Brothers as heirs to the reformism of al-Afghani, 'Abduh and Rida.⁶⁶ Like those reformers, he began with the problem of Muslim decline, which, he believed, had begun with the passing of the 'rightly guided' caliphs and reached its nadir in modern times with the dismantling of the caliphate, the prevalence of *madhhab*-zealotry and other forms of Muslim disunity, and the spread of Western imperialism, Zionism and communism, all of which were based on a philosophy of materialism.⁶⁷ The way to rectify the situation was through action, for God, as the Qur'anic verse beloved of the reformers stated, would not change the condition of a people unless they changed themselves.⁶⁸ Action meant returning to true Islam, the principles and teachings of which, al-Banna asserted, 'are all inclusive, encompassing the affairs of the people in this world and the hereafter'. Far from being purely a spiritual message or a body of ritual, Islam was 'a faith and a ritual, a nation and a nationality, a religion and a state, spirit and deed, holy text and sword'.⁶⁹ Islam, al-Banna argued, did not teach 'a rendering to Caesar that which is Caesar's and to God that which is God's' as Christ had done. Rather, he said, 'Caesar and what belongs to Caesar is for God Almighty alone.'⁷⁰ The goal, therefore, was the creation of *al-nizam al-islami*, 'the Islamic system', where the Qur'an itself was the constitution.⁷¹ This meant not so much the creation of a theocracy or Islamic state as a society permeated with the spirit of the Qur'anic message, a goal that was to be achieved, as al-Banna put it, 'through learning, education, and jihad'.⁷²

The Muslim Brothers, al-Banna wrote in a key 1943 text, *The Obstacles in Our Path*, were to be 'a new soul in the heart of this nation to give it life by means of the Qur'an', 'a new light which shines to destroy the darkness of materialism through knowing God' and a 'strong voice which rises to recall the message of the Prophet'.⁷³ The society, he said, was 'a Salafi message, a Sunni way, a Sufi truth, a political organization, an athletic group, a cultural-educational union, an economic company, and a social idea'.[74] It was led by *al-murshid al-'amm* – 'the General Guide', a term with Sufi connotations – to whom Brothers pledged unquestioning obedience, and organized into various 'sections' covering missionaries (who spread the Brotherhood beyond the borders of Egypt), workers and peasants, white-collar professionals, a scout-like group called the 'rovers', the family and a women's group known as 'the Muslim Sisters'. There was also a militant section called 'the Secret Apparatus'.[75] Though al-Banna spoke often of jihad, which he regarded as an obligation on every Muslim, the emphasis, in the first instance, was on spreading true Islam through *al-tarbiyah wa-al-da'wah* – education and missionary work.[76]

Sayyid Qutb, who like al-Banna was a graduate of Dar al-'Ulum, had begun his career as a literary critic, teacher and civil servant at the Egyptian Ministry of Education. From the mid-1940s, he began to turn towards Islamism, publishing, in 1949, *Social Justice in Islam*, a book which combined Marxist-inspired themes with the characteristic Islamist idea that Islam is a comprehensive 'system' that covers the political as well as the more purely 'religious' dimensions of life.[77] In late 1948, he went to the United States on behalf of the Egyptian Ministry of Education, an experience that seems to have convinced him of the moral and spiritual decadence of Western culture.[78] On his return to Egypt, he fell increasingly under the influence of the ideas of Mawdudi. By 1951, nine of Mawdudi's most important works, including *The Four Fundamental Concepts of the Qur'an, The Political Theory of Islam, The Renewal and Revival of Religion* and *Jihad in Islam*, were available in Arabic translation.[79] Besides these translations, another channel of influence was Abu l-Hasan 'Ali Nadwi (d. 1999), a prominent figure in the Nadwat al-'Ulama' of Lucknow, who toured the Middle East in 1951.

Though he had turned against Mawdudi ten years previously, Nadwi helped to popularize Mawdudi's transhistorical understanding of *jahiliyyah* through his widely read book, *What the World Lost with the Decline of the Muslims*, which had been published in Arabic in 1947. Qutb wrote the preface to the second edition of Nadwi's book, which was published in 1952.[80] In March of the following year, Qutb formally joined the Muslim Brotherhood, becoming the head of its propaganda section and editor of its official journal.

This was a period of dramatic upheaval for Egypt and the Muslim Brothers. In July 1952, the Free Officers, led by Gamal Abdel Nasser, had overthrown the monarchy. The relationship between the Free Officers and the Brotherhood was an uneasy one at best. Nasser and Anwar Sadat, another of the Free Officers, may have been affiliated at one stage to the Brotherhood, yet Hasan al-Hudaybi (d. 1973), who had been elected the General Guide of the Society in October 1952, was slow to support the revolution, and was equivocal about his organization's commitment to the principle of Egyptian nationalism. When al-Hudaybi sought a more prominent role for the Brothers in the new government, and Nasser refused, the relationship began to spiral into open hostility, a process exacerbated by the Brotherhood's vocal opposition to the agreement Nasser made with Britain for the withdrawal of British troops from Egypt. In October 1954, Nasser used a failed attempt on his life by a former member of the Secret Apparatus as an opportunity to crush the Brotherhood. The day after the failed assassination attempt, the Society's headquarters were destroyed by a mob, and there were soon waves of arrests. Seven Muslim Brothers were sentenced to death, including al-Hudaybi, whose sentence, however, was commuted to life imprisonment with hard labour. Among the hundreds of Brothers who were imprisoned in 1954 was Sayyid Qutb, who would spend most of the next twelve years in prison, before he was himself executed in 1966.[81]

Influenced by his reading of Mawdudi and Nadwi, the brutal conditions of his confinement and his unfiltered meditation upon the Qur'anic message, Qutb developed his own radical version of Islamist ideology. He set down this vision in several revised editions of *Social Justice in Islam*, and most influentially in a highly personal and emotive commentary on the Qur'an titled *In the Shade of the Qur'an*, which was eventually published in six volumes, and *Signposts on the Path*, a summary of the most radical elements of his vision of renewal. At the core of this vision was the notion of a perennial conflict between Islam and *jahiliyyah*. Even more than Mawdudi, Qutb elevated this idea into a metaphysical statement about the very nature of reality.[82] Commenting on Qur'an 5:49–50, which commands people to judge according to what God has revealed rather than by *hukm al-jahiliyyah* – 'the judgement of the days of ignorance' – Qutb explains that the term *jahiliyyah* denotes not a particular period of time but 'a certain condition'. Specifically, it means 'the rule of people over people' and human beings' submission to other people rather than to God. As such, it is a denial of God's *uluhiyyah*, or divinity, and an ascription of that divinity to other humans – the classic definition of *shirk* or polytheism.[83] In his commentary on Qur'an 12:40 – which announces that 'judgement (*hukm*) belongs only to God' – Qutb makes the same point using the language of divine sovereignty or *hakimiyyah*, another concept which he borrowed from Mawdudi. Sovereignty, he writes, 'is among the characteristic features of divinity', and 'whoever lays claim to sovereignty – whether it is an individual, a class, a party, an institution, a community or humanity at large in the form of an international organization – disputes the primary characteristic of [God's] divinity' and so 'is guilty of unbelief in the most blatant manner'.[84]

Qutb regarded Nasser's Egypt – along with other nominally Muslim states which refused to recognize God's sovereignty by implementing the Shari'ah in its original Qur'anic form – as a manifestation of *jahiliyyah*. 'Our whole environment, people's beliefs and ideas, habits and art, rules and laws,' he writes in *Signposts*, 'is *jahiliyyah*, even to the extent that what we consider to be Islamic culture, Islamic sources, Islamic philosophy, and Islamic thought, are also constructs of *jahiliyyah*.' Any form of compromise with this state of affairs was inconceivable, for 'Islam cannot accept or agree to a situation which is half-Islam and half-*jahiliyyah*'.[85] This being the case, Qutb calls for the formation of a revolutionary 'vanguard' of true believers prepared to separate themselves from *jahili* society – a move he calls *hijrah* or 'emigration' – and to wage armed struggle against its representatives. Drawing on Mawdudi's work on jihad as well as the writings of Ibn Taymiyyah's chief disciple Ibn Qayyim al-Jawziyyah, Qutb declares that Qur'an 9:123 – 'O believers, fight the unbelievers who are near to you; and let them find in you a harshness' – permits offensive struggle for the purpose of establishing Islam and is the Qur'an's 'conclusive judgement' on the question of jihad, abrogating less militant verses.[86] Rulers who illegitimately assume God's authority for themselves, he says, are 'idols', and both they and their helpers are unbelievers who deserved to be killed.[87]

Smuggled out of prison by Qutb's sister Hamidah (d. 2012) and the Muslim Sister Zaynab al-Ghazali (d. 2005), *Signposts* became the ideological charter of the 'Qutbist' wing of the Muslim Brotherhood, led by Sayyid Qutb's brother Muhammad (d. 2014), which took a more radical line on the question of *takfir* – that is, of the conditions for declaring a Muslim an unbeliever.[88] It was out of this wing that the global jihadist movement would later emerge in the 1980s and 1990s. Qutb was the major source of inspiration for 'Abd Allah 'Azzam (d. 1989), a Palestinian scholar with a doctorate in Islamic law from al-Azhar who became the chief ideologue of the jihad against the Soviet Union in 1980s Afghanistan. 'Azzam joined the Jordanian branch of the Muslim Brotherhood in 1954, became close to Muhammad Qutb while studying in Cairo and firmly identified with the Qutbist wing. 'No author of books on Islamic thought,' he recalled later in life, 'has influenced me more than Sayyid Qutb.'[89]

This influence runs through the pages of *The Jihad*, the monthly Arabic-language magazine that 'Azzam edited during the Soviet-Afghan war. History and society, 'Azzam declares in one issue, operate according to certain laws that have been instituted by God. One of these laws is that human souls only flourish when they follow 'the method of divine lordship' and remain under God's protection. All human methods to solve the problems of man – 'from capitalism to communism, socialism and nationalism' – are therefore doomed to failure. The existence of this law, 'Azzam writes, is proven by the contemporary Arab-Islamic world, which has become 'a plantation for the implementation of man-made *jahili* methods', and so abounds in human misery and economic, military and social decay. Another law is the inevitability of the struggle between truth and error, a struggle which has been going on 'since Adam set foot out of paradise'. On the one side in this perennial struggle stand the divine messengers and their followers, on the other, Satan and his followers, who include 'the Jews and Christians (the People of the Book), the idolaters, the Buddhists, the Hindus, the Baha'is, the Qadiyanis [a pejorative name for the Ahmadiyyah], the socialists, the atheists, the polytheists and the hypocrites'. Today, 'Azzam says, the focal point in the struggle is Palestine, which is the victim of 'international Crusaderism and global Judaism'.[90] (Like Qutb, whose books include *Our Battle with the Jews*, 'Azzam often resorted to anti-Semitic tropes.[91])

Given this eternal struggle between Islam and *jahiliyyah*, jihad, as 'Azzam saw it, was the highest expression of faith – or, as he put it in a favourite phrase, 'the summit of the mount of Islam'.[92] The first article of the first issue of *The Jihad*, published in 1984, declares that 'the flourishing of the world and of religion is founded on jihad'. Jihad, 'Azzam thought, was the means for re-establishing the Muslim unity that the Prophet had brought. While the jihad for Palestine – in which the Muslim Brothers had played a key role since the Arab–Israeli War of 1948 – remained a priority (indeed it was 'a part of the religion'), the Afghan jihad was a 'golden opportunity' to 'revive the spirit of jihad' in the souls of Muslims and to 'renew their covenant with their Lord'. Participation in the jihad would weigh heavily on the scales of divine judgement, and to stay at home was a sin that could only be atoned for by repenting and joining the jihad. 'Azzam developed these ideas in a fatwa that he published in book form in March 1985 titled *The Defence of Muslim Lands: The Most Important of Individual Duties*. This fatwa brought together the classical legal position that it is a religious duty to respond to the foreign invasion of Muslim lands with defensive jihad and the militant Islamist idea that the obligation to wage jihad was universal and did not depend on the approval of individual nation-states.[93] Reportedly the bestselling book in Islamist bookshops in 1990s Britain, *The Defence of Muslim Lands* gave scholarly heft to the nascent global jihadist movement, and both Ayman al-Zawahiri (d. 2022) and Osama Bin Laden (d. 2011), the founders of Al-Qaeda, thought highly of 'Azzam, 'the Sayyid Qutb of Jordan', just as they esteemed the original Qutb.[94]

By no means all Muslim Brothers thought this way, however. Opposed to the Qutbist wing of the Brotherhood was the 'Bannaist' wing, which took a more moderate and pragmatic line on the question of *takfir* and other contentious issues.

The position of this moderate wing is set out in *Preachers Not Judges*, a book completed in 1969 and published in 1977 under the name of Hasan al-Hudaybi, the General Guide of the Society, though its authorship has been questioned. Whereas, for Qutb, a Muslim must 'cut off his relationship of loyalty to the *jahili* society' to be included within the community of believers, *Preachers Not Judges* takes the view that anyone who pronounces the Islamic testimony of faith – even if he or she is a sinner – is to be considered a Muslim, the only exception being when 'impious deeds are accompanied by impious utterances'. Even then, only a judge has the authority to declare someone an unbeliever, and the Brothers are 'preachers, not judges'. Though the book never mentions Sayyid Qutb by name, it does respond directly to Mawdudi, rejecting his theory of a perennial conflict between Islam and *jahiliyyah*. The book also aims to undermine the radical Islamists' weaponization of jihad, arguing that Muslims should tolerate oppressive rulers on the condition that they do not defend their actions in terms of the legitimacy of man-made laws.[95]

Two important voices in this debate – and in twentieth-century Islam more broadly – were the Azhar-educated Muslim Brothers Muhammad al-Ghazali (d. 1996) and Yusuf al-Qaradawi (d. 2022), the intellectual leaders of the so-called *sahwah islamiyyah* or 'Islamic awakening' of the 1970s. Born, respectively, in 1917 and 1926, and educated at al-Azhar between the late 1930s and early 1950s, al-Ghazali and al-Qaradawi came of age in a difficult period for the ulema. Newly independent nation states were continuing the work of their colonial predecessors in dismantling the traditional institutions of Islamic law and learning – principally through the confiscation of their *awqaf*, the charitable endowments on which they depended – or incorporating them into state bureaucracies; more state funding was directed to modern universities teaching secular subjects; and alternative sources of religious authority were emerging in the form of activist journalists such as Mawdudi and Salafi scholars who were unattached to the schools of law.[96] In 1961, Nasser's government subjected al-Azhar to sweeping reforms, placing the venerable institution under the authority of the Ministry of Endowments, making the rector a government-appointed official and introducing colleges of engineering and medicine.[97] While these changes did significantly curtail the independence of institutions such as al-Azhar, many ulema were able to adapt to the new circumstances, as Muhammad 'Abduh had done before them, and retain their status as respected and influential religious authorities, presenting themselves (to use Muhammad Qasim Zaman's apt phrase) as 'custodians of change' from their vantage point as representatives of the Islamic scholarly tradition.[98] Muhammad al-Ghazali and Yusuf al-Qaradawi were particularly adept at this. Writing in the late twentieth century, the Islamic studies scholar Haifaa Khalafallah observed that there was 'a prevailing sense among many Egyptians that Ghazali is the spokesman of "Islam"'.[99] In the same period, Yusuf al-Qaradawi established a reputation as a 'global mufti' through his appearances on the Al Jazeera TV programme *Shari'ah and Life* and his leadership of international organizations such as the European Council for Fatwa and Research and the International Union of Muslim Scholars.[100]

As Muslim Brothers committed to what al-Qaradawi referred to as 'the renewal of the religion from within', both al-Ghazali and al-Qaradawi were critical, just as 'Abduh had been in his day, of what they regarded as the outdated curriculum and teaching methods employed at al-Azhar, and more generally of conservative ulema and their juristic hairsplitting.[101] The field of jurisprudence covering the acts of ritual worship, al-Ghazali once said, had 'grown into a cancer'.[102]

The obsession with the rules around ritual purity, for instance, made jurisprudence seem irrelevant, and only served the interests of tyrannical authorities by distracting religious scholars from the key questions of daily life.[103] In place of this outmoded jurisprudence, they called for a renewal of *ijtihad* and the development of a form of jurisprudence that took into account the *maqasid* or overarching aims of the Shariʿah; was conducive to the common interest or *maslahah* of the community; and was attuned to the *waqiʿ* or lived reality facing Muslims today – including Muslims living in Europe and other non-Muslim countries, a topic that was a special interest of al-Qaradawi's.[104] In this regard they were continuing a project which had been initiated by another Azhar-educated Muslim Brother, al-Sayyid Sabiq (d. 2000), who had compiled *The Jurisprudence of the Sunnah* in the 1940s at the instigation of Hasan al-Banna.[105] The stated aim of this legal manual, which was based on the Zaydi traditionalist al-Shawkani's Hadith-based book of law, was to treat issues in Islamic law and their scriptural proof texts in a way that was easy to understand, and 'to put an end to disagreement and the innovation of partisanship for the schools of law', as well as the 'superstition' that 'the gate of *ijtihad*' had been closed.[106] With the same aim in mind, Sabiq also edited *God's Conclusive Proof* by Shah Wali Allah, whom he saw as a model of traditionalist religious reform.

Another influence on the Azhari Muslim Brothers was Mahmud Shaltut (d. 1963), a modernist in the tradition of Muhammad ʿAbduh who served as rector of al-Azhar at the end of his life. He is best known for a Qur'an commentary in which, like ʿAbduh and Rida, he attempts to draw out the essential meaning of the scriptural text and show its applicability to contemporary life, as well as for his leadership of an initiative for rapprochement between Sunnis and Shiʿah.[107] Al-Qaradawi was one of the compilers of Shaltut's collection of fatwas, in which he claimed to rely 'only upon the beloved Book and the true Sunna and the basic and eternal principles of Islam', always providing reasons for the opinions given and often taking the public interest into consideration.[108]

Like Shaltut, al-Ghazali and al-Qaradawi stressed the lenient and balanced nature of the divine law and its adaptability to new circumstances. This stance is reflected in the permissive position that both scholars took on the acceptability of music in Islam, and especially in their more liberal views on legal questions related to the status of women in Muslim society – an issue to which Shaltut, too, had devoted considerable attention, arguing for a more expansive role for women's testimony.[109] In his most famous work, *The Prophetic Sunnah between the Jurists and the Traditionalists* (1989), al-Ghazali, drawing on the Zahiri jurist Ibn Hazm, advances the innovative view that there is nothing in the Qur'an or Sunnah prohibiting a woman from assuming the political leadership of the Muslim community. According to al-Ghazali, who was critical of the tendency to 'grab a ruling from any passing Hadith',[110] the Hadith report usually cited to support this prohibition – 'A people that is led by and entrusts its affairs to a woman will never flourish' – is a historically specific statement applying only to the Sasanian monarchy of Iran at the time of the Muslim conquests, not a universally applicable description of reality. The capacity of female leaders to lead flourishing nations, he says, is demonstrated not only by the Qur'anic story of the Queen of Sheba, 'who led her people to faith and salvation through her wisdom and intelligence', but also in the present day by the success of India under Indira Gandhi, Israel under Golda Meir, and Britain under Margaret Thatcher.[111] 'I testify that Thatcher is superior to seventy men with beards and moustaches,' al-Ghazali once declared.[112] Al-Qaradawi, who was generally more conservative than his teacher, did not go as far as al-Ghazali, arguing that the prohibition on women assuming leadership over a nation was set down in explicit scriptural texts.[113] Yet he did contradict a legal opinion issued by al-Azhar's fatwa council in 1952 by arguing that women are permitted in Islamic law to participate – whether as voters or as candidates – in parliamentary elections. Like al-Ghazali, he supported his position by citing the Qur'anic example of the Queen of Sheba and claiming that the Qur'anic verses and Hadith reports cited in support of limiting women's participation in public life were restricted to specific contexts.[114]

In keeping with their commitment to the methods of Hasan al-Banna and what al-Qaradawi called *wasatiyyah* ('moderation'), both al-Ghazali and al-Qaradawi were critics of Sayyid Qutb and his followers within the Muslim Brotherhood and beyond. Qutb's knowledge of Islamic jurisprudence, al-Ghazali observed, was 'shallow', hence 'he sometimes said things that no scholar could have possibly uttered'.[115] Expelled from the Brotherhood for challenging al-Hudaybi's autocratic style of leadership, al-Ghazali attacked the Muslim Brothers for their 'non-enthusiasm for democracy'.[116] Al-Qaradawi, too, was critical of what he described as the extremist positions that Sayyid Qutb had adopted in the final stage of his life, particularly his view that contemporary Muslim societies were mired in *jahiliyyah* and unbelief and his commitment to offensive jihad on the grounds that the most militant Qur'anic verses on jihad constituted God's 'conclusive judgement' on the issue.[117]

That said, al-Qaradawi did not reject the core Islamist concept of *hakimiyyah*, the sovereignty of God; indeed, in a book on the principles of Islamic moderation published in 2010, he defined monotheism as the recognition of God's unique lordship (*tawhid al-rububiyyah*), God's unique divinity (*tawhid al-uluhiyyah*) and God's unique sovereignty (*tawhid al-hakimiyyah*), a definition that marries Islamist ideology to the theology of the Salafi and Wahhabi movements.[118] Like

Mawdudi, he argued that divine sovereignty was not incompatible with democracy – albeit not democracy in the secular liberal sense, but what he called 'true democracy', meaning democracy within the limits of the divine law.[119] Certainly, neither Muhammad al-Ghazali nor Yusuf al-Qaradawi were liberals in the Western meaning of the term. Al-Ghazali declared that secularism, the separation of religion and state, was 'unadulterated unbelief', and justified the Islamic Jihad group's assassination of the Egyptian secularist Faraj Foda (d. 1992) (who, like 'Abd al-Raziq, had argued that the caliphate was a purely worldly institution) on the grounds that secularism is apostasy, which is punishable by death.[120] Al-Qaradawi, who shared the view that politics could not be separated from religion, was a social conservative who declared homosexuality 'a depraved act that contravenes innate human nature'.[121] While he held that women ought to be 'liberated from the effects of the period of backwardness and recession in Islam', he also thought, echoing Rashid Rida's critique of the aping of Western egalitarianism, that Muslim women needed to be 'freed from the evil results of the cultural invasion by the West'.[122] And though he was opposed to offensive jihad, he defended suicide bombing in the context of the Israel–Palestine conflict as a legitimate form of defensive jihad.[123]

It was in light of views such as these that Nasr Hamid Abu Zayd (d. 2010), another Egyptian secular liberal, argued in his 1994 book, *The Critique of Religious Discourse*, that representatives of 'moderation' such as Muhammad al-Ghazali and al-Qaradawi shared the same intellectual premises and strategies as the extremists. These commonalities, as Abu Zayd saw it, included a commitment to the principle of divine sovereignty and the use of force in defence of that sovereignty, a readiness to declare other Muslims unbelievers, conflating their own interpretations with 'true Islam', relying on the authority of tradition and the *salaf*, intellectual dogmatism, and an ahistorical approach to religious questions. Referring repeatedly to al-Ghazali and al-Qaradawi as examples of the so-called 'moderate' approach, Abu Zayd alleged that they differed from extremists such as Qutb and his militant heirs only on *when* violence ought to be used to impose true Islam, not on the principle itself.[124] Abu Zayd, an academic scholar of the Qur'an who was inspired by the hermeneutics of the Muʿtazilah and Ibn ʿArabi, was himself the victim of the 'religious discourse'. When he applied for a promotion to the rank of full professor at Cairo University in 1992, one of the assessors, a philology professor and popular preacher named ʿAbd al-Sabur Shahin (d. 2015), accused him of being a Marxist and atheist and violating the fundamental tenets of Islam. The following year, a case was brought against him, accusing him of apostasy, and arguing that, as an apostate, his marriage to a Muslim woman was no longer valid. In June 1995, a court ruled that Abu Zayd's marriage was annulled, and the couple were forced to flee to the Netherlands.

Abu Zayd, who wrote the introduction to a later edition of ʿAli ʿAbd al-Raziq's *Islam and the Fundamental Principles of Government*, was committed to the separation of religion and politics, and argued that the essence of the Islamic message was 'to give a primary role to reason in the domain of thought, and to justice in the domain of social conduct'.[125] His greatest crime, in the eyes of the Islamists, however, was to read the Qur'an, which he distinguished both from *kalam Allah* (the speech of God) and *wahy* (the revelation or inspiration received by Muhammad) as a historical and literary text.[126]

The hegemony of this type of religious discourse, as Abu Zayd saw it, was not a problem confined to Egypt or the Arab world. Lamenting the intolerant attitude of both 'moderate' ulema and 'extremist' Islamists to literature and the arts, Abu Zayd cited the *Satanic Verses* incident, when Ayatollah Khomeini (d. 1989), the Supreme Leader of the

Islamic Republic of Iran, issued a fatwa declaring that the novelist Salman Rushdie was an unbeliever who ought to be killed by any Muslim who had the opportunity.[127] Along with Mawdudi and Sayyid Qutb, Khomeini was the other leading twentieth-century theorist of the sovereignty of God, a principle enshrined in the second article of Iran's constitution following the Islamic Revolution of 1979.

Unlike Mawdudi and Qutb, Khomeini was a religious scholar, trained in the Usuli tradition of Shi'i jurisprudence. Among his teachers was Shaykh 'Abd al-Karim Ha'iri Yazdi (d. 1937), an Usuli scholar widely recognized as the *marja' al-taqlid* or 'source of emulation' of his day, who established a major Shi'i seminary in the holy city of Qom in 1922. Notably, Khomeini was also deeply immersed in the Sufi metaphysics of the school of Ibn 'Arabi and the Shi'i philosophical tradition of Mulla Sadra. Having followed Ha'iri Yazdi to Qom, Khomeini studied Mulla Sadra's *The Four Journeys of the Intellect* and commentaries on the works of Ibn 'Arabi with Mirza Muhammad 'Ali Shahabadi (d. 1950), and also received instruction from Mirza 'Ali Akbar Hakim (d. 1925), a student of the great nineteenth-century Sadrian philosopher Mulla Hadi Sabzavari. Besides his books on law and legal theory, Khomeini's own written works include an independent treatise on Shi'i mystical philosophy titled *The Lamp Showing the Right Way to Viceregency and Sainthood* and glosses on important texts in the Sufi tradition of Ibn 'Arabi.[128]

Both these elements in Khomeini's education – the training in Usuli jurisprudence and in Shi'i mystical philosophy – were crucial to the development of his political thought. Khomeini's distinctively Shi'i contribution to Islamist political theory was his interpretation of the doctrine of *wilayat al-faqih*, 'the authority of the jurist'. This concept was taken from the nineteenth-century Usuli jurist Ahmad Naraqi (discussed in chapter five), but Khomeini extended its scope to mean the executive and administrative authority of the Shi'i jurist over the political sphere. This theory is already outlined in embryonic form in *The Unveiling of Mysteries*, a 1943 book in which he argued that only 'the law of Islam' and 'the government of God' were able to achieve *madinah-yi fazilah*, 'the virtuous city' of the Platonic philosophical tradition, and that authority in the time of the occultation of the Twelfth Imam therefore belonged not to secular rulers like the Pahlavi Shah of Iran or Mustafa Kemal Ataturk, but to the jurists, who should form a council tasked with establishing a government.[129] It was fully developed in a series of thirteen lectures that Khomeini delivered while in exile from the Shah of Iran's regime – of which he had become the leading clerical critic in the early 1960s – in the Iraqi shrine city of Najaf between January and March 1970. These lectures were collected by his students and published in Beirut under the title *The Authority of the Jurist: Islamic Government* later that year.[130]

As with all theorists of political Islam, Khomeini's starting point is the all-encompassing nature of Islam. 'Islam,' he says, 'is a comprehensive religion providing for every aspect of human life.' Invoking an idea that goes back to al-Afghani, he stresses Islam's essentially revolutionary nature – Islam, in his reading, is 'a religion of militant individuals ... who desire freedom and independence' and 'struggle against imperialism'.[131] Yet the true nature of Islam, he thinks, has been distorted in the minds of Muslims – the masses and the educated alike – by the 'evil propaganda' of the enemies of Islam, among whom Khomeini (whose worldview, like Sayyid Qutb's and 'Abd Allah 'Azzam's, was deeply anti-Semitic) includes 'the Jews', Western imperialists, orientalists and their agents in the universities, government institutions and even the Shi'i seminaries of Iran. Khomeini alleges that these enemies have portrayed Islam as a religion primarily of ritual laws pertaining to things like menstruation, separating religion from politics as part of their 'plan to keep us backward ... so that they can exploit our riches, our underground wealth, our lands, and our human resources'. It is this anti-Islamic propaganda, then, that explains the disparity between, on the one hand, the Qur'an and Hadith, which are primarily concerned with social affairs and contain all the guidance that man needs in order to flourish, and, on the other hand, the books of jurisprudence studied in the seminaries, which, Khomeini protests – echoing Muhammad al-Ghazali – are primarily concerned with ritual matters.[132]

For Khomeini, once the true nature of Islam is recognized, it will be seen that Islamic government needs to be established. The Islamic form of government, he explains, 'does not correspond to any of the existing forms of government', because 'in Islam the legislative power and competence to establish laws belongs exclusively to God' – which is to say, in characteristic Islamist fashion, that 'sovereignty belongs to God alone, and law is His decree and command'.[133] Constitutionalism and the nation state, with which the agents of imperialism have tried to deceive Muslims, violate the laws of Islam, and Islam likewise 'proclaims monarchy and hereditary succession wrong and invalid'.[134] These non-Islamic political systems are systems of unbelief led by *tawaghit* (the plural of *taghut*, a false god or idol), who are the heirs of Pharaoh, the Qur'anic archetype of tyranny. Such systems ought to be eradicated, for they only produce what the Qur'an describes as 'corruption on earth'.[135]

Turning to the form that the Islamic government which will be established in their place will take, Khomeini explains that, because Islamic government is a system of divine law, the leader must be the person who is most knowledgeable in the law – an idea inspired by the Usuli principle that the *marja' al-taqlid*, 'the source of emulation' to whom other Shi'ah look for religious guidance, ought to be the 'most learned' of the

Shi'ah. Knowledge of Islamic law and justice are the only two qualities required of the holder of authority. This means that, in the period of the occultation of the Twelfth Imam, authority falls on 'the just *faqih* (jurist)', who 'has the same authority as the Most Noble Messenger and the just Imams had' and is tasked with establishing a government that will implement God's laws and protect Muslim territory.[136]

Khomeini, of course, saw himself as that 'just *faqih*'. Though he cautioned that the political authority enjoyed by the most knowledgeable jurist did not grant him a special spiritual status, he did indicate that the jurist inherits the Prophet's role as God's deputy or 'viceregent' – that is, His caliph – a status which, in his mystical writings, Khomeini describes in terms of Ibn 'Arabi's theory of the perfect human.[137] In a 1988 letter to Mikhail Gorbachev, Khomeini recommended that the Soviet leader study the writings of Ibn 'Arabi, Mulla Sadra, the Illuminationist philosopher al-Suhrawardi and the Aristotelians al-Farabi and Ibn Sina – indicating the value that he continued to attribute to the mystical and philosophical traditions of pre-modern Islam as sources of political as well as spiritual wisdom.[138] It is possible, then, that Khomeini saw himself as the Platonic philosopher-king or Sufi perfect human of his age, who, having completed the 'four journeys' outlined by Mulla Sadra, was tasked by God with delivering the world from corruption and establishing a reign of righteousness on earth.[139] Within the mainstream Twelver Shi'i tradition, this was a task reserved for the Hidden Imam on his return as the Mahdi. In assuming the title of Imam for himself – and in not laying to rest his more radical followers' suggestion that he was the Mahdi himself – Khomeini rejected the politically quietist strand of the mainstream Shi'i tradition and replaced it with a millenarian doctrine that was, in this respect at least, close to that of the Babi movement and its successor Baha'ism, which he so abhorred.[140] This impression is reinforced by

Khomeini's decree in January 1988 that the guardian jurist has the right to suspend God's laws – even those pertaining to prayer, fasting and pilgrimage – in the name of *maslahah* or public interest.[141]

Besides becoming the ideological basis of clerical rule in post-revolutionary Iran, Khomeini's revolutionary reading of Islam has also been influential among Islamists in the Sunni world. One prominent example of this influence is Rached Ghannouchi, the leader of the Muslim Brotherhood-affiliated Ennahda party in Tunisia, which in 2016 announced that it was transitioning from Islamism to a commitment to 'Muslim democracy'. He has spoken of the influence on his thought of Sayyid Qutb's vision of Islam as 'a comprehensive system of life', and the accompanying principle of divine sovereignty.[142] Yet Ghannouchi also describes how, following the Iranian revolution, Khomeini's ideology gave his movement the 'tools' to express the social conflict between 'the oppressed and the mighty' – a conflict which, borrowing from Khomeini, Ghannouchi has expressed in terms of a perennial struggle between 'Moses' (standing for righteousness) and 'Pharaoh' (representing tyranny).[143] Similar language has also been used by al-Qaradawi, who, under Shi'i influence, himself acquired the status of a *marja'* or authoritative source of reference in contemporary Sunni Islam.[144]

Among high-ranking Shi'i ulema, however, *wilayat al-faqih* has been controversial. At the time of the Islamic Revolution, the most widely recognized Shi'i *marja' al-taqlid* was Ayatollah Abu al-Qasim al-Khoei (d. 1992) of Najaf. Though he, like Khomeini, was a critic of the Shah, he rejected Khomeini's reading of 'the authority of the jurist', asserting that, in the period of the occultation, 'the *wilayah* of the jurists cannot be established by any proof'; that authority in the wide sense meant by Khomeini was exclusive to the Prophet and Imams; and that the jurists' authority was restricted to judging legal cases and issuing fatwas. His student, Ayatollah 'Ali Sistani, who is widely acknowledged as the leading *marja' al-taqlid* in the Shi'i world today, holds a similar view.[145] Within Iran, Ayatollah Hossein 'Ali Montazeri (d. 2009), a supporter of the revolution who was initially designated as Khomeini's successor, became the most prominent critic of Khomeini's assertion of the unrestricted authority of the leading jurist, arguing that 'Islam is for the separation of powers and does not recognize the concentration of power in the hand of a fallible human being'.[146]

When he described Islamic government as a government of law, Khomeini laid particular stress on the implementation of the *hudud*, the penalties fixed by God for certain crimes. Just as Muhammad 'implemented the penal provisions of Islam', cutting off the hand of the thief and administering lashings and stonings to the wine drinker and the fornicator, he says, so must the Prophet's successor, the guardian jurist.[147] Following the Islamic Revolution, the *hudud* were incorporated into Iranian criminal law, and the penalty for *zina*, sexual immorality, was set at death by stoning for married men and women and flogging for unmarried perpetrators.[148] The imposition of Islamic family and penal law had a disproportionate impact on the lives of Iranian women. Khomeini insisted that 'in the Islamic system, women do have the same rights as men', and, like al-Qaradawi, argued that women should have the right to vote and to run in parliamentary elections, as well as to study, work and own property. He was equally insistent, however, that it was obligatory for women to wear the hijab. Khomeini justified the necessity of veiling on the grounds of the essential biological differences between men and women, and condemned women who refused to wear it as 'corrupt manifestations of the monarchical regime and the West'.[149]

Questions pertaining to the rights and status of women were coming to the forefront of religious debate throughout the Islamic world in this period. In February 1979, the same month that the Islamic Revolution toppled the Shah of Iran, General Zia-ul-Haq, the president of Pakistan, promulgated the Hudood Ordinance, which enshrined into Pakistani law the penalties set down in the Qur'an and Sunnah for *zina*, false accusations of sexual immorality, theft and the consumption of alcohol. In Egypt and the wider Arab world, the 1980s saw the resurgence of the veil as a visible marker of female Muslim piety as part of the wider 'Islamic awakening' associated with the rise to prominence of figures such as Yusuf al-Qaradawi and Muhammad al-Ghazali and the growing strength of Islamist movements. In defining the relationship between the sexes, these Islamist groups adhered to the principle of *takamul* or gender 'complementarity' (a term that was also appearing in conservative Christian discourse at this time).[150] At the same time, a Muslim feminist movement was emerging which sought to develop specifically Islamic arguments for gender egalitarianism, principally through a critical rereading of the Islamic jurisprudential tradition or gender-focused exegesis of the Qur'an.

Following in the wake of their early twentieth-century predecessors, the principal strategy adopted by these Muslim feminists has been to make a distinction between Islam in its ideal form and Islam as it has been interpreted and practised by Muslims. While the true Islam of the Qur'an, they argue, echoing 'Abduh and Qasim Amin, is a religion of complete gender equality, the legal and theological traditions of Islam have been overlaid with man-made patriarchal ideas and institutions. In her pioneering 1975 book *Beyond the Veil*, the Moroccan sociologist Fatema Mernissi (d. 2015) asserts that, whereas the inequality of the sexes in the West is based on a belief in the essential biological inferiority of women, 'Islam does not advance the thesis of women's inherent inferiority'. On the contrary, Islam 'affirms the potential equality between the sexes' and recognizes women as inherently powerful.[151] The trouble, however, is that 'the Muslim social order' has been constructed to 'subjugate' women's power and to 'neutralize its disruptive effects'.[152] 'The entire Muslim social structure', she writes, singling out practices such as segregation, arranged marriage, the domineering role played by mothers in their sons' lives, divorce by repudiation and polygamy – 'can be seen as an attack on, and a defence against, the disruptive power of female sexuality'.[153] The Iranian legal anthropologist Ziba Mir-Hosseini has similarly written of how, attending the family courts in post-revolutionary Iran, she came to realize 'the gap between the ideals of Islam' and actual legal practices in countries claiming to implement the Shari'ah. 'If justice is an intrinsic value in Islam' and equality is 'an essential principle in contemporary conceptions of justice', she asks, 'why have women been treated as second-class citizens in the Islamic legal tradition?'[154] In forming her answer, she argues for a distinction between Shari'ah, meaning God's law, the essence of which is justice, and *fiqh*, the fallible – and often deeply unjust – human attempt to interpret that law.[155]

Perhaps the most impactful genre of Islamic feminist writing in recent decades has been Qur'anic exegesis, particularly the work that has been produced by Muslim women writing in English. Female exegetes such as Amina Wadud, an African–American convert to Islam engaged in what she describes as a 'gender jihad', and 'Azizah al-Hibri, a Lebanese-born law professor who is also based in the United States, have sought to get behind the patriarchal traditions of classical Qur'anic commentary and jurisprudence in order to rediscover what they see as the essentially egalitarian ethos of the Qur'anic message. In her ground-breaking 1992 work *Qur'an and Woman: Rereading the Sacred Text from a Woman's Perspective*, Amina Wadud attempts to show, through 'an analysis of the concept of woman drawn directly from the Qur'an', how 'it was not the text which restricted women, but the interpretations of that text which have come to be held in greater importance than the text itself'. 'If [the Qur'an] had been fully implemented in the practical sense,' she argues, invoking an argument of earlier modernists, 'then Islam would have been a global motivating force for women's empowerment.'[156]

As the scholar of feminist exegesis Aysha Hidayatullah has pointed out, these writers have principally relied on three interpretative strategies in their approach to the Qur'an.[157] First, they contextualize Qur'anic verses – for instance, pertaining to polygamy, giving testimony or the punishment of disobedient wives – which have traditionally been understood in patriarchal ways, limiting the application of these verses to the specific historical or social contexts in which they are believed to have been revealed.[158] 'Overall,' Wadud writes, 'my analysis tends to restrict the meaning of many passages to a particular subject, event, or context.'[159] For example, verses 2:228 ('men have a degree above [women]') and Qur'an 4:34 ('men are the maintainers [or 'in charge'] of women insofar as God has favoured some of them over others') have often been taken as statements of men's general superiority over women, but Wadud reads them as contextually specific statements that apply only to the context of divorce (in the case of verse 2:228) and inheritance (in the case of 4:34).[160] This strategy is inspired by the influential South Asian Muslim modernist Fazlur Rahman (d. 1988), who argued that 'the Qur'an is the divine response, through the Prophet's mind, to the moral–social situation of the Prophet's Arabia', which means that its interpreters should separate out the general principles underlying particular Qur'anic rules from the rules themselves, which are specific to the seventh-century Arabian context. He gives the example of polygamy, which the Prophet permitted as a concession to pre-Islamic Arabic practice while limiting the number of wives a man could take so as to lay out the 'moral ideal towards which the society was expected to move'.[161]

In keeping with this distinction between historically specific injunctions and universally valid moral principles, the second strategy employed by feminist exegetes is to read the sacred text holistically, interpreting problematic verses in the light of what they regard as the overarching egalitarian message of the Qur'an.[162] In the view of Wadud, the Qur'an lays out a 'trajectory' of 'justice towards humankind, human dignity, equal rights before the law and before Allah, mutual responsibility, and equitable relations between humans'.[163] In tracing this trajectory, feminist exegetes begin with the Qur'an's account of the creation of Adam and Eve – in which, unlike in Genesis and the Hadith, Eve is not created from Adam's rib – before turning their focus to those Qur'anic verses which stress the equal moral responsibility of men and women before God. In the Qur'an, Wadud argues, 'the individual is not distinguished on the basis of gender, but on the basis of faith and deeds'.[164] Accompanying this holistic approach to the Qur'an is an ambivalent attitude towards the Hadith, which (as the example of the creation of Eve shows), the feminist exegetes tend to regard as a repository of spurious patriarchal traditions that have been foisted on the egalitarian Qur'an.[165]

Finally, feminist exegetes employ what they call 'the *tawhidic* paradigm'. This paradigm, which Wadud describes as 'a basic theoretical principle for removing gender asymmetry', takes its name from the fundamental Islamic doctrine of *tawhid*, the affirmation of God's unity. For the feminist exegetes, affirming God's unity means acknowledging that God is superior to and in charge of His creation. To put some human beings above others, therefore, means to put them in the place of God. To say that men are superior to women and in charge of them, or that wives must be obedient or submit to their husbands, in other words, is a form of *shirk* or polytheism, which, in the words of the feminist exegete Asma Barlas, involves 'the symbolic extension of God's Sovereignty to others' and is therefore 'the gravest of all sins'. Patriarchal interpretations of the Qur'an are based on what both Wadud and 'Azizah al-Hibri refer to as a kind of 'Satanic logic', that is, an attitude of being, like Satan, too proud to submit to the one God. Feminist exegetes use these concepts to explain away problematic verses of the Qur'an, as well as to insist on a distinction between the meaning of the Qur'an itself and the interpretations of those who read it.[166]

Hard and fast distinctions between *tawhid* and *shirk*, the recognition and denial of God's sovereignty, and 'divine' and 'Satanic' logic are reminiscent of the kind of language used by Islamists. Amina Wadud in fact refers frequently to Sayyid Qutb's Qur'an commentary, and the feminists share with the Islamists a deeply critical attitude to much of the Islamic scholarly tradition and a desire to get behind that tradition and return directly to scripture. Yet the feminists clearly differ from the Islamists in their commitment to egalitarianism rather than complementarianism, their affirmation of progressive values and their strong scepticism of programmes for reviving and implementing the Shari'ah as a form of statutory law – the *raison d'être* of all Islamist movements.

This scepticism towards the Islamist project is shared by contemporary Muslims of various ideological persuasions. Alongside secular liberals such as Nasr Hamid Abu Zayd, both politically quietist Salafis and conservative adherents of the legal *madhhabs* and Sufi orders have been vocal critics of political Islam. Nasir al-Din al-Albani, the Salafi Hadith scholar whom we met at the end of the last chapter, accused Sayyid Qutb of professing the heretical Sufi doctrine of *wahdat al-wujud*, the unity of existence, and Hasan al-Banna of taking positions that were 'contrary to the Sunnah'.[167] His main criticism of the Muslim Brothers and other participants in the Islamic awakening was that, in focusing their attention on politics rather than religious knowledge, they had got things back to front. Though he acknowledged that 'all Muslims agree on the need to establish an Islamic state', such a state, al-Albani thought, could only be established once Muslims understood and practised their religion correctly, and that would only be achieved once it had been determined which Hadith reports were authentic and which were forgeries. The founding of a state, therefore, needed to be preceded by *al-tasfiyah wa-al-tarbiyah*, the purification of belief and actions, and education in Islamic doctrine on the basis of the Qur'an and the authentic Sunnah. In line with this view, al-Albani famously issued a fatwa calling on Muslim Palestinians living under Israeli occupation in the West Bank and Gaza to emigrate to Muslim-controlled territory, on the basis that they were no longer able to practice their religion properly – an opinion that demonstrates the distance separating quietist Salafis from activist Islamists such as Yusuf al-Qaradawi.[168]

Al-Albani has himself been subjected to harsh criticism not only from Islamists but also from conservative or 'neo-traditionalist' scholars, so called on account of their self-conscious commitment to the scholarly tradition of the legal *madhhabs*, the Ash'ari or Maturidi schools of theology and the mystical tradition of the Sufi brotherhoods. (They should not be confused with 'traditionalists', those who take their legal doctrine directly from Hadith reports.) Leading neo-traditionalists include the present rector of al-Azhar, Ahmed al-Tayyib, 'Ali Jum'a, the former chief mufti of Egypt, and the Mauritanian scholar 'Abd Allah bin Bayyah, a Maliki jurist who is currently the chief mufti of the United Arab Emirates – as well as prominent Western converts to Islam such as Hamza Yusuf, a student of Bin Bayyah and co-founder of Zaytuna College, a Muslim liberal arts college located in

Berkeley, California, and the British Muslim Timothy Winter (also known as Abdal Hakim Murad), who is a lecturer at the University of Cambridge's Faculty of Divinity and the founder of the Cambridge Muslim College.

In the view of Hamza Yusuf and his fellow American convert Nuh Ha Mim Keller, the problem with the Salafi approach is that there are few, if any, Muslims alive today who have sufficient mastery of Arabic and knowledge of the religious sciences to take their legal doctrine directly from the Qur'an and Sunnah without the mediation of the legal schools, which have developed, over many centuries, a finely tuned system for deriving legal rules from those sources. To blame the *madhhabs* for tribalism – as Salafis and many other reformers do – Hamza Yusuf says, is like blaming all wars on religion – for tribalism, like war, is a sadly inevitable feature of human nature. Those who follow al-Albani's views on Hadith, he further argues, are following al-Albani rather than the Prophet, and it would be better for them to follow the interpretations of the *madhhabs*, which represent a long and living tradition, rather than a single self-taught scholar like al-Albani.[169] Timothy Winter sees anti-madhhabism as an unfortunate legacy of the reformism of 'Abduh and Rida, who, 'dazzled by the West ... urged Muslims to throw off the shackles of *taqlid*, and to reject the authority of the Four Schools', with the result that the 'unity, credibility, and effectiveness of the Islamic movement' were damaged, as 'issues settled by the great Imams [meaning the founders of the legal schools] over a thousand years ago' were reopened and made the subject of often violent debate.[170] In Winter's view, there are simply too many Hadith reports for a Muslim fundamentalism to make sense, meaning that 'you cannot have a fundamentalism in Islam'.[171]

The neo-traditionalist critique of Islamism has been similarly sharp. Timothy Winter criticizes those who claim that the purpose of Islam is to establish the Shari'ah on the grounds that 'no jurist of the past ever said this'. The purpose of Islam, he says, is to achieve salvation. Invoking the Deobandi scholar Husayn Ahmad Madani (d. 1957), who dismissed Mawdudi as a journalist who ought not to be issuing legal opinions, Winter observes that the Shari'ah has never been understood as a form of statutory law. Though Islam as a religion is socially conservative, it was never imposed on the population by the central state on the 'caeseropapist model' (a term used by the sociologist Max Weber to denote the situation where the secular ruler enjoys supreme authority over religious matters).[172] Indeed, he argues, citing the literary historian Thomas Bauer's thesis that premodern Islamic culture was 'a culture of ambiguity', classical Islam was inherently pluralistic, undermining the Islamist attempt to impose a reading of the Shari'ah that brooks no argument.[173] The neo-traditionalists also take issue with the victimization narrative – or what Winter calls 'the atmosphere of grievance and complaint' – that pervades contemporary Islamist discourse. Hamza Yusuf criticizes this narrative on theological grounds. Drawing on the classical Sufi view of this world as 'the abode of injustice and a place of tribulation from Allah', he argues that 'all suffering has a redemptive value'; hence the ulema 'traditionally were opposed to revolution'.[174] In keeping with this traditional attitude of the religious scholars, neo-traditionalists have tended to align themselves with incumbent regimes in the Middle East, adopting a critical stance towards the Arab revolutions of 2011 and supporting the violent suppression of Islamist movements.[175] 'Exalting the leaders is the basis for society,' Hamza Yusuf once declared on Emirati television. 'We do not accept any rebellion against our leaders or our public affairs even if they are oppressive.'[176]

Heavily invested in Sufi piety and metaphysics as well as the jurisprudential tradition of the schools of law, the neo-traditionalists lament what Max Weber described as the 'disenchantment' of the modern world.[177] They lay the blame for this process at the door of the Protestant Reformation in Christian Europe and the rise of Wahhabism and similarly puritanical movements in the Muslim world.[178] To those who say that Islam needs its own Reformation, Yusuf says that what is in fact needed is 'restoration' – meaning the restoration of the Islamic tradition of scholarship and spirituality. Such a restoration, the neo-traditionalists argue, would be true *tajdid*.[179] 'It is our contention,' Yusuf writes in the first issue of the journal of Zaytuna College, which is pointedly named *Renovatio*, 'that, in essence, the foundations of the Abode of Islam are sound, but the house that harbors this civilization has fallen into deep dereliction. It is in need of renovation, not reformation.'[180]

The positions taken by the neo-traditionalists remind us that, as Frank Griffel has pointed out, it is erroneous to assume that 'all modern Muslims are either Aligarh-style modernists or outright fundamentalists'.[181] At the same time, the scholar of Islamic law and gender Kecia Ali rightly observes that 'modern Islam is a profoundly Protestant tradition', in the sense that 'believers read scriptural texts in isolation from their commentarial traditions and often without expert guidance'.[182] The neo-traditionalists Bin Bayyah and Hamza Yusuf speak in this regard of the 'crisis of the fatwa', where 'charlatan muftis' issue erroneous opinions in the name of Islam.[183] However their conclusions are judged, the turn to the original sources has undoubtedly created space for modern Muslims – whether they are liberal-progressives, Islamists or Salafists – to think in fresh ways about fundamental questions such as the status of women in Islam, the relationship between religion and politics and the correct method of serving God and observing His law.

As this and the previous two chapters have highlighted, this process was catalyzed by the encounter with Western modernity, which induced many Muslim thinkers to locate the apparent decline of Muslim societies in what they saw as the failure of Muslims to practise true Islam. It has been accelerated in previously unimaginable ways by the internet, which not only allows anyone to set themselves up as an authority on Islamic theology or law, but also gives ordinary Muslims access to the Qur'an and Hadith – as well as to countless modern and premodern texts and the fatwas, sermons and interviews of a 'global mufti' like Yusuf al-Qaradawi – at the press of a button. Yet it would be a mistake to assume that the renewal of Islam on 'Protestant' lines originated in the encounter with the modern West. In fact, the movements which have defined modern Islam are in many ways the heirs of the reformist movements of the eighteenth and early nineteenth centuries, which themselves drew deeply from the well of the classical Islamic heritage. The Islamists' defence of God's sovereignty, the feminists' case for gender equality and the neo-traditionalists' plea for the Islam of the *madhhabs* are all part of a longer struggle to define true Islam and explain how it can be renewed.

One Ramadan night in 1930, Rashid Rida gave a lecture at the Egyptian Geographical Society at the invitation of the Society of the Oriental League. The objectives of the Oriental League, the pioneering historian of nationalism Hans Kohn relates, were 'to spread scientific knowledge as the basis of all social progress; to strengthen the ties of solidarity and brotherhood between the peoples of the East without distinction of race or religion: to revive Oriental culture by fostering what is characteristic of it at its best, while at the same time adopting everything in European culture which may serve the cause of this revival and be compatible with the spirit of the Orient'.[184] Rida's lecture, which he later published in *The Lighthouse*, was titled 'Renewal, Renewing, and Renewers'.[185]

At a time, Rida said, when Egypt and the wider Muslim world were afflicted by 'ideological, intellectual, political, Communist, and Bolshevik upheavals' and 'religious, literary, and social chaos', there was a 'dire need for renewal and renewers'. What was needed, however, was genuine religious renewal, of the kind embodied by Jamal al-Din al-Afghani and Muhammad 'Abduh, not the 'imitative renewal' of secular liberals like Ataturk who unthinkingly emulated the 'heretics of Europe'. Invoking the *mujaddid* Hadith, Rida explained that the Prophet's words urged Muslims to 'return to the simplicity and guidance of religion as it was in the beginning', to unite around what they shared in common, and to practise *ijtihad*, if they were able, or else to engage in *taqlid* while avoiding the 'divisive extremism' of *madhhab*-partisanship.

Renewal, Rida proposed, was a general law of existence – one of the 'universal divine customs' through which God gave order to His creation. Through renewal, a balance was struck between the old and the new, each of which had their place in the life of man. 'Humans at all times,' he said, 'need both the old and the new. In each there is good and ill, benefit and harm.' It is in the quest for balance between the new and the old – between the duty to be faithful to the Sunnah of the Prophet and the requirement to adapt to the needs of the age – that modern Islam has been made. Yet Rida also quotes the famous words of Ecclesiastes: 'There is nothing new under the sun.' For the proponents of Islamic renewal, what was good and true in the new was identical to what was good and true in the old. As they saw it, to make Islam modern meant nothing more than to recover Islam as it had originally been.

Acknowledgements

The initial research for this book was carried out at All Souls College, Oxford. I remain forever grateful to the Warden, Fellows and Staff of the college for six wonderful years that taught me the true meaning of 'fellowship'. Most of the book was written between Pembroke College, Oxford, and the Faculty of Asian and Middle Eastern Studies. The Master and Fellows of Pembroke, and my colleagues both at Pembroke and at AMES, have likewise been tremendously supportive, while also teaching me many things, sharing helpful ideas (often without realizing they were doing so) and encouraging me by their example. Ron Nettler, in particular, remains a constant source of guidance and stimulating conversation. I am grateful, too, to the staff of the Bodleian Libraries, especially the Nizami Ganjavi Library, for their help in locating a number of hard-to-come-by books and journals, and for providing an ideal environment for conducting research.

That I have been able to turn this research into a book is down to Georgina Capel, whose enthusiasm for serious yet accessible books on intellectual history has been a great source of encouragement, and to Neil Belton at Head of Zeus and Timothy Bent at Oxford University Press, whom I've been very fortunate to have as my editors. Sincere thanks, as well, are due to Emily Wood and Egle Zigaite, for their hard work

ACKNOWLEDGEMENTS

in bringing the book into the world, and to Kate Wands for her help with publicizing it.

In writing the book, as in everything that I do, I have leaned heavily on my family. I particularly thank my parents, for always encouraging me to pursue my academic interests, my late parents-in-law, Marilena and Johannes, both of whom I miss greatly, my siblings, for being a tremendous source of fun and interesting conversation, my wife Dyedra, not only for her loving support, generosity with her time and energy and belief in my work, but also for managing to be even more passionate about theology than I am, and our son Monty, for bringing so much joy into our home.

As the discerning reader may have sensed, in thinking about the issues confronting modern Islamic thinkers, I have often been guided by questions and challenges arising from my personal attempt to live out my own Christian faith in the modern world. Though I do not share the religious commitments of these thinkers, I have tried to give as fair and objective an account of their thought as possible. In this endeavour, I have taken inspiration from the following words of an earlier, pioneering Christian scholar of Islam: 'Islamicate culture,' wrote Marshall Hodgson, 'is supremely important because it represents the highest creative aspirations and achievements of millions of people. Whoever we are, the hopes, the triumphs, and the failures too of any human being are properly of concern to us; in the moral economy of mankind they are also our own hopes and failures. In studying and sharing in them we know ourselves better, understand better who we truly have been and are, we human beings.'[1]

Notes

Preface: Reform, Resistance and Renewal

1. Bernard Lewis, 'Introduction', in Ignaz Goldziher, *Introduction to Islamic Theology and Law*, tr. Andras and Ruth Hamori (Princeton, NJ: Princeton University Press, 1981), vii.
2. D. B. Macdonald to Ignaz Goldziher, 17.7.07, http://real-ms.mtak.hu/8644/1/000756944.pdf, last accessed 11 February 2025.
3. Josef van Ess, 'Goldziher as a Contemporary of Islamic Reform', in *idem.*, *Kleinere Schriften: Volume 1*, ed. Hinrich Biesterfeldt (Leiden: Brill, 2018), 497–511: 508–510; Joseph H. Escovitz, '"He was the Muḥammad 'Abduh of Syria": A Study of Ṭāhir al-Jazā'iri and His Influence', *International Journal of Middle East Studies* 18/3 (1986), 293–310.
4. Ahmed El Shamsy, *Rediscovering the Islamic Classics: How Editors and Print Culture Transformed an Intellectual Tradition* (Princeton, NJ: Princeton University Press, 2020), 160.
5. van Ess, 'Goldziher as a Contemporary', 501.
6. Goldziher, *Introduction*, 231–42.
7. J. O. Hunwick (ed.) and Michael Barry (tr.), 'Ignaz Goldziher on al-Suyūṭī', *The Muslim World* 68/2 (1972), 79–99.
8. cf. Wael Hallaq, 'Was the Gate of *Ijtihād* Closed?', *International Journal of Middle East Studies* 16 (1984), 3–41: 27.
9. Ella Landau-Tasseron, 'The "Cyclical Reform": A Study of the *Mujaddid* Tradition', *Studia Islamica* 70 (1989), 79–117.
10. *Encyclopaedia of Islam*, 2nd edition, 'al-Suyūṭī' (E. Geoffroy).
11. Hunwick and Barry, 'Ignaz

Goldziher on al-Suyūṭī', 96; Landau-Tasseron, 'The "Cyclical Reform"', 83, 87.
12 Goldziher, Introduction, 244.

1: Dreaming of Renewal

1 Barbara von Schlegell, 'Sufism in the Ottoman Arab World: Shaykh 'Abd al-Ghanī al-Nābulusī (d. 1143/1731)' (PhD thesis, University of California, Berkeley, 1997), 62; Elizabeth Sirriyeh, *Sufi Visionary of Ottoman Damascus: 'Abd al-Ghanī al-Nābulusī, 1641–1731* (London: Routledge, 2005), 63.
2 Sirriyeh, *Sufi Visionary*, 67; Elizabeth Sirriyeh, *Dreams & Visions in the World of Islam: A History of Muslim Dreaming and Foreknowing* (London: I.B. Tauris, 2015), 97.
3 Al-Nabulusi, *Ta'tir al-anam fi ta'bir al-manam*, in two vols. (Cairo: al-Matba'ah al-Azhariyyah, 1301 AH [= 1883/4]), 2:212.
4 von Schlegell, *Sufism*, 62.
5 Al-Nabulusi, *Takmil al-nu'ut fi luzum al-buyut*, ed. Majdi ibn Mansur ibn Sayyid al-Shura (Cairo: Mu'assasat al-Ahram li-l-nashr wa-al-tawzi', 1998), 25.
6 Samer Akkach, *'Abd al-Ghani al-Nabulusi: Islam and the Enlightenment* (Oxford: Oneworld, 2007), 55–8; von Schlegell, *Sufism*, 66–9.
7 Al-Nabulusi, *al-Sulh bayn al-ikhwan fi hukm 'ala ibahat al-dukhan* (British Library MS 19547), fols. 10a-b, 14a, https://www.qdl.qa/العربية/archive/81055/vdc_100000000041.0x0001c1, last accessed 13 July 2022; al-Nabulusi, *Kashf al-sirr al-ghamid fi sharh Diwan Ibn al-Farid*, ed. Khalid al-Zar'i (Damascus: Dar Ninawa, 2017), 161, 164.
8 Al-Nabulusi, *Idah al-dalalat fi sam' al-alat* (MS Ḥājī Maḥmūd 3213), fol. 5a, https://www.quranicthought.com/books/إيضاح-الدلالات-في-سماع-الآلات-للشيخ-عب/, last accessed 21 February 2024.
9 Al-Nabulusi, *Idah al-dalalat*, fol. 3b; al-Nabulusi, *al-Sulh bayn al-ikhwan*, fols. 3a–b.
10 Madeline C. Zilfi, 'The Kadizadelis: Discordant Revivalism in Seventeenth-Century Istanbul', *Journal of Near Eastern Studies* 45/4 (1986), 251–69.
11 Mustapha Shaykh, *Ottoman Puritanism and its Discontents: Ahmad al-Rumi al-Aqhisari and the Qadizadelis* (Oxford:

12 Khaled El-Rouayheb, *Islamic Intellectual History in the Seventeenth Century: Scholarly Currents in the Ottoman Empire and the Maghreb* (Cambridge: Cambridge University Press, 14–15; Shaykh, *Ottoman Puritanism*, 43–7.
13 Shaykh, *Ottoman Puritanism*, 50.
14 Ahmad ibn ʿAbd al-Qadir Rumi, *Majalis al-abrar wa-masalik al-akhyar wa-mahaʾiq al-bidaʿ wa-maqamiʿ al-ashrar* (Ann Arbor University of Michigan Isl. Ms. 481), fol. 263b, https://babel.hathitrust.org/cgipt?id=mdp.39015079127935&seq=1, last accessed 23 February 2024.
15 Katharina A. Ivanyi, *Virtue, Piety and the Law: A Study of Birgivī Meḥmed Efendī's al-Ṭarīqah al-Muḥammadīyah* (Leiden: Brill, 2020), 3.
16 *Ibid.*, 72.
17 See *ibid.*, 119–20.
18 *Ibid.*, 160–99.
19 Hallaq, 'Was the Gate of Ijtihad Closed?', 17.
20 Ivanyi, *Virtue, Piety and the Law*, 97, 207.
21 Jon E. Mandaville, 'Usurious Piety: The Cash Waqf Controversy in the Ottoman Empire', *International Journal of Middle East Studies* 10/3 (1979), 289–308: 289.
22 Ivanyi, *Virtue, Piety and the Law*, 304–6.
23 *Ibid.*, 153.
24 Shaykh, *Ottoman Puritanism*, 3.
25 Ahmad ibn ʿAbd al-Qadir Rumī, *Against Smoking: An Ottoman Manifesto*, tr. Yahya Michot (Markfield: Kube Publishing, 2010), 12.
26 Bernard Lewis, *Istanbul and the Civilization of the Ottoman Empire* (Norman, OK: University of Oklahoma Press, 1963), 132–3.
27 *Ibid.*, 134.
28 *Ibid.*, 135; Zilfi, 'The Kadizadelis', 257.
29 Umar Shareef, '*Taqyīd al-Mubāḥ* and Tobacco: Between Administrative and Legislative Authority', *Islamic Law and Society* 30/3 (2023), 1–30.
30 Katib Çelebi, *The Balance of Truth*, tr. Geoffrey Lewis (London: George Allen and Unwin Ltd, 1957), 52.
31 *Ibid.*, 61.
32 Von Schlegell, *Sufism*, 84.
33 Jonathan Parkes Allen, 'Reading Mehmed Birgivi with ʿAbd al-Ghanī al-Nābulusī', in Lejla Demiri and Samuela Pagani (eds), *Early Modern Trends in Islamic Theology: ʿAbd*

al-Ghanī al-Nābulusī and His Network of Scholarship (Tübingen: Mohr Siebeck, 2019), 153–70: 157.
34 Al-Nabulusi, *al-Sulh bayn al-ikhwan*, fols. 6b, 8a; al-Nabulusi, *Kashf al-sirr al-ghamid*, 160; Astrid Meier, 'Words in Action: 'Abd al-Ghanī al-Nābulusī as a Jurist', in Demiri and Pagani, *Early Modern Trends*, 107–36: 126–7.
35 Al-Bukhari, *Sahih al-Bukhari* (Damascus; Beirut: Dār Ibn Kathīr, 1423/2002), *kitab bad' al-wahy, bab kayf kana bad' al-wahy ila rasul Allāh*, 7, no. 1; *Encyclopaedia of Islam*, 2nd edition, 'al-Bukhārī, Muḥammad b. Ismāʿīl' (J. Robson).
36 Al-Nabulusi, *Idah al-dalalat*, fol. 14a.
37 Ibid., fol. 16b.
38 Al-Nabulusi, *al-Sulh bayn al-ikhwan*, fols. 105a–106b; Bakri Aladdin, "Abd al-Ghanī al-Nābulusī, the Doctrine of the Unity of Being and the Beginnings of the Arab Renaissance', in Demiri and Pagani, *Early Modern Trends*, 31–48: 47; Meier, 'Words in Action,' 127.
39 Al-Nabulusi, *Idah al-dalalat*, fol. 18a.
40 Ibid., fol. 52a.
41 Steve Tamari, 'Confounding Dichotomies: Elite and Popular, Spiritual and Secular, Pious and Joyous in the Travel Writings of 'Abd al-Ghanī al-Nābulusī', in Demiri and Pagani, *Early Modern Trends*, 225–36: 228.
42 von Schlegell, *Sufism*, 46, 49–50.
43 Denis Gril, '*Jawāhir al-nuṣūṣ fī ḥall kalimāt al-Fuṣūṣ*: 'Abd al-Ghanī al-Nābulusī's Commentary on Ibn ʿArabī's *Fuṣūṣ al-ḥikam*', in Demiri and Pagani, *Early Modern Trends*, 49–57: 50.
44 Jawad Anwar Qureshi, 'Some of 'Abd al-Ghanī al-Nābulusī's Kalām Writings', in Demiri and Pagani, *Early Modern Trends*, 59–72: 63; Steven Styer, 'The Relationship between Kalām and Akbarian Theology in the Thought of 'Abd al-Ghanī al-Nābulusī', in Demiri and Pagani, *Early Modern Trends*, 73–95: 79–80.
45 Styer, 'The Relationship', 85–6.
46 El-Rouayheb, *Islamic Intellectual History*, 131–72.
47 Ibid., 191.
48 Akkach, *'Abd al-Ghanī al-Nābulusī*, 107–8; Samer Akkach, *Intimate Invocations: al-Ghazzī's Biography of 'Abd al-Ghanī al-Nābulusī*

(Leiden: Brill, 2012), 86–7; Lejla Demiri and Samuela Pagani, "Abd al-Ghanī al-Nābulusī and the Intellectual and Religious History of the 17th–18th-Century World of Islam', in Demiri and Pagani, *Early Modern Trends*, 1–27: 11; Abdul-Karim Rafeq, "Abd al-Ghani al-Nablusi: Religious Tolerance and Arabness in Ottoman Damascus', in Camille Mansour and Leila Fawaz (eds), *Transformed Landscapes: Essays on Palestine and the Middle East in Honor of Walid Khalidi* (Cairo: American University of Cairo Press, 2009), 1–18.

49 Michael Winter, 'A Polemical Treatise by ʿAbd al-Ghanī al-Nābulusī against a Turkish Scholar', *Arabica* 35 (1988), 92–103: 98.

50 *Ibid.*, 99.

51 Lejla Demiri, "Abd al-Ghanī al-Nābulusī', *Christian-Muslim Relations 1500–1900*, https://referenceworks.brillonline.com/entries/christian-muslim-relations-ii/abd-al-ghani-l-nabulusi-COM_28512, last accessed 26 February 2024.

52 *Ibid.*; Sirriyeh, *Sufi Visionary*, 131.

53 Sirriyeh, *Sufi Visionary*, 18.

54 El-Rouayheb, *Islamic Intellectual History*, 332–44; Aladdin, "Abd al-Ghanī al-Nābulusī'; Alexander Knysh, *Ibn al-ʿArabi in the Later Islamic Tradition: The Making of a Polemical Image in Medieval Islam* (Albany, NY: State University of New York Press, 1998); William C. Chittick, 'Rūmī and *waḥdat al-wujūd*', in Amin Banani, Richard G. Hovannisian, and George Sabagh (eds), *Poetry and Mysticism in Islam: The Heritage of Rūmī* (Cambridge: Cambridge University Press, 1994), 70–111.

55 Fitzroy Morrissey, *Sufism and the Scriptures: Metaphysics and Sacred History in the Thought of ʿAbd al-Karīm al-Jīlī* (London: I. B. Tauris, 2021), 26–7.

56 Quoted in Jan Assmann, *From Akhenaten to Moses: Ancient Egypt and Religious Change* (Cairo: American University in Cairo Press, 2014), 13.

57 Demiri, "Abd al-Ghanī al-Nābulusī'.

58 Samer Dajani, *Sufis and Sharīʿa: The Forgotten School of Mercy* (Edinburgh: Edinburgh University Press, 2022).

59 Styer, 'The Relationship'.

60 El-Rouayheb, *Islamic Intellectual History*, 291.
61 See Jon Hoover, *Ibn Taymiyya* (London: Oneworld, 2019), 32, 108–10; Wael B. Hallaq (tr.), *Ibn Taymiyya against the Greek Logicians* (Oxford: Clarendon, 1993).
62 El-Rouayheb, *Islamic Intellectual History*, 272–90, 320–32; Khaled El-Rouyaheb, 'From Ibn Hajar al-Haytami (d. 1566) to Khayr al-Din al-Alusi (d. 1899): Changing Views of Ibn Taymiyya amongst Sunni Islamic Scholars', in Shahab Ahmed and Yossef Rapoport (eds), *Ibn Taymiyya & His Times* (Karachi: Oxford University Press, 2010), 269–318.
63 Atallah S. Copty, 'The Legacy of Ibrāhīm al-Kūrānī and its Influence on the Writings of ʿAbd al-Ghanī al-Nābulusī', in Demiri and Pagani, *Early Modern Trends*, 97–106; Edward Badeen, *Sunnitische Theologie in Osmanischer Zeit* (Würzburg: Ergon, 2008), 57–61.
64 Michel Chodkiewicz, *Seal of Saints: Prophethood and Sainthood in the Doctrine of Ibn ʿArabī*, tr. Liadain Sherrard (Cambridge: Islamic Texts Society, 1999), 128–46.
65 *Ibid.*, 136; von Schlegell, *Sufism*, 56.
66 Shahab Ahmed, *What is Islam? The Importance of Being Islamic* (Princeton, NJ: Princeton University Press, 2015), 167–8.
67 Akkach, *ʿAbd al-Ghani al-Nabulusi*; Aladdin, 'ʿAbd al-Ghanī al-Nābulusī'.

2: Harmonizing the Tradition

1 Shah Wali Allah, *Hujjat Allah al-balighah*, ed. al-Sayyid Sabiq in two vols. (Cairo: Dar al-Kutub al-Hadithah, 1964), 1:23; Shāh Walī Allāh, *The Conclusive Argument from God*, tr. Marcia K. Hermansen (Leiden: Brill, 1996), 7.
2 *Ibid.*; Shah Wali Allah, *Fuyud al-haramayn maʿa Urdu tarjamah saʿadat-i kawnayn* (Delhi: al-Matbaʿ al-Ahmadi, 1307/1889/90), 31–2.
3 Mawlawi M. Hidayat Hasan, 'The Persian Autobiography of Shāh Walīullah bin ʿAbd al-Raḥīm al-Dihlavī: its English translation and a list of his works', *Journal and Proceedings of the Royal Asiatic Society of Bengal* 8 (1912), 162–75: 166.
4 Frances Robinson, *The*

'Ulama of Farangi Mahall and Islamic Culture in South Asia* (London: Hurst, 2001), 2, 15.
5. Hasan, 'The Persian Autobiography', 163.
6. Yohanan Friedmann, *Shaykh Aḥmad Sirhindī: An Outline of His Thought and a Study of His Image in the Eyes of Posterity* (Montreal: McGill University Institute of Islamic Studies, 1971), 15–17, 33–4.
7. Waleed Ziad, *Hidden Caliphate: Sufi Saints beyond the Oxus and Indus* (Cambridge, MA: Harvard University Press, 2021), 61–2; Arthur F. Bueler, *Revealed Grace: The Juristic Sufism of Ahmad Sirhindi (1564–1624)* (Louisville, KY: Fons Vitae, 2011).
8. Hasan, 'The Persian Autobiography', 164–5.
9. Ibid., 166.
10. Shah Wali Allah, *al-Tafhimat al-ilahiyyah* in two vols. (Barqa, 1936), 1:81ff.
11. Shah Wali Allah, *Hujjat Allah al-balighah*, 1:25.
12. Shāh Walī Allāh, *The Conclusive Argument from God*, xxix–xxxiii; Marcia Hermansen (tr.), *Shāh Walī Allāh's Treatises on Juristic Disagreement and Taqlīd: al-Inṣāf fī Bayān Sabab al-Ikhtilāf and ʿIqd al-Jīd fī Aḥkām al-Ijtihād wa-l-Taqlīd* (Louisville, KT: Fons Vitae, 2010); Jonathan A. C. Brown, *Misquoting Muhammad: The Challenge and Choices of Interpreting the Prophet's Legacy* (London: Oneworld, 2014), chapter 2; R. Stephen Humphreys, *Islamic History: A Framework for Inquiry* (Princeton, NJ: Princeton University Press, 1991), 212.
13. Henri Laoust, *Essai sur les doctrines sociales et politiques de Taḳī-d-Dīn Aḥmad b. Taimīya* (Cairo: Impr. de l'Institut français d'archéologie orientale, 1939), 229–30.
14. Daud Rahbar, 'Shah Waliullah and Ijtihad: A Translation of Selected Passages from His *ʿIqd al-Jid fi Ahkam al-Ijtihad*', *The Muslim World* 45/4 (1955), 346–58; Ahmad S. Dallal, *Islam Without Europe: Traditions of Reform in Eighteenth-Century Islamic Thought* (Chapel Hill, NC: The University of North Carolina Press, 2018), 71–2, 80–1, 195–6; Muhammad Qasim Zaman, 'Shāh Walī Allāh of Delhi, His Successors, and the Qur'ān', in Bettina Gräf, Birgit Krawietz, and Schirin Amir-Moazami (eds),

Ways of Knowing Muslim Cultures and Societies: Studies in Honour of Gudrun Krämer (Leiden: Brill, 2018), 280–97: 285.
15 Shah Waliyullah, *al-Fauz al-kabir fi usul al-tafsir*, tr. G. N. Jalbani (Islamabad: National Hijra Council, 1985), 2; G. N. Jalbani, *Teachings of Shāh Walīyullāh of Delhi* (Lahore: Sh. Muhammad Ashraf, 1967), 22.
16 J. M. S. Baljon, *Religion and Thought of Shah Wali Allah Dihlawi, 1703–1762* (Leiden: E. J. Brill, 1986), 73; Shah Waliyullah, *al-Fauz al-kabir*, 75.
17 Baljon, *Religion and Thought*, 72; Jalbani, *Teachings*, 8.
18 Shah Waliyullah, *al-Fauz al-kabir*, 2 (adapted); Baljon, *Religion and Thought*, 72.
19 Simon Leese, 'Arabic Utterances in a Multilingual World: Shāh Walī-Allāh and Qur'anic Translatability in North India', *Translation Studies* 14, no. 2 (2021), 242–61.
20 Travis Zadeh, *The Vernacular Qur'an: Translation and the Rise of Persian Exegesis* (London: Oxford University Press in association with the Institute of Ismaili Studies, 2012), 17.
21 Ibid., 53–91.
22 Al-Wansharisi, *al-Miʿyar al-muʿrib wa-al-jamiʿ al-mughrib ʿan fatawa ʿulamaʾ Ifriqiyah wa-al-Andalus wa-al-Maghrib*, ed. Muḥammad Ḥajjī in two vols. (Rabat: Wizarat al-Awqaf wa-al-Shuʾun al-Islamiyyah li-l-Mamlakat al-Maghribiyyah, 1981), 1:186.
23 SherAli Tareen, 'South Asian Qur'an Commentaries and Translations: A Preliminary Intellectual History', *ReOrient* 5/2 (2020), 233–56: 239.
24 Zadeh, *The Vernacular Qur'an*, 20.
25 See Tareen, 'South Asian Qur'an Commentaries', 234.
26 Baljon, *Religion and Thought*, 77; Muhammad Qasim Zaman, 'Shāh Walī Allāh of Delhi', 282.
27 Zaman, 'Shāh Walī Allāh of Delhi', 282.
28 Ibid., 283–4.
29 Shah Wali Allah, *Hujjat Allah al-balighah*, 1:21.
30 Ibid., 1:230.
31 Ibid., 1:231.
32 Yasin Dutton, *The Origins of Islamic Law: The Qurʾan, the Muwaṭṭaʾ and Madinan ʿAmal* (Richmond: Curzon, 1999), 16–17.
33 Shah Wali Allah, *Hujjat Allah al-balighah*, 1:231.

34 *Ibid.*
35 *Ibid.*, 1:22–3.
36 *Ibid.*, 1:26–8.
37 *Encyclopaedia of Islam*, 2nd edition, 'Maḳāṣid al-Sharīʿa' (R. Gleave).
38 Bernard Weiss, *The Search for God's Law: Islamic Jurisprudence in the Writings of Sayf al-Dīn al-Āmidī* (Salt Lake City, UT: University of Utah Press, 1992), 593–632.
39 Wael Hallaq, *A History of Islamic Legal Theories: An Introduction to Sunnī uṣūl al-fiqh* (Cambridge: Cambridge University Press, 1997), 89.
40 Mawardi, *Maverdii Constitutiones politicae*, ed. Maximilian Enger (Bonn: A. Marcum, 1853), 3.
41 Christopher Melchert, 'Māwardī's Legal Thinking', *al-ʿUsur al-wusta* 23 (2015), 68–86: 73.
42 Felicitas Opwis, *Maṣlaḥa and the Purpose of the Law: Islamic Discourse on Legal Change from the 4th/10th to 8th/14th century* (Leiden: Brill, 2010), 65–87; *Encyclopaedia of Islam*, 2nd edition, 'Istiḥsān and Istiṣlāḥ' (R. Paret) and 'Maṣlaḥa' (M. Khaddouri).
43 Al-Zabidi, *Ithaf sadat al-muttaqin bi-sharh Ihyaʾ ʿulum al-din*, in ten vols. (Miṣr: al-Maṭbaʿah al-Maymaniyyah, 1311/1893/4), 4:194.
44 Ibn ʿArabi, *al-Futuhat al-Makkiyyah*, in four vols. (Egypt: Dar al-kutub al-ʿarabiyyah al-kubra, 1910), 1:604. See also *ibid.*, 2:187; Atif Khalil, 'White Death: Ibn al-ʿArabī on the Trials and Virtues of Hunger and Fasting', *Journal of the American Oriental Society* 141, no. 3 (2021), 577–86: 580; Dajani, *Sufis and Shariʿa*, esp. 100–28.
45 Shah Wali Allah, *Hujjat Allah al-balighah*, 1:54–5; Franz Rosenthal, *The Classical Heritage in Islam* (London: Routledge, 1992), 94, 96.
46 Shah Wali Allah, *Hujjat Allah al-balighah*, 1:102
47 *Ibid.*, 1:61.
48 *Ibid.*, 1:64; 112.
49 Baljon, *Religion and Thought*, 106.
50 Shah Wali Allah, *Hujjat Allah al-balighah*, 1:93.
51 'Reagan cites Islamic Scholar', *The New York Times*, 2 October 1981, 26, https://www.nytimes.com/1981/10/02/us/reagan-cites-islamic-scholar.html, last accessed 15 March 2024.
52 Shah Wali Allah, *Hujjat Allah al-balighah*, 1:83–4.
53 *Ibid.*, 1:86.
54 *Ibid.*, 1:86–90.

55 Ibid., 1:84.
56 Muhsin Mahdi, *Alfarabi and the Foundation of Islamic Political Philosophy* (Chicago, IL: University of Chicago Press, 2001).
57 Shah Wali Allah, *Hujjat Allah al-balighah*, 1:92.
58 Ibid., 1:94–5.
59 Ibid., 1:85, 97–8.
60 Ibid., 1:65.
61 Ibid., 1:156.
62 Patricia Crone and Martin Hinds, *God's Caliph: Religious Authority in the First Centuries of Islam* (Cambridge: Cambridge University Press, 1986).
63 Ziad, *Hidden Caliphate*, 11–2.
64 Shah Wali Allah, *Hujjat Allah al-balighah*, 1:97.
65 Ibid., 1:179.
66 Ibid., 1:149, 160.
67 Ibid., 1:122.
68 See ibid., 1:142, 223.
69 Ibid., 1:206–7.
70 Ibid., 1:177.
71 Ibid., 1:141.
72 Ibid., 1:219–21.
73 Ibid., 1:21, 80; *Encyclopaedia of Islam* THREE, 'Fiṭra' (Jon Hoover).
74 Shah Wali Allah, *Hujjat Allah al-balighah*, 1:214–15, 217–23.
75 Ibid., 1:207–8.

3: Returning to Fundamentals

1 Al-Shawkani, *al-Badr al-taliʿ bi-mahasin man baʿd al-qarn al-sabiʿ*, in two vols (Cairo: Dar al-kutub al-islami, n.d.), 2:138.
2 Ibid.
3 Bernard Haykel, *Revival and Reform in Islam: The Legacy of Muhammad al-Shawkānī* (Cambridge: Cambridge University Press, 2003), 82.
4 Etan Kohlberg, 'The Term *Muḥaddath* in Twelver Shīʿism', in *Studia Orientalia Memoriae D.H. Baneth Dedicata* (Jerusalem: Magnes Press, 1979), 34–47.
5 Haykel, *Revival and Reform*, 6–7; Najam Haider, 'Zaydism: A Theological and Political Survey', *Religion Compass* 4/7 (2010), 436–42: 438–40.
6 Haider, 'Zaydism', 437; Haykel, *Revival and Reform*, 6, 26–7.
7 Haykel, *Revival and Reform*, 16–17.
8 Ibid., 36–48.
9 Al-Shawkani, 'Al-Qawl al-mufid fi adillat al-ijtihad wa-al-taqlid', in Muhammad ibn ʿAli al-Shawkani, *al-Rasaʾil al-salafiyyah fi ihyaʾ sunnat khayr al-bariyyah* (Beirut: Dar al-Kitab al-ʿarabi, 1994), 192.
10 Haykel, *Revival and Reform*, 10–11.

11 Hallaq, 'Was the Gate of *Ijtihād* Closed?'; Wael Hallaq, 'From Fatwās to Furūʿ: Growth and Change in Islamic Substantive Law', *Islamic Law and Society* 1/1 (1994), 29–65; Talal al-Azem, *Rule-Formulation and Binding Precedent in the Madhhab-Law Tradition: Ibn Quṭlūbughā's Commentary on* The Compendium *of Qudūrī* (Leiden; Boston: Brill, 2017).

12 Sherman Jackson, '*Taqlīd*, Legal Scaffolding and the Scope of Legal Injunctions in Post-Formative Theory: *Muṭlaq* and *ʿĀmm* in the Jurisprudence of Shihāb al-Dīn al-Qarāfī', *Islamic Law and Society* 3/2 (1996), 165–92.

13 Mohammad Fadel, 'The Social Logic of Taqlīd and the Rise of the *Mukhataṣar*', *Islamic Law and Society* 3/2 (1996), 193–233.

14 Jonathan A. C. Brown, *The Canonization of al-Bukhārī and Muslim: The Formation and Function of the Sunnī Ḥadīth Canon* (Leiden: Brill, 2007), 311; Ibn al-Amir al-Sanʿani, *Irshad al-nuqqad ila taysir al-ijtihad* (Cairo: al-Tibaʿah al-Muniriyyah, 1984), 12, https://www.quranicthought.com/ar/books/-إرشاد-النقاد-إلى-تيسير-الاجتهاد/, last accessed 12 November 2024.

15 Dallal, *Islam without Europe*, 173, 181.

16 Ibid., 87.

17 Al-Shawkani, *Qatr al-wali ʿala hadith al-wali*, ed. Ibrahim Ibrahim Hilal (Cairo: Dar al-kutub al-hadithah, 1969), 345.

18 Al-Shawkani, *al-Badr al-taliʿ*, 2:135.

19 Dallal, *Islam without Europe*, 170.

20 Al-Shawkani, *al-Badr al-taliʿ*, 2:134.

21 Dallal, *Islam without Europe*, 184–7.

22 Dallal, *Islam without Europe*, 86.

23 Haykel, *Revival and Reform*, 81.

24 Al-Sanʿani, *Irshad al-nuqqad*, 11–12; Haykel, *Revival and Reform*, 98–9.

25 Haykel, *Revival and Reform*, 81–2.

26 Al-Shawkani, *al-Badr al-taliʿ*, 2:133; Haykel, *Revival and Reform*, 19.

27 Al-Shawkani, *al-Badr al-taliʿ*, 2:133–4.

28 Ibid., 2:136; Haykel, *Revival and Reform*, 65–6.

29 Maribel Fierro, 'La polémique à propos de *rafʿ al-yadayn fī l-ṣalāt* dans al-Andalus', *Studia Islamica* 65 (1987), 69–90: 69.

30 Ibn Rushd, *The Distinguished Jurist's*

Primer: Bidāyat al-Mujtahid, tr. Imran Ahsan Khan Nyazee in two vols. (Reading: Garnet, 1994–6), 1:146–7.
31 Fierro, 'La polémique', 69, 72; Abu Dawud, *Sunan Abi Dawud wa-maʻalim al-sunan: kitab al-manasik bab fi rafʻ al-yadayn idha raʻa al-bayt.*
32 For this Hadith, see M.J. Kister, 'Do Not Assimilate Yourselves ... *Lā Tashabbahū*', *Jerusalem Studies in Arabic and Islam* 12 (1989), 321–71; Youshaa Patel, *The Muslim Difference: Defining the Line between Believers and Unbelievers from Early Islam to the Present* (New Haven, CT: Yale University Press).
33 Muhammad ibn Ismaʻil al-Amir al-Sanʻani, *Subul al-salam al-muwsilah ila bulugh al-maram*, ed. Muhammad Subhi Hasan Hallaq in nine vols. (Dammam: Dar Ibn al-Jawzi, 1433 AH), 2:182.
34 Al-Shawkani, *Nayl al-awtar min asrar Muntaqa al-abrar*, ed. Muhammad Subhi Hasan Hallaq in sixteen vols. (Dammam: Dar Ibn al-Jawzi, 1327 AH], 4:41–3.
35 Haykel, *Revival and Reform*, 105–6.
36 *Ibid.*, 107. See also Dallal, *Islam without Europe*, 85.
37 Dallal, *Islam without Europe*, 89.
38 Haykel, *Revival and Reform*, 102–3.
39 Dallal, *Islam without Europe*, 72–3.
40 Haykel, *Revival and Reform*, 103; Dallal, *Islam without Europe*, 206.
41 Haykel, *Revival and Reform*, 116–17.
42 Mark Cohen, 'What was the Pact of ʻUmar? A Literary-Historical Study', *Jerusalem Studies in Arabic and Islam* 23 (1999), 100–57: 106–7.
43 S. D. Goitein, *Jews and Arabs: A Concise History of their Social and Cultural Relations* (Mincola, NY: Dover Publications, 2005), 74.
44 Haykel, *Revival and Reform*, 117–18.
45 *Ibid.*, 122–3; Mohamed A. Moustafa, 'Jawāb al-suʼāl ʻan ijlāʼ ahl al-kitāb min al-Yaman', *Christian-Muslim Relations Online II*, https://referenceworks-brill-com.ezproxy-prd.bodleian.ox.ac.uk/display/entries/CMR2/COM-31290.xml?ebody=article%20details, last accessed 11 July 2024.
46 Haykel, *Revival and Reform*, 123.
47 *Ibid.*, 125–6; Ahmad Dallal, 'On Muslim Curiosity and the Historiography of the Jews

of Yemen', in Joseph V. Montville (ed.), *History as Prelude: Muslims and Jews in the Medieval Mediterranean* (Lanham, MD: Lexington Books, 2011), 71–107: 76.
48 Dallal, 'On Muslim Curiosity', 75.
49 *Ibid.*, 82–3.
50 Alexander Knysh, 'The *Tariqa* on a Landcruiser: The Resurgence of Sufism in Yemen', *Middle East Journal* 55/3 (2001), 399–414: 401.
51 Haykel, *Revival and Reform*, 130–3; Bernard Haykel, 'A Zaydī-Yemeni Response to the Wahhābī doctrine on Intercession' (MPhil thesis, University of Oxford, 1991).
52 Cole Bunzel, *Wahhābism: The History of a Militant Islamic Movement* (Princeton, NJ: Princeton University Press, 2023), 128–32.
53 Muhammad ibn Isma'il ibn Salah ibn al-Amīr al-San'ani, *Tathir al-i'tiqad 'an adran al-ilhad*, ed. Abu al-'Abbas Muhammad ibn Jibril al-Shuhri (Sa'da: Maktabat al-Imam al-Wadi'i li-al-nashr wa-al-tawzi', 1340/2009), 22–3, 34–5.
54 Goldziher, *Introduction*, 242.
55 Michael Cook, 'On the Origins of Wahhābism', *Journal of the Royal Asiatic Society* (1992), third series, 2/2, 191–202: 191–8.
56 *Ibid.*, 192. The translation of the Qur'anic verse is A. J. Arberry's. See *The Koran Interpreted*, tr. A. J. Arberry (London: George Allen & Unwin Ltd., 1955), 187.
57 Natana J. DeLong-Bas, *Wahhabi Islam: From Revival and Reform to Global Jihad* (New York: Oxford University Press, 2004); Cook, 'On the Origins', 199–200.
58 Michael Crawford, *Ibn 'Abd al-Wahhab* (London: Oneworld, 2014), 27.
59 Ibn 'Abd al-Wahhab, *Kitab al-Tawhid* (Riyad: Jami'at al-Imam Muhammad Ibn Sa'ud al-Islamiyyah, 1999), 32ff., 41, 42–4, 56ff., 90; Bunzel, *Wahhābism*, 40–1.
60 DeLong-Bas, *Wahhabi Islam*, 22; David Commins, *The Wahhabi Mission and Saudi Arabia* (London: I. B. Tauris, 2009), 13; Bunzel, *Wahhābism*, 41.
61 DeLong-Bas, *Wahhabi Islam*, 23–4.
62 Bunzel, *Wahhābism*, 1.
63 Cook, 'On the Origins', 201; Dallal, *Islam without Europe*, 36.
64 Bunzel, *Wahhābism*, 1–2.
65 *Ibid.*, 2.
66 Crawford, *Ibn 'Abd*

al-Wahhab, 61–6; Bunzel, *Wahhābism*, chapter four.
67 Crawford, *Ibn 'Abd al-Wahhab*, 66; Bunzel, *Wahhābism*, 158.
68 Laoust, *Essai*, 529; Crawford, *Ibn 'Abd al-Wahhab*, 69–70.
69 DeLong-Bas, *Wahhabi Islam*, 27–9.
70 Crawford, *Ibn 'Abd al-Wahhab*, 36.
71 Laoust, *Essai*, 510.
72 'Uthman ibn 'Abd Allah ibn Bishr, *'Unwan al-majd fi tarikh najd*, ed. 'Abd al-Rahman Al al-Shaykh in two vols. (Riyad: Matba'at Darat al-malik 'Abd al-'Aziz, 1402/1982), 1:33. See also Crawford, *Ibn 'Abd al-Wahhab*, 36.
73 Crawford, *Ibn 'Abd al-Wahhab*, 77–8; Bunzel, *Wahhābism*, 13.
74 Bunzel, *Wahhābism*, 206.
75 Ibn Bishr, *'Unwan al-majd*, 1:34.
76 DeLong-Bas, *Wahhabi Islam*, 24–5.
77 Esther Peskes, 'The Wahhābiyya and Sufism in the Eighteenth Century', in Frederick de Jong and Berndt Radtke (eds), *Islamic Mysticism Contested* (Leiden: Brill, 1999), 145–61: 149–51; Crawford, *Ibn 'Abd al-Wahhab*, 24, 85.
78 Zachary Wright, *Realizing Islam: The Tijaniyya in North Africa and the Eighteenth-century Muslim World* (Chapel Hill, NC: University of North Carolina Press, 2020), 19; Laoust, *Essai*, 522.
79 Sulayman ibn 'Abd Allah ibn al-Shaykh Muhammad ibn 'Abd al-Wahhab, *al-Tawdih 'an tawhid al-khallaq* (Riyad: Dar al-Tayba, 1404/1984), 349–50.
80 Jon Hoover, *Ibn Taymiyya* (London: Oneworld, 2019), 45.
81 Sulayman ibn 'Abd Allah, *al-Tawdih*, 346.
82 Crawford, *Ibn 'Abd al-Wahhab*, 84; Bunzel, *Wahhābism*, 60.
83 Rachida Chih, 'Prophetic Piety, Mysticism, and Authority in Premodern Arabic Devotional Literature: al-Jazuli's *Dala'il al-Khayrat* (15th Century)', *International Journal of Middle East Studies* 54 (2022), 462–83.
84 Hamid Algar, *Wahhabism: A Critical Essay* (Oneonta, NY: Islamic Publications International, 2002), 28.
85 Richard F. Burton, *Personal Narrative of a Pilgrimate to Al-Madinah & Meccah*, in two vols. (London: George Bell & Sons, 1898), 1:12.
86 Bunzel, *Wahhābism*, 47.
87 George, Viscount Valentia, *Voyages and Travels to*

India, Ceylon, The Red Sea, Abyssinia, and Egypt in the Years 1802, 1803, 1804, 1805, and 1806, in four vols. (London: F., C., and J. Rivington, 1811), 2:367–8.
88 John Lewis Burckhardt, Notes on the Bedouins and Wahabys, in two vols. (London: Henry Colburn and Richard Bentley, 1831), 1:102.
89 Peskes, 'The Wahhābiyya and Sufism', 153.
90 Esther Peskes, Muḥammad b. ʿAbdalwahhāb (1703–92) im Widerstreit: Untersuchungen zur Rekonstruktion der Frühgeschichte der Wahhābīya (Beirut: Franz Steiner Verlag Stuttgart, 1993), 25–6, n. 54.
91 Peskes, 'The Wahhābiyya and Sufism', 153.
92 Hoover, Ibn Taymiyya, 38.
93 Burckhardt, Notes on the Bedouins and Wahabys, 2:108.
94 Viscount Valentia, Voyages and Travels, 2:373.
95 Algar, Wahhabism, 26; Hoover, Ibn Taymiyya, 69.
96 Ibn Bābawayh al-Qummī, A Shiʿite Creed, tr. Asaf A. A. Fyzee (London: Oxford University Press, 1942), 96.
97 Ingvild Flaskerud, 'Twelver Shiʿa Pilgrimage: Ziyara', in Oliver Leaman (ed.), Routledge Handbook of Islamic Ritual and Practice (London: Routledge, 2022), 385–401: 390.
98 Crawford, Ibn ʿAbd al-Wahhab, 87–8.
99 Meir Litvak, 'Encounters between Shiʿi and Sunni ʿUlama' in Ottoman Iraq', in Ofra Bengio and Meir Litvak (eds), The Sunna and Shiʿa in History: Division and Ecumenism in the Muslim Middle East (New York: Palgrave Macmillan, 2011), 69–86: 74–5.
100 Hamid Dabashi, Shiʿism: A Religion of Protest (Cambridge, MA: Harvard University Press, 2011), 80.
101 Bunzel, Wahhābism, 218.
102 Laoust, Essai, 264.
103 Crawford, Ibn ʿAbd al-Wahhab, 88.
104 Bunzel, Wahhābism, 77–8.
105 See ibid., 70–71, 78, 81, 88, 189, 223, 255, 257.
106 Henri Laoust, Les schismes dans l'Islam: introduction à une étude de la religion musulmane (Paris: Poyot, 1965), 331.
107 Bunzel, Wahhābism, 48.
108 Dallal, Islam without Europe, 37.
109 Bunzel, Wahhābism, 58.
110 Dallal, Islam without Europe, 5–6, 20–2.
111 Bunzel, Wahhābism, 64.
112 Crawford, Ibn ʿAbd al-Wahhab, 12.
113 Burckhardt, Notes on the Bedouins and Wahabys, 1:102; Bunzel, Wahhābism, 16.

114 See e.g. Valentia, *Voyages and Travels*, 2:372; Michael Cook, *Commanding Right and Forbidding Wrong in Islamic Thought* (Cambridge: Cambridge University Press, 2000), chapter 8.
115 Ibn Bishr, *'Unwan al-majd*, 1:25; Peskes, *Muḥammad b. 'Abdalwahhāb*, 209.
116 Cook, 'On the Origins', 203; Bunzel, *Wahhābism*, 63.
117 Ibn Bishr, *'Unwan al-majd*, 1:33; Algar, *Wahhabism*, 6; Bunzel, *Wahhābism*, 41.
118 Ibn Bishr, *'Unwan al-majd*, 1:25.

4: Following the Prophet

1 Valerie Hoffman, 'Annihilation in the Messenger of God: Development of a Sufi Practice', *International Journal of Middle East Studies* 31/3 (1999), 351–69.
2 See Mark Sedgwick, *Saints and Sons: The Making and Remaking of The Rashīdi Aḥmadi Sufi Order, 1799–2000* (Leiden: Brill, 2005), 27.
3 Ivanyi, *Virtue, Piety, and the Law*, 81, 101–2.
4 Annemarie Schimmel, *Pain and Grace: A Study of Two Mystical Writers of Eighteenth-Century Muslim India* (Leiden: Brill, 1976), 34; Ziad, *Hidden Caliphate*, 79.
5 Schimmel, *Pain and Grace*, 14, 35–6; Neda Saghaee, *Sufism in Eighteenth-Century India: Muḥammad Nāṣir 'Andalīb's Lament of the Nightingale and Ṭarīqa-yi Khāliṣ Muḥammadiyya* (London: Routledge, 2022), 41–3, 233–4.
6 Homayra Ziad, 'Poetry, Music and the Muḥammadī Path: How Khvājah Mīr Dard Brought Three Worlds Together in Eighteenth-Century Delhi', *Journal of Islamic Studies* 21/3 (2010), 345–76: 361. See also Homayra Ziad, 'Quest of the Nightingale: The Religious Thought of Khvājah Mīr Dard (1720–1785)' (PhD thesis, Yale University, 2008), 55; Schimmel, *Pain and Grace*, 41–2; Saghaee, *Sufism*, 131–2, 135.
7 Saghaee, *Sufism*, 136.
8 Ibid., 52; Ziad, *Quest of the Nightingale*, 46.
9 Saghaee, *Sufism*, 80–1.
10 Ibid., 50–1; Schimmel, *Pain and Grace*, 45; Soraya Khodamoradi and Carl Ernst, 'Yoga and the "Pure Muhammadi Path" of Muhammad Nasir 'Andalib', *Religions MDPI* 15/3 (2024).
11 Saghaee, *Sufism*, 150.
12 Ibid., 146.
13 Khodamoradi and Ernst,

'Yoga and the "Pure Muhammadi Path"'.
14. Saghaee, *Sufism*, 139.
15. Muhammad U. Faruque, 'Sufism *contra* Shariah? Shāh Walī Allāh's Metaphysics of *Waḥdat al-Wujūd*', *Journal of Sufi Studies* 5 (2016), 27–57: 45.
16. Saghaee, *Sufism*, 168–9.
17. Schimmel, *Pain and Grace*, 39.
18. Saghaee, *Sufism*, 176–8; Schimmel, *Pain and Grace*, 43; Khodamoradi and Ernst, 'Yoga and the "Pure Muhammadi Path"'.
19. Saghaee, *Sufism*, 141–3.
20. *Ibid.*, 143; Ziad, *Quest of the Nightingale*, 62, n. 232.
21. Schimmel, 38, 40, 66; Ziad, *Quest of the Nightingale*, 66.
22. Ziad, *Quest of the Nightingale*, 3, 10.
23. *Ibid.*, 214, n. 812.
24. *Ibid.*, 215–6.
25. Schimmel, *Pain and Grace*, 46.
26. Ziad, *Quest of the Nightingale*, 55.
27. Schimmel, *Pain and Grace*, 49.
28. Ziad, *Quest of the Nightingale*, 76, 100.
29. *Ibid.*, 77–8, 233; Yohanan Friedmann, *Prophecy Continuous: Aspects of Aḥmadī Religious Thought and its Medieval Background* (Berkeley, CA: University of California Press, 1989).
30. Ziad, *Quest of the Nightingale*, 107 (adapted).
31. *Ibid.*, 194.
32. Fitzroy Morrissey, *Sufism and the Perfect Human* (Abingdon: Routledge, 2020), chapter 5.
33. Ziad, *Quest of the Nightingale*, 157.
34. Schimmel, *Pain and Grace*, 38.
35. Ziad, *Quest of the Nightingale*, 234–5.
36. *Ibid.*, 164.
37. *Ibid.*, 201–5, 141.
38. *Ibid.*, 223–7.
39. Frederick de Jong, 'Mustafa Kamal al-Din al-Bakri (1688–1749): Revival and Reform of the Khalwatiyya Tradition?', in Nehemia Levtzion and John Voll (eds), *Eighteenth-Century Islamic Renewal and Reform* (Syracuse: Syracuse University Press, 1987), 117–32.
40. G. W. J. Drewes, 'A Note on Muhammad al-Samman, his writings, and 19th century Sammàniyya practices, chiefly in Batavia, according to written data', *Archipel* 43 (1992), 73–87: 74.
41. *Ibid.*, 75; Michel Chodkiewicz, *The Meccan Revelations*, tr. David Speight (New York: Pir Press, 2004), 36.

42 Drewes, 'A Note', 74.
43 Muhammad ibn 'Abd al-Karim al-Samman, *Mawlid al-nabi* (Egypt: Matba'at al-Taqaddum, 1908), 2.
44 Abdul Muthalib, 'The Mystical Teachings of Muḥammad 'Abd al-Karim al-Sammān, an 18th Century Ṣūfī' (PhD thesis, McGill University, 2007), 101.
45 *Ibid.*, 99.
46 *Ibid.*, 142.
47 *Ibid.*, 142, 127.
48 *Ibid.*, 128.
49 Wright, *Realizing Islam*, 37.
50 Marion Holmes Katz, *The Birth of the Prophet Muḥammad: Devotional Piety in Sunni Islam* (Abingdon: Oxford, 2007), 171; C. Snouck Hurgronje, *Mekka in the Latter Part of the 19th Century*, tr. J. H. Monahan (Leiden: Brill, 2007), 54.
51 C. Snouck Hurgronje, *The Achenese*, tr. A. W. S. O'Sullivan (Leiden: Brill, 1906), 216–18.
52 Stefan Reichmuth, *The World of Murtaḍā al-Zabīdī: Life, Networks, and Writings* (Cambridge: E. J. W. Gibb Memorial Trust, 2009), 35.
53 Rachid Abdallah El-Nasser, 'Morocco, From Kharijism to Wahhabism: The Quest for Religious Purism' (PhD thesis, University of Michigan, 1983); Mohamed El Mansour, *Morocco in the Reign of Mawlay Sulayman* (Wisbech: Middle East & North African Studies Press, 1990).
54 Wright, *Realizing Islam*, 180; Jamil M. Abun-Nasr, *The Tijaniyya: A Sufi Order in the Modern World* (London: Oxford University Press, 1965), 21.
55 Wright, *Realizing Islam*, 100.
56 *Ibid.*, 128.
57 Abun-Nasr, *The Tijaniyya*, 24.
58 Wright, *Realizing Islam*, 114–15.
59 *Ibid.*, 1.
60 Abun-Nasr, *The Tijaniyya*, 43.
61 Wright, *Realizing Islam*, 3–4.
62 *Ibid.*, 160.
63 *Ibid.*, 143, 153–4.
64 Abun-Nasr, *The Tijaniyya*, 28–36, 39–40; Wright, *Realizing Islam*, 88, 169.
65 Wright, *Realizing Islam*, 56–9.
66 Al-Lamati, *Pure Gold from the Words of Sayyidī 'Abd al-'Azīz al-Dabbāgh*, tr. John O'Kane and Bernd Radkte (Leiden: Brill, 2007), xii.
67 Al-Lamati, *Pure Gold*, 662.
68 R. S. O'Fahey, *Enigmatic Saint: Ahmad ibn Idris*

and the Idrisi Tradition (London: Hurst & Company, 1990).
69 Bernd Radkte et al., The Exoteric Ahmad Ibn Idris: A Sufi's Critique of the Madhahib and the Wahhabis: Four Arabic Texts with Translation and Commentary (Leiden: Brill, 2000).
70 Ibid., 48.
71 Ibid., 59–60, 65, 66, 77.
72 Dajani, Sufis and Shariʿa, 282; Sedgwick, Saints and Sons, 15.
73 Radkte, Exoteric, 54.
74 Ibid., 50, 54–5.
75 Ibid., 156–7.
76 O'Fahey, Enigmatic Saint, 74.
77 Radkte, Exoteric, 149–50.
78 Ibid., 159–60; O'Fahey, Enigmatic Saint, 103.
79 Radkte, Exoteric, 168–70; Dajani, Sufis and Shariʿa, chapter 10.
80 Sedgwick, Saints and Sons, 20.
81 Ibid., 13.
82 O'Fahey, Enigmatic Saint, 3–4.
83 Knut S. Vikør, Sufi and Scholar on the Desert Edge: Muhammad b. ʿAli al-Sanusi and His Brotherhood (Evanston, IL: Northwestern University Press, 1995), 59–60; O'Fahey, Enigmatic Saint, 132.
84 Vikør, Sufi and Scholar, 95–6.
85 Ibid., 110, 112; O'Fahey, Enigmatic Saint, 133.
86 Vikør, Sufi and Scholar, 115–18.
87 Dajani, Sufis and Shariʿa, 255.
88 Radkte, Exoteric, 2; Vikør, Sufi and Scholar, 221–3; Dajani, Sufis and Shariʿa, 289.
89 Dallal, Islam without Europe, 79.
90 Vikør, Sufi and Scholar, 223–4; Dajani, Sufis and Shariʿa, 289.
91 John Obert Voll, A History of the Khatmiyyah Tariqah in the Sudan (PhD thesis, Harvard University, 1969); Sedgwick, Saints and Sons.
92 Burton, Traveller's Narrative, 2:24–5, n. 3.
93 Vikør, Sufi and Scholar, 154–6.
94 Nicola A. Ziadeh, Sanūsīyah: A Study of a Revivalist Movement in Islam (Leiden: Brill, 1983), 52.
95 Mervyn Hiskett, The Sword of Truth: The Life and Times of the Shehu Usuman dan Fodio (New York: Oxford University Press, 1973), 4.
96 Ibid., 33, 37.
97 Ibid., 60.
98 ʿUthman ibn Fudi, Ihyaʾ al-sunnah wa-ikhmad al-bidʿah (Cairo: Matbaʿat Mashhad al-Husayni, 1382 [1963]), 13, 15.

99 Nana Asma'u, *Collected Works of Nana Asma'u, daughter of Usman dan Fodiyo, (1793–1864)*, ed. Jean Boyd and Beverly B. Mack (East Lansing: Michigan State University Press, 1997), 23–4, 503–4.

100 Mervyn Hiskett, 'Kitāb Al-Farq: A Work on the Habe Kingdoms Attributed to 'Uthmān Dan Fodio', *Bulletin of the School of Oriental and African Studies Press* 23/3 (1960), 558–79: 561–3, 566–9.

101 Hiskett, *Sword of Truth*, 66.

102 Murray Last, *The Sokoto Caliphate* (London: Longmans, 1967), 13, 46.

103 *Ibid.*, 10.

104 Hiskett, *Sword of Truth*, 119–20.

105 *Ibid.*, 108; Muhammad Sani Zahradeen, ''Abd Allah Ibn Fodio's contributions to the Fulani Jihad in Nineteenth Century Hausaland' (PhD thesis, McGill University, 1976), 30–1.

106 Humphrey Fisher, 'The Western and Central Sudan and East Africa', in P. M. Holt, Ann K. S. Lambton, and Bernard Lewis (eds), *The Cambridge History of Islam. Volume 2 A, The Indian Sub-Continent, South-East Asia, Africa and the Muslim West* (Cambridge: Cambridge University Press, 1977), 345–405: 353.

107 Hiskett, *Sword of Truth*, 121; Michael Cook, *Commanding Right and Forbidding Wrong*.

108 Nana Asma'u, *Collected Works*, 22, 502.

109 B. G. Martin, *Muslim Brotherhoods in Nineteenth-Century Africa* (Cambridge: Cambridge University Press, 1976), 35.

110 Hiskett, *Sword of Truth*, 123–4.

111 *Ibid.*, 125.

112 Dajani, *Sufis and Sharī'a*, chapter 8.

113 Martin, *Muslim Brotherhoods*, 38.

114 Abun-Nasr, *The Tijaniyya*, 109; Martin, *Muslim Brotherhoods*, 71.

115 Abun-Nasr, *The Tijaniyya*, 112; Martin, *Muslim Brotherhoods*, 83.

116 Abun-Nasr, *The Tijaniyya*, 122–3; Martin, *Muslim Brotherhoods*, 92.

117 Abun-Nasr, *The Tijaniyya*, 33; Martin, *Muslim Brotherhoods*, 84.

118 Martin, *Muslim Brotherhoods*, 76.

119 *Ibid.*, 79.

120 Bernd Radkte, 'Studies on the Sources of the *Kitāb Rimāḥ ḥizb al-raḥīm* of al-Ḥajj 'Umar', *Sudanic Africa* 6 (1995), 75–113.

121 *Ibid.*, 77; Bernd Radkte,

'Ijtihad and neo-Sufism', *Asiatische Studien* 48 (1994), 909–21: 917; Dajani, *Sufis and Shariʿa*, 291.
122 Gavin Picken, 'The "Greater" Jihad in Classical Islam', in Elisabeth Kendall and Ewan Stein (eds), *Twenty-First Century Jihad* (London: I. B. Tauris, 2015), 126–38.
123 Martin, *Muslim Brotherhoods*, 82.
124 Ibid., 89.
125 Radkte, 'Studies on the Sources', 76; Abun-Nasr, *The Tijaniyya*, 48.
126 Max Weber, *Economy and Society: An Outline of an Interpretative Sociology*, ed. Guenther Roth and Claus Wittich (Berkeley, Los Angeles and London: University of California Press, 1978), 542.
127 P. M. Holt, *The Mahdist State in the Sudan, 1881–1898* (Nairobi; Oxford: Oxford University Press, 1979), 106.
128 Aharon Layish, *Shariʿa and the Islamic State in 19th-century Sudan: The Mahdi's Legal Methodology and Doctrine* (Leiden; Boston: Brill, 2016), 26–55.
129 Marc Gaborieau, *Le Mahdi incompris* (Paris: CNRS Éditions, 2010), 61, 63–5.
130 Ibid., 94; SherAli Tareen, *Defending Muhammad in Modernity* (Notre Dame, IN: University of Notre Dame Press, 2020), 52–4.
131 Tareen, *Defending Muhammad*, 56ff.
132 Gaborieau, *Le Mahdi incompris*, 78–82.
133 Ibid., 102.
134 Shah Ismail Shaheed, *Taqwiyat-ul-Imân (The Strengthening of Faith)* (Saudi Arabia: Dar-us-Salam Publications, n.d.), 38; Shah Ismaʿil Shahid, *Taqwiyat-ul-iman* (Riyad: Maktab Daʿwat wa-tawʿiyat al-jaliyat, n.d.), 40.
135 Gaborieau, *Le Mahdi incompris*, 151–7.
136 Shah Ismail Shaheed, *Taqwiyat-ul-Imân*, 42.
137 Tareen, *Defending Muhammad*, 97–8.
138 Shah Ismail Shaheed, *Taqwiyat-ul-Imân*, 47.
139 Ibid., 50–5.
140 Gaborieau, *Le Mahdi incompris*, 111–14.
141 Ayesha Jalal, *Partisans of Allah: Jihad in South Asia* (Cambridge, MA: Harvard University Press, 2008), 68; Gaborieau, *Le Mahdi incompris*, 44.
142 Tareen, *Defending Muhammad*, 107.
143 Ibid., 106, 111.
144 Ibid., 117–18.
145 Ibid., 107–10.
146 Gaborieau, *Le Mahdi incompris*, 223.
147 Ibid., 217.

148 John Calvin, *Institutes of the Christian Religion: Volume II*, tr. Henry Beveridge (Edinburgh: The Calvin Translation Society, 1845), 159.

5: Following the Imams

1 Ibn Bābawayh al-Qummī, *A Shi'ite Creed*, 95.
2 George Warner, *The Words of the Imams: Al-Shaykh al-Ṣadūq and the Development of Twelver Shī'ī Hadith Literature* (London: I. B. Tauris, 2022), 38.
3 Abū Ḥanīfah Nu'mān ibn Muḥammad, *Disagreements of the Jurists: A Manual of Islamic Legal Theory*, ed. and tr. Devin J. Stewart (New York, NY: New York University Press, 2015), 29.
4 Devin J. Stewart, *Islamic Legal Orthodoxy: Twelver Shiite Responses to the Sunni Legal System* (Salt Lake City, UT: University of Utah Press, 1998), 177.
5 Edmund Hayes, *Agents of the Hidden Imam: Forging Twelver Shi'ism* (Cambridge: Cambridge University Press, 2022).
6 *Encyclopaedia Iranica*, 'ĠAYBA' (Said Amir Arjomand), https://www.iranicaonline.org/articles/gayba, last accessed 20 September 2024.
7 Abdulaziz Sachedina, *Islamic Messianism: The Idea of the Mahdi in Twelver Shi'ism* (Albany, NY: SUNY Press, 1981), 101.
8 Stewart, *Islamic Legal Orthodoxy*, 182.
9 Norman Calder, 'Doubt and Prerogative: The Emergence of an Imāmī Shī'ī Theory of Ijtihād', *Studia Islamica* 70 (1989), 57–78: 59 (adapted).
10 Christopher Melchert, 'The Imāmīs between Rationalism and Traditionalism', in Lynda Clarke (ed.), *Shī'ite Heritage: Essays on Classical and Modern Traditions* (Binghamton, NY: Global Publications, 2001), 273–83: 274; Stewart, *Islamic legal Orthodoxy*, 54, 120, 125ff.
11 Robert Gleave, 'Between Ḥadīth and Fiqh: The "Canonical" Imāmī Collections of Akhbār', *Islamic Law and Society* 8/3 (2001), 350–82.
12 Stewart, *Islamic Legal Orthodoxy*, chapter 4.
13 Hossein Modarressi, 'Rationalism and Traditionalism in Shī'ī Jurisprudence: A Preliminary Survey', *Studia Islamica* 59 (1984), 141–58.
14 Hassan Ansari and Sabine

Schmidkte, 'The Shīʿī Reception of Muʿtazilism (II): Twelver Shīʿīs', in Sabine Schmidkte (ed.), *The Oxford Handbook of Islamic Theology* (Oxford: Oxford University Press, 2014), 196–214.

15 Stewart, *Islamic Legal Orthodoxy*, 16; Calder, 'Doubt and Prerogative', 67.

16 Calder, 'Doubt and Prerogative', 68; Robert Gleave, *Inevitable Doubt: Two Theories of Shīʿī Jurisprudence* (Leiden: E. J. Brill, 2000), 5.

17 Calder, 'Doubt and Prerogative', 72.

18 Saïd Amir Arjomand, *The Shadow of God and the Hidden Imam: Religion, Political Order, and Societal Change in Shiʿite Iran from the Beginning to 1890* (Chicago; London: University of Chicago Press, 1984), 139; Stewart, *Islamic Legal Orthodoxy*, 183, 207, 213.

19 Calder, Doubt and Prerogative', 73.

20 *Ibn*, 70; Stewart, *Islamic Legal Orthodoxy*, 72.

21 Arjomand, *Shadow of God*, 133–4; Abbas Amanat, *Iran: A Modern History* (New Haven, CT: Yale University Press, 2017), 64.

22 Arjomand, *Shadow of God*, 142.

23 Robert Gleave, *Scripturalist Islam: The History and Doctrines of the Akhbārī Shīʿī School* (Leiden; Boston: Brill, 2007), 33–4. See also Stewart, *Islamic Legal Orthodoxy*, 180.

24 Stewart, *Islamic Legal Orthodoxy*, 184.

25 Gleave, *Scripturalist Islam*, 64.

26 Muhammad Amin al-Astarabadi, *al-Fawāʾid al-madaniyyah wa-yalihi al-Shawāhid al-makkiyyah*, ed. al-Shaykh Rahmat Allah al-Rahmati al-Araki (Qom: Muʾassasat al-Nashr al-islami, 1426 AH), 76; Stewart, *Islamic Legal Orthodoxy*, 184.

27 Gleave, *Scripturalist Islam*, 66–8.

28 Al-Astarabadi, *al-Fawāʾid al-madaniyyah*, 75.

29 Gleave, *Scripturalist Islam*, 72–4.

30 Stewart, *Islamic Legal Orthodoxy*, 184.

31 Gleave, *Scripturalist Islam*, 79, 87.

32 Juan R. Cole, 'Imami Jurisprudence and the Role of the Ulama: Mortaza Ansari on Emulating the Supreme Exemplar', in Nikki Keddie (ed.), *Religion and Politics in Iran: Shiʿism from Quietism to Revolution* (New Haven, CT: Yale University Press, 1983),

33–46: 43; Juan R. Cole, *Roots of North Indian Shī'ism in Iran and Iraq: Religion and State in Awadh, 1722–1859* (Berkeley, CA: University of California Press, 1988), 124.
33 Al-Astarabadi, *al-Fawa'id al-madaniyyah*, 77.
34 Stewart, *Islamic Legal Orthodoxy*, 185–6.
35 Gleave, *Scripturalist Islam*, 46.
36 Andrew Newman, 'The Nature of the Akhbārī/Uṣūlī Dispute in Late Ṣafawid Iran. Part 1: 'Abdallah al-Samāhijī's *Munyat al-Mumārisīn*', *Bulletin of the School of Oriental and African Studies* 55/1 (1992), 22–51; The Andrew Newman, 'The Nature of the Akhbārī/Uṣūlī Dispute in Late Ṣafawid Iran. Part 2: The Conflict Reassessed', *Bulletin of the School of Oriental and African Studies* 55/2 (1992): 250–61.
37 Juan R. Cole, 'Shi'i Clerics in Iraq and Iran, 1722–1780: The Akhbari-Usul Conflict Reconsidered', *Iranian Studies* 18/1 (1985), 3–34: 5–6.
38 Hamid Algar, *Religion and State in Iran, 1785–1906: The Role of the Ulama in the Qajar Period* (Berkeley, CA: University of California Press, 1969), 28, n. 7, 30; Abbas Amanat, *Resurrection and Renewal: The Making of the Babi Movement in Iran, 1844 to 1850* (Ithaca, NY; London: Cornell University Press, 1989), 37, 41, n. 22; Arjomand, *Shadow of God*, 133; Gleave, *Scripturalist Islam*, 31, 45.
39 Algar, *Religion and State in Iran*, 34–5.
40 Gleave, *Inevitable Doubt*, esp. 31–59, 103–5, 133, 251–2.
41 Algar, *Religion and State in Iran*, 35.
42 Cole, 'Shi'i Clerics', 19.
43 Ibid., 21–2.
44 Gleave, *Inevitable Doubt*, 244.
45 Ibid., 133–6.
46 Muhammad Baqir al-Wahid al-Bihbahani, '*Risalat al-ijtihad wa-al-akhbar*', in *al-Rasa'il al-usuliyyah* (Qom: Mu'assasat al-'Allamah al-Mujaddid al-Wahid al-Bihbahani, 1416), 25.
47 Gleave, *Inevitable Doubt*, 238.
48 Devin J. Stewart, 'Islamic Juridical Hierarchies and the Office of Marji' al-Taqlīd', in Clarke (ed.), *Shī'ite Heritage*, 137–58: 139.
49 Ann K. S. Lambton, 'A Reconsideration of the Position of Marja'

al-Taqlīd and the Religious Institution', *Studia Islamica* 20 (1964), 115–35: 119; Abbas Amanat, 'In Between the Madrasa and the Marketplace: The Designation of Clerical Leadership in Modern Shi'ism', in Said Amir Arjomand (ed.), *Authority and Political Culture in Shi'ism* (Albany, NY: SUNY Press, 1988), 98–132: 99.
50 Cole, 'Imami Jurisprudence', 40, 44.
51 *Encyclopaedia Iranica*, 'Hojjat-al-Eslām' (Hamid Algar), https://www.iranicaonline.org/articles/hojjat-al-eslam, last accessed 25 September 2024.
52 Arjomand, *Shadow of God*, 224.
53 *Ibid.*, 232, 236; Saïd Amir Arjomand, 'Political Ethic and Public Law in the Early Qajar Period', in Robert Gleave (ed.), *Religion and Society in Qajar Iran* (London; New York: RoutledgeCurzon, 2005), 21–40: 30.
54 Arjomand, 'Political Ethic', 30.
55 Cole, 'Imami Jurisprudence', 41.
56 Arjomand, 'Political Ethic', 29.
57 Ahmad al-Naraqi, *'Awa'id al-ayyam* (Qom: Markaz al-Abhath wa-al-dirasat al-islamiyyah, 1417 AH), 536–82.
58 Arjomand, 'Political Ethic', 29; cf. Hamid Dabashi, 'Early Propagation of *Wilayat-e Faqih* and Mulla Ahmad Naraqi', in S. H. Nasr, H. Dabashi, and S. V. R. Nasr (eds), *Expectation of the Millennium: Shi'ism in History* (Albany, NY: SUNY Press, 1988), 287–300.
59 Sabine Schmidtke, 'Ibn Abī Jumhūr al-Aḥsā'ī (d. after 1491) and his *Kitāb Mujlī Mir'āt al-munjī*', in Khaled El-Rouayheb and Sabine Schmidtke (eds), *The Oxford Handbook of Islamic Philosophy* (New York: Oxford University Press, 2016), 397–414: 397.
60 Jon McGinnis, 'Naṣīr al-Dīn al-Ṭūsī (d. 1274): *Sharḥ al-Ishārāt*', in El-Rouayheb and Schmidtke (eds), *Oxford Handbook of Islamic Philosophy*, 327–47; *Encyclopaedia Iranica*, 'Ṭusi, Naṣir-al-Din' (George E. Lane), https://www.iranicaonline.org/articles/tusi-nasir-al-din-bio, last accessed 25 September 2024.
61 *Encyclopaedia Iranica*, 'Āmolī, Sayyed Bahā'-al-Din' (Etan Kohlberg), https://www.iranicaonline.org/articles/amoli-sayyed

-baha-al-din-haydar-b, last accessed 25 September 2024.
62 Schmidtke, 'Ibn Abī Jumhūr al-Aḥsā'ī'
63 Encyclopaedia Iranica, 'Mollā Ṣadrā Šīrāzī' (Sajjad Rizvi), https:// www.iranicaonline.org/articles/molla-sadra-sirazi, last accessed 25 September 2024.
64 Pierre Hadot, What is Ancient Philosophy?, tr. Michael Chase (Cambridge, MA; London: Harvard University Press, 2002); Sajjad Rizvi, 'Philosophy as a Way of Life in the World of Islam: Applying Hadot to the Study of Mullā Ṣadrā Shīrāzī (d. 1635)', Bulletin of the School of Oriental and African Studies 75/1 (2012), 33–45.
65 Sadr al-Din Shirazi, al-Hikmah al-mutaʿaliyah fī al-asfar al-arbaʿah, ed. R. Lutfi, I. Amini, and F. Ummi, in 9 vols. (Beirut: Dar Ihya' al-turath al-ʿArabi, 1402/1981), 1:20; Ahmed, What is Islam?, 17; Fitzroy Morrissey, 'What is Islamic Philosophy? The Islamic Reception of a Greek Idea', Antigone, https://antigonejournal.com/2021/05/islamic-reception-greek-philosophy/, last accessed 25 September 2024.
66 Encyclopaedia Iranica, 'Mollā Ṣadrā Šīrāzī' (Rizvi).
67 Fazlur Rahman, The Philosophy of Mullā Ṣadrā (Ṣadr al-Dīn al-Shirāzī) (Albany, NY: SUNY Press, 1975), 27–34; Sajjad H. Rizvi, Mullā Ṣadrā and Metaphysics: Modulation of Being (London: Routledge, 2009), 104–6.
68 Rizvi, Mullā Ṣadrā and Metaphysics, 109.
69 Rahman, Philosophy of Mullā Ṣadrā, 37.
70 Rizvi, Mullā Ṣadrā and Metaphysics, 110.
71 Ibid., 29.
72 Encyclopaedia Iranica, 'Mollā Ṣadrā Šīrāzī' (Rizvi).
73 Shirazi, al-Hikma al-mutaʿaliya, 1:5–6; Arjomand, Shadow of God, 149.
74 Arjomand, Shadow of God, 151–9.
75 Sajjad Rizvi, 'Whatever Happened to the School of Isfahan? Philosophy in 18th-Century Iran', in Michael Axworthy (ed.), Crisis, Collapse, Militarism and Civil War: The History and Historiography of 18th Century Iran (New York: Oxford University Press, 2018), 71–104: 73–4.
76 Reza Pourjavady, 'Introduction', in idem. (ed.), Philosophy in Qajar Iran (Leiden; Boston: Brill, 2019), 1–35: 14.

77 Algar, *Religion and State in Iran*, 34; Amanat, *Resurrection and Renewal*, 77.
78 Rizvi, 'Whatever Happened', 78.
79 Pourjavady, 'Introduction', 15, 18–19.
80 Rizvi, 'Whatever Happened', 72.
81 *Ibid.*, 76.
82 Juan R. I. Cole, 'Ideology, Ethics, and Philosophical Discourse in Eighteenth Century Iran', *Iranian Studies* 22/1 (1989), 7–34: 17; Rizvi, 'Whatever Happened', 77; Pourjavady, 'Introduction', 12, 52.
83 Cole, 'Shi'i Clerics', 15, 21; Cole, 'Ideology', 19.
84 Cole, 'Ideology', 19; Cole, 'Shi'i Clerics', 22; Rizvi, 'Whatever Happened', 80.
85 Cole, 'Ideology', 19–20.
86 Rizvi, 'Whatever Happened', 93–4; Pourjavady, 'Introduction', 45, 50, 57.
87 Al-Naraqi, *Jami' al-sa'adat*, in two vols. (Qom: Intisharat Isma'iliyan, 1428 AH), 1:16; Cole, 'Ideology', 21; Pourjavady, 'Introduction', 43.
88 Al-Naraqi, *Jami' al-sa'adat*, 1:51.
89 *Ibid.*, 1:87–8; Cole, 'Ideology', 21–2.
90 *Ibid.*, 25–6.
91 Pourjavady, 'Introduction', 17, 28; Rizvi, 'Whatever Happened', 94; Sajjad Rizvi, 'Mulla 'Ali Nuri', in Pourjavady (ed.), *Philosophy in Qajar Iran*, 125–78: 158.
92 Pourjavady, 'Introduction', 59.
93 Algar, *Religion and State in Iran*, 58; Rizvi, 'Mulla 'Ali Nuri', 154, n. 149.
94 Rizvi, 'Mulla 'Ali Nuri', 163.
95 Sajjad Rizvi, 'Being (*Wujud*) and Sanctity (*Wilaya*)', in Gleave (ed.), *Religion and Society in Qajar Iran*, 113–26: 120; Hamed Naji Esfahani, ''Aqa Muhammad Rida Qumsha'i', in Pourjavady (ed.), *Philosophy in Qajar Iran*, 259–82: 279.
96 Edward G. Browne, *A Year Amongst the Persians* (London: Adam and Charles Black, 1893), 85; also *ibid.*, 131.
97 Mahdi Muhaqqiq and Toshihiko Izutsu, *The Metaphysics of Sabzavari* (Delmar, NY: Caravan Books, 1977), 12.
98 *Ibid.*, 13; Pourjavady, 'Introduction', 20.
99 Browne, *A Year Amongst the Persians*, 132–3, 135.
100 Muhaqqiq and Izutsu, *Metaphysics*, 20; Browne, *A Year Amongst the Persians*, 133.
101 Rizvi, 'Mulla 'Ali Nuri', 133.

102 Browne, *A Year Amongst the Persians*, 134–5.
103 Muhaqqiq and Izutsu, *Metaphysics*, 15–16; Browne, *A Year Amongst the Persians*, 134.
104 Fatemeh Fana, 'Mullā Hādī Sabzawārī', in Pourjavady (ed.), *Philosophy in Qajar Iran*, 259–82: 201.
105 Muhaqqiq and Izutsu, *Metaphysics*, 1; Fana, 'Mullā Hādī Sabzawārī', 193; Pourjavady, 'Introduction', 23–4.
106 Fana, 'Mullā Hādī Sabzawārī', 201, 212–16.
107 Muhaqqiq and Izutsu, *Metaphysics*, 7.
108 Browne, *A Year Amongst the Persians*, 136.
109 Muhaqqiq and Izutsu, *Metaphysics*, 9.
110 Muhaqqiq and Izutsu, *Metaphysics*, 10; Browne, *A Year Amongst the Persians*, 137.
111 Browne, *A Year Amongst the Persians*, 137–9; Muhaqqiq and Izutsu, *Metaphysics*, 189, 234.
112 Sayyid Muhammad Husayn Husayni Tehrani, *Shining Sun*, tr. Tawus Raja (London: ICAS Press, 2011), 61; Muhammad Husayn Tabataba'i, *Shi'ite Islam*, tr. Seyyed Hossein Nasr (Albany, NY: SUNY Press, 1975), 94–6.
113 Denis MacEoin, *The Messiah of Shiraz: Studies in Early and Middle Babism* (Leiden: Brill, 2009), 61.
114 Denis Hermann, *Le Shaykhisme à la période qajare: histoire sociale et doctrinale d'une école chiite* (Turnhout: Brepols, 2017), 45.
115 Juan R. I. Cole, 'Shaykh Ahmad al-Ahsa'i on the Sources of Religious Authority', in Linda S. Walbridge (ed.), *The Most Learned of the Shi'a: The Institution of the* Marjaʿ Taqlid (New York: Oxford University Press, 2001), 82–93: 86–7; MacEoin, *Messiah of Shiraz*, 67–8.
116 Zackery M. Heern, *The Emergence of Modern Shi'ism: Islamic Reform in Iraq and Iran* (Oxford: Oneworld, 2015), 92–4.
117 MacEoin, *Messiah of Shiraz*, 78–9.
118 Cole, 'Shaykh Ahmad al-Ahsa'i', 84; see also Hermann, *Le Shaykhisme*, 76–7; Mangol Bayat, *Mysticism and Dissent: Socioreligious Thought in Qajar Iran* (Syracuse, NY: Syracuse University Press, 1989), 39; cf. Arjomand, *Shadow of God*, 252.
119 MacEoin, *Messiah of Shiraz*, 83.
120 Algar, *Religion and State in Iran*, 67.

121 MacEoin, *Messiah of Shiraz*, 87.
122 Ibid., 94; Hermann, *Le Shaykhisme*, 48.
123 Pourjavady, 'Introduction', 24.
124 Rizvi, 'Mulla ʿAlī Nūrī', 136; Henry Corbin, *History of Islamic Philosophy*, tr. Liadain Sherrard and Philip Sherrard (London: Kegan Paul International in association with the Institute of Ismaili Studies, 1993), 306; Muhaqqiq and Izutsu, *Metaphysics*, 14.
125 Todd Lawson, 'Orthodoxy and Heterodoxy in Twelver Shiʿism: Aḥmad al-Aḥsāʾī on Fayḍ Kāshānī (the *Risālat al-ʿIlmiyya*)', in Gleave (ed.), *Religion and Society in Qajar Iran*, 127–54: 130.
126 Cole, 'Shaykh Ahmad al-Ahsaʾi', 82, 86, 87.
127 Juan R. I. Cole, 'The World as Text: Cosmologies of Shaykh Ahmad al-Ahsaʾi', *Studia Islamica* 80 (1994), 145–63: 154.
128 Bayat, *Mysticism and Dissent*, 48–9.
129 Henry Corbin, *Spiritual Body and Celestial Earth: From Mazdean Iran to Shīʿite Iran*, tr. Nancy Pearson (Princeton, NJ: Princeton University Press, 1977), 191.
130 Lawson, 'Orthodoxy and Heterodoxy', 134.
131 John Walbridge, *The Science of Mystic Lights: Quṭb al-Dīn Shīrāzī and the Illuminationist Tradition in Islamic Philosophy* (Cambridge, MA: Harvard University Press, 1992), 149; Lawson, 'Orthodoxy and Heterodoxy', 134; Todd Lawson, 'Shaykh Aḥmad al-Aḥsāʾī and the World of Images', in Denis Hermann and Sabrina Mervin (eds), *Shiʿi Trends and Dynamics in Modern Times* (Beirut: Ergon Verlag Würzburg, 2010), 19–31: 26.
132 Denis Gril, 'Hadith in the work of Ibn ʿArabī', *Journal of the Muhyiddin Ibn ʿArabi Society* 50 (2011), online version, https://ibnarabisociety.org/ahadith-in-the-work-of-ibn-arabi-denis-gril/, last accessed 4 October 2024; al-Lamati, *Pure Gold*, 12.
133 Muhammad U. Faruque, 'Life after Life: Mullā Ṣadrā on Death and Immortality', *Religious Studies* 60 (2024), 104–16; Walbridge, *Science of Mystic Lights*, 149–59.
134 Corbin, *Spiritual Body*, 185.
135 MacEoin, *Messiah of Shiraz*, 95–8.
136 Ibid., 98, 100, 103.
137 Hermann, *Le Shaykhisme*, 54.
138 Bayat, *Mysticism and Dissent*, 40; MacEoin,

139 Idris Samawi Hamid, 'Shaykh Aḥmad al-Aḥsā'ī', in Pourjavady (ed.), *Philosophy in Qajar Iran*, 66–124: 78.
140 MacEoin, *Messiah of Shiraz*, 116–17.
141 Ibid., 69, 117–18; Hermann, *Le Shaykhisme*, 53, 58.
142 MacEoin, *Messiah of Shiraz*, 118.
143 Bayat, *Mysticism and Dissent*, 66–7, 75–6; Amanat, *Resurrection and Renewal*, 53–4; MacEoin, *Messiah of Shiraz*, 192; Hermann, *Le Shaykhisme*, 82–4.
144 cf. MacEoin, *Messiah of Shiraz*, 193.
145 Bayat, *Mysticism and Dissent*, 69.
146 Ibid., 66–7.
147 Ibid., 67–8, 70.
148 Ibid., 75.
149 MacEoin, *Messiah of Shiraz*, 170–1.
150 Mirjam Künkler and Devin J. Stewart, 'Introduction', in *idem*. (eds), *Female Religious Authority in Shi'i Islam: Past and Present* (Edinburgh: Edinburgh University Press, 2020), 1–17.
151 MacEoin, *Messiah of Shiraz*, 226–45.
152 Ibid., 199; Amanat, *Resurrection and Renewal*, 142.
153 MacEoin, *Messiah of Shiraz*, 200.
154 Ibid., 245.
155 Bayat, *Mysticism and Dissent*, 79–80; Algar, *Religion and State*, 149–50.
156 Amanat, *Resurrection and Renewal*, 11.
157 *Encyclopaedia Iranica*, 'Bahaism, i. The Faith' (J. Cole), https://iranicaonline.org/articles/bahaism-i, last accessed 3 October 2024.
158 Arjomand, *Shadow of God*, 259.
159 Amanat, *Resurrection and Renewal*, 168.

6: Engaging with Modernity I

1 Hadrat Maulana Ashiq Ilahi Meeruti, *Tadhkiratur Rashid: Biography of Hadrat Maulana Rashid Ahmed Gangohi*, in two vols. (Delhi: Idara Impex, 2016), 1:116.
2 Lawrence James, *Raj: The Making and Unmaking of British India* (London: Little, Brown and Company, 1998), 233.
3 Syed Ahmad Khan Bahadur, *The Causes of the Indian Revolt* (Benares: Medical Hall Press, 1873), 16.
4 Barbara D. Metcalf, *Islamic Revival in British India: Deoband, 1860–1900* (Princeton, NJ: Princeton University Press, 1982), 84.
5 James, *Raj*, 270.

6 Ibid., 256.
7 SherAli Tareen, *Perilous Intimacies: Debating Hindu-Muslim Friendship after Empire* (New York: Columbia University Press, 2023), 80.
8 Justin Jones, 'Remembrances of Rashīd: Life-Histories as Lessons in the Dēōband Movement', *Journal of the Royal Asiatic Society*, 33/4 (2023), 933–48: 945–7.
9 Meeruti, *Tadhkiratur Rashid*, 1:117–26.
10 Metcalf, *Islamic Revival*, 82.
11 Brannon Ingram, *Revival from Below: The Deoband Movement and Global Islam* (Oakland, CA: University of California Press, 2018), 18–19, 14.
12 Ibid., 129.
13 Metcalf, *Islamic Revival*, 91.
14 Ibid., 92.
15 Ibid., 101.
16 Muhammad Qasim Zaman, 'Religious Education and the Rhetoric of Reform: The Madrasa in British India and Pakistan', *Comparative Studies in Society and History* 41/2 (1999), 294–323: 304.
17 Muhammad Qasim Zaman, *Ashraf 'Ali Thanawi: Islam in Modern South Asia* (Oxford: Oneworld, 2008), 27.
18 Ibid., 28.
19 Reichmuth, *The World of Murtaḍā al-Zabīdī*, 70.
20 Abdul-Rahman Mustafa, *On Taqlid: Ibn al-Qayyim's Critique of Authority in Islamic Law* (New York: Oxford University Press, 2013), 1.
21 Ingram, *Revival from Below*, 41; Metcalf, *Islamic Revival*, 101.
22 Metcalf, *Islamic Revival*, 129.
23 Ingram, *Revival from Below*, 52, 41–2.
24 Metcalf, *Islamic Revival*, 107.
25 George Makdisi, *The Rise of Colleges: Institutions of Learning in Islam and the West* (Edinburgh: Edinburgh University Press, 1984), 39.
26 Jonathan P. Berkey, 'Madrasas Medieval and Modern: Politics, Education, and the Problem of Muslim Identity', in Robert W. Hefner and Muhammad Qasim Zaman (eds), *Schooling Islam: The Culture and Politics of Modern Muslim Education* (Princeton, NJ: Princeton University Press, 2007), 40–60: 43.
27 Metcalf, *Islamic Revival*, 93.
28 Margrit Pernau, 'Introduction: Entangled Translations: The History of the Delhi College', in

Margrit Pernau (ed.), *The Delhi College: Traditional Elites, the Colonial State and Education Before 1857* (Delhi: Oxford University Press, 2006), 1–32: 18.
29 Metcalf, *Islamic Revival*, 97; Ingram, *Revival from Below*, 39.
30 Metcalf, *Islamic Revival*, 98; Muhammad Qasim Zaman, *Islam in Pakistan: A History* (Princeton, NJ: Princeton University Press, 2018), 16.
31 Metcalf, *Islamic Revival*, 128.
32 *Ibid.*, 136.
33 SherAli Tareen, *Defending Muhammad in Modernity* (Notre Dame, ID: University of Notre Dame Press, 2020), 171.
34 Metcalf, *Islamic Revival*, 100.
35 Ingram, *Revival from Below*, 26; Brannon Ingram, 'Sufis, Scholars and Scapegoats: Rashīd Ahmad Gangohī (d. 1905) and the Deobandi Critique of Sufism', *Muslim World* 99/3 (2009), 478–501: 480.
36 Barbara Daly Metcalf, *Perfecting Women: Maulana Ashraf ʿAli Thanawi's* Bihishti Zewar (Delhi: Oxford University Press, 1992), 20, 49. See also Brannon D. Ingram, 'Crises of the Public in Muslim India: Critiquing "Custom" at Aligarh and Deoband', *South Asia: Journal of South Asian Studies* 38/3, 403–18: 414.
37 Muhammad Qasim Zaman, *Islam in Pakistan*, 14; Metcalf, *Islamic Revival*, 136.
38 *Encyclopaedia of Islam Three*, 'Anglo-Muhammadan Law' (Muhammad Khalid Masud), https://referenceworks-brill-com.ezproxy-prd.bodleian.ox.ac.uk/display/entries/EI3O/COM-22716.xml?rskey=Bd6shV&result=1, last accessed 21 October 2024.
39 Muhammad Qasim Zaman, *The Ulama in Contemporary Islam: Custodians of Change* (Princeton, NJ: Princeton University Press, 2002), 51.
40 Metcalf, *Islamic Revival*, 140.
41 *Ibid.*, 146–7; Muḥammad Khālid Masʿūd, 'Trends in the Interpretation of Islamic Law as Represented in the *Fatāwā* Literature of the Deoband School' (MA thesis, University of McGill, 1969), 12.
42 Metcalf, *Islamic Revival*, 148; Ingram, *Revival from Below*, 56 and chapter 2.
43 Jones, 'Remembrances of Rashīd', 942.

44 Mas'ūd, 'Trends in the Interpretation of Islamic Law', 17 (adapted).
45 Ingram, *Revival from Below*, 2–3.
46 Moin Ahmad Nizami, *Reform and Renewal in South Asian Islam: The Chishti-Sabris in 18th–19th Century North India* (Delhi: Oxford University Press, 2017), 232; Tareen, *Defending Muhammad*, 199; Ingram, 'Crises of the Public', 415.
47 Metcalf, *Islamic Revival*, 150; Ingram, *Revival from Below*, 65; Tareen, *Defending Muhammad*, 224.
48 Ingram, *Revival from Below*, 66.
49 Ibid., 67.
50 Sunil Sharma, *Amir Khusraw: The Poet of Sultans and Sufis* (Oxford: Oneworld, 2005), 55.
51 Metcalf, *Islamic Revival*, 79; Nizam, *Reform and Renewal*, 146, 165, 183–4, 198.
52 Nizami, *Reform and Renewal*, 200–1, 215, 222, 225; Ingram, *Revival from Below*, 70–1.
53 Metcalf, *Islamic Revival*, 77; Ingram, 'Sufis, Scholars and Scapegoats', 489; Jones, 'Remembrances of Rashīd', 939.
54 Metcalf, *Islamic Revival*, 157.
55 Ali Altaf Mian, 'Surviving Modernity: Ashraf 'Alī Thānvī (1863–1943) and the Making of Muslim Orthodoxy in Colonial India' (PhD dissertation, Duke University, 2015), 69; Muhammad Umar Faruque, 'Eternity Made Temporal: Ashraf 'Alī Thānavī, a Twentieth-Century Indian Thinker and the Revival of Classical Sufi Thought', *Journal of Sufi Studies* 9/2 (2020): 215–246.
56 Mian, 'Surviving Modernity', 111, 143, 148.
57 Metcalf, *Perfecting Women*, 70.
58 Metcalf, *Islamic Revival*, 139.
59 Ingram, 'Sufis, Scholars and Scapegoats', 488.
60 Jones, 'Remembrances of Rashīd', 939; Ingram, *Revival from Below*, 27.
61 Ingram, *Revival from Below*, 27 and chapter 4; Jones, 'Remembrances of Rashīd', 940; Nizami, *Reform and Renewal*, 194.
62 Ingram, *Revival from Below*, 131.
63 Ibid., 128.
64 Metcalf, *Perfecting Women*, 49–50; Mian, 'Surviving Modernity', 218.
65 Metcalf, *Perfecting Women*, 1, 3; Ingram, *Revival from Below*, 105.
66 Metcalf, *Perfecting Women*, 47–8.

67 Ibid., 48–50.
68 Mian, 'Surviving Modernity', 226.
69 Metcalf, *Perfecting Women*, 67–8.
70 Ibid., 68–72.
71 Ibid., 72–4.
72 Ibid., 74.
73 Ibid., 74–5.
74 Ibid., 77.
75 Tareen, *Perilous Intimacies*, chapter 2.
76 Metcalf, *Islamic Revival*, 276; Martin Riexinger, *Sanā'ullāh Amritsarī (1868–1948) und die Ahl-i-Ḥadīs im Punjab unter britischer Herrschaft* (Würzburg: Ergon, 2004), 122–8; Julia Anne Stephens, *Governing Islam: Law, Empire, and Secularism in Modern South Asia* (Cambridge: Cambridge University Press, 2018), 118.
77 Stephens, *Governing Islam*, 118–20; Shawkani, 'Al-Qawl al-mufid', 191–2.
78 Saeedullah, *The Life and Works of Muhammad Siddiq Hasan Khan, Nawab of Bhopal, 1248–1307 (1832–1890)* (Lahore: Sh. Muhammad Ashraf, 1973), 13, 28.
79 Ibid., 35–7; Barbara Metcalf, 'A Way with Words: Nawab Siddiq Hasan Khan (1832–1890) and the Unexpected Power of Print', *Journal of the Royal Asiatic Society* 33/4 (2023), 949–69: 954.
80 Saeedullah, *Life and Works*, 43; Metcalf, 'A Way with Words', 956.
81 El Shamsy, *Rediscovering the Islamic Classics*, 173–4; Metcalf, 'A Way with Words', 961.
82 Saeedullah, *Life and Works*, 14.
83 Ibid., 64.
84 Ibid., 14.
85 Metcalf, 'A Way with Words', 949.
86 El Shamsy, *Rediscovering the Islamic Classics*, 173.
87 Metcalf, 'A Way with Words', 958; Saeedullah, *Life and Works*, 101.
88 Saeedullah, *Life and Works*, 132, 136.
89 Ibid., 136, 153; El-Shamsy, *Rediscovering the Islamic Classics*, 167.
90 Saeedullah, *Life and Works*, 119–20.
91 Ibid., 102.
92 Ibid., 118–19.
93 Metcalf, 'A Way with Words', 959–60.
94 Francis Robinson, 'Technology and Religious Change: Islam and the Impact of Print', *Modern Asian Studies* 27/1 (1993), 229–51: 242.
95 Nile Green, *Terrains of Exchange: Religious Economies of Global Islam* (New York: Oxford University Press,

2015), chapter 4; Arian Hopf, *Translating Islam, Translating Religion: Conceptions of Religion and Islam in the Aligarh Movement* (Heidelberg: CrossAsia-eBooks, 2021), 49.
96 Ulrike Gleixner, 'Pietism', in Ulinka Rublach (ed.), *The Oxford Handbook of the Protestant Reformations* (New York: Oxford University Press, 2015), 329–49: 330.
97 C. G. Pfander, *The Mizan ul Haqq; or Balance of Truth*, tr. R. H. Weakley (London: Church Missionary House, 1866), x.
98 A. A. Powell, 'Maulānā Raḥmat Allāh Kairānawī and Muslim-Christian Controversy in India in the Mid-19th Century', *Journal of the Royal Asiatic Society of Great Britain and Ireland* 1 (1976), 42–63.
99 Christian Troll, *Sayyid Ahmad Khan: A Reinterpretation of Muslim Theology* (New Delhi: Vikas Publishing House, 1978), 28; Hopf, *Translating Islam*, 8.
100 Troll, *Sayyid Ahmad Khan*, 29–30; Schimmel, *Pain and Grace*, 31.
101 Christian W. Troll, Charles M. Ramsey and Mahboob Basharat Mughal (tr.), *The Gospel according to Sayyid Ahmad Khan (1817–1898): An Annotated Translation of* Tabyīn al-kalām *(part 3)* (Leiden: Brill, 2020), xv; Ziad, *Quest of the Nightingale*, 45.
102 J. M. S. Baljon, *The Reforms and Religious Ideas of Sir Sayyid Ahmad Khan* (Leiden: Brill, 1958), 8, n. 2.
103 Troll, *Sayyid Ahmad Khan*, 37.
104 Baljon, *Reforms and Religious Ideas*, 60; Troll, *Sayyid Ahmad Khan*, 38; Hopf, *Translating Islam*, 26.
105 Hopf, *Translating Islam*, 27.
106 Baljon, *Reforms and Religious Ideas*, 61.
107 Troll, *Sayyid Ahmad Khan*, 44–6.
108 Hopf, *Translating Islam*, 39–40; Troll, *Sayyid Ahmad Khan*, 40.
109 Baljon, *Reforms and Religious Ideas*, 19.
110 Hopf, *Translating Islam*, 56.
111 Troll, *Sayyid Ahmad Khan*, 70; Hopf, *Translating Islam*, 64.
112 Troll, *Sayyid Ahmad Khan*, 69, 80; Hopf, *Translating Islam*, 57, 69–70.
113 Hopf, *Translating Islam*, 65; Troll, *Sayyid Ahmad Khan*, 90, 93–4.
114 Ahmad Khan, *Causes*, e.g. 39–40.

115 Troll, *Sayyid Ahmad Khan*, 95–6.
116 Troll, Ramsey, and Mughal, *The Gospel*, 3.
117 William Muir, *The Life of Mahomet*, in four vols. (London: Smith, Elder & Co., 1861), 1:iii.
118 Troll, *Sayyid Ahmad Khan*, 113.
119 Sir Sayyid Ahmad Khan, *A Series of Essays on the Life of Mohammed and Subjects Subsidiary Thereto* (Delhi: Idarah-i Adabiyat-i Delli, 1981), xvii–xviii.
120 Ibid., xix.
121 G. F. I. Graham, *The Life and Work of Syed Ahmed Khan* (Edinburgh and London: William Blackwood and Sons, 1885), 98–9.
122 Ahmad Khan, *A Series of Essays*, ix–xi.
123 Troll, *Sayyid Ahmad Khan*, 128.
124 Ibid., 128, 130.
125 Ahmad Khan, *A Series of Essays*, xii.
126 Troll, *Sayyid Ahmad Khan*, 137–42.
127 Metcalf, *Islamic Revival*, 269.
128 William Muir, *The Life of Mahomet*, 4:321.
129 Ahmad Khan, 'Essay on the Question Whether Islam has been Beneficial or Injurious to Human Society in General, and to the Mosaic and Christian Dispensations', in *idem.*, *A Series of Essays*.
130 Cherágh Ali, *A Critical Exposition of the "Popular Jihad"* (Calcutta; Thacker, Spink & Co., 1885), esp. lxx, lxxxvii–lxxxix, 16–26, 114–15, 158–61.
131 Syed Ameer Ali, *The Spirit of Islâm: A History of the Evolution and Ideals of Islâm* (London: Christophers, 1953), esp. xlv–lii, 122.
132 Ibid., 175.
133 Aziz Ahmad, *Islamic Modernism in India and Pakistan, 1857–1964* (London: Oxford University Press, 1967), 36.
134 Ingram, *Revival from Below*, 51–2.
135 David Lelyveld, *Aligarh's First Generation: Muslim Solidarity in British India* (Princeton, NJ: Princeton University Press, 1978), 129.
136 Ibid., 125.
137 Gail Minault, 'Sir Sayyid on "The Present State of Education among Muhammadan Females"', in Yasmin Saikia and M. Raisur Rahman (eds), *The Cambridge Companion to Sayyid Ahmad Khan* (Cambridge: Cambridge University Press, 2019), 55–68.
138 William C. Lubenow, *The Cambridge Apostles*,

1820–1914: Liberalism, Imagination, and Friendship in British intellectual and Professional Life (Cambridge: Cambridge University Press, 1998), 256.
139 Thomas W. Arnold, The Preaching of Islam: A History of the Propagation of the Muslim Faith (London: Constable & Company, 1913); Ruchama Johnston-Bloom, '"Dieses wirklich westöstlichen Mannes": The German-Jewish Orientalist Josef Horovitz in Germany, India, and Palestine', in Susannah Heschel and Umar Ryad (eds), The Muslim Reception of European Orientalism: Reversing the Gaze (London: Routledge, 2018), 168–83.
140 Gregory Maxwell Bruce, 'Translator's Afterword', in Shibli Nuʿmani, Turkey, Egypt, and Syria: A Travelogue, tr. Gregory Maxwell Bruce (Syracuse, NY: Syracuse University Press, 2020), 202–26: 203–4, 208; Metcalf, Islamic Revival, 333, 337.
141 Arnold, The Preaching of Islam, ix.
142 Metcalf, Islamic Revival, 341.
143 Usha Sanyal, Devotional Islam and Politics in British India: Ahmed Riza Khan Barelvi and his Movement, 1870–1920 (Delhi: Oxford University Press, 1996), 217; Nizami, Reform and Renewal, 208.
144 Metcalf, Islamic Revival, 335–6; Sanyal, Devotional Islam, 217; Zaman, Islam in Pakistan, 25.
145 Bruce, 'Translator's Afterword', 208–9; Metcalf, Islamic Revival, 337.
146 Baljon, Reforms and Religious Ideas, 33; Ingram, 'Crises of the Public', 408.
147 Ingram, 'Crises of the Public', 411.
148 Baljon, Reforms and Religious Ideas, 114; Troll, Sayyid Ahmad Khan, 100, 313.
149 Troll, Sayyid Ahmad Khan, 165, 317.
150 Ibid., 155.
151 Ibid., 156.
152 Baljon, Reforms and Religious Ideas, 64, 73; David Lelyveld, 'Naicari Nature: Sir Sayyid Ahmad Khan and the Reconciliation of Science, Technology, and Religion', in Saikia and Rahman (eds), Cambridge Companion to Sayyid Ahmad Khan, 69–86: 80.
153 Metcalf, Islamic Revival, 144–5.
154 Mian, 'Surviving Modernity', 98.

155 Ingram, 'Crises', 405.
156 Yohanan Friedmann, *Prophecy Continuous: Aspects of Aḥmadī Religious Thought and Its Medieval Background* (Berkeley, CA: University of California Press, 1989), 105.
157 Hadrat Mirza Ghulam Ahmad, *Barāhīn-e Ahmadiyya: Parts 1 & II* (Tilford: Islam International Publications, 2012), 74.
158 Friedmann, *Prophecy Continuous*, 4–10.
159 Ghulam Ahmad, *Barāhīn*, xx–xxi; Friedmann, *Prophecy Continuous*, 132.
160 Friedmann, *Prophecy Continuous*, 108–9.
161 *Ibid.*, 110; Suliman Bashear, 'The Title "Fārūq" and its Association with ʿUmar I', *Studia Islamica* 72 (1990), 47–70.
162 Friedmann, *Prophecy Continuous*, 142–3.
163 *Ibid.*, 116–17.
164 *Ibid.*, 109.
165 *Ibid.*, 88.
166 *Ibid.*, 133.
167 *Ibid.*, 130.
168 *Ibid.*, 128.
169 *Ibid.*, 175.
170 Hadrat Mirza Ghulam Ahmad, *The British Government and Jihad*, tr. Tayyba Seema Ahmed and Lutfur Rahman (Tilford: Islam International Publications, 2006), 10.
171 Friedmann, *Prophecy Continuous*, 177.
172 *Ibid.*, 5.
173 *Ibid.*, 30.
174 *Ibid.*, 115, 117–18.
175 Mian, 'Surviving Modernity', 96.
176 Sanyal, *Devotional Islam*, 55.
177 *Ibid.*, 56–7.
178 Metcalf, *Islamic Revival*, 304.
179 Sanyal, *Devotional Islam*, 153, 164.
180 *Ibid.*, 245.
181 *Ibid.*, 259–62.
182 *Ibid.*, 257–8.
183 Tareen, *Defending Muhammad*, 176.
184 Sanyal, *Devotional Islam*, 145.
185 *Ibid.*, 132.
186 *Ibid.*, 204.
187 *Ibid.*
188 *Ibid.*, 221–3.
189 *Ibid.*, 226–7, 229.
190 *Ibid.*, 184–5.
191 *Ibid.*, 231, 234, 237–9; Ingram, *Revival from Below*, 100.
192 Sanyal, *Devotional Islam*, 5.

7: Engaging with Modernity II

1 Eugene Rogan, *The Damascus Events: The 1860 Massacre and the Destruction of the Old Ottoman World* (London: Allen Lane, 2024), 160–3.
2 *Ibid.*, chapter 2.

3 *Ibid.*, 91.
4 *Ibid.*, 185–6.
5 *Ibid.*, 149.
6 Alexandre Bellemare, *Abd-El-Kader, sa vie politique et militaire* (Paris: Hachette, 1863), 443–4.
7 Tom Woerner-Powell, *Another Road to Damascus: An Integrative Approach to 'Abd al-Qadir al-Jazā'irī (1808–1883)* (Berlin; Boston: de Gruyter, 2017), 149.
8 Rogan, *Damascus Events*, 97.
9 Itzchak Weismann, *Taste of Modernity: Sufism, Salafiyya, and Arabism in Late Ottoman Damascus* (Leiden: Brill, 2001), 148.
10 Vikør, *Sufi and Scholar*, 125–7; O'Fahey, *Enigmatic Saint*, 136–7.
11 'Abd al-Qadir al-Jaza'iri, *Kitab al-Mawaqif fi al-tasawwuf wa-al-wa'z wa-al-irshad*, in three vols. (Cairo: n.p., 1911), 1:143; Weismann, *Taste of Modernity*, 140.
12 Albert Hourani, 'Sufism and Modern Islam: Mawlana Khalid and the Naqshbandi Order', in *The Emergence of the Modern Middle East* (Berkeley and Los Angeles, CA: University of California Press, 1981), 75–89; Weismann, *Taste of Modernity*, 31.
13 James McDougall, *A History of Algeria* (Cambridge: Cambridge University Press, 2017), 50.
14 Bellemare, *Abd-El-Kader*, 37.
15 McDougall, *A History of Algeria*, 61.
16 Weismann, *Taste of Modernity*, 149.
17 Tom Woerner-Powell, "Abd al-Qādir al-Jazā'irī, Migration, and the Rule of Law: "A Reply to Certain Persons of Distinction"', *Studia Islamica* 106/2 (2011), 214–40; Woerner-Powell, *Another Road to Damascus*, chapter 2.
18 Woerner-Powell, *Another Road to Damascus*, 107, n. 89, 172.
19 Muhammad ibn 'Abd al-Qadir al-Jaza'iri, *Tuhfat al-za'ir fi ma'athir 'Abd al-Qadir wa-akhbar al-jaza'ir*, in two vols. (Alexandria: Matba'at al-Tijariyyah, 1903), 2:161–85, esp. 162, 163–5, 166–7, 169, 172.
20 Woerner-Powell, *Another Road to Damascus*, 112.
21 Ibn 'Abd al-Qadir al-Jaza'iri, *Tuhfat al-za'ir*, 2:17.
22 'Abd al-Qadir al-Jaza'iri, *Dhikra al-'aqil wa-tanbih al-ghafil* (Beirut: n.d.) https://archive.org/details/zikra3aqel/page/n139/mode/1up, last accessed 25 September 2025, esp. 3–7, 12–13, 33–5, 40,

50–1, 71–6; cf. Woerner-Powell, *Another Road to Damascus*, 131–40.
23 Al-Jaza'iri, *Dhikra al-ʿaqil*, 40; Weismann, *Taste of Modernity*, 150.
24 Butrus Abu-Manneh, 'Four Letters of Šayḫ Ḥasan al-ʿAṭṭār to Šayḫ Ṭāhir al-Ḥusaynī of Jerusalem', *Arabica* 50/1 (2003), 79–95: 80.
25 F. de Jong, 'The Itinerary of Hasan al-ʿAṭṭār (1766–1835): A Reconsideration and its Implications', *Journal of Semitic Studies* XXVIII/1 (1983), 99–128; Khaled El-Rouayheb, 'Aḥmad al-Mallawī (d. 1767): *Commentary on the Versification of the Immediate Implications of Hypothetical Propositions*', in El-Rouayheb and Schmidkte (eds), *The Oxford Handbook of Islamic Philosophy*, 509–34: 529–30.
26 Rifāʿah Rāfiʿ al-Ṭahṭāwī, *An Imam in Paris: Account of a Stay in France by an Egyptian Cleric (1826–1831)*, tr. Daniel L. Newman (London: Saqi, 2011), 105.
27 *Ibid*., 48.
28 Juan Cole, 'Rifāʿah al-Ṭahṭāwī and the Revival of Practical Philosophy', *The Muslim World* 70/1 (1980), 29–46: 41–2.
29 J. Heyworth-Dunne, 'Rifāʿah Badawī Rāfiʿ aṭ-Ṭahṭāwī: The Egyptian Revivalist', *Bulletin of the School of Oriental Studies* 9/4 (1939), 961–7: 966; al-Ṭahṭāwī, *An Imam in Paris*, 47.
30 Indira Falk Gensink, *Islamic Reform and Conservatism: Al-Azhar and the Evolution of Modern Sunni Islam* (London: I. B. Tauris, 2009), 66–71; al-Tahtawi, *al-Aʿmal al-kamilah*, ed. Muhammad ʿAmara in five vols. (Cairo: Maktabat al-Usrah, 2010), 5:17–63.
31 Al-Ṭahṭāwī, *An Imam in Paris*, 209–10.
32 Albert Hourani, *Arabic Thought in the Liberal Age* (Cambridge: Cambridge University Press, 1983), 78, 80.
33 Leila Ahmed, *Women and Gender in Islam: Historical Roots of a Modern Debate* (New Haven, CT: Yale University Press, 2021), 133.
34 *Ibid*., 136; Hourani, *Arabic Thought*, 78; Marilyn Booth, *The Career and Communities of Zaynab Fawwaz: Feminist thinking in Fin-de-Siècle Egypt* (Oxford: Oxford University Press, 2021), 201, n. 100.
35 Ibn Miskawayh, *Tahdhib al-akhlaq*, ed. ʿAbd al-ʿAlim

Salih (Egypt: Matbaʿat al-Taraqqi, 1317 [= 1899), 91.
36 Cole, 'Rifāʿah al-Ṭahṭāwī', 36–7.
37 Woerner-Powell, *Another Road to Damascus*, 122.
38 Weismann, *Taste of Modernity*, 152.
39 al-Jazaʾiri, *Kitab al-Mawaqif*, 1:69–70.
40 Woerner-Powell, *Another Road to Damascus*, 163–7.
41 al-Jazaʾiri, *Kitab al-Mawaqif*, 1:134.
42 Michel Chodkiewicz, *The Spiritual Writings of Amir ʿAbd al-Kader*, tr. James Chrestensen and Tom Manning (Albany, NY: SUNY Press, 1995), 13.
43 Oliver Scharbrodt, 'The Salafiyya and Sufism: Muḥammad ʿAbduh and his *Risālat al-Wāridāt* (Treatise on Mystical Inspirations)', *Bulletin of the School of Oriental and African* Studies 70/1 (2007), 89–115: 91; Charles C. Adams, *Islam and Modernism in Egypt: A Study of the Modern Reform Movement inaugurated by Muḥammad ʿAbduh* (London: Oxford University Press, 1933), 21–2.
44 W. Montgomery Watt (tr.), *The Faith and Practice of al-Ghazālī* (London: George Allen and Unwin Ltd., 1952), 22–6; Adams, *Islam and Modernism in Egypt*, 25, n. 2; ʿUthman Amin, *Muhammad ʿAbduh: essai sur ses idées philosophiques et religieuses* (Cairo: Imprimerie Misr, 1944), 4.
45 Nikki R. Keddie, *Sayyid Jamāl ad-Dīn "al-Afghānī": A Political Biography* (Berkeley, CA: University of California Press, 1972), 89.
46 Scharbrodt, 'The Salafiyya and Sufism', 98; Adams, *Islam and Modernism in Egypt*, 32–3.
47 Pourjavady, 'Introduction', 20.
48 Nikki R. Keddie, *An Islamic Response to Imperialism: Political and Religious Writings of Sayyid Jamāl al-Dīn ʿAl-Afghānī*' (Berkeley and Los Angeles, CA: University of California Press, 1968), 10–11.
49 Wilfrid Scawen Blunt, *Secret History of the English Occupation of Egypt* (London: T. Fisher Unwin, 1907), 100.
50 Edward G. Browne, *The Persian Revolution of 1905–1909* (Cambridge: The University Press, 1910), 2–3.
51 Scharbrodt, 'The Salafiyya and Sufism', 98; Muhammad Rashid Rida, *Tarikh al-ustadh al-imam al-shaykh Muhammad*

52 Browne, *The Persian Revolution*, 3.
53 George F. Hourani, *On the Harmony of Religion and Philosophy: A translation, with introduction and notes, of Ibn Rushd's Kitāb faṣl al-maqāl* (London: Luzac, 1976); Fazlur Rahman, *Prophecy in Islam: Philosophy and Orthodoxy* (London: Allen & Unwin, 1958); Muhsin Mahdi, *Alfarabi*.
54 Niyazi Berkes, *The Development of Secularism in Turkey* (Montreal: McGill University Press, 1964), 180.
55 Cole, 'Rifā'ah al-Ṭahṭāwī', 33.
56 Rida, *Tarikh*, 1:30–1.
57 *Ibid.*, 1:32.
58 Oliver Scharbrodt, *Muhammad 'Abduh: Modern Islam and the Culture of Ambiguity* (London: I. B. Tauris, 2022), 43; Nathan Spannaus, 'Theology in Central Asia', in Sabine Schmidtke (ed.), *The Oxford Handbook of Islamic Theology* (New York: Oxford University Press, 2014), 587–605: 588; al-Taftazani, *al-Talwih ila kashf haqa'iq al-Tanqih*, Maktabat 'Arif Hikmat 251.9 / 216.1 SMT, fol. 2 'Abduh, in three vols. (Cairo: Dar al-Fadilah, 2006), 1:y. https://dar.kawla.gov.sa/ar/dar/altlwyh-aly-kshf-hqayq-altnqyh, last accessed 3 October 2024.
59 Scharbrodt, 'The Salafiyya and Sufism', 98–112; Scharbrodt, *Muhammad 'Abduh*, 48–52; Jami, *The Precious Pearl*, tr. Nicholas Heer (Albany, NY: SUNY Press, 1979).
60 Muhammad Haddad, *Le réformisme musulman: une histoire critique* (Milan; Paris: Éditions Mimésis, 2016), 43–5; Scharbrodt, *Muhammad 'Abduh*, 52–8; Robert Wisnovksy, 'Avicenna's Islamic Reception', in Peter Adamson (ed.), *Interpreting Avicenna: Critical Essays* (Cambridge: Cambridge University Press, 2013), 190–213: 210–13.
61 Adams, *Islam and Modernism*, 39, 44; Hourani, *Arabic Thought*, 132; Mark Sedgwick, *Muhammad Abduh* (Oxford: Oneworld, 2009), 30–1; Andrew Hammond, *Late Ottoman Origins of Modern Islamic Thought: Turkish and Egyptian Thinkers on the Disruption of Islamic Knowledge* (Cambridge: Cambridge University Press, 2022), 5, 10–11.
62 M. Guizot, *General History of Civilization in Europe, from the Fall of the Roman*

Empire to the French Revolution (New York, NY: D. Appleton and Co., 1838), 75.
63 Hourani, *Arabic Thought*, 132; al-Ṭahṭāwī, *An Imam in Paris*, 293; Robert Irwin, *Ibn Khaldun: An Intellectual Biography* (Princeton, NJ: Princeton University Press, 2018), 164.
64 El Shamsy, *Rediscovering the Islamic Classics*, 150.
65 Malcolm H. Kerr, *Islamic Reform: The Political and Legal Theories of Muḥammad ʿAbduh and Rashīd Riḍā* (Berkeley and Los Angeles, CA: University of California Press, 1966), 137, n. 101; Sedgwick, *Muhammad Abduh*, 16–17.
66 William Ryle-Hodges 'Muḥammad ʿAbduh's Politics of Adab: Knowledge, Journalism and Policing Public Sociability in 19th century Egypt' (PhD dissertation, University of Cambridge, 2020); El Shamsy, *Rediscovering the Islamic Classics*, 150.
67 Adams, *Islam and Modernism*, 46–51.
68 al-Ṭahṭāwī, *An Imam in Paris*, 194; Khaldun S. Al-Husry, *Origins of Modern Arab Political Thought* (Delmar, NY: Caravan Books, 1980), 23, 49.
69 Kerr, *Islamic Reform*, 134.
70 *Encyclopaedia Iranica*, 'DAHRĪ' (Daniel Gimaret), https://www.iranicaonline.org/articles/dahri-ar#pt2, last accessed 9 January 2025.
71 Keddie, *An Islamic Response*, 21, 53–9.
72 Keddie, *Sayyid Jamāl ad-Dīn "al-Afghānī"*, 126, 171.
73 Al-Sayyid Jamal al-Din al-Afghani, *al-Radd ʿala al-dahriyyin*, tr. Muhammad ʿAbduh with the assistance of ʿArif Efendi Abi Turab al-Afghani (Egypt: Matbaʿat al-Mawsuʿat, 1300), 61–8; cp. Keddie, *An Islamic Response*, 161–73.
74 Ernest Renan, 'Islam and Science', tr. Sally Ragep with the assistance of Faith Wallis (McGill University, 2011), https://www.mcgill.ca/islamicstudies/files/islamicstudies/renan_islamism_cversion.pdf, last accessed 9 January 2025.
75 Keddie, *An Islamic Response*, 84–7, 182–3.
76 Sayyid Jamal al-Din al-Afghani, *al-Aʿmal al-kamilah*, ed. Sayyid Hadi Khusrawshahi in seven vols. (Tehran: Shuruq, 1379), 1:68–9.
77 Al-Afghani, *al-Radd ʿala al-dahriyyin*, 69; Keddie, *An Islamic Response*, 173; al-Afghani, *al-Aʿmal al-kamilah*, 128, 195; Kerr, *Islamic Reform*, 130–1.

78 Browne, *The Persian Revolution*, 9.
79 Algar, *Religion and State in Iran*, 196; al-Afghani, *al-A'mal al-kamilah*, 71.
80 Amin, *Muhammad 'Abduh*, 15.
81 Adams, *Islam and Modernism*, 64; Hurgronje, *Mekka in the Latter Part*, 178–9.
82 Ammeke Kateman, *Muhammad 'Abduh and his Interlocutors: Conceptualizing Religion in a Globalizing World* (Leiden: Brill, 2019), 41–2.
83 Muhammad 'Abduh, *The Theology of Unity*, tr. Ishaq Musa'ad and Kenneth Cragg (London: George Allen & Unwin, 1966), 27–8; Muhammad 'Abduh, *Risalat al-Tawhid*, ed. Muhammad 'Amara (Cairo: Dar al-Shuruq, 1994), 13–14.
84 'Abduh, *The Theology of Unity*, 30–1; 'Abduh, *Risalat al-Tawhid*, 18–19.
85 'Abduh, *The Theology of Unity*, 132–6; 'Abduh, *Risalat al-Tawhid*, 150–3.
86 'Abduh, *The Theology of Unity*, 32–40.
87 Ibid., 28; 'Abduh, *Risalat al-Tawhid*, 14.
88 'Abduh, *The Theology of Unity*, chapters 2–5.
89 Ibid., 22.
90 'Abduh, *Risalat al-Tawhid*, 177.
91 Adams, *Islam and Modernism*, 68–70.
92 Ibid., 70–5.
93 El Shamsy, *Rediscovering the Islamic Classics*, 24, 154.
94 Ibid., 151.
95 Adams, *Islam and Modernism*, 76.
96 Wilfrid Scawen Blunt, *My Diaries*, in two vols. (New York: Alfred A. Knopf, 1922), 2:42.
97 Rashid Rida, *Tafsir al-Fatihah mulakhkhas min durus al-imam al-'alim wa-al-ustadh al-hakim al-shaykh Muhammad 'Abduh* (Egypt: Matba'at al-Mawsu'at, 1319), 5–21.
98 Johannes J. G. Jansen, *The Interpretation of the Koran in Modern Egypt* (Leiden: Brill, 1974), 18–34; *Encyclopaedia of the Qur'ān*, 'Exegesis: Modern' (Rotraud Wielandt).
99 Adams, *Islam and Modernism*, 136, 138; Kerr, *Islamic Reform*, 129.
100 Kerr, *Islamic Reform*, 130; Marwa Elshakry, *Reading Darwin in Arabic* (Chicago: The University of Chicago Press, 2013), chapter 5.
101 Elshakry, *Reading Darwin*, 167, 172; Blunt, *My Diaries*, 2:66; Adams, *Islam and Modernism*, 125.
102 Adams, *Islam and Modernism*, 86–7; Kateman, *Muhammad*

'Abduh and his Interlocutors, 167–8; Booth, *The Career and Communities*, 330–6.
103 Kateman, *Muhammad 'Abduh and his Interlocutors*, 166.
104 Muhammad 'Abduh, *al-A'mal al-kamilah*, ed. Muhammad 'Amara in five vols. (Cairo: Dar al-Shuruq, 1993), 3:219–37.
105 Kateman, *Muhammad 'Abduh and his Interlocutors*, 253–5.
106 Jakob Skovgaard-Petersen, *Defining Islam for the Egyptian State: Muftis and Fatwas of the* Dār al-Iftā (Leiden: Brill, 1997), 121.
107 Charles C. Adams, 'Muḥammad 'Abduh and the Transvaal Fatwā', in *The Macdonald Presentation Volume* (Princeton, NJ: Princeton University Press, 1933), 11–30: 14; cf. Skovgaard-Petersen, *Defining Islam*, 121.
108 *Al-Fatāwá al-islāmiyyah min dār al-iftā' al-miṣriyyah*, in 39 vols (Cairo: Dār al-Iftā' al-Miṣriyyah, 2010), 17:7–9; Adams, 'Muḥammad 'Abduh and the Transvaal Fatwā', 16–18.
109 Skovgaard-Petersen, *Defining Islam*, 124–5.
110 Ibid., 130.
111 Ibid., 127–30.
112 El Shamsy, *Rediscovering the Islamic Classics*, 157.
113 Junaid Quadri, *Transformations of Tradition: Islamic Law in Colonial Modernity* (New York: Oxford University Press, 2021), 40.
114 Hammond, *Late Ottoman Origins*, 77; Andrew Hammond, '"The Imam of Modern Egypt was a Sceptic": Mustafa Sabri's Radical Critique of Muhammad 'Abduh and Modernist Theology', *Journal of the Royal Asiatic Society* 32/2 (2022), 463–85.
115 Leor Halevi, *Modern Things on Trial: Islam's Global and Material Reformation in the Age of Rida, 1865–1935* (New York: Columbia University Press, 2019), chs 1 and 5.
116 Adams, *Islam and Modernism*, 152; Ahmed, *Women and Gender in Islam*, 139.
117 Ahmed, *Women and Gender in Islam*, 138.
118 Adams, *Islam and Modernism*, 230; Ahmed, *Women and Gender in Islam*, 140.
119 Mohammad Fadel, 'Two Women, One Man: Knowledge, Power, and Gender in Medieval Sunni Legal Thought', *International Journal of Middle East Studies* 29/2 (1997), 185–204: 187;

Karen Bauer, *Gender Hierarchy in the Qur'ān: Medieval Interpretations, Modern Responses* (Cambridge: Cambridge University Press, 2015), 69–70.
120 Booth, *The Career and Communities*, 172, 177.
121 *Ibid.*, 169.
122 *Ibid.*, 208, 224–5.
123 *Ibid.*, 207, n. 117, 199, 208.
124 Qasim Bek Amin, *Tahrir al-mar'ah* (Egypt: Al-Maktabah al-Sharqiyyah, n.d.), 9, https://mc.dlib.nyu.edu/files/books/columbia_aco003336/columbia_aco003336_lo.pdf, last accessed 17 January 2025.
125 *Ibid.*, 12.
126 *Ibid.*, 13–15.
127 *Ibid.*, 7.
128 *Ibid.*, 25, 50.
129 *Ibid.*, 19.
130 *Ibid.*, 27–9.
131 *Ibid.*, 43–50.
132 *Ibid.*, 51–2.
133 *Ibid.*, 68, 79.
134 *Ibid.*, 75–6.
135 *Ibid.*, 73–4.
136 *Ibid.*, 77; Marion Holmes Katz, *Women in the Mosque: A History of Legal Thought and Social Practice* (Columbia, NY: Columbia University Press, 2014), chapter 1.
137 Bahithat al-Badiyah, 'A Lecture in the Club of the Umma Party, 1909', in Margot Badran and Miriam Cooke (eds), *Opening the Gates: A Century of Arab Feminist Writing* (Bloomington, IN: Indiana University Press, 1990), 227–38.
138 Nazira Zein-ed-Din, 'Veiling and Unveiling', in Charles Kurzman (ed.), *Liberal Islam: A Sourcebook* (Oxford: Oxford University Press, 1996), 127–38.
139 Juan Ricardo Cole, 'Feminism, Class, and Islam in Turn-of-the-Century Egypt', *International Journal of Middle East Studies* 13/4 (1981), 387–407: 392.
140 *Ibid.*, 403.
141 Omnia Shakry, 'Schooled Mothers and Structured Play: Child Rearing in Turn-of-the-Century Egypt', in Lila Abu-Lughod (ed.), *Remaking Women* (Princeton, NJ: Princeton University Press, 1998), 126–70: 147.
142 Muhammad Rashid Rida, *Nida' li-al-jins al-latif* (Egypt: Matba'at al-Manar, 1351), 121–2.
143 Henri Lauzière, 'The Construction of Salafiyya: Reconsidering Salafism from the Perspective of Conceptual History', *International Journal of Middle East Studies* 42/3

(2010): 369–89; Frank Griffel, 'What Do We Mean By 'Salafi'? Connecting Muḥammad 'Abduh with Egypt's Nūr Party in Islam's Contemporary Intellectual History', *Die Welt des Islams* 55/2 (2015): 186–222.
144 El Shamsy, *Rediscovering*, 184–9.
145 Basheer M. Nafi, 'Salafism Revived: Nu'mān al-Alūsī and the Trial of Two Aḥmads', *Die Welt des Islams* 49/1 (2009) 49–97: 76.
146 David Commins, *Islamic Reform: Politics and Social Change in Late Ottoman Syria* (New York: Oxford University Press, 2023), 50–5.
147 Ibid., 54.
148 Ibid., 71–2.
149 El Shamsy, *Rediscovering*, 193.
150 James Grehan, *Twilight of the Saints: Everyday Religion in Ottoman Syria and Palestine* (New York: Oxford University Press, 2014), 198.
151 Commins, *Islamic Reform*, 39.
152 Hourani, *Arabic Thought*, 225.
153 Scharbrodt, 'The Salafiyya and Sufism', 95.
154 cf. Simon A. Wood, *Christian Criticisms, Islamic Proofs: Rashid Rida's Modernist Defence of Islam* (New York: Oneworld, 2012), 148–50; Muhammad Qasim Zaman, *Modern Islamic Thought in a Radical Age: Religious Authority and Internal Criticism* (Cambridge: Cambridge University Press, 2012), 8 and chapter 2.
155 Scharbrodt, *Muhammad 'Abduh*, 186; Ahmad Dallal, 'Appropriating the Past: Twentieth-Century Reconstruction of Pre-Modern Islamic Thought', *Islamic Law and Society* 7/3 (2000), 325–58: 340.
156 Dallal, 'Appropriating the Past', 338–9.
157 Toby Matthiesen, *The Caliph and the Imam: The Making of Sunnism and Shiism* (Oxford: Oxford University Press, 2023), 280.
158 John Willis, 'Debating the Caliphate: Islam and Nation in the Work of Rashid Rida and Abul Kalam Azad', *The International History Review* 32/4 (2012), 711–32: 720.
159 Muhammad Rashid Rida, *al-Wahhabiyyun wa-al-Hijaz* (Egypt: Matba'at al-Manar, 1344), 4–6.
160 Henri Lauzière, *The Making of Salafism: Islamic Reform in the Twentieth Century* (New York:

161 Bernard Haykel, 'On the Nature of Salafi Thought and Action', in Roel Meijer (ed.), *Global Salafism: Islam's New Religious Movement* (New York: Oxford University Press, 2014), 34–57.

162 Aaron Rock-Singer, *In the Shade of the Sunna: Salafi Piety in the Twentieth-Century Middle East* (Oakland, CA: University of California Press, 2022).

163 Stéphane Lacroix, 'Between Revolution and Apoliticism: Nasir al-Din al-Albani and his Impact on the Shaping of Contemporary Salafism', in Meijer (ed.), *Global Salafism*, 58–80; Brown, *Canonization*, 301–34; Christopher Melchert, 'Muḥammad Nāṣir al-Dīn al-Albānī and Traditional Hadith Criticism', in Elisabeth Kendall and Ahmad Khan (eds), *Reclaiming Islamic Tradition: Modern Interpretations of the Classical Heritage* (Edinburgh: Edinburgh University Press, 2016), 33–51.

164 Rida, *Tarikh*, 1:11; Hourani, *Arabic Thought*, 140–1; Kerr, *Islamic Reform*, 108–9.

8: Defending God's Sovereignty

1 'Ali 'Abd al-Raziq, *al-Islam wa-usul al-hukm: bahth fi al-khilafah wa-al-hukumah fi al-islam* (Egypt, Matba'at Misr, 1925), 64–80.

2 Ibid., 12–20-, 21–8.

3 Ibid., 24–5, 95–103.

4 Ibid., 35.

5 Ibid., 103.

6 Ibid., 11.

7 Ibid., 15; Thomas W. Arnold, *The Caliphate* (Oxford: The Clarendon Press, 1924), 42, 47–8.

8 Troll, *Sayyid Ahmad Khan*, 133.

9 *Encyclopaedia of Islam* THREE, "Abd al-Rāziq, Muṣṭafā' (Anke von Kügelgen), https://referenceworks-brill-com.ezproxy-prd.bodleian.ox.ac.uk/display/entries/EI3O/SIM-0275.xml?rskey=aR8oj6&result=1, last accessed 22 January 2025.

10 Quadri, *Transformations of Tradition*, 165–6.

11 Andrew March, *The Caliphate of Man: Popular Sovereignty in Modern Islamic Thought* (Cambridge, MA: Harvard University Press, 2019), 40.

12 Hammond, *Late Ottoman Origins*, 44.

13 Hourani, *Arabic Thought*, 190.

14 Ana Belén Soage, 'Rashīd

Ridā's Legacy', *The Muslim World* 98/1 (2008), 1–23: 6.
15 Muhammad Rashid Rida, *The Caliphate or the Supreme Imamate*, tr. Simon A. Wood (New Haven, CT: Yale University Press, 2024), 51.
16 March, *Caliphate of Man*, 59.
17 Rida, *The Caliphate*, 127–8.
18 March, *Caliphate of Man*, 44–5.
19 Rida, *The Caliphate*, 141–2; March, *Caliphate of Man*, 53.
20 Rida, *The Caliphate*, 66.
21 *Ibid.*, 64; Kerr, *Islamic Reform*, 161–6.
22 Rida, *The Caliphate*, 140; March, *The Caliphate*, 64.
23 March, *The Caliphate*, 56.
24 Rida, *The Caliphate*, 69.
25 Gail Minault, *The Khilafat Movement: Religious Symbolism and Political Mobilization in India* (New York: Columbia University Press, 1982), 92; Willis, 'Debating the Caliphate', 723, 725.
26 Minault, *Khilafat Movement*, 93–4.
27 Zaman, *Islam in Pakistan*, 30.
28 Willis, 'Debating the Caliphate', 724.
29 Minault, *Khilafat Movement*, 39.
30 Willis, 'Debating the Caliphate', 723; Minault, *Khilafat Movement*, 41.
31 Muhammad Qasim Zaman, 'The Sovereignty of God in Modern Islamic Thought', *Journal of the Royal Asiatic Society* 25/3 (2015), 389–418: 396.
32 Minault, *Khilafat Movement*, 219, n. 26.
33 *Ibid.*, 55.
34 Annemarie Schimmel, *Gabriel's Wing: A Study of the Religious Ideas of Sir Muhammad Iqbal* (Leiden: Brill, 1963), 38; Muhammad Iqbal, *The Development of Metaphysics in Persia: A Contribution to the History of Muslim Philosophy* (Lahore: Bazm-i Iqbal, 1964), 96–116, 116–33, 134–43.
35 Iqbal, *The Development of Metaphysics*, 143–6.
36 Schimmel, *Gabriel's Wing*, 21, 42, 60; Sir Muhammad Iqbal, *The Reconstruction of Religious Thought in Islam* (London: Oxford University Press, 1934), 141.
37 Schimmel, *Gabriel's Wing*, 40–1.
38 *Ibid.*, 42; Sheikh Muhammad Iqbal, *The Secrets of the Self*, tr. Reynold A. Nicholson (London: Macmillan and Co., 1920), esp. chapters VI–VIII.

39 Iqbal, *The Secrets of the Self*, chapter IX.
40 Sir Muhammad Iqbal, *The Mysteries of Selflessness: A Philosophical Poem*, tr. Arthur J. Arberry (London: John Murray, 1953), 29–39.
41 Zaman, 'The Sovereignty of God', 398.
42 *Ibid.*, 400–1.
43 Jan-Peter Hartung, *A System of Life: Mawdūdī and the Ideologisation of Islam* (London: Hurst & Co., 2020), 12.
44 Seyyed Vali Reza Nasr, *Mawdudi and the Making of Islamic Revivalism* (New York: Oxford University Press, 1996), 10, 12; Hartung, *A System of Life*, 14.
45 Hartung, *A System of Life*, 15.
46 *Ibid.*, 35.
47 *Ibid.*, 18, 37; Nasr, *Mawdudi*, 22–3.
48 Abu Ala Mawdudi, *Islamic Law and the Constitution*, tr. Khurshid Ahmad (Lahore: Islamic Publications Ltd., 1960), 431–2.
49 Nasr, *Mawdudi*, 23; Mawdudi, *Islamic Law and the Constitution*, 8.
50 Hartung, *A System of Life*, 128.
51 Mawdudi, *Towards Understanding Islam*, tr. Abdul Ghani (Lahore: Sh. Muhammad Ashraf, 1940), 55, 66.
52 Hartung, *A System of Life*, 98.
53 March, *Caliphate of Man*, 88; Zaman, *Islam and Pakistan*, 6.
54 Hartung, *A System of Life*, 172 (adapted).
55 James D. Bratt, *Abraham Kuyper: A Centennial Reader* (Grand Rapids, MI: Paternoster Press, 1998), 461. I am grateful to Joel Knight for this reference.
56 Hartung, *A System of Life*, 93 (adapted).
57 *Ibid.*, 140–55.
58 March, *Caliphate of Man*, 82.
59 *Ibid.*, 98.
60 Zaman, 'The Sovereignty of God', 401.
61 March, *Caliphate of Man*, 93–7, 104–5.
62 Hartung, *A System of Life*, 68.
63 *Ibid.*, 65.
64 *Ibid.*, 78–83.
65 Zaman, *Islam in Pakistan*, 152–63.
66 Richard P. Mitchell, *The Society of the Muslim Brothers* (London: Oxford University Press, 1969), 1–8.
67 *Ibid.*, chapter VIII.
68 *Ibid.*, 234.
69 *Ibid.*, 232–3.
70 *Ibid.*, 244.
71 *Ibid.*, 234.
72 *Ibid.*, 214.

73 *Ibid.*, 30.
74 *Ibid.*, 14.
75 *Ibid.*, chapter VI.
76 *Ibid.*, 207; chapter VII.
77 William Shepard, 'The Development of the Thought of Sayyid Quṭb as Reflected in Earlier and Later Editions of Social Justice in Islam', *Die Welt des Islams* 32/2 (1992), 196–236: esp. 208, 218–19, 224.
78 John Calvert, *Sayyid Qutb and the Origins of Radical Islamism* (London: Hurst, 2010), chapter 4.
79 Hartung, *System of Life*, 194.
80 *Ibid.*, 195.
81 Mitchell, *The Society of the Muslim Brothers*, chapter V; Fawaz Gerges, *Making the Arab World: Nasser, Qutb, and the Clash that Shaped the Middle East* (Princeton, NJ: Princeton University Press, 2018), esp. chapter 3.
82 Ronald L. Nettler, 'Guidelines for the Islamic Community: Sayyid Qutb's Political Interpretation of the Qur'an', *Journal of Political Ideologies* 1/2 (1996), 183–96: 185.
83 Hartung, *System of Life*, 202–3.
84 Zaman, 'The Sovereignty of God', 393.
85 Gerges, *Making the Arab World*, 245.
86 Hartung, *System of Life*, 213. The translation of the Qur'anic verse is A. J. Arberry's. See *The Koran Interpreted*, 222.
87 Hartung, *System of Life*, 209.
88 Thomas Hegghammer, *The Caravan: Abdallah Azzam and the Rise of Global Jihad* (Cambridge: Cambridge University Press, 2020), 73.
89 *Ibid.*, 40.
90 'Abd Allah 'Azzam, 'Qafuhum ... innahum mas'ulun', *al-Jihad* 9/1 (1985), 1–7, Afghan Serials Collection. Partisan Publications from The Wahdat Library (DA-ASC), last accessed 25 April 2022.
91 Hegghammer, *The Caravan*, 125, 502–3.
92 'Abd Allah 'Azzam, 'Muqaddimah', *al-Jihad* 1/1 (1984), 3, Afghan Serials Collection. Partisan Publications from The Wahdat Library (DA-ASC), last accessed 20 April 2022.
93 Hegghammer, *The Caravan*, 302–3.
94 *Ibid.*, 88, 464, 474–5; Hartung, *System of Life*, 214.
95 Barbara H. E. Zollner, *The Muslim Brotherhood: Hasan al-Hudaybi and Ideology* (London: Routledge, 2009), chapter 3; Sebastian Elsässer,

'Between Preaching and Judging: the Muslim Brotherhood and the Predicament of takfīr (1960s–1980s)', *Islamic Law and Society* 31/3 (2024), 235–59.

96 Christopher Melchert, 'The Relation of Ibn Taymiyya and Ibn Qayyim al-Jawziyya to the Ḥanbalī School of Law', in Birgit Krawietz and Georges Tamer (eds), *Islamic Theology, Philosophy and Law: Debating Ibn Taymiyya and Ibn Qayyim al-Jawziyya* (Berlin: De Gruyter, 2013), 146–61: 161; Jakob Skovgaard-Petersen, 'Yūsuf al-Qaraḍāwī and al-Azhar', in Bettina Gräf and Jakob Skovgaard-Petersen (eds), *Global Mufti: The Phenomenon of Yūsuf al-Qaraḍāwī* (New York: Columbia University Press, 2009), 27–53: 29.

97 Muhammad Qasim Zaman, *The Ulama in Contemporary Islam: Custodians of Change* (Princeton, NJ: Princeton University Press, 2002), 60.

98 *Ibid., passim.*

99 Haifaa G. Khalafallah, 'Rethinking Islamic Law: Genesis and Evolution in the Islamic Legal Method and Structures' (PhD Dissertation, Georgetown University, 1999), 55, n. 8.

100 Bettina Gräf and Jakob Skovgaard-Petersen, 'Introduction', in Gräf and Skovgaard-Petersen (eds), *Global Mufti*, 1–15: 4, 12.

101 Sagi Polka, *Shaykh Yūsuf al-Qaraḍāwī: Spiritual Mentor of Wasaṭī Salafism* (Syracuse, NY: Syracuse University Press, 2019), 330; Skovgaard-Petersen, 'Yūsuf al-Qaraḍāwī and al-Azhar', 33; Khalafallah, 'Rethinking Islamic Law', 65.

102 Khalafallah, 'Rethinking Islamic Law', 98.

103 *Ibid.*, 128.

104 *Ibid.*, chapter five; Armando Salvatore, 'Qaraḍāwī's *Maṣlaḥa*: From Ideologue of the Islamic Awakening to Sponsor of Transnational Public Islam', in Gräf and Skovgaard-Petersen (eds), *Global Mufti*, 239–50; Tauseef Ahmad Parray, 'The Legal Methodology of "*Fiqh al-Aqalliyyat*" and its Critics: An Analytical Study', *Journal of Muslim Minority Affairs* 31/1 (2012), 88–107; Polka, *Shaykh Yūsuf al-Qaraḍāwī*, 271–8, 330.

105 Husam Tammam, 'Yūsuf Qaraḍāwī and the Muslim Brothers: The Nature of a Special Relationship', in Gräf and

106 Skovgaard-Petersen (eds), *Global Mufti*, 55–83: 55.
106 Al-Sayyid Sabiq, *Fiqh al-sunnah*, in three vols (Beirut: al-Maktabah al-ʿAṣriyyah, 2014), 1:5.
107 Kate Zebiri, *Maḥmūd Shaltūt and Islamic Modernism* (Oxford: Clarendon Press, 1993), chapter 8; Rainer Brunner, *Annäherung und Distanz: Schia, Azhar und die islamische Ökumene im 20. Jahrhundert* (Berlin: K. Schwarz, 1996), chapters 6 and 9.
108 Zebiri, *Maḥmūd Shaltūt*, 120, 122.
109 Khalafallah, 'Rethinking Islamic Law', 102, 112, 142; Tammam, 'Yūsuf Qaraḍāwī and the Muslim Brothers', 58; Zebiri, *Maḥmūd Shaltūt*, 64.
110 Daniel Brown, *Rethinking Tradition in Modern Islamic Thought* (Cambridge: Cambridge University Press, 1996), 117.
111 Muḥammad al-Ghazālī, *al-Sunnah al-nabawiyyah bayn ahl al-fiqh wa-ahl al-ḥadīth* (Cairo: Dār al-Shurūq, n.d.), 55–8; Khalafallah, 'Rethinking Islamic Law', 144; Brown, *Misquoting Muhammad*, 137–9.
112 Khalafallah, 'Rethinking Islamic Law', 146.
113 Brown, *Misquoting Muhammad*, 140.
114 Barbara Freyer Stowasser, 'Yūsuf al-Qaraḍāwī on Women', in Gräf and Skovgaard-Petersen (eds), *Global Mufti*, 181–211: 201–6.
115 Khalafallah, 'Rethinking Islamic Law', 101.
116 *Ibid.*, 68, 99.
117 Skovgaard-Peterson, 'Yūsuf al-Qaraḍāwī and al-Azhar', 38; Polka, *Shaykh Yūsuf al-Qaraḍāwī*, 20–1.
118 Polka, *Shaykh Yūsuf al-Qaraḍāwī*, 156, 329.
119 *Ibid.*, 161.
120 Fauzi M. Najjar, 'The Debate on Islam and Secularism in Egypt', *Arab Studies Quarterly* 18/2 (1996), 1–21: 3–4.
121 Polka, *Shaykh Yūsuf al-Qaraḍāwī*, 302.
122 *Ibid.*, 330.
123 Alexandre Caeiro and Mahmoud al-Saify, 'Qaraḍāwī in Europe, Europe in Qaraḍāwī: The Global Mufti's European Politics', in Gräf and Skovgaard-Petersen (eds), *Global Mufti*, 109–48: 124.
124 Nasr Hamid Abu Zayd, *Critique of Religious Discourse*, tr. Jonathan Wright (New Haven, CT: Yale University Press, 2018), chapter 1.
125 *Ibid.*, 81.
126 Katajun Amirpur, *New*

Thinking in Islam: The Jihad for Democracy, Freedom and Women's Rights, tr. Eric Ormsby (London: Gingko Library, 2015), chapter 3.
127 Abu Zayd, *Critique of Religious Discourse*, 45.
128 Alexander Knysh, '"*Irfan*" Revisited: Khomeini and the Legacy of Islamic Mystical Philosophy', *Middle East Journal* 46/4 (1992), 631–53.
129 Eskandar Sadeghi-Boroujerdi, *Revolution and its Discontents: Political Thought and Reform in Iran* (Cambridge: Cambridge University Press, 2019), 86–7; Ruh Allah Khumayni, *Kashf al-asrar* (no date or place of publication), 178–9, 257, https://archive.org/details/1_20201121_202011 21_1425/page/n298/mode/1up?q=قوامة& view=theater, last accessed 7 February 2025.
130 Sadeghi-Boroujerdi, *Revolution and its Discontents*, 94.
131 Ruh Allah Khumayni, *Islam and Revolution: Writings and Declarations of Imam Khomeini*, tr. Hamid Algar (Berkeley, CA: Mizan Press, 1981), 28.
132 *Ibid.*, 28–9, 33, 34, 44.
133 *Ibid.*, 55–6.
134 *Ibid.*, 30, 49–50.
135 *Ibid.*, 48–9.
136 *Ibid.*, 59–60, 62.
137 *Ibid.*, 62–6; Sadeghi-Boroujerdi, *Revolution and its Discontents*, 101.
138 Arshin Adib-Moghaddam, 'What is Power in Iran? The Shifting Foundations of the *Velayat-e Faqih*', in Mahmood Monshipouri (ed.), *Inside the Islamic Republic: Social Change in Post-Khomeini Iran* (London: Hurst, 2016), 23–36: 26.
139 Knysh, '"*Irfan*" Revisited', 652; Vanessa Martin, *Creating an Islamic State: Khomeini and the Making of a New Iran* (London: I. B. Tauris, 2003), 34–5; cf. Lloyd Ridgeon, 'Hidden Khomeini', in Arshin Adib-Moghaddem (ed.), *A Critical Introduction to Khomeini* (Cambridge: Cambridge University Press, 2014), 193–210: 200–4.
140 Arjomand, *The Shadow of God*, 269.
141 Sadeghi-Boroujerdi, *Revolution and its Discontents*, 108–9.
142 Rached Ghannouchi with Andrew F. March, *On Muslim Democracy: Essays and Dialogues* (New York: Oxford University Press, 2023), 157.
143 *Ibid.*, 166–7, 42–3.
144 Al-Azami, *Islam and the Arab Revolutions:*

The Ulama between Democracy and Autocracy (London: Hurst, 2022), 39; Motaz al-Khateeb, 'Yūsuf al-Qaraḍāwī as an Authoritative Reference (Marji'iyya)', in Gräf and Skovgaard-Petersen (eds), Global Mufti, 85–108.

145 Hamid Mavani, Religious Authority and Political Thought in Twelver Shi'ism: from Ali to post-Khomeini (Abingdon: Routledge, 2013), 196–7.

146 Geneive Abdo, 'Re-Thinking the Islamic Republic: A "Conversation" with Ayatollah Hossein 'Ali Montazeri', Middle East Journal 55/1 (2001), 9–24: 11.

147 Khumayni, Islam and Revolution, 38, 40, 63.

148 Arzoo Osanloo, 'Women and Criminal Law in Post-Khomeini Iran', in Monshipouri (ed.), Inside the Islamic Republic, 91–112: 99.

149 Azadeh Kian, 'Gendered Khomeini', in Adib-Moghaddem (ed.), A Critical Introduction to Khomeini, 170–92: 184–5.

150 Leila Ahmed, A Quiet Revolution: The Veil's Resurgence from the Middle East to America (New Haven, CT: Yale University Press, 2011), chapters 5 and 6; Ghannouchi, On Muslim Democracy, 23.

151 Fatima Mernissi, Beyond the Veil: Male-Female Dynamics in Muslim Society (Bloomington and Indianapolis, IN: Indiana University Press, 1987), 19.

152 Ibid., 33.

153 Ibid., 45.

154 Ziba Mir-Hosseini, Journeys towards Gender Equality in Islam (London: Oneworld, 2022), 1.

155 Ibid., 72–4.

156 Amina Wadud, Qur'an and Woman: Rereading the Sacred Text from a Woman's Perspective (New York: Oxford University Press, 1999), x-xxii.

157 Aysha A. Hidayatullah, Feminist Edges of the Qur'an (New York: Oxford University Press, 2013), 33, and part II.

158 Ibid., chapter 4.

159 Wadud, Qur'an and Woman, 63.

160 Ibid., 65–71.

161 Fazlur Rahman, Islam & Modernity: Transformation of an Intellectual Tradition (Chicago, IL: University of Chicago Press, 1982), 5; Fazlur Rahman, Major Themes of the Qur'an (Chicago, IL: University of Chicago Press, 2009), 48. Rachel M. Scott, 'A Contextual Approach to Women's Rights in the Qur'ān: Readings of 4:34',

162 *The Muslim World* 99/1 (2009), 60–85.
162 Hidayatullah, *Feminist Edges*, chapter 5.
163 Wadud, *Qur'an and Woman*, xiii; Hidayatullah, *Feminist Edges*, 96.
164 Wadud, *Qur'an and Woman*, 58; Hidayatullah, *Feminist Edges*, 93.
165 Hidayatullah, *Feminist Edges*, 81–6, 91.
166 Hidayatullah, *Feminist Edges*, chapter 6; Saadia Yacoob, 'Islamic Law and Gender', in Anver M. Emon and Rumi Ahmed (eds), *The Oxford Handbook of Islamic Law* (New York: Oxford University Press, 2015), 75–102: 84.
167 Lacroix, 'Between Revolution and Apoliticism', 69; Hegghammer, *The Caravan*, 93–4.
168 Lacroix, 'Between Revolution and Apoliticism', 69–70.
169 Nuh Ha Mim Keller, 'Why Muslims Follow Madhhabs' (1995), https://www.masud.co.uk/ISLAM/nuh/madhhabstlk.htm, last accessed 5 February 2025; Hamza Yusuf, 'Maliki Fiqh – Part 1' (2017), https://muslimcentral.com/hamza-yusuf-maliki-fiqh-part-1/, last accessed 5 February 2025.
170 Abdal Hakim Murad, 'Understanding the Four Madhhabs' (1995), https://www.masud.co.uk/ISLAM/ahm/newmadhh.htm, last accessed 4 February 2025.
171 Abdal Hakim Murad, 'Paradigms of Leadership: Imam Malik' (2021), https://muslimcentral.com/abdal-hakim-murad-imam-malik-paradigms-of-leadership/, last accessed 6 February 2025.
172 Richard Swedberg and Ola Agevall, *The Max Weber Dictionary: Key Words and Central Concepts* (Stanford, CA: Stanford Social Sciences), 24.
173 Abdal Hakim Murad, 'Paradigms of Leadership: Hussain Ahmad Madani' (2021), https://muslimcentral.com/abdal-hakim-murad-hussain-ahmed-madani-paradigms-of-leadership/, last accessed 6 February 2025; Murad, 'Imam Malik'; Thomas Bauer, *A Culture of Ambiguity: An Alternative History of Islam*, tr. Hinrich Biesterfeldt (New York: Columbia University Press, 2021).
174 Walaa Quisay, *Neo-Traditionalism in Islam in the West: Orthodoxy, Spirituality and Politics* (Edinburgh: Edinburgh University Press, 2023), 128, 132, 158.
175 Al-Azami, *Islam and the Arab Revolutions*, chapters 3–5, 7, 9; Masooda Bano,

'Al-Azhar University: A Crisis of Authority', in Masooda Bano (ed.), *Modern Islamic Authority and Social Change, Volume 1* (Edinburgh: Edinburgh University Press, 2018), 55–78.
176 Quisay, *Neo-Traditionalism*, 136.
177 Swedberg and Agevall, *Max Weber Dictionary*, 86.
178 Quisay, *Neo-Traditionalism*, 13, 46.
179 Ibid., 53; Nathan Spannaus and Christopher Pooya Razavian, 'Zaytuna College and the Construction of an American Muslim Identity', in Masooda Bano (ed.), *Modern Islamic Authority and Social Change, Volume 2* (Edinburgh: Edinburgh University Press, 2017), 37–71: 56.
180 Hamza Yusuf, 'Letter from the Editor: Why Renovatio?', *Renovatio* (28 April 2017), https://renovatio.zaytuna.edu/article/letter-from-the-editor, last accessed 6 February 2025.
181 Frank Griffel, 'Contradictions and Lots of Ambiguity: Two New Perspectives on Premodern (and Postclassical) Islamic Societies', *Bustan: The Middle East Book Review* 8/1 (2017), 1–21: 20.
182 Kecia Ali, *The Lives of Muhammad* (Cambridge, MA: Harvard University Press, 2014), 239.
183 Quisay, *Neo-Traditionalism*, 197.
184 Hans Kohn, *A History of Nationalism in the East* (London: George Routledge and Sons, 1929), 53–4.
185 Muhammad Rashid Rida, 'Renewal, Renewing, and Renewers', in Charles Kurzman (ed.), *Modernist Islam, 1840–1940: A Sourcebook* (New York: Oxford University Press, 2002), 77–85; Muhammad Rashid Rida, *Kitab Majallat al-Manar*, in 35 vols, 32:49, https://shamela.ws/book/6947/4151, last accessed 12 February 2025.

Acknowledgements

1 Marshall G. S. Hodgson, *The Venture of Islam: Conscience and History in a World Civilization*, in three vols. (Chicago, IL: University of Chicago Press, 1977), 1:99.

Index

'Abbas I, Shah 117
'Abbas II, Shah 119
'Abd al-'Aziz Al Sa'ud 233, 234
'Abd Allah ibn al-Sayf, 51
'Abd al-'Aziz, Shah 23, 58–9, 92, 95–6, 160, 165, 184
'Abd al-Hayy, Mawlana 163
'Abd al-Qadir, Shah 92, 160, 162
'Abd al-Qadir al-Jaza'iri 188–96, 209, 231
  France, confinement in 195
  Ibn 'Arabi, following 199–200
'Abd al-Qadir al-Jilani 191, 231
'Abd al-Rahman, Mawlay 191
'Abd al-Rahman, Mubarakpuri 163
'Abd al-Raziq, 'Ali 237–40
'Abd, al-Raziq, Mustafa 238
'Abd al-Rahim, Shah 16, 17
'Abduh, Muhammad x, 209
  and al-Azhar 207, 215–16
  exiled 209
  and Islam 214–15, 218–23, 235–6
  and Rashid Rida 232, 234, 238, 239, 240, 259, 277, 281
  early schooling 200–1
  Women's status, reforms proposed to 224–6
  teaching and publishing 208–9
  writings 205–6, 212–13
Abraham 53
Abu Bakr 58, 59, 97, 156, 237
Abu Hanifah 24, 161, 175
Abu Yusuf 24
Abu Zayd, Nasr Hamid 263–5, 275
Afghan jihad 257
al-Afghani, Jamal al-Din ix–x, 201–5, 206, 207, 209, 209–13, 214, 266, 281
Aga Khan 102
Agra 164, 167
The Agreement of Religions in the Oneness of God, the Hereafter, and Prophethood 48
Ahl-i Hadith 158, 161, 163–4, 166, 176, 184
Ahl-i Sunnat wa-Jama'at 182
Ahmad, Inayat, Mufti 175
Ahmad, Mahmud 181
Ahmad, Mirza Ghulam 178–82
Ahmadi Mosque 200
Ahmadiyyah 178, 181
  and Christianity 181
  and England, success in 181
  Muslim opposition to 181–2
  split into two branches, Qadiyani and Lahori factions 181
Al-Ahsa 109, 128
al-Ahsa'i, Ahmad, Shaykh 127–33, 135

al-Ahsa'i, Ibn Abi
    Jumhur 127
Akbar, Mughal
    Emperor 17
Akhbarism 108–10,
    111–12, 129
'Alamgir 16
al-Albani, Nasir al-
    Din 234–5, 275,
    276, 277
Algiers 190–1
Ali, Kecia 279
'Ali, Amir, Sayyid
    172–3
'Ali, Chiragh 172
'Ali ibn Abi Talib 36
'Ali Jawhar,
    Muhammad 279
'Ali Jawhar, Shawkat
    243, 244
'Ali Mubarak 199
'Ali, Muhammad 197,
    245
'Ali, Sayyid
    Muhammad 136,
    137–9
Aligarh Anglo-
    Muhammadan
    Oriental College
    173–4, 209, 238,
    242, 243, 244, 246
Aligarh movement of
    Islamic modernism
    165, 174
Aligarh Muslim
    University see
    Aligarh Anglo–
    Muhammadan
    Oriental College
The All-
    Comprehensive
    Words 130
al-Alusi, Mahmud
    Shukri 230
al-Alusi, Nu'man
    Khayr al-Din
    230–1

al-Alusi, Shihab al-
    Din 231
al-'Amili, al-Hurr 109
Amin, Qasim 226–8,
    229, 239
Amuli, Haydar 116
'Andalib, Nasir
    Muhammad 64–7
Anglo–Muhammadan
    Law 149
Annesley, George
    (Viscount Valentia)
    57
Ansar al-Sunnah al-
    Muhammadiyyah
    234
Ansari, Murtada 113,
    114–15
Antun, Farah 220,
    223
al-Aqhisari, Ahmad
    al-Rumi 4
Aristotelian logic 12,
    22
Aristotle 5, 28
Arjomand, Saïd Amir
    116
Arnold, Thomas W.
    174, 175, 238, 244
Asadabad 201
Ash'arism 3, 9, 100,
    117, 195, 207,
    214, 276
al-'Askari, Hasan
    102
Asma'u, Nana 85, 87
al-Astarabadi,
    Muhammad Amin
    107–9, 110, 111,
    112
Ataturk, Mustafa
    Kemal 266
Athanasius Dabbas 11
al-'Attar, Hasan,
    Shaykh 197
Aurangabad 246
Authentic Collections

(of Hadith) of
    al-Bukhari and
    Muslim, 24 37, 44,
    103, 170, 235
The Authority of
    the Jurist: Islamic
    Government 266
al-'Ayn, Qurrat 136–7
'Ayn Madi 192
Azad, Abu l-Kalam
    242–3, 247
al-Azhar 197, 201
al-Azhar, Sunni Islam
    centre of learning
    ix, 76–7, 81, 207,
    215–16, 223,
    258–9, 260
Azurdah, Sadr al-Din
    160
'Azzam, 'Abd Allah
    255–7

Babism 135–9
Badasht 137
al-Badawi, Ahmad 57,
    200–1
Baha'ism 138–9
Baha' Allah 138
Baha'i, Shaykh 117
al-Bahrani, Yusuf
    111–12, 121
Bakhit al-Muti'i,
    Muhammad 239,
    240
al-Bakri, Mustafa 70
Balakot 97
The Balance of Truth
    164
Balıkesir 5
al-Banna, Hasan
    250–1, 260, 262,
    275
al-Baraghani,
    Muhammad Taqi
    132
Bareilly 160, 182
Barelwi, Ahmad Riza

INDEX

Khan 182–6
Barelwi, Sayyid
  Admad 92–4,
  95–6, 97, 152,
  158, 166, 182
Barlas, Asma 275
Basra 52
Bauer, Thomas 278
al-Baytamani 1–2
Beck, Theodore 174,
  177
Bedouins 54
Begum, Shah Jahan
  161
Bello, Muhammad 86,
  87, 89
Berkey, Jonathan P.
  147
Beyond the Veil
  271–2
Bhopal 160, 161
bid'ah x–xi, 3, 149,
  157, 162, 166–7,
  168, 226
Bihbahan 111
Bihbahani,
  Muhammad 'Ali
  120
Bihbahani,
  Muhammad Baqir
  110–13, 121, 128
Bin Bayyah, 'Abd
  Allah 276, 279
Bin Laden, Osama
  257
Birgivi, Mehmed 4–5,
  10, 13, 63–4
al-Bitar, 'Abd al-
  Razzaq 230, 231–2
Blunt, Wilfrid Scawen
  202, 216
Bohra Isma'ili 102
*The Book for Those
  Who Do Not Have
  a Jurist with Them*
  103
*The Book of
  Monotheism* 51
*The Book of Pure
  Gold* 76, 90
*The Book of Spiritual
  Stations* 200
*The British
  Government and
  Jihad* 180–1
British Raj 142
Browne, Edward
  Granville 124,
  125, 126–7, 202,
  213, 216
al-Bukhari,
  Muhammad, Imam
  7, 24, 34, 42–3
  see also Authentic
  Collections (of
  Hadith) of al-
  Bukhari and
  Muslim
Bunzel, Cole 53
Burckhardt, Johann
  Ludwig 57, 58, 61
*Burnishing the Mirror
  of the One Who
  Saves Regarding
  Theology, the Two
  Philosophies, and
  Sufism* 117
Bursa 199
Burton, Richard 56,
  83
al-Busiri 56–7
al-Bustani, Butrus 202
Buyid dynasty 104

Cairo 204
Calcutta 164
Calder, Norman 105
*The Caliphate and
  Kingship* 248
Calvin, John 23
Carlyle, Thomas 170
*The Causes of the
  Indian Revolt* 141,
  168
Çelebi, Katib *see*
  Katib Çelebi
Chhindwara 244
*The Clarifier of the
  Qur'an* 23
Cole, Juan 108
*The Commentary of
  the Lighthouse*
  216–17
*The Commentary on
  a Philosophical
  Poem* 126
*The Compendium of
  Happiness* 122
The Complaint 244
Comrade 243
*The Councils of the
  Pious* 4, 5–6
Crawford, Michael
  53, 58, 61
The Crescent 243
*A Critical Exposition
  of the Popular
  "Jihad"* 172
*The Critique
  of Religious
  Discourse* 263
Cyrenaica 82

al-Dabbagh, 'Abd al-
  'Aziz 76, 90
Dahlan, Ahmad ibn
  Zayni 213
Dallal, Ahmed 44, 61
Damascus x, 2, 11,
  199
the Damascus Events
  187–9
Dan Fodio, Usman
  83–8, 89, 90, 191,
  192
Dar al-Funun 203–4
Dar al-'Ulum 145,
  146–8, 208
Dard, Khwaja Mir 64,
  65, 67, 68–9, 70,
  165–6

Daumas, Eugène
and 'Abd al-Qadir,
questions and
answers 193–4
al-Dawani, Jalal al-
din 206
al-Dawlah, Zahir 134
Decisive Treatise on
the Connection
between
Religion and
Philosophy 203
The Defence of
Muslim Lands: The
Most Important of
Individual Duties
257
Degel 86
Delhi 95, 141, 142
The Deliverer from
Error 201
Deoband 144–5,
146–8
see also Dar al-
'Ulum
school
Deobandi scholars
143–52, 153–4,
157–8
The Development of
Metaphysics in
Persia 244
The Difference
between the Rule
of the Muslims
and the Rule of the
Unbelievers 85
Dihlawi, Rafi' al-Din
144–5
al-Din, Khayr see
al-Tunisi, Khayr
al-Din
al-Din, Nasir, Shah
120, 125
al-Din, Rafi', Shah 23,
166

Dir'iyyah 53–4
The Disagreements of
the Jurists 104
The Disavowal
of Those Who
Disavow the
Blessings
of Religion,
Caliphate, and
Community
239–40
The Divine
Elucidations 18,
31
The Divine
Revelations 71

East India Company
140, 149, 160,
165, 166
Ebu-s-Su'ud 5
Ecclesiastes 281
The Effusions of the
Two Sanctuaries 15
Egypt School of
Languages 198
The Egyptian Events
208
Egyptian
Geographical
Society 280
Egyptian girls,
education of
199, 227–8
Egyptian revolution of
1952 253
Ennahda party
(Tunisia) 269
The Epistle on
Monotheism
213–14, 232, 238
An Epistle Refuting
the Partisans of
Opinion 77
The Etiquette of
Learning 44

European Council
for Fatwa and
Research 259
The Everlasting of the
Names 137
An Explanation of
God's Servants'
Obligation to
Emigrate 86
The Exposition 137,
138
The Extraction
of Gold in the
Distillation of
Paris 197–8

A Fair Explanation
of the Cause of
Difference 20
Farangi Mahall 16,
147–8, 163, 242
Fath 'Ali Shah 120,
129
Fathpuri Mosque 246
Fatimah 36, 69, 92,
131, 133, 136
The Fatwas of
'Alamgir 16
Fawwaz, Zaynab
225–6
Fayz-i 'Amm
Madrasah
(Kanpur) 175
Fez 73, 76
al-Fiqi, Muhammad
Hamid 234
The Firmest Handle
212–13, 243
Foda, Faraj 263
The Four
Fundamental
Concepts of the
Qur'an 247, 248
The Four Journeys of
the Intellect 119,
126, 265

INDEX

Free Officers (Egypt) 253
Futa-Toro 88

Gandhi, Indira 261
Gangohi, Rashid Ahmad 140, 142, 143–4, 146, 147, 150, 151, 152, 153
General History of Civilization in Europe: From the Fall of the Roman Empire to the French Revolution 207
Ghannouchi, Rached 269
al-Ghazali 4–5, 26, 27, 153, 175, 201, 206
al-Ghazali, Muhammad 258–9, 261–2, 267, 271
al-Ghazali, Zaynab 255
Ghilzai Afghans 110
al-Ghita', Kashif 114
Gibbon, Edward 172
Gleave, Robert 26
Gleixner, Ulriche 164
God's Conclusive Proof 19, 24, 28, 260
Goitein, S.D. 46
Goldziher, Ignaz ix–xiii, 50, 231
Gorbachev, Mikhail 268
Gordon, General 91
The Great Victory on the Principles of Exegesis 21–2
The Greatest and All-Comprehensive Visitation 130
Green, Nile 164

Griffel, Frank 279
Guidance for Students 88
Guizot, François 207, 208
Gulshan, Shah Sa'd Allah 64

Hadawi madhhab *see* Zaydi school of law
al-Hadi, Imam 36
Hadith 7, 17–19, 20, 21, 23–5, 37, 66, 69, 72, 75, 90, 92, 98, 100, 103, 105, 108, 112, 128–9, 145–7, 153, 158–9, 162–3, 170–1, 234–5, 267
ritual prayer and *raf' al-yadayn* 42–3
women's role and treatment of 261, 262, 274
Hagia Sophia (Grand Mosque) 3
Ha'iri Yazdi, 'Abd al-Karim 265
Hakim, Mirza 'Ali Akbar 265
Hali 167, 169
Hallaq, Wael 38
Hamza, Mahmud Efendi 188
Hanafi school of Islamic law 3, 24, 26, 40
Hanotaux, Gabriel 218–19
Harazim, 'Ali 74, 90
Hartford Theological Seminary, Connecticut ix
Hasan ibn 'Ali 15, 64, 68

Hastings, Warren 165
Hausaland 83, 85, 86, 87
The Healing 121
Heavenly Ornaments 154–5
al-Hibri, 'Azizah 272, 275
Hidayatullah, Aysha 273–4
Hijaz 72
al-Hilli, al-'Allamah 105–6, 109
al-Hilli, al-Muhaqqiq 105
Hiskett, Mervyn 88
History of the Decline and Fall of the Roman Empire 172
Hobbes, Thomas 238
Hoover, Jon 55–6
Horovitz, Josef 174
How is an Islamic State Established? 248
al-Hudaybi, Hasan 253, 258, 262
Hudood Ordinance 271
Huraymila 51, 60
Hurgronje, Snouck 72–3
Husayn bin 'Ali, Sharif of Mecca 233
Husayn ibn 'Ali 15
tomb, desecration of 59

Ibn 'Abd al-Wahhab, Muhammad 50–1, 95, 98, 233–4
hostility against 59–62
Ibn Sa'ud, pact with 54

monotheism and polytheism 51–5, 56–8
Shi'i Muslims and 59
takfir, use of 60, 61
Ibn 'Abd Allah, Jabir 42
Ibn Abi Jumhur al-Ahsa'i 117
Ibn al-Amir 37, 39–42, 46, 60–1
Islam, renewal of 48, 49, 52
Ibn al-Amir al-San'ani 34–5
Ibn 'Arabi 74–5, 98, 116–17, 123, 152, 162, 180, 190, 205, 244
'Abd al-Qadir and 199–200
Abu Zayd and 264
Al-Ahsa'i and 130–1
Al-Nabulusi's following of 8, 9, 10, 11–12, 13, 14, 23, 44, 64
Ayatollah Khomeini and 265, 268
Dan Fodio and 84, 88, 90
Ibn Idris and 79, 81, 116
Ibn Taymiyyah and 12, 13
Mir Dard and 68–9, 77
Mulla Sadra and 117–19, 121, 126, 130–1
Shah Wali Allah and 18–19, 27, 31–2, 56
Ibn Babawayh 101, 103
Ibn Bishr 54, 55, 59, 61

Ibn al-Farid 56, 77
Ibn Hajar al-'Asqalani 40
Ibn Hazm 40, 42, 232, 261
Ibn Idris, Ahmad 76–80, 81, 82, 100
Ibn Khaldun 28, 208, 239
Ibn al-Khatib, Muhibb al-Din 233, 251
Ibn Miskawayh 198, 199, 207
Ibn Mu'ammar, 'Uthman 52, 54, 55, 97
Ibn Muhammad, 'Abd Allah 86
Ibn Qayyim al-Jawziyyah 146, 255
Ibn Rushd 177, 203, 220
Ibn Sa'ud, Muhammad 52
and Ibn 'Abd al-Wahhab, pact with 54
Ibn Sina 116, 118
Ibn Sudah 76
Ibn Taymiyyah xi, 12, 13, 18, 40, 49, 81, 158, 231
Abu l-Kalam Azad and 243
Ibn 'Abd al-Wahhab influenced by 51, 52, 53, 55, 57–8, 59–60
Shah Muhammad Isma'il and 95
Rashid Rida and 232–3, 234
saints' tombs, visitations to 57–8, 59

Shah Wali Allah and 21
Siddiq Hasan Khan and 160, 162, 230
Ibn 'Umar, Jibril 84, 85
Ibn al-Wazir, Muhammad bin Ibrahim 37, 40
al-Iji, 'Adud al-Din 206
ijtihad 20–1, 36, 37–8, 40, 43, 63, 98, 111, 112–13
Imami Shi'ah *see* Twelver Shi'ism
Imdad Allah, Hajji 142–3, 150, 152, 175
Important Issues 86
In the Shade of the Qur'an 254
The Incoherence of the Philosophers 206
Indian Mutiny 140–3
Indian Penal Code (1860) 149
Ingram, Brannon 148, 153
International Union of Muslim Scholars 259
The Interpreter of the Qur'an 247
Introduction to History 208, 239
An Invitation to the Gentle Sex: Women's Rights in Islam and their Share of the Universal Muhammadan Reform 229–30
Iqbal, Muhammad 244–5, 247, 250

INDEX

Iran 58, 106-39, 164, 165, 202, 204, 205, 261, 264-71, 272
Iran, Shah of see Pahlavi, Mohammad Reza, Shah of Iran
Iraq 110
Isfahan 110, 114, 119
Ishaq, Shad Muhammad 150
Islam and the Fundamental Principles of Government 237-8, 239, 240, 264
Islam and politics 275
Islamic law and women, treatment of 154-5, 261-2, 263, 270-5
Islamic Revolution (1979) 265, 271
Isma'il, Shah Muhammad 92-7, 148, 156, 157, 158, 160, 166, 245-6
Isma'il Khwaju'i 120-1
Istanbul 6, 203
Izutsu, Toshihiko 126

Jabal Barat tribes 41
Jabal 'Amil 107
Jackson, Sherman 38
Jama'at al-Ikhwan al-Muslimin *see* Muslim Brotherhood
Jama'at-i Islami, 246, 247, 250
James, Lawrence 140, 141
Jam'iyyat-i'ulama-i Hind 246

al-Jaza'iri, Tahir x, 230, 231, 233
Al Jazeera TV 259
al-Jazuli 56
Jesus 11, 17, 69, 72, 117, 168, 178, 179, 196, 211
The Jewels of Spiritual Meanings 74, 90
The Jewels of Theology 114
The Jihad 256-7
al-Jilani, 'Abd al-Qadir 57, 86
al-Jili, 'Abd al-Karim 12, 244
Journal des Débats 212
Le Journal 218
Jum'a, 'Ali 276
The Jurisprudence of the Sunnah 260

Kairanawi, Rahmat Allah 164-5, 167, 168
al-Karaki, 'Ali 106-7, 110
Karbala 59, 109, 111, 133, 136
Kashan 121
al-Kashani, Fayd 109, 117, 122, 130-1
Katib Çelebi 7
Ka'bah 1-2
Keller, Nuh Ha Mim 277
Kemal, Mustafa 239, 240
Kerr, Malcolm 209
Khadir, Shaykh Darwish 201
Khalafallah, Haifaa 259
Khalid, Shaykh 190

Khalidiyyah 190
Khalwatiyyah order 70
Khan, Sir Sayyid Ahmad 103, 140-1, 165-71, 208-9, 238, 242
  Bible, commentary on the 167-8
  Indian Muslims' education 173-4
  and Islam, writings on 169-71, 176-8
  and Wahhabism 166-7
Khan, al-Hajj Muhammad Karim 134-5, 137
Khan, Siddiq Hasan 158, 159-163, 171, 230
Khartoum 91
Khatmiyyah 82
Khayrabadi, Fazl-i Haqq 141
Khayyam, 'Umar 175
Khilafat Movement 242, 243
al-Khoei, Abu al-Qasim 269-70
Khomeini, Ayatollah Ruhollah 107, 115, 264
  Islam, nature of 266-7
  Islamic government 267-70
  Islamist political theory 265-6
Khusraw, Amir 151
al-Kindi, Khawlah bint al-Azwar 228-9
Kiranwi, Habib Ahmad 146
Kirman 134
Kirmanshah 130

347

Knowers of Mystical Truths 68
The Knowledge of the Book 68–9
Knowles, Samuel 158
Knysh, Alexander 48
Kohn, Hans 280
al-Kubaybi, Nasir ibn Muhammad 78
al-Kurani, Ibrahim 12–3, 18, 50
al-Kurdi, Abu Tahir Muhammad 18, 50
Kuyper, Abraham 248

al-Lamati, Ahmad ibn Mubarak 76
The Lamp Guiding the Brethren to the Most Important Things Needed at this Time 87
The Lamp Showing the Right Way to Viceregency and Sainthood 265
The Lances of the Party of the All-Merciful against the Throats of the Party of the Accursed Satan 89, 90
Landau-Tasseron, Ella xii
Laoust, Henri 54
Lauzière, Henri 230
The Leader of Qadiyan 182
Lectures on Islam ix, x
Lelyveld, David 173
The Liberation of Woman 226–8, 239
The Life of Jesus 211

Life of Mahomet 169, 171
The Lighthouse 220, 224, 229, 232, 235, 240, 242, 280
Locke, John 238
London 169–70
Lucknow 16, 140, 147, 152, 176
Ludhiana 181

Macdonald, Duncan Black ix, xii
McGinnis, Jon 116
Madani, Husayn Ahmad 278
madhhabism 39
madhhabs, Sunni xii, 3, 20–1, 90, 184, 276
al-Maghili 87, 192
Mahall, Farangi 147, 148
al-Mahdi, Muhammad 83
al-Mahdi Ahmad ibn al-Husayn, Imam 49
Majlisi, Muhammad Baqir 109, 119
Majlisi, Muhammad Taqi 109
Mali 89
Malik 18, 24
Maliki school of law 19, 76, 80, 81, 82, 83, 87, 88, 189, 192, 195, 222, 276
Mandaville, Jon E. 5
The Manifest 223
The Mantle Ode 56, 83
al-Maqbali, Salih 46
March, Andrew 239, 241
Maronite Christians, massacre of 187
Masina, king of 89
Maturidism xii, 3, 100, 197, 204, 206, 207, 276
al-Mawardi 26
Mawdudi, Abu l-'Ala' 246–50, 252, 253, 254, 255, 258, 263, 278
Mawlay Muhammad 73, 76
Mawlay Sulayman 73, 76
mawlid (celebration of the Prophet's birthday) 72, 150–1, 166, 183
Mecca 1, 15, 18, 42, 45, 58, 60, 72–3, 77, 78, 81, 84, 107, 143, 152, 185, 190, 233
The Meccan Revelations 84, 199
Medina 15, 18, 21, 42, 50, 57–8, 70–2, 133, 185, 190, 233, 237
Meerut 140
Meir, Golda 261
Mernissi, Fatema 271
Metcalf, Barbara 145, 155, 163
Mevlevi order 232
millenarianism 83, 92
Milton, John 171
Minault, Gail 174, 243
Mir Damad 117
Mir-Hosseini, Ziba 272
al-Mirghani, Muhammad 'Uthman 82

INDEX

Miruti, 'Ashiq Ilahi 140, 142, 143, 147, 150
Mohammadan Common Law 172
Mohammedan Educational Congress 176
monotheism and polytheism 49–50, 94–5
Montazeri, Ayatollah Hossen 'Ali 270
The Most Holy Book 138
The Mother of Proofs 9
Muhammad x, xi, 13, 15, 17, 18, 56–7, 65, 74, 169, 237, 270
  non-Muslims, treatment of 45
Muhammad Ahmad 91–2
Muhammad 'Ali 77
Muhammadan Light 69, 71
The Muhammadan Path 4, 5, 7, 10, 12
Muhammadan Reality 69, 73, 74, 123, 131
Muhaqqiq, Mahdi 126
Muir, William 169, 171, 193
mujaddid xi, xii, 2, 4, 15, 17, 18, 35, 62, 78, 87, 88, 110, 134, 143, 161, 178, 179, 182, 184, 232, 233, 250, 281
Mujaddidi order 16–7, 64, 67, 70
mujtahid xii, 20, 36, 40–1, 43–4, 81, 88, 106, 108, 110, 112, 113, 115, 198, 215, 231, 232, 241
Müller, Max 172
Murad IV (Sultan) 6–7
Muradabadi, Fazl-i Rahman, Shah 175
al-Murtada, al-Sharif 104, 106
Muslim Brotherhood 250–2, 255, 256, 262, 269
  Bannist wing 257–8
  Qutbist wing 257–8
Muslim feminist movement 271–5
Muslim ibn al-Hajjaj al-Naysaburi 24
  see also Authentic Collections (of Hadith) of al-Bukhari and Muslim
Muslim Protestants 164
al-Mutawakkil Isma'il, Imam 46
Mu'tazilism x, 105, 117, 166, 206, 207, 215, 232, 264
al-Muti'i, Muhammad Bakhit 223
The Mysteries of Selflessness 245

al-Nabulusi, Abd al-Ghani 1–3, 4, 7–14, 15, 18, 19, 22, 23, 44, 56, 64, 75, 138–9
  Bethlehem, Church of the Nativity 10–11
  Jaffa, Armenian monastery 11
  Muslim hierarchy of beliefs 9
  rational sciences 12
  religious pluralism 10–11
Nader Shah 110
Nadwat al-'Ulama' – 'The Council of Religious Scholars' 175–6, 252–3
Nadwi, Abu l-Hasan 'Ali 252
Naim, C.M. 154
Najaf 107, 109, 266, 269
Najafi, Muhammad Hasan 114
Najd 51, 54–5
Nanautvi, Muhammad Qasim 142, 143, 146, 147, 152, 157, 178
Napoleon III 195
Napoleonic Code 215
Naqshbandi order 3, 16
Naraqi, Ahmad 115–16, 265
Naraqi, Muhammad Mahdi 116, 120–2, 126
Nasif, Malak Hifni 228, 229, 238
Nasser, Gamal Abdel 253, 255, 259
Nawab of Bhopal *see* Khan, Siddiq Hasan
Nazir Husayn 158–9
The Necklace on the Rules of Ijtihad and Taqlid 20
The New Woman 228

The Nightingale's Lament 65–6
Nuri, Mulla 'Ali 122–4, 125, 132
al-Nu'man, al-Qadi 102, 104, 109
Nu'mani, Shibli 174–5

The Obstacles in Our Path 251
occultation 102–3, 136
Oriental League, Society of 280
Origins of the Species 218
Our Battle with the Jews 256

Pact of 'Umar 45–6, 187
Pahlavi, Mohammad Reza, Shah of Iran 266
Pakistan 250, 271
Palestine 276
Peçevi, Ibrahim 6
The Perfecting of the Attributes in Staying at Home 2
The Perfuming of Mankind in the Interpretation of Dreams 1
Pfander, Carl Gottlieb 164–5, 167, 169
The Philosophy of Society and History 208
The Pleasant Breeze 163
Poem of the Way 77
Pointers and Reminders 116, 204
The Polishing of Hearts 166
The Political Theory of Islam 247–8, 249
polytheism *see* monotheism and polytheism
Pratt, John H. 177
Preachers Not Judges 258
The Preaching of Islam 174, 175
The Precious Pearl 206
The Problem of the Caliphate 242
The Profits of Days 115
The Proofs of Ahmad 178–9
The Proofs of Good Deeds 56, 72
The Prophetic Sunnah between the Jurists and the Traditionalists 261
Protestant Reformation 207, 279
Punjab 96
Pure Muhammadan Path 65–70, 73, 166
Purifying Doctrine from the Filth of Heresy 49

Qadizadeh Mehmed 3, 5, 6
Qadizadeli movement 3–4, 5–6, 7–8, 9–10, 35
Al Qaeda 257
Qajar dynasty 112, 114
al-Qaradawi, Yusuf 258–61, 262–3, 269, 271, 276, 280
Qarawiyyin mosque, Fez 76
al-Qasimi, Jamal al-Din 230, 231
Qasimi dynasty 36, 37, 38
Qazvin 132, 202
Qom 265
Qumsha'i, Muhammad Rida 123–4
Quraysh Arab tribe 241
Qur'an 26, 28, 31, 32, 37, 53, 61, 68, 75, 77–8, 105, 159, 162, 168, 170–2, 177, 180, 189, 203, 212–4, 216–8, 224–5, 229, 245, 248, 261
 marriage and treatment of women 193, 198, 208–9, 224–30, 271–5
 translation of 22–3
Qur'an and Woman: Rereading the Sacred Text from a Woman's Perspective 272–3
Qutb, Hamidah 255
Qutb, Muhammad 255, 256
Qutb, Sayyid 250, 252, 253–6, 258, 262, 269, 275

Rahimiyyah madrasah 16, 17–18
Rahman, Fazlur 273
The Rank of the Imamate 96

INDEX

The Rare Gardens 111
al-Rashid, Ibrahim 82
Rashidiyyah 82
Rashti, Sayyid Kazim 128, 133–4, 135
rational theology (*kalām*) 9, 12, 13, 177, 223, 232
al-Razi, Fakhr al-Din 116
The Refinement of Morals 198, 207
The Reformation of Customs 144
The Reformation of the Vicissitudes of the Muslim Community 144
The Reformation of Thought 144
Refutation of the Logicians 160
The Refutation of the Materialists 209–10, 213
A Reminder to the Intelligent and a Warning to the Ignorant 195
Renan, Ernest 211–12, 220
The Renewal and Revival of Religion 250
Renovatio 279
The Response to the Complaint 244–5
The Revival of the Muhammadan Sunnah and the Extinguishing of Innovations 84, 87
The Revival of the Religious Sciences 5, 27, 122, 235

Rida, Muhammad Rashid 204, 215, 216, 217–18, 220, 224, 229–30, 233, 235, 241–2, 263, 280–1
and Wahhabism 233–4
see also under 'Abduh, Muhammad
al-Rijal, Sahib 107
The Ringstones of Wisdom 8–9, 68, 77, 152, 168
ritual prayer
rafʿ al-yadayn issue 41–3
Rizvi, Sajjad 120
Robinson, Francis 16, 164
Rogan, Eugene 187, 189
Rumi, Jalal al-Din 125, 152, 163, 175, 245
Rushdie, Salman 265

Sabbatai Zevi 46
al-Sabri, Mustafa 223, 239–40
Sabiq, al-Sayyid 260
Sabya 77, 78
Sabzavar 124
Sabzavari, Mulla Hadi 124–7, 130, 244, 265
Sadat, Anwar 253
al-Sadiq, Jaʿfar 105
Sadra, Mulla 117–19, 120, 121, 126, 244, 265, 268
Saharanpuri, Khalil Ahmad 151
Salafi movement 161
Salafism 230, 234–5

Salafiyyah Bookshop and Publishing House 233
al-Samahiji, ʿAbd Allah 110
al-Samman, Muhammad ʿAbd al-Karim 70, 71–2, 73, 75
Sanaa, Great Mosque of 34, 37, 41, 44
Sanaa, Mosque of Expulsion 46
al-Sanusi, Muhammad ibn ʿAli 80–2, 190
al-Sanusi, Muhammad ibn Yusuf 9, 10, 195
Sanusi order 82–3
Sarasvati, Dayananda 157
Satanic Verses 264
Saʿud ibin Abd al-ʿAziz 58, 59
Saudi Arabia, Kingdom of 54
Seal of Muhammadan Sainthood 13
The Secrets of the Self 245
The Secrets of Wisdom 125
The Selection 218
A Series of Essays on the Life of Muhammad and Subjects Subsidiary Thereto 169–70
The Sermons of Ahmad 169
al-Shafiʿi 24
Shafiʿi school xii, 20, 36–7, 42, 106, 184, 198, 221
Shafti, Muhammad Baqir 114, 133
Shah ʿAlam II 67

351

Shah II, Bahadur 141
Shahabadi, Mirza
  Muhammad Ali
  265
Shahin, 'Abd al-Sabur
  264
Shaltut, Muhammad
  260–1
al-Sha'rani, 'Abd al-
  Wahhab 88
Shari'ah 77, 85, 153,
  241, 247, 272, 278
Shari'ah and Life 259
al-Shawkani,
  Muhammad
  34–5, 37, 38,
  39–41, 42–3,
  44–5, 230, 232,
  260
  and *ijtihad* 43–4, 63
  Islam, renewal of
  48–9
  and Yemen Jews 47
al-Shaybani,
  Muhammad 24
al-shaykh al-akbar 11
Shaykhism 133–5,
  136
Sheba, Queen of 261,
  262
al-Shihr 36–7
Shi'ism 35–6, 55,
  58–9, 101–2, 156
al-Shirbini, 'Abd al-
  Rahman 223
Signposts on the Path
  254, 255
al-Sindi, Muhammad
  Hayat 50–1
Singh, Ranjit 96
Sirhindi, Ahmad
  16–17, 64
Sistani, Ayatollah 'Ali
  270
Skovgaard-Peterson,
  Jakob 222

Social Justice in Islam
  252, 254
Society for the Revival
  of the Arabic
  Sciences 216
The Society of the
  Muslim Brothers
  see Muslim
  Brotherhood
  see also Jama'at
  al-Ikhwan
  al-Muslimin
Sokoto Caliphate 86,
  88–9
Spencer, Herbert 218
The Spirit of Islam
  172
The Spiritual Couplets
  125–6, 152, 245
Stewart, Devin 113
The Straight Path 93
*The Strengthening of
  Faith*
  93, 96, 156–7,
  170, 182
Sufism 3, 4, 6, 10, 14,
  17, 55–6, 151–3,
  165
al-Suhrawardi, 'Umar
  68
Suhrawardi, Yahya
  70, 116–9, 121,
  124, 131, 204,
  205, 244, 268
Sulayman ibn
  'Abd Allah Al
  al-Shaykh 55–6
Sulayman ibn 'Abd
  al-Wahhb 60
Sunnah x–xi, 4, 11,
  12, 38, 43, 44, 77,
  90, 93, 94, 108,
  159, 162, 166,
  237, 261, 271,
  276, 277
The Sunnah and

  *the Rejection of
  Innovations* 166–7
Sunnism 101, 103–5,
  106
The Support 218–19
al-Suyuti, Jalal al-Din
  xi–xii, 5, 20
*The Sword of Religion
  for Cutting the
  False Claims of the
  Apostates* 191
*The Sword of the
  Two Sanctuaries
  upon the Throat
  of Unbelief and
  Falsehood* 185

Tabarsi, Shaykh 138
Tabataba'i,
  Muhammad
  Husayn 127
Tabataba'i,
  Muhammad
  Mahdi, Sayyid
  128, 129
al-Taftazani 207
Tahmasp, Shah 106
al-Tahtawi, Rifa'ah
  Rafi' 197–200,
  208, 209
tajdid (renewal)
  xi–xii, 13, 88,
  143–4, 279
Tamari, Steve 8
Tanzimat reforms 188
taqlid (blind
  emulation) 3, 9,
  13, 20, 21, 38, 39,
  44, 48, 51, 81,
  88, 98, 106, 113,
  118, 145–6, 159,
  160–3, 170, 195,
  198, 211, 215,
  219, 223, 224,
  230, 231, 233,
  234, 235, 277, 281

taqyid al-mubah
(restricting the permissible) 7
Tareen, SherAli 142, 150
Tariqah-yi Muhammadiyyah 148, 158, 160, 182
Tawney, R.H. 169
Taylor, Isaac 213
al-Tayyib, Ahmed 276
Tehran 120, 123–4, 129
Thana Bhawan 142–3, 152
Thanawi, Ashraf 'Ali 144, 148, 150, 152–7, 178, 182
Thatcher, Margaret 261
al-Tijani, Ahmad 73–6, 89
Tijani order 75, 89–90, 192
Towards Understanding Islam 247
The Transcendent Philosophy in the Four Journeys of the Intellect 117
Transvaal fatwa 221–3
Treatise Explaining the Unity of Existence 152
The Treatise on Mystical Inspirations 205, 206, 232
Tripoli (Lebanon) 232
The Truth about Islam and the Principles of Government 239
The Truth of the Naichari Sect and an Explanation of the Condition of the Naichariyyah 210
al-Tunisi, Khayr al-Din 209
Tunisia 269
al-Tusi, Nasir al-Din 116, 118
al-Tusi, al-Ta'ifah, Shaykh 105
Twelver Shi'ism 36, 58, 102–7, 108, 109, 127, 137–8, 179, 268
Tyndale, William 23

al-'Ulum, Bahr *see* Tabataba'i, Muhammad Mahdi, Sayyid
'Umar, Pact of 45, 46, 187
'Umar ibn al-Khattab 59, 97
'Umar Tal, al-Hajj 88–91, 99–100
Umayyad caliphate 35
Umayyad Mosque of Damascus 8, 44
The Unifier 220
United Arab Emirates 276
Unveiling and the Hijab 229
The Unveiling of Mysteries 266
'Urabi, Colonel Ahmad 209
'Urabi revolt (1882) 209
The Useful Lessons of Medina 107–8, 109
al-Ustuwani, Muhammad Sa'id 188
Usulism 106–7, 108, 109, 109–10, 111–12, 112, 116
'Uyaynah 50, 52, 55

Voegelin, Eric 12

Wadud, Amina 272–3, 274, 275
wahdat al-wujud ('the unity of existence') 11, 12, 32, 66, 69, 93, 116, 121, 126, 205, 275
Wahhabis and Wahhabism xii–xiii, 50–62, 71–3, 77, 78–80, 83, 87, 95, 98, 99, 128, 166, 182, 213, 233–4, 262, 279
The Wahhabis and the Hijaz 233
Waking the Somnolent to Act upon the Qur'an and Hadith 81
Wali Allah, Shah 35, 40, 44, 56, 142, 145, 165, 222, 260
civilization and politics 29–32
dreams and visions 15, 18
early life 16
Hadith studies 18–9, 23–5
and the 'heavenly religions' 32–3
ijtihad, advocacy of 20–2
Mughal society decay, response to 28–9

Qur'an, translation of 22–3
and the Shari'ah 25–8
al-Waqidi 169
A Warning to the Ignorant and Reminder to the Rational of the Ways of the Pious 85, 87
Weber, Max 91, 278
The Well-Strung Pearl on the Sincere Expression of Monotheism 48
The Well-Trodden Path 18, 24, 84
What the World Lost with the Decline of the Muslims 253
Winter, Timothy 277–8
Women's Matters 228

The Word of Truth 166

Yan Taru educational movement 85
Yazd 129, 130
Yemen 36–43, 82
Jews, suppression of and expulsion 45–8
Yusuf, Hamza 276, 277, 278, 279

al-Zabidi, Murtada 145, 190
Zahhar, Ahmad Sharif 190
Zayn al-Din, Nazirah 229
Zaman, Muhammad Qasim 145, 242, 259

al-Zawahiri, Ayman 257
Zayd b. 'Ali 35, 43
Zaydi school of law 36, 37, 38, 39, 41, 45
Zaydi traditionalism 37–9, 40, 42, 43, 52, 98, 99
non-Muslims, treatment of 45–6
Zaydis 35, 36–43, 45
Zaytuna College, Berkeley 276, 277, 279
Zia-ul-Haq, General 271
Ziad, Homayra 68
Zubayr, Pir Muhammad 64, 65
Zunuzi, 'Ali Mudarris 123–4